200 Years of the Republic
in Retrospect

200 Years of the Republic
in Retrospect

Edited by
William C. Havard
and
Joseph L. Bernd

University Press of Virginia
Charlottesville

THE UNIVERSITY PRESS OF VIRGINIA
Copyright © 1976 by the Southern Political Science Association

Originally published as
A Special Bicentennial Issue of the
Journal of Politics
Volume 38, Number 3, August 1976

Library of Congress Cataloging in Publication Data

Main entry under title:
200 years of the Republic in retrospect.

"Originally published as a special bicentennial issue of the
Journal of politics, volume 38, August 1976."

1. United States—Constitutional history—Addresses, essays,
lectures.   2. United States—Politics and government—
Addresses, essays, lectures.   3. Political Science—History—
United States—Addresses, essays, lectures.   I. Havard,
William C.   II. Bernd, Joseph L.   III. The Journal of
politics.

JK21.T9   320.9′73   76–45777

ISBN 0–8139–0690–3

Printed in the United States of America

Contents

PREFACE

Conservative Revolution and Liberal Rhetoric: The
Declaration of Independence
    Alan P. Grimes   1

"Time Hath Found Us": The Jeffersonian
Revolutionary Vision
    Robert J. Morgan   20

The Impact of the American Independence and the
American Constitution: 1776-1848; With a Brief Epilogue
    Manning J. Dauer   37

The American Contribution to a Theory of
Constitutional Choice
    Vincent Ostrom   56

The Symbolism of Literary Alienation in the
Revolutionary Age
    Lewis P. Simpson   79

British and European Commentaries on the
American Political Experience
    René de Visme Williamson   101

Towards the Restoration of the American Political Tradition
    George W. Carey and James McClellan   110

Bicentennial Reflections on Party Government
    Jasper B. Shannon   128

Revitalization and Decay: Looking Toward the Third
Century of American Electoral Politics
    Walter Dean Burnham   146

Judicial Review: Vagaries and Varieties
    Robert J. Harris   173

Congress: Retrospect and Prospect
    Ralph K. Huitt   209

The Presidency in 1976: Focal Point of Political Unity?
    George E. Reedy   228

The South and Sectionalism in American Politics
    Numan V. Bartley   239

Continuity and Discontinuity: Dour Reflections on the
National Security
    Charles Burton Marshall   258

Democracy and Tyranny in America: The Radical Paradox
of the Bicentennial and Blacks in the American
Political System
    Samuel DuBois Cook   276

Women's Place in American Politics: The
Historical Perspective
    Louise M. Young   295

Ethnics in American Politics
    Louis L. Gerson   336

CONTRIBUTORS TO THIS ISSUE   347

Preface

ALTHOUGH THE *Journal of Politics,* in a manner characteristic of
many scholarly publications, has tended to cater to the changing
fads of the profession, its editors have never failed to recognize that
Political Science is an eclectic discipline, as well as one which has
"practical" implications in both the ordinary and special epistemo-
logical meanings of that term.   Thus, even when the scientific mode
was so much in the ascendency that its most dedicated proponents
could argue that only one whose epistemology was thoroughly
positivist and whose methodology was strictly quantitative could
properly be labelled a political scientist, the *Journal of Politics* continued to carry a few pieces to serve as reminders that the historical
and philosophical modes of perception have something to contribute
to the understanding of politics.   And despite a considerable propensity towards ideological orthodoxy among members of the profession, the contents of the *Journal* have continued to reflect not
only a diversity of perspective and due attention to the role of
criticism in the development of scholarship, but also something of
the way in which the dialectics of pragmatic politics lead to the
resolution or amelioration of social conflict.   Just as unremitting
conformity to the dominant paradigm can stultify scholarship, so
too, does the effort to eliminate all contingency from politics tend
to push states towards absolutism.   The aims of the *Journal of
Politics* have, we trust, been appropriately modest in not claiming
too much in the way of certainty on behalf of the discipline, or in
becoming so abstract in the effort to explain political phenomena
theoretically, that its contents have lost all contact with the frequently intractable world of practical politics.

All of this may seem an unnecessary *apologia* for deviating from
the *Journal's* standard format to produce a special issue as a tribute
to the bicentennial.   After all, the *Journal of Politics* has previously
published several special issues on topics of current interest, includ-

ing one on its own twenty-fifth anniversary, so this departure from standard form is hardly without precedent. Furthermore, one might suggest that the very idea that a magazine whose purpose is to advance the understanding of politics should produce a special issue on occasion of the two-hundredth anniversary of the formal inauguration of the American Republic is so obvious as to be pedestrian. The American Revolution was undoubtedly one of the great political events of history; what could be more natural than for *any* publication exclusively concerned with politics to take advantage of this opportunity to do something special on the subject? Our reservation, then, was less about the appropriateness of the conception than the possibility that we might be undertaking something that every other magazine devoted to politics, whether professional or popular, would be doing. Redundancy can be embarrassing to a periodical which insists that its contents be works of "original" scholarship.

To our surprise, casual inquiry and scrutiny of the literature did not disclose any sources that appeared to duplicate what we proposed to do. Although one or two symposia seemed to be close to our plans, most of the floodtide of writing generated by the bicentennial has been of a local nature, or has been related exclusively to issues arising out of the origins of the Republic, or has been simply esoteric, although not lacking in commercial appeal. Perhaps the notion of surveying the major ideas and institutions involved in two hundred years of republican government under essentially self-perpetuating political arrangements, by means of topical essays written by specialists from several disciplines, is too risky for most publishing outlets and for those who control the bicentennial public purses to consider seriously. Not only is the terrain too vast to cover in more than an ephemeral way, but the possibility of achieving interpretative cohesion in so loosely organized a project seems hopelessly remote.

We were not deterred by the obviousness of the idea, which may be a slur on our imaginations, but certainly says something for our persistence. Two hundred years of survival as an independent state under essentially the same set of political institutions is no mean feat when measured against the norms of most political units in most periods of history. It is hardly to be expected that every student of American political history in general, or of its institutions and special working arrangements in particular, would perceive the bases of this continuity in the same way. Some might even go so far as to suggest that the contradictions inherent in the major events of American political history and its institutional carriers are too great to permit us to say with any assurance that we have persisted through 200 years as essentially the same Republic. But whatever differences may be discerned in geography, demography, institutional patterns, scope of governmental activity and scale of the issues between the incipient Republic of 1776 and the massive American Republic of 1976, and however often reference is made to certain epochs as having produced the birth or re-birth of the nation, the country has not adhered to Jefferson's advice on the need for a complete renewal of the foundations of government each generation. As John Adams would have preferred it, the Republic's existence has been assured because of its implantation in the hearts and minds of the people rather than by reason of specific occurrences in particular times and places.

Thus even in the face of diversity of interpretation and a variety of temporal and ideological perspectives on the topics covered in this symposium, the essays cohere in at least two respects: the idea of the continuity of the Republic from its revolutionary beginnings to its entry into a third century of existence is either an underlying assumption or a declared premise of each contributor. A closely related, but sometimes more subtly projected, common feature of the essays is a concern for the maintenance of the Republic into the indefinite future under guiding principles which are accepted as being coeval not only with the origins of the nation, but with its total experience (even though differences about the precise implications of these principles abound). Even the authors who are most critical of the pragmatically conditioned lapses from adherence to the precepts of constitutional democracy, or of the apparently deliberate deviations from proclaimed ideals, somehow manage to affirm the abiding validity of the nation's self-interpretation. And even those most pessimistic about the possibility of national survival under conditions deemed fundamental to a constitutional order based on experience with this self-interpretation have not entirely abandoned hope for the future.

The topics that could have been included in such a survey are virtually limitless. Our intention was to secure breadth without claim to comprehensiveness, so the assignment of general subjects is as obvious as the theme. The origins had to be presented at some length, so essays on the Declaration, the Constitution and the ideas of some early political leaders were planned to cover the essentials without attempting to bring forth a catalogue of the interpretations which have been advanced in the past and are still being offered. Essays which might be included in this category, although extending somewhat beyond the scope of the standard topics, are those which assess the place of the literary figure in America, the impact of the American experience abroad, and the view of America from Europe. Chapters on the working arrangements of the American political system and the durability of its institutions occupy the central section of the issue, and are followed by contributions on some persisting problems in American politics, including sectionalism, national security in a polarized world, and the politics of exclusion and inclusion with respect to certain major components of American pluralism.

The essays vary greatly in length, as well as in mode of analysis and temporal perspective. Although a standard length was suggested, it is evident that the editors did not police the authors very effectively on this point, and we did not attempt to regulate them at all with respect to the ways in which they handled their topics. Although the resulting eclecticism may have a superficial impression that every essay is discrete, close examination discloses unifying elements other than those mentioned earlier. Some of the essays stay almost entirely within the historical framework of the revolutionary and constitutional periods, others range over the entire history of their subjects, several deal primarily with contemporary issues, and one or two focus mainly on the future. Almost invariably, however, the dominating perspective is affected by consideration of accretions from the past and the relative openness of the future. Thus the retrospective we hoped to achieve, and the historicism we sought to avoid, constitute loose boundaries beyond which the authors have not strayed. In almost every case their contributions reflect not only their accumulated knowledge and wisdom, but also the extent to which their intellectual and practical experiences have been congruent with the standards they discern in the foundations of the American Republic.

The persons we contacted in the bureaucratic circles charged with administering the "official" celebrations of the bicentennial did not appear to be interested in our proposal to assess in broad terms the foundations and operations of the American political system in the perspective of 200 years of experience with it. On the other hand, we owe a debt of gratitude to a number of others who were both interested in the idea and supportive of its execution. The Editorial Board and all those associated directly with the *Journal of Politics* were enthusiastic about the special issue, as were the officers and members of the Southern Political Science Association. We are especially grateful to the American Council of Learned Societies for a grant which underwrote part of the cost of having the special issue made available in book form through the University Press of Virginia. To the extent that this collection of essays is both a useful contribution to the general understanding of American politics and a worthy (though not officially sanctioned) tribute to the two-hundredth anniversary of the founding of the Republic which that politics has sustained, these organizations and the individuals who comprise them are due a major share of the credit.

WILLIAM C. HAVARD

200 Years of the Republic
in Retrospect

Conservative Revolution
and
Liberal Rhetoric:
The Declaration
of
Independence

ALAN P. GRIMES

IT IS A COMMON CHARACTERISTIC of modern political systems that
their legitimatizing myths are derived from the rhetoric of their
founding revolutions. Nations born out of revolutions turn back
to their revolutions for their statement of political principles, as
though the revolutions themselves had placed the stamp of a national imprimatur upon their political ideology. In the United
States to return to the principles of the Revolution is to return to
the principles of the Declaration of Independence. We have no
formidable treatises on philosophical systems such as Marx and
Engels brought forth for later revolutionaries; we have neither
Rousseaus nor Condorcets to fire us with broad sweeps of intuited
anthropology and history and future prospects; nor do we have
Hobbeses or Harringtons or Lockes (though much diluted we inherited all three); what we have as a revolutionary philosophy is
a short, elegantly phrased paragraph, simple enough to be commonplace and whose ultimate significance rests upon its being
accepted as commonplace. For only commonplace statements can
be called self-evident truths.

This ideology of political legitimacy, this revolutionary creed,
is found in one paragraph of the Declaration of Independence.

The creed is almost a set of slogans which are found in the first three sentences of the second paragraph, as that document is usually printed.

We hold these truths to be self-evident, that all men are created equal, that they are endowed by their Creator with certain unalienable Rights, that among these are Life, Liberty and the pursuit of Happiness. That to secure these rights, Governments are instituted among Men, deriving their just powers from the consent of the governed. That whenever any Form of Government becomes destructive of these ends, it is the Right of the People to alter or to abolish it, and to institute new Government, laying its foundation on such principles and organizing its powers in such form, as to them shall seem most likely to effect their Safety and Happiness.

These three sentences are the only statements in the entire Declaration which were thought to be of such an obvious character that they needed no further argument or demonstration but could stand forth on their own ground not only as truths, but as truths which were self-evident. One cannot berate the ideology for being banal; banality was the essence of the proposition. The self-evident truths consist of five statements, each prefaced by the word "that." The first of these presumed axioms asserted the equality of all mankind; the second, that rights were given by God and were unalienable; the third, that these rights included life, liberty and the pursuit of happiness (among others not mentioned); the fourth, that the legitimate function of government was to preserve these rights, a function which was dependent upon the consent of the governed; and the fifth, that should the people refuse consent to the government, they reserved the right to alter or abolish it.

In essence, these five statements are truly remarkable propositions, no less so in 1976 than they were in 1776. They present us at the outset with an equalitarian ethic which has helped shape the nation's history, and through the process of amendment greatly influenced the course of constitutional development. The whole concept of equal rights is but a merging or an amalgamation of the first three propositions. The concept of political consent as the basis for determining whether the functions of government are being legitimately performed has been so operationalized as to make Americans probably the most thoroughly enfranchised citizens of any modern democracy. Of the 26 amendments which have been added to the Constitution, only a few do not define or extend the equalitarian ethic, or the meaning of consent. Indeed, six of the last eleven amendments have been concerned with the elimination of discriminations which had previously limited the franchise. In other words, the unmistakable thrust of our constitutional amendment has been in the direction of equal rights and popular consent. In a constitutional sense, the truths of the Declaration of Independence are more nearly realized at the time of our bicentennial anniversary than at any time in our history. Furthermore, no amendment has been added to the Constitution which supported the cause of inequality; and only one amendment (the 22nd), could be thought of as one which restricted the opportunity for consent of the governed. And Thomas Jefferson himself had been an advocate of the two term limitation on the office of president. The normative content of the Declaration has clearly been approximated, in a formal sense at least, in the equalitarian amendments to the Constitution.

Impressive as this correspondence in values is, between the Declaration and the amendments, one must be very cautious as to what statements might reasonably be made to explain this correspondence. It would be absurd, for example, to attribute some superior wisdom to the Revolutionary fathers which set the national norms, so to speak, for all subsequent generations without regard to changed conditions and circumstances and political interests. It would be equally absurd to see in this sequence of amendments, which collectively point in the same direction, although each was enacted in response to some special political circumstance, only an extraordinary coincidence. Obviously there has been an interaction of political values and political interests. As Talcott Parsons has written, "Beliefs and values are actualized, partially and imperfectly, in realistic situations of social interaction, and the outcomes are *always* co-determined by the values and the realistic exigencies; conversely . . . 'interests' are by no means independent of the values which have been institutionalized in the relevant groups."[1] Where there is a congruence of values and interests in effective measure, political action takes place, and revolutions, proclamations, statutes, and constitutional amendments record the results.

In most concrete political contests the issues usually become ones of specific claims, immediate goals or ends, the victory of this person or that party, in which the more abstract statement of gen-

[1] Talcott Parsons, *Structure and Process in Modern Societies* (Glencoe, Illinois: The Free Press, 1960), 173.

erality called values takes a subordinate, if albeit necessary, role. If this generalization is correct, then we may say that political activities which seek to put a man in or out of office, or a law on or off the books, to effect structural arrangements of the political system, and so on, are direct political activities. Values are of course involved in the selection of issues, of candidates, of positions on public policy, and so forth. But the direct ends of politics are specific and determinable. In addition, however, values often emerge as by-products of direct political activity and serve an instrumental role in identifying issues and unifying partisans. The value propositions, the ideological statements, which emerge from a political conflict, however, may be of far more lasting importance in political history (and socialization) than the direct political struggle which brought them forth. For, to be trite, heroes, parties, and movements die; but the words they left behind live on; and the values these words convey hold meaning for new generations in vastly changed circumstances.

The American Revolution, and the interpretation of it in recent literature, clearly illustrates how the values this event gave rise to have had a lasting impact on our history. The primary and direct goal of the Revolution, at least during its early phase, was concerned with eliminating certain English taxes and regulations which the colonists found objectionable. As part of the strategy to achieve these immediate goals, arguments were formulated which employed terms and phrases drawn from English legal precedents, constitutional history, and modern natural rights philosophy. Relatively late in the conflict, independence of the former colonies was advocated as the desired means to achieve the initial goal of avoidance of English taxes and regulations. As a part of the movement toward independence, the Declaration of Independence was authorized, and a final draft approved, by the Continental Congress. The lengthier part of the Declaration, seldom read today, is concerned with the enumeration of felt abuses which it was the primary goal of the colonists to have eliminated. The brief paragraph of general political philosophy was in the way of preamble to the enumerated grievances, which in turn lead to the declaratory part of the entire statement, the announcement of independence. It is quite possible that had the direct or primary goals been met early in the conflict, the issue of independence would not have arisen.[2]

[2] In July, 1775, the Continental Congress published a Declaration of the

Once, however, the issue of independence became an additional goal, the equalitarian and consent theory of the Declaration were supportive reasoning to justify the specific declaratory act of independence. But they were by-products or indirect consequences of the specific act of revolution. In 1776, doubtless, the enumerated grievances were thought to be of more importance than the statement of self-evident truths; but in historical consequence this order of importance has been reversed.

What makes the unraveling of action and rhetoric, of direct goals and ideology, so complicated is that the script lives on after the actors have left, and the lines are interpreted by new generations in quite new circumstances, and the actual politics which brought forth the script are reinterpreted in the light of the script. Liberal rhetoric is thus thought to reveal liberal politics; and conservative rhetoric, conservative politics.

On June 7, 1776 Richard Henry Lee offered a resolution of independence which in fact contained the words of the last paragraph of the Declaration of Independence. On June 10, 1776 the Continental Congress voted in favor of a resolution to authorize a committee to "prepare a declaration to the effect of the said first [Lee] resolution." On July 2, Congress passed Lee's June 7 resolution, proclaiming thereby independence from Great Britain. On July 4, Congress passed the committee's draft of what has come to be known as the Declaration of Independence, and which constituted the arguments for the proclamation of independence which had in fact been proclaimed two days earlier. In other words, the direct goal of independence had already been proclaimed before the formal statement of justification for the action, in effect the ideology, had been officially approved. Thomas Jefferson was well aware of the legitimatizing function of the document he drafted, for he noted many years later: "When forced, therefore, to resort to arms for redress, an appeal to the tribunal of the world was deemed proper for our justification. This was the object of the Declaration of Independence. Not to find out new principles, or new arguments . . . but to place before mankind the common sense of the subject,

---

Causes and Necessity of Taking up Arms, which proclaimed, in part: "We have not raised armies with ambitious designs of separating from Great Britain. . . ." See Carl Becker, *The Declaration of Independence* (New York: Vintage Books, 1958), 126-127.

in terms so plain and firm as to command their assent, and to justify ourselves in the independent stand we are compelled to take."[3]

With time, however, the second paragraph of the Declaration, with its enumeration of self-evident truths, came to acquire an existence almost independent of the rest of the document. The propositions which were intended to justify the act of separation from the British empire, transcended that issue and occasion to become values which constituted the ultimate tests of democratic political legitimacy. Whenever the issue of democracy, with government by the consent of the governed, has been at stake, the rhetoric of the Declaration has been invoked; whenever the equalitarian ethic has been challenged, the sacred text of self-evident truths has been called upon. In other words, the philosophic principles became detached from the historic occasion which brought them forth. A good illustration of this transcendence of history, whereby the philosophic principles derived from the past took on meaning for the future, is found in Lincoln's claims during his celebrated debate with Douglas. What had prompted the discussion of the Declaration of Independence, in 1857, had been the Dred Scott decision in which Chief Justice Taney had held that the equalitarian principles of the document had been intended by the authors to apply only to Englishmen. What had the authors meant by equality? Lincoln declared:

They meant to set up a standard maxim for free society, which should be familiar to all, and revered by all; constantly looked to, constantly labored for, and even though never perfectly attained, constantly approximated, and thereby constantly spreading and deepening its influence and augmenting the happiness and value of life to all people of all colors everywhere. The assertion that 'all men are created equal' was of no practical use in effecting our separation from Great Britain; and it was placed in the Declaration not for that, but for future use. Its authors meant it to be—as, thank God, it is now proving itself—a stumbling-block to all those who in after times might seek to turn a few people back into the hateful paths of despotism.[4]

Any other view, Lincoln held, such as the view that it was intended only to justify the separation of the American colonies from Great Britain, would make "a mere wreck—mangled ruin" of "our once glorious Declaration." "I had thought the Declaration contemplated

---

[3] Saul K. Padover, *Thomas Jefferson on Democracy* (New York: Penguin Books, Inc., 1946), 13.

[4] John G. Nicolay and John Hay, eds., *Complete Works of Abraham Lincoln* (Lincoln Memorial Library, 1894), II, 331.

the progressive improvement in the condition of all men everywhere . . . ." But if it was adopted only to justify independence then "the Declaration is of no practical use now—mere rubbish—old wadding left to rot on the battlefield after the victory is won." And so Lincoln challenged his audience:

And now I appeal to all . . . are you really willing that the Declaration shall thus be frittered away?—thus left no more, at most, than an interesting memorial of the dead past?—thus shorn of its vitality and practical value, and left without the germ or even the suggestion of the individual rights of man in it? . . .

What has been at one time an instrumental measure, a justifying statement to legitimatize the act of separation from Great Britain, so became the national normative statement of democratic political theory. The historic Declaration became superseded by the ideological Declaration, and the historic Revolution became idealized into a mythological Revolution which was fought to make manifest the eternal principles of the self-evident truths. In the course of this transformation of history into myth, Jefferson became apotheosized, and the Declaration of Independence became our sacred scripture.[5]

This is not to say, however, that the authors of the Declaration were not themselves well aware of the historic consequences of the document they drafted, as well as of the future significance of the Revolution itself. One cannot help be impressed in reading the records of this period with the self-conscious awareness on the part of many of the Revolutionary leaders of the high historic importance of the steps they had undertaken. And in their own interpretation of these events political values were of the utmost importance. For example, looking back on the Revolution some forty odd years later, John Adams wrote:

The American Revolution was not a common event. Its effects and consequences have already been awful over a great part of the globe. And when or where are they to cease? But what do we mean by the American Revolution? Do we mean the American war? The Revolution was effected before the war commenced. The Revolution was in the minds and hearts of the people; a change in their religious sentiments of their duties and obligations . . . This radical change in the principles, opinions, sentiments, and affections of the people, was the real American Revolution.[6]

[5] See Merrill D. Peterson, *The Jeffersonian Image in the American Mind* (New York: Oxford University Press, 1962), prologue.

[6] Harry R. Warfel, Ralph H. Gabriel, Stanley T. Williams, eds., *The American Mind* (New York: American Book Company, 1937), 203.

So singular an event was the American Revolution, bringing in so short a time political cohesion out of customary separateness, that Adams believed that scholars should collect and treasure every scrap of paper, "all the records, pamphlets, newspapers, and even handbills, which in any way contributed to change the temper and views of the people, and compose them into an independent nation."[7] The results of such research, however, would give scant comfort to future revolutionaries; for the records would show the moderation, temperateness, and sagacity of the American people at that time. Not any people could carry through a revolution, nor did any grievance warrant one.

> They [the records] may teach mankind that revolutions are no trifles; that they ought never to be undertaken rashly; nor without a deliberate consideration and sober reflection; nor without a solid, immutable, eternal foundation of justice and humanity; nor without a people possessed of intelligence, fortitude, and integrity sufficient to carry them with steadiness, patience, and perseverance, through all the vicissitudes of fortune, the fiery trials and melancholy disasters they may encounter . . .[8]

Writing to his wife, Abigail, the day after the passage of the Declaration of Independence by the Continental Congress, Adams declared the enactment to be "the most memorable epocha in the history of America." And he exclaimed, prophetically: "I am apt to believe that it will be celebrated by succeeding generations as the great anniversary festival. . . . It ought to be solemnized with pomp and parade, with shows, games, sports, guns, bells, bonfires, and illuminations, from one end of this continent to the other, from this time forward forevermore."[9]

This buoyancy, this enthusiasm, this ecstatic sense that something truly remarkable had happened in the history not only of Americans but of all mankind is found in much of the literature of this first generation of Americans. In Abigail Adams' diary, written aboard the *Active* in which she was sailing from Boston to join her husband in France, we find after daily notations about the weather, the passengers, and the ravages of seasickness, this entry dated July 4, 1784:

> This is the anniversary of our Glorious Independence.
> O thou! by whose Almighty Nod the Scale,
> of Empires rises, or alternate falls,

[7] *Ibid.*, 204.
[8] *Ibid.*
[9] *Ibid.*, 203.

> Send forth the Saveing virtues round our land
> In bright patrol; white peace, and Social Love,
> The tender looking Charity, intent
> on Gentle Deeds, and sheding tears through Smiles,
> Undaunted Truth, and Dignity of mind
> Courage composed and keen; sound temperance
> Healthfull in Heart and look; Clear Chastity
> with blushes reddening as she moves along
> Disordered at the deep regard she draws;
> Rough Industry; Activity untir'd,
> With copious Life informed and all awake;
> While in the Radient front, superiour shines
> That first parental virtue, publick Zeal;
> Who throws o'er all an equal wide survey;
> And ever museing on the Common Weal,
> Still Labours glorious with some great design;

Whilst the Nations of Europe are enveloped in Luxury and dissipation; and a universal venality prevails throughout Britain, may the new empire, Gracious Heaven, become the Guardian and protector of Religion and Liberty, of universal Benevolence and Phylanthropy. May those virtues which are banished from the land of our Nativity, find a safe Assylum with the inhabitants of this new world.[10]

In her stilted eighteenth-century verse, rich with religious feeling, Abigail Adams was expressing the sentiment that the less devout Tom Paine had expressed in the closing lines of *Common Sense*: "Every spot of the old world is overrun with oppression. Freedom hath been hunted round the Globe . . . O! receive the fugitive, and prepare in time an asylum for mankind."[11]

What emerges, again and again, in the early patriotic literature is the beginnings of a theme that would later be called American exceptionalism. According to this view, there was something distinct, indeed unique, about this country which would make it take a different route in its development, make it exceptional to the general historical configurations which had shaped the character of the old world countries. In the new world was to be found a new man, who would provide an asylum for the banished virtues from abroad, even as the land would provide an asylum for the banished men. In the old world were found tyranny and vice; in the old world, according to John Adams, were found the corrupting influences of the feudal and the canon law. Americans had escaped

---

[10] L. H. Butterfield, ed., *The Adams Papers* (New York: Atheneum, 1964), III, 162-163.

[11] Warfel, etc., *op. cit.*, 153.

these old world systems, and had buttressed man's new estate with a broad system of public education "in a manner that I believe has been unknown to any other people ancient or modern." It was rare in America, Adams wrote in 1765, to find one who could not read and write. "It has been observed," he noted, "that we are all of us lawyers, divines, politicians, and philosophers. And I have good authorities to say that all candid foreigners who have passed through this country and conversed freely with all sorts of people here will allow that they have never seen so much knowledge and civility among the common people in any part of the world."[12] This notion of exceptionalism came to be interpreted in many ways: the freedom of the press; the diversity of religious expression; the absence of feudalism; the presence of the frontier; the extent of property holding, and of the franchise; the abundance of natural resources; the distinctiveness of capitalistic development; the high degree of literacy ,and so on. But whatever the interpretation the theme remained essentially the same; America was exceptional, and its politics and culture could not be simply explained by the formulas derived from either ancient history or European experience.

This exceptional character of American politics was to be found, according to the early New England settlers, in the opportunities to do simultaneously God's work and man's work, untrammelled by ancient customs, institutions, and practices. In the early Puritan writings are found many references to an awareness of this remarkable opportunity, presented in the new land, to create institutions in both church and state which were in accord with what they believed to be God's plan. In the new world lay the promised land where men might start anew and fashion institutions to His purpose, rather than live under the corrupt institutions which had heretofore fashioned men. But it was not, of course, only the religiously motivated who saw in the new land a new world of opportunity. The thousands upon thousands of families who crowded aboard the little vessels with their unhealthy and primitive accommodations to make the perilous voyage to the new world staked their health, possessions and lives on the promise that the new land would offer something better than the old.

If the American colonial experience was exceptional, the Revolu-

[12] George A. Peek, Jr., *The Political Writings of John Adams* (Indianapolis: The Bobbs-Merrill Co., 1954), 12.

tion which brought forth "the first new nation," to adopt Seymour Lipset's felicitious expression, was exceptional too.[13] If one looked at the great modern revolutions, the English in the seventeenth century, the French in the eighteenth, the Russian in the twentieth, certain similarities were observable. Class antagonisms were generated under an old regime which proved to be inept in coping with them. A revolutionary leadership of moderates arose, who were in turn displaced by extremists. A reign of terror followed which brought forth a thermidorean reaction. Where did the American Revolution fit into this general pattern?

Crane Brinton, in his pioneering study of these four revolutions, found the American Revolution to be exceptional primarily in its lack of truly sharp and clear class alignments. "Men like John Adams and Washington were not attempting to overturn our social and economic system, but rather to set the English North American colonies up as an independent nation-state." On the other hand, Brinton believed, "Sam Adams, Tom Paine, Jefferson himself, were trying to do more than just cut us off from the British Crown; they were trying to make us a more perfect society according to the ideals of the Enlightenment."[14] In studying revolutions comparatively, Brinton noted again and again how similar the patterns of the English, French, and Russian revolutions were, but that the American never quite fit the pattern of the others. His four revolution analysis really turned out to be a three nation analysis with an American exception. So that we are frequently met with such statements as: "But we must always remember that the American Revolution was as a social revolution in a sense an incomplete one, that it does not fit perfectly our conceptual scheme, that it does not show the victory of the extremists over the moderates."[15]

Brinton, who had first presented his four revolution analysis in 1938, had difficulty accounting for the American exception because the concept of moderation was hardly compatible with a thesis of social class upheaval, even such a modified class conflict as he employed. For in effect the singular element which seemed to dominate and characterize the American exception was its fundamental

[13] Seymour Martin Lipset, *The First New Nation* (New York: Basic Books, Inc., 1963).

[14] Crane Brinton, *The Anatomy of Revolution* (New York: Vintage Books, revised edition, 1964), 22.

[15] *Ibid.*, 24.

conservatism. In the 1950's however, many writers came to see American politics, past and present, as being characterized by a deep underlying conservatism. Indeed, the more remote the event became in time, the more conservative it came to appear in character. The inherent conflict between a social class upheaval on the one hand, and a moderate or conservative revolution on the other, became resolved by many writers by disclaiming the thesis of a social revolution at all. For example, a leading college textbook today notes:

The American Revolution was no social revolution, like those of France and Russia. No class as such was expropriated, slavery was not abolished, the structure of society was not altered . . . Even the confiscation of loyalist property affected the relations of persons rather than of classes: one set of proprietors was impoverished, and another enriched; and it was not long before the patriots who obtained Tory farms and mansions were just as conservative as the former owners.[16]

This absence of a social revolution, of a social upheaval, at a time that a political upheaval was taking place, may be of momentous importance in understanding the climate of opinion in which the Declaration of Independence was formulated. If there were not hard and fast class cleavages, if society was indeed essentially open and fluid, then one might say that in such a society all men were created equal even though such a proposition was contrary to all European experience. This would further explain why the five moderate to conservative members of the committee appointed to draft the Declaration of Independence, a committee composed of four lawyers and a publisher, could endorse the self-evident truths without fear that they would incite a rebellion at home. If the key phrases of the self-evident truths were but a paraphrase of John Locke's *Second Treatise on Civil Govern-*

16 Samuel Eliot Morison and Henry Steele Commager, *The Growth of the American Republic* (New York: Oxford University Press, 1961), I, 246. For a contrary view see Richard B. Morris, *The American Revolution Reconsidered* (New York: Harper & Row, 1967). Morris notes, "Striking though the similarities are between the American and the French Revolutions, the two movements have obvious differences, as obvious as the contrast in the characters and temperaments of a Washington and a Robespierre. The trouble is that recent commentators have made the differences appear more obvious than the facts warrant. They have refused to give to the American Revolution any dimension other than that of a political movement of liberation, whereas they have invested the French Revolution with all the trappings of class war." (p. 54).

ment, this was only further proof of how well established in the colonies those principles were; for the very strength and efficacy of these principles lay in the fact that they had the approval of respected and conservative members of the community. For in an essentially open society there was nothing really radical about these opinions at all.

One further aspect of the exceptional character of the American Revolution is pertinent to this discussion of revolutionary ideology and its relation to a conservative political movement. That is the heavily legalistic and constitutional character of the colonists' argument. In Daniel Boorstin's view, the Revolution was less of a break with the past than an effort to continue and perpetuate it. The British Constitution, as understood by the colonists, was the norm, the "given"; as a result arguments tended to be legal rather than philosophical. Even the Declaration of Independence, he noted, once we get past the first two paragraphs which were "merely a succinct restatement of the Whig theory of the British revolution of 1688," was more "a document of imperial legal relations rather than a piece of high-flown political philosophy."[17] More recently, Bernard Bailyn has stressed the constitutional nature of the conflict, noting that the Revolution "was above all else an ideological-constitutional struggle and not primarily a controversy between social groups undertaken to force changes in the organization of society."[18] Clinton Rossiter in his analysis of the pamphlets, sermons and articles written during the Revolution was also impressed by the heavy emphasis upon legal and constitutional arguments. "The Revolutionary crisis marked the climax of an historic process that had been generations in the making: the seizure of political power by the legal profession."[19]

Even when the Revolutionary writers passed beyond the arguments from their ancient colonial charters, their technical and seemingly nit-picking discussions of internal versus external taxes, their refined constitutional arguments on the jurisdictional limits on Parliament in matters of trade and defense, their evolving theories

[17] Daniel Boorstin, *The Genius of American Politics* (Chicago: The University of Chicago Press, 1953), 81-85.

[18] Bernard Bailyn, *Pamphlets of the American Revolution, 1750-1776* (Cambridge, Mass: Harvard University Press, 1965), I, viii.

[19] Clinton Rossiter, *The Political Thought of the American Revolution,* Part Three of *Seedtime of the Republic* (New York: Harcourt, Brace & World, 1963), 39.

of the British empire, they chose to rest their claims on the vener-
able tradition of natural law. As constitutional law led back to
Blackstone and Coke, so their study of natural law led them back
to Pufendorf, Locke and Hooker. But the appeal was always to
a tradition that seemed immutably secure. If law led to philosophy, so that in time the rights of Englishmen could be seen as
the rights of man, philosophy gave to the law a sense of universal
appeal which could, with time, transcend the experience of the
Revolution itself. In Rossiter's assessment:

Perhaps the most remarkable characteristic of this system of political ideas was
its deep-seated conservatism. However radical the principles of the Revolution may have seemed to the rest of the world, in the minds of the colonists
they were thoroughly preservative and respectful of the past . . . By 1765 the
colonies had achieved a society more open, and more constitutional than anything Europeans would know for years to come. Americans had secured and
were ready to defend a condition of freedom that other liberty-minded men
could only hope for in the distant future or plot for in the brutal present.
The political principles of the American Revolution, in contrast to those of
the French Revolution, were not designed to make the world over. The
world—at least the American corner of it—had already been made over as
thoroughly as any sensible man could expect.[20]

This was undoubtedly hyperbole; yet after allowance has been
made for the exaggeration of one who saw consensus rather than
conflict as the fundamental theme of American politics, a large
element of truth remains.

In the two decades which have passed since the 1950's, when
the American Revolution became reinterpreted as a War of Independence rather than as a two-fold revolution (one at home, one
abroad), there has been much dispute over the proper interpretation of this signal event. Robert Brown, Forrest McDonald and
Edmund Morgan have stressed the degree of democracy already
present in the colonies at the time of the Revolution and accordingly find little support for the class conflict thesis with its corollary
of a democratic revolution at home.[21] On the other hand, Merrill

---

[20] *Ibid.*, 229.

[21] Robert E. Brown, *Middle-Class Democracy and the Revolution in Massa-
chusetts, 1691-1780* (Ithaca: Cornell University Press, 1955), and Robert E.
Brown and Katherine Brown, *Virginia, 1705-1786: Democracy or Aristocracy*
(East Lansing: Michigan State University Press, 1964); Forrest McDonald,
We the People (Chicago, 1958); Edmund Morgan, *The Birth of the Republic*
(Chicago, 1956); also see F. B. Tolles, "The American Revolution Considered
as a Social Movement," *American Historical Review*, (1954), LX, 1-12.

Jensen, Jackson Main and Richard Morris have pointed up the degree of inequality in American society and have in effect rejected the "consensus" or conservative view as an oversimplification of what was presumably a class structured society.[22] Indeed, in a sharp attack on the "consensus" writers, Morris has noted: "It is a pity to mar the charming landscape of social affability and homogeneity which contemporary commentators on the Revolution are painting, but it is required of scholars that they look below the surface, and if they do they may find that in the Thirteen Colonies on the eve of the Revolution the rich were getting richer while a class of depressed and indigent persons was growing up."[23] In spite of conflicts over interpretations, however, there does seem to be a large area of agreement about the nature of colonial society which is relevant to this discussion. There were gradations in rank, which tended to follow gradations in property holding, so that the upper ranks were referred to as "gentlemen," and the term "esquire" was used to define the upper members of this rank; while "yeoman" and "goodman" applied to small property holders. There were, as one might expect, differences in status. But there seems to be little evidence that these alignments, whether large as opposed to small property holders, or of propertied versus nonpropertied persons, shaped in any consistent pattern the political division into Loyalists or Revolutionaries. Property qualifications for voting existed throughout the colonies; but most recent studies indicate that these qualifications produced only a relatively minor degree of disfranchisement.[24] Property was apparently generally

[22] Merrill Jensen, The Articles of Confederation (Madison: The University of Wisconsin Press, 1959 printing); Jackson Main, The Antifederalists (Chapel Hill: The University of North Carolina Press, 1961); Richard B. Morris, The American Revolution Reconsidered (New York: Harper & Row, 1967).

[23] Morris, op. cit., 59-60.

[24] The degree of disfranchisement of white, adult males due to the property qualifications for voting is a matter of much speculation and relatively meager evidence. After careful research in the records of colonial Massachusetts, Robert E. Brown found: "While it is true that property ownership was a prerequisite for province and town voting, it is also true that the amount of property required for the franchise was very small and that the great majority of men could easily meet the requirements." Op. cit., 402. This view is supported by Chilton Williamson, American Suffrage from Property to Democracy, 1760-1860 (Princeton: Princeton University Press, 1960) where it is noted that "in the history of colonial suffrage and elections, contests arose more frequently than might be expected from matters involving religion, ethnic, and

easy to acquire and was widely held. As far as the economic aspect of the Revolution was concerned, property was the crux of the issue precisely because it was so widely held. As Edmund Morgan has observed:

The Americans fought England because Parliament threatened the security of property. They established state constitutions with property qualifications for voting and officeholding in order to protect the security of property. And when the state governments seemed inadequate to the task, they set up the Federal government for the same purpose . . . Devotion to security of property was not the attitude of a privileged few but the fundamental principle of the many, inseparable from everything that went by the name of freedom and adhered to the more fervently precisely because it did affect most people so intimately.[25]

Today, when the issue of human rights is often raised in opposition to claims of property rights, it is difficult, as Morgan has noted, to see that property rights were once an instrument for achieving human rights. The colonists did not need to turn back to Aristotle, for they could cite James Harrington to argue the intimate connection between widely distributed property and widely distributed political power. This wide distribution of property had been fortuitously achieved by the happy combination of an expansive continent, a resourceful people, and an adaptable legal system. This wide distribution of property not only gave to the colonists a supporting economic base, for the country was pri-

---

national origins rather than from the issue of property per se. With property so widely diffused, differences and distinctions of other kinds appeared more significant." (Pp. 53-4) Jackson Main, op. cit., observed: "The majority of white Americans, and by far the largest number of voters, were farmers who owned their land and who lived at a subsistence-plus level." (p. 5) However, he qualified this sentence by noting, "What percentage of the men could vote is a moot point. In the South, where it was usually necessary to own land, about half were disfranchised, but in New England probably between 60 and 90 percent had the suffrage." (Fn. 10, p. 5) Yet Forrest McDonald, E Pluribus Unum (Boston: Houghton Mifflin Co., 1965) reports that "Virginia (which was what people most often meant when they said 'the South') was scarcely aristocratic at all, at least by contemporary standards. The suffrage was widespread: a far greater percentage of its adult males regularly went to the polls than was the case in 'democratic' Connecticut or Massachusetts. The rate of turnover of elected officials was great, considerably more rapid than in New Hampshire or even the 'licentious republic,' Rhode Island." (p. 67) Also for Virginia, see Robert E. and Katherine Brown, op. cit.

    25 Edmund S. Morgan, The American Revolution: Two Centuries of Interpretation (Englewood Cliffs, N. J.: Prentice-Hall, 1965), 176.

marily agricultural then, which made possible a large measure of economic independence; but it also gave to the colonists a clear stake in society. Property rights were at the core of their system of rights. Property holding has always had political consequences; with a vested interest to protect, civic interest is easily acquired. Citizen participation in public affairs followed quite naturally from citizen concern over the protection of property. For property holders, traditionally, taxes have been an issue of utmost importance. When taxes and restrictive regulations upon trade were imposed by Parliament, a property holders' revolt was a natural consequence even as was the democratic form it took. For implicit in the slogan "no taxation without representation" was the message that a representation of property holders would not have enacted such taxation. Such an aroused citizenry could safely be trusted with the powers of government, because the property they would be protecting would be their own. Furthermore, only in a system in which the power to tax lay with representatives of their own choosing, could their property be considered truly safe. In this view then, it was the wide distribution of property, and the universal respect in which property was held, which made for the War of Independence to escape perceived unjust taxation and regulation of trade; it was the wide distribution of property, furthermore, which made for representative government, home rule in effect, as the surest means to protect property in the future.

Coupled with the theory of representative government was the belief in limited government. As *Cato's Letters*, widely read at the time of the Revolution, had observed, the people must see that governments use power sparingly. "All history affords but few Instances of Men trusted with great Power without abusing it, when with Security they could." Governments should be "narrowly watched, and checked with Restraints stronger than their Temptation to break them."[26] This was the same point often made by Thomas Jefferson in noting that he was not a friend of energetic government; free government was founded on a prudent sense of caution and suspicion; the price of liberty was eternal vigilance. Again it is instructive to remember that in the eighteenth century there was felt, at least on the part of most English and American writers, to be no incompatability between the concept of limited government and the concept of representative government. In the

[26] Quoted in Main, *op. cit.*, 9.

.same way that a representative government of property holders was thought to be an effective means to see that no unjust taxes were levied, so was it thought that a truly representative government would not seek to augment its powers at the expense of popular liberty. It was this same sense of limitation which would later find expression in written constitutions, with circumscribed powers for the different branches of government, checks and balances, and bills of rights.

In a society in which property was widely if unevenly held, the lawyers, merchants, farmers and other property holders who constituted the Second Continental Congress would not be thought of as unrepresentative figures; nor would the distinguished committee composed of Jefferson, John Adams, Franklin, Sherman and Livingston which was charged with the task of drafting the Declaration be thought of as molded from a different clay than their fellow man for all of their extraordinary talents and education. Nor would the Continental Congress, itself a product of a property-conscious society which had over the years enjoyed a large measure of home rule, find the phrases of the Declaration of Independence at all exceptional in philosophy. For barring slavery generations of colonial experience had demonstrated the openness of the opportunity structure for the acquisition of property (if only a small farm), of education (if only literacy), and some political power (if only to vote). In such a society it could be said that men were created equal, for no man could comfortably accept the superiority of another, and least of all the political superiority of Englishmen across the sea. In such a society men were jealous guardians of their rights, and believed these rights were best protected by a government of their own choosing. And in such a society men were then proving in 1776 their right to replace one government with another when the former failed to protect and preserve their rights.

Equality is not a doctrine that is likely to be enthusiastically supported by an aristocracy in a society in which there are clear and rigid class cleavages, for it would threaten their very existence. Nor in such a society is equality likely to find wide support if its champions are spokesmen for peasants and proletarians. In a society imbued with middle class norms, however, equality is a doctrine of almost infallible appeal, reassuring to both those above and those below the average level. To those above this level it brings the comfort of being more equal than others without subjecting them to the hazards of a higher system of gradations; to those below this level it brings the reassurance that no matter what advantages others may possess, no man need feel the humility of ascriptive inferiority. In American society the equalitarian ethic has continued to hold its appeal precisely because it has reflected this middle class orientation. It has been, in other words, the conservative middle class orientation of American society which today, as in 1776, has made the equalitarian ethic an essential component of our liberal value structure.

"Time Hath Found Us":
The Jeffersonian
Revolutionary
Vision

ROBERT J. MORGAN

IN JANUARY, 1776, Thomas Paine jubilantly predicted that, if Americans would recognize "the ripeness . . . of the Continent for independence," they could "begin the world all over again" by forming "the noblest, purest constitution on the face of the earth."[1] Just this once John Adams agreed heartily with him. The lawgivers of antiquity certainly would have wished to live at that moment, when Americans had the opportunity to serve posterity by founding the "wisest and happiest government" within the power of human prudence.[2] Looking back fifty years to those exhilarating days, Jefferson rejoiced that "our Revolution . . . presented us with an album on which we were free to write what we pleased."[3]

We are probably too jaded by subsequent events to share the jubilation of those men who believed that they had lived life to some purpose. Generally, we are inclined to agree with their

[1] Thomas Paine, "Common Sense" in *The Complete Writings of Thomas Paine,* ed. Philip S. Foner (2 vols.; New York: The Citadel Press, 1945), I, 31, 45; cited hereafter as *Writings.*

[2] John Adams, *The Works of John Adams,* ed. Charles Francis Adams (10 vols.; Boston: Little Brown and Co., 1850-56), IV, 200; cited hereafter as *Works.*

[3] Thomas Jefferson, *The Writings of Thomas Jefferson,* ed. Albert Emery Bergh (20 vols.; Washington: D. C., The Thomas Jefferson Memorial Association, 1903), XVI, 44; cited hereafter as *Writings.*

contemporary, the Abbé Raynal, that the American Revolution was no more than a colonial rebellion, albeit one which the world has scarcely been able to ignore. Yet, even among the Founders, who made the revolution without being utopians, were men like Hamilton who said that Americans might be deciding for mankind the question whether good governments may be the consequence of deliberate choice, or must rest on accident and force.[4] Both the sober and the visionary among them believed they were joined in a revolutionary political experiment.

There is no mystery why Paine and Jefferson, who shared in both the American and French Revolutions, believed that the first one was no less important than the second. The world would have paid little attention to America's political separation from Britain, Paine said, were it not that it had produced "revolution in the principles and practices of government" which linked republicanism with the progress of civilization being wrought by advances in "science and commerce."[5] When the Abbé Raynal dismissed the American Revolution as a mere colonial revolt over taxes, Paine answered that he mistakenly judged it by outdated ideas of a revolution. Properly understood, it was a revolution because it was an unprecedented political change. "All the revolutions till [sic] then had been worked in the atmosphere of a court, and never on the great floor of a nation . . ." made up of people from many sources, speaking different languages and worshipping in diverse faiths.[6] To the end of his life, Jefferson held that our experience

[4] Alexander Hamilton, John Jay and James Madison, *The Federalist*, introduction by Edward Meade Earle (New York: Modern Library, 1937), 3; cited hereafter as *Federalist*.

[5] Paine, *Writings*, I, 240; II, 354.

[6] *Ibid*; I, 217; II, 360. Probably the most widely cited work which repeats the Abbé Raynal's criticism is Louis Hartz, *The Liberal Tradition in America* (New York: Harcourt, Brace and World, Inc., 1955). American thought has never been revolutionary because it has not been directed to the destruction of an existing "society" and the reconstruction "of a new society on the ruins of an old one . . .," 66. The meaning of "society" in such arguments is usually vague, but it is clear that a violent overthrow of existing public office holders and their wholesale replacement by former outsiders is the *minimal* political element in a revolution. For a Marxist, such a change brings a new "class" to power for the purpose of giving "rational" direction to a wide range of human affairs after public expropriation of the means of production. Obviously, the American and French Revolutions were not of this latter sort. They were purely changes in the forms of previous regimes and were, therefore, political only.

was truly revolutionary because we had reached a new understanding of politics. We had learned the importance of emancipat-
ing the human mind from superstition and ignorance by which
mankind had been rendered dependent upon traditional elites for
rule during all previous time. The Declaration of Independence
had proclaimed principles "pregnant . . . with fate of the world"
because they revealed the source of human misery: "one single
curse—that of a bad form of government."[7]   Early in his public
career, John Adams denounced the "confederacy of temporal and
spiritual powers" found in Europe where aristocracy depended for
its status upon war and clerics hoodwinked the people with authority founded upon superstition and mysteries.   This combination held people in a condition of *dependence,* whereas Americans
were learning the form of knowledge which traditional rulers
dreaded most—"the characters and conduct of their rulers. . . ."
Therefore, Adams proclaimed, "let every sluice of knowledge be
opened. . . ."[8]

Paine, Jefferson and Adams shared a common belief in the primacy of politics inherited from Classical thought and combined
it with a conviction that opinions are powerful weapons in any
struggle to effect decisive political and social changes.   In addition,
they claimed a special sense of destiny based upon their unique
perceptions of irreversible and fundamental changes facing Europe
and America alike.   These perceptions were to provide the foundation of American institutions and the example for Europe.   For
fifteen years before 1775, John Adams said, a debate over imperial
relations was waged until it effected a revolution in the minds of
the American people.[9]   With hostilities, Paine claimed, Americans
began "to see with other eyes . . . hear with other ears; and think
with other thoughts" to a point where their "thinking underwent
a revolution."[10]   In *Common Sense* Paine called for separation
followed by a republican union established after cool and deliberate
debate.   Otherwise, some "Massanello" [Massaniello] might rouse
the desperate and discontented to "sweep away the liberties of the

---

[7] Jefferson, *Writings,* XVI, 181-182; Thomas Jefferson, *The Papers of Thomas*
Jefferson, ed. Julian Boyd (19 vols.; Princeton: The Princeton University Press,
1950 to date), VIII, 403-404; cited hereafter as *Papers.*

[8] Adams, *Works,* III, 448-464, *passim;* IV, 292-293.

[9] *Ibid.,* IX, 172.

[10] Paine, *Writings,* I, 242.

continent like a deluge."[11] Congress issued a declaration of our independent *political* status because the members had a decent respect for the opinions of mankind. Although this change was effected by arms, it was a true revolution because it produced a political change and not a violent and convulsive upheaval of the "whole fabric of opinions" which would destroy habit and custom totally.[12] It pleased Jefferson to report that even in the seventh year of the war no one had been executed for treason, although persons who declined to swear allegiance to Virginia were deprived of their property.[13] In carrying the lesson of the American Revolution to France in 1792, Paine defined it as a change in the moral condition of governments through discussion, persuasion and conviction.[14] His experience with the Terror coupled with a term in jail confirmed his belief that the "moral principle of revolution is to instruct, not to destroy."[15]

This understanding of revolution as tuition in political reconstruction partially confirmed and, yet, rejected as well, a number of ideas inherited from the body of Western political thought. Simultaneously, it carried the promise of a new political and social age directed to the achievement of commonwealth, the elusive goal of English theorists during the seventeenth century. The idea of revolution as political change was inherited from the Classical Greek writers, although the English usage of the term first appeared during the Civil War and then chiefly as a metaphor. Prior to that development, revolution was treated analytically as a series of degenerations of good forms of constitutions into bad ones. Thu-

[11] *Ibid.*, I, 29-30.

[12] Joel Barlow, *Advice to the Privileged Orders in the Several States of Europe* (Ithaca, N.Y.: Cornell University Press, 1956; first published in London, 1792), 196; cited hereafter as *Advice*.

[13] Thomas Jefferson, *Notes on the State of Virginia* (New York: Harper and Row, 1964; first published in Paris, 1785), 148-149.

[14] Paine, *Writings*, I, 396, 400.

[15] *Ibid.*, II, 587. Contrast this belief with that of those rebels who are tormented by what Albert Camus called Hegel's "philosophy of the guilty conscience" and announce that their mission is "to destroy, not to construct." *The Rebel* (New York: Knopf, Vintage Books, 1956), 144. A contemporary version of this form of what Camus called metaphysical rebellion is found in Marcuse's "great refusal" to accept the natural necessity of work. He teaches withdrawal into sexual fantasies in symbolic rebellion against a mythical, universal father whose authority denies his "sons" the gratification of their lust. Readers must judge whether the aim is moral or immoral.

cydides vividly portrayed the alternating triumph of democratic and oligarchic parties in cities involved in the Peloponnesian War. Plato formulated a psychological theory of the deterioration of best to worst forms, making democracy the last stage before tyranny. Aristotle assigned both general and specific causes to changes from one constitution to another. Among the moderns, Machiavelli revived interest in this matter and added his own emphasis upon the idea that all "mixed" regimes, supposedly the most durable styles, were necessarily subject to degeneration through corruption. Machiavelli referred to such changes as *"mutazione di stato,"* rather than *"revoluzione."*[16] His usage suggests a mood of scientific detachment, rather than ideological frenzy, and it appealed to his great admirer, James Harrington, as well as the latter's many disciples in America. Machiavelli taught, in addition, that a sound form of constitution which has been corrupted can be restored deliberately by recurrence to first principles. This idea was commonplace among Americans of the revolutionary age.

A more proximate source of their ideas of revolution was the body of theory and history prompted by the English Civil War. The Jeffersonians chose eclectically from this source. From "the incomparable Harrington," as James Otis called him, they drew upon the attempt to explain changes in the forms of regimes on a naturalistic, scientific basis. His chief purpose was to demonstrate that the change from monarchy to republic is naturally inevitable, irreversible and progressive. He also laid down the much broader proposition that the "corruption" of one regime is simply the generation of a new one. This idea and others related to it greatly influenced American revolutionary thought as I intend to show presently. From Locke, Jefferson seems to have drawn the idea that a dissolution of government does not entail a dissolution of society. In addition, Americans absorbed his teaching that such an act is undertaken against "tyranny" collectively, rather than individually, and, therefore, it does not lay "a ferment for frequent rebellion."[17] Locke's prescription guided Congress in declaring the end of the imperial tie and the states as they framed constitutions. The latter,

16 Melvin J. Laskey, "The Birth of a Metaphor: On the Origins of Utopia and Revolution," *Encounter,* XXXIV (February 1970), 35-45; (March 1970), 30-42, 31.

17 John Locke, *The Second Treatise of Civil Government,* ed. T. W. Gough (Oxford: Basil Blackwell, 1946), 109; chap. 19, par. 224.

however, required the collective action of the people in the form of a specially elected convention to frame a constitution, according to Jefferson, if the government were to be legitimate. Consent to be governed under a given regime was not to be inferred merely from the election of public officials.[18]

The Jeffersonians' knowledge of the English Civil War seems to have turned them quite strongly against the "modern" conception of revolution which some scholars have perceived in the literature of the period.[19] The language of revolutionary ideology was theological rather than secular and scientific, but it conveyed metaphorical visions of utopian moral and material deliverance to be attained in one final, purifying fury of fire and blood. Heaven was to come to earth so man need not wait for the hereafter. Paradise reached through the fiery passage would never again be lost. Certainly, the expectation of a total and irreversible moral reconstruction has become a basic component of modern millenarian secularism. This development, among others, makes the definition of rebellion inescapably ideological.[20]

The apocalyptic notion of final and total moral purification had a distinctively negative effect on the Jeffersonians and their opponents, alike. If moral perfection is a possibility for man, the public sword is not the proper instrument of his redemption. A union of faith and sword is a violation of the natural right of conscience and its consummation leads only to the support of "roguery and error all over the earth," Jefferson charged.[21] When Madison defended the rights of dissenting sectarians in Virginia, he did so despite the offense which their "enthusiasm" gave to orthodox religionists. Moreover, religion as moral tuition had never re-

---

[18] Jefferson, *Notes on Virginia*, 122-123.

[19] Laskey, *op. cit.*; Michael Walzer, *The Revolution of the Saints* (New York: Atheneum, 1968), 1-4.

[20] John Dunn, *Modern Revolutions* (Cambridge: The University Press, 1972). Modern revolutions undertaken in the name of Marx have been far more "political" than Marxist ideologues care to admit. They have established national states in contradiction of their promise of non-capitalist internationalism and they have displaced old governments with new ones composed of persons previously excluded from offices. Inequalities of power certainly have not been eliminated. See 248-249 and 255-256, especially. For the argument that revolution must consist of violent change on the model of the French, Russian, and Chinese revolutions see Chalmers Johnson, *Revolutionary Change* (Boston: Little Brown and Co., 1966), 7, 11-12.

[21] Jefferson, *Notes on Virginia*, 153.

strained the abuse of power. Utopian communitarians mean well, but they confuse man's first and second natures in assuming the permanency of their experiments.[22] Even John Adams was moved to defend early Massachusetts theocrats against the charge of being excessively "enthusiastical, superstitious and republican. . . ." They were guilty, he explained, only of the "noble infirmity" of passionately wishing for human happiness.[23] There was much agreement with Harrington's warning that religious ideologues are to be dreaded for their totalitarian attempts to "reduce the commonwealth to a party" by gaining power under the pretence of religion which they have never failed to dishonor.[24] When man's nature is unmasked, the motives for both ceaseless conflict and cooperation are evident. There is in human nature, Madison remarked, a degree of "depravity" which requires "circumspection," but there are certain other qualities which justify some "esteem and confidence . . ." essential to the governance of republics. Without some degree of virtue among men, they would be fit only for despotism to restrain them from mutual destruction.[25]

Despite their rejection of moral perfection as the end of revolution, the Founders were deeply conscious of living in an age of irreversible change with the prospect of *improving* the mental, moral and material condition of mankind. The Classical heritage infused them, however, with a sense of what Madison called "the necessity of moderating . . . our expectations and hopes from the efforts of human sagacity" in establishing "the institutions of man."[26] But, if Hume and Paine were both correct, Classical beliefs about the conditions which trigger the cycle of corruption, degeneration and restoration in various regimes no longer provided unequivocal, or even useful, instruction in political life. If Aristotle had been correct, Jefferson would never have been required to recant his confirmation of the former's dictum: *Agricolarum democratica respublica optima.* The ancient writers on politics, and even Ma-

---

[22] James Madison, *The Writings of James Madison,* ed. Gaillard Hunt, (9 vols.; New York: G. P. Putnam's Sons, 1900-10), V, 27; IX, 361. Ralph L. Ketchem, "James Madison and the Nature of Man," *Journal of the History of Ideas,* XIX (January 1958), 62-76.

[23] Adams, *Works,* III, 453.

[24] James Harrington, *The Oceana of James Harrington and His Other Works,* ed. John Toland (London: 1700), 75; cited hereafter as *Oceana.*

[25] *Federalist,* 365.

[26] *Ibid.,* 228-229.

chiavelli, had failed to consider the importance of trade, Hume contended. It was the "opulence, grandeur and military achievements of the two maritime powers" of modern Europe which were teaching mankind the importance of commerce. Above all, the ancient *opinion* that trade, arts ands science could flourish to the greatest degree only in the free republican cities of Europe had been found wrong. Under the British monarchy it was no longer necessary for merchants to waste their profits by purchasing "employments to which privileges and honors are attached," because the royal government was now honoring such men on a plane of equality with the traditional ecclesiastical and military elites.[27]

American revolutionaries understood fully the implications of the new changes unknown to the ancients. In his *Summary View of the Rights of British America,* Jefferson denounced the British government for using unconstitutional legislation to deprive Americans of their "natural right" of "a free trade with all parts of the world. . . ." Imperial policy was calculated to gratify the inordinate avarice of a few Britons through colonial exploitation. Willing hands were found to administer this policy which rewarded ministers and their favorites with the "sale of lucrative and easy office." These royal servants "hope to gain the dignity of a British knighthood." The total design of policy was to secure "the dependency of his majesty's dominions in America upon the crown and parliament. . . ." By instituting novel policies controlling the sale of lands, "the population of our country is likely to be checked." By claiming absolute authority over the colonies and subordinating their civil governments to military authority, Britain was ignoring the truth that "force cannot give right." This was the first occasion, Paine complained, when tyranny was established by law, instead of against, or outside, of it. British America was being governed by 1775 as a military fiefdom.[28]

The readiness of Americans for independence was evident to Paine because the relation of England to America reversed the order of nature which never makes a satellite larger than its primary planet.[29] Americans had a natural right to independence because they had reached a "pitch of greatness, trade and population, be-

[27] David Hume, *Hume's Moral and Political Philosophy,* ed. Henry D. Aiken (New York: Hofner Publishing Co., 1948), 316-319.

[28] Jefferson, *Papers,* I, 121-135 *passim;* Paine, *Writings,* I, 217, 219.

[29] *Ibid.,* I, 24.

yond which it was the interest of Britain not to suffer her to pass, lest she should grow too powerful to be kept subordinate."[30] We must ask, therefore, "Is the power who is jealous of our prosperity, a proper power to govern us?"[31] Self-interest impels Britain to suppress American "growth . . . in every case which doth not promote her advantage, or in the least interferes with it."[32] Without independence, America could not be a free country, independent of the will of Britain whose interest was trade, the principal source of wealth.[33] Moreover, with the outbreak of wars involving Britain, American trade goes to ruin because of the British connection.[34] Free trade is a "pacific system, operating to cordialize mankind." Allowed full development, it would "extirpate war" and become the greatest force ever known for extending civilization.[35] This idea was the "small spark kindled in America," from which "a flame has risen."[36]

The order of nature requires separation from Britain in order to establish a republic, because the republics of Europe are all at peace, now and always. Monarchies, however, are perpetually and restlessly engaged in wars which republics would avoid because they, alone, are founded on "natural principles. . . ."[37] Alexander Hamilton sourly denounced this passivist republican rhetoric, contending that the causes of war are numerous, but unrelated to the form of a regime. "Have republics in practice been less addicted to war than Monarchies?" The ancient republics were "never sated of carnage and lust. . . ." Has commerce done anything but "change the objects of war" and whet the appetite for it?[38] Paine's answer was that the "idea of conquering countries, like the ancient Greeks and Romans . . . for profit" has been exploded and, consequently, they could no longer serve as examples of republics to be imitated by Americans who had discovered the truth that free trade is the policy of republics and the antidote to imperial exploitation.[39]

[30] *Ibid.*, I, 78.
[31] *Ibid.*, I, 25.
[32] *Ibid.*, I, 26.
[33] *Ibid.*, I, 80.
[34] *Ibid.*, I, 21.
[35] *Ibid.*, I, 400-401.
[36] *Ibid.*, I, 398.
[37] *Ibid.*, I, 26-27.
[38] *Federalist*, 30-31.
[39] Paine, *Writings*, I, 242.

Perceptive Loyalists agreed with Paine, Jefferson and their fellow republicans that the dynamics of the struggle between Britain and its colonials seeking to escape imperialism would have profound and predictable political consequences. Samuel Seabury admitted that profits were concentrated in England, and Americans were becoming restless because they lacked exclusive control over their potential for a vast increase in population and wealth in lands and commerce. That was why they were claiming a right of representation based upon a republican principle which would subvert the British monarchy. They were engaged in sedition to destroy the Empire and erect a commonwealth on its ruins.[40] Daniel Leonard predicted that, if the Americans separated from Britain and instituted governments, they would be unable to establish anything like the British constitution which was claimed as their right by heritage. The provincial assemblies were but pale imitations of Parliament. Upon separation, therefore, they would become either wholly monarchical or republican, but there was no foundation for mixed governments upon which their liberties supposedly depended.[41]

These loyalists and Patriots like John Adams understood that the growing tension between Britain and the colonies was fully consistent with Harrington's prophetic vision of an eventual separation. Starting with his fundamental axiom that power is founded upon property, he held it to be a law of the natural science of politics that a crisis and eventual separation will occur between a "national" government and its "provinces," if the property of the latter ever overbalances that of the former. It follows, therefore, that free republics which are founded upon balance deny such governments to their provinces. Venice, the greatest, freest and most durable of all republics, refused its provinces "balance," he said, "lest the foreign interest should root out the national . . . and by diffusing the commonwealth through her territories lose the advantage of her situation, by which in great part she subsists." In 1656 Britain's American colonies were "yet babes that cannot live without sucking the breasts of their mother cities," but he would be greatly mistaken "if when they come of age they do not wean themselves."[42] When Paine's *Common Sense* burst upon

---

[40] Quoted in Alpheus T. Mason, *Free Government in the Making*, 3rd ed. (New York: Oxford University Press, 1965), 116-117.

[41] *Ibid.*, 120.

[42] Harrington, *Oceana*, 43-44.

the American consciousness in 1776, it confirmed Harrington's prediction that empires are subject to a natural law of disunion. Miraculously, it simultaneously confirmed the pacific and civilizing consequences of free trade implied in Montesquieu's teaching that republics are devoted to commerce, not to war, and need, therefore, only a citizen army without the leadership of hereditary aristocrats.

This vision of the peaceful, civilizing mission of modern republics based upon enlightened public opinion and devoted to raising mankind's standard of living was instruction aimed at both a domestic and a foreign audience. Certainly, Jeffersonians attached the highest importance to Aristotle's warning that control of military power involves control of "the future destiny of a constitution."[43]   From the Bill of Rights and the controversy in England over a standing army after 1697, all had learned that standing armies in time of peace are dangerous to liberties. Jefferson proposed in his constitution for Virginia, 1776, such an explicit declaration. The Virginians tried without success to incorporate one in the Constitution of 1787. When Anti-Federalists denounced this omission, Alexander Hamilton characteristically excoriated these "clamors as the dishonest artifices of a sinister and unprincipled opposition."[44] Madison thought it prudent to assuage this stinging attack with assurances that a popular militia organized in each state would serve as the natural barrier to what he called ambitious encroachments upon liberty.[45]

When the militia was organized on a federal basis, the Jeffersonians justified the action as being characteristic of a republic and a reaffirmation of ancient teaching inscribed in the Second Amendment to become part of the American creed. At the same time, they attacked changes occurring in British civil-military relations because they were novel and dangerous departures from the Glorious Revolution. In the British Empire, the military power was no longer subordinate to the civil. Instead, there was "a cordial coalition and mutual support" between the military and commercial elites who formerly had been opponents. The new policy of expanding the public debt had multiplied capital to stimulate a vast

---

[43] Aristotle, *Politics*, ed. Ernest Barker (Oxford: at the Clarendon Press, 1946), 302; Book VII, chap. 9, 1329a.

[44] *Federalist*, 150.

[45] *Ibid.*, 309.

increase in commerce and the expectation of a handsome return to investors. War was being fought for the "wholly modern" purpose of "profit among merchants and ministers," instead of honor for the military alone, according to the traditional theory of monarchy advanced by Montesquieu. In Britain, despite Burke's objections, "the spirit of commerce . . . has become predominant over that of chivalry and . . . church."[46] Madison added his judgment that this symbiotic relationship between those who profited from war and those who waged it left only the facade of liberty to cover the new prosperity.[47]

This criticism of changes in British civil-military relations was a part of a general strategy of giving political instruction in republicanism. "Every species of government has its specific principles. Ours perhaps are more peculiar than those of any other in the universe," Jefferson explained.[48] When Americans framed their new constitutions upon declaring independence, their whole experience had been with monarchy and their political science was derived from European theorists who inspired fear of urban revolutionary mobs called democrats. Americans still thought that republicanism was achieved merely by revolting from monarchy. Consequently, their new constitutions were republican in so far as they banished monarchy and its hereditary orders, but not so in so far as they revealed distrust of popular control of institutions. He agreed with Paine and Adams that America provided the natural conditions for establishing republicanism because we had nothing like the European system of hereditary orders. In America there were differences of offices, but not of men who were all of the same official status out of office. A few "natural" aristocrats had influence, however, according to Adams.[49] Madison, too, recognized the importance of defining republicanism by reference to basic characteristics. Otherwise, even Americans would fall back on European writers and the classical heritage derived from the ancient republics. Such people called both Poland and England republics quite improperly because they were mixtures of aristocracy and monarchy.[50] Montesquieu's argument that the clergy, nobility and

[46] Barlow, Advice, 106-112, passim.
[47] Madison, Writings, VI, 94, 193.
[48] Paine, Writings, I, 354.
[49] Adams, Works, IV, 54, 359, 380, 395-396, 587-588.
[50] Federalist, 243.

certain magistracies stood as barriers between king and people to protect their liberty rested upon the failure to understand that the only legal barrier to autocratic rule is a constitution supported by public opinion.[51] Such instruction in republicanism was necessary to overcome the traditional identification of it with turbulent and unjust democracy. To make their case, the Jeffersonians had to reverse the inherited belief that monarchy is the most virtuous form of regime and a republic the form most likely to degenerate into tyranny.

For the Jeffersonians, the full significance of the Revolution as instruction in politics could not be comprehended without a clear grasp of the ways in which traditional elites impeded the progress of science and common well-being. To make their point, they republicanized Bolingbroke's denunciation of cabinet government. Corruption was the essential lubricant of cabinet government which was destroying the ancient orders and forms of the balanced constitution. Ambitious adventurers seeking their fortunes were rewarded with "titles and ribbands" and offices paid out of the public treasury. Given the dynamics of imperialism and industrialization, the Jeffersonians could not conceive of any way in which Americans could restore such a system to what Bolingbroke called its primitive integrity as a barrier to arbitrary power consistent with the first principles of republicanism.[52] They were certainly aware that John Adams and Hamilton frequently praised the British constitution as the best example of free government known to man. If it were imitated in America, it would destroy the virtuous republics which had been idealized in public discourse, but scarcely realized in fact, as the result of the Revolution.[53]

Jefferson and Madison were much too sophisticated to believe in this idealized rhapsody in praise of republicanism which merged the individual and his rights with the public good in 1776. The myth of a public good rooted in homogeneity was faced with the reality of diversity which, Paine predicted, might well make Union impossible, if it were postponed half a century hence. The vast variety of interests, occasioned by an increase of trade and popula-

[51] Jefferson, *Papers*, XIII, 405-406; *Notes on Virginia*, 83.

[52] Henry St. John, Viscount Bolingbroke, *The Idea of a Patriot King* (Indianapolis: The Bobbs-Merrill Co., 1965; first published in London, 1749), 35-41.

[53] Gordon Wood, *The Creation of the American Republic* (Chapel Hill, N.C.: The University of North Carolina Press, 1969), chaps. 1-3.

tion would set opposing groups against each other. The struggle for advantage would become intensely political and the most precious fruit of the Revolution for Jefferson would perish in the scuffle to control the distribution of the vast increase in wealth. *Independence* is the essential condition for the self-governance of individuals as it is for nations. No right can be inalienable without independence in both an intellectual and physical sense. Harrington was right. He who has the property to feed a nation has dominion over it. If every man has the property to feed himself, he is a freeman owing no dues, feudal or modern. Farming made men virtuous, Jefferson said in his *Notes on Virginia,* because it made them independent, whereas dependence begets venality, the parent of corruption. The mobs of cities were to be feared because of their dependence upon others for their bread, opinions and political leadership.

So, the attack upon Europe's traditional aristocracies was not intended to destroy "society," but to teach that aristocracy is not natural, but artificial and politically and economically dependent for support of its fraudulent claims of autonomy and virtue. In Britain, the traditional aristocracy was being bought by the merchant class and both were instruments of the state and not the independent pillars of "society." A political revolution must occur before society is renovated. The "adulterous connection of church and state" must be severed, Paine thundered, if the human mind is to be genuinely freed. The capacity of traditional elites to manipulate the mass of mankind through ignorance and superstition must be destroyed first by the abolition of formal government which, Paine insisted, is not the "dissolution of society," but the occasion for recurrence to first principles.[54] Madison warned that the strong bias favoring this "old error" that government and church require a reciprocal "alliance or coalition" must be opposed vigilantly because it corrupts all concerned.[55]

The Jeffersonians' restorative principle upon which the good of the American republic would rest, therefore, was the Renaissance republican ideal that public office would be given only on the basis of talent and training so that civic virtue might pervade all levels of government. Full political and civil rights coupled with control of their own arms would be extended to independent yeomen

[54] Paine, *Writings,* I, 358.
[55] Madison, *Writings,* IX, 101.

linked to a natural aristocracy of talent in freedom and common civic virtue. Each would perform public service at the level commensurate with his talents and training. Jefferson, more than any of his associates—and especially Madison—never could shake this vision completely, and yet he was too shrewd to be taken in completely by his own best hopes. He warned against the innocent assumption that Americans would never create an artifical aristocracy of wealth and influence in imitation of Britain. Human nature, he remarked in his *Notes on Virginia*, is the same on both sides of the Atlantic. The sources of wealth and dominion are the same everywhere and are linked easily to mankind's corrupting passions.[56]

If civic virtue were to be maintained, it would be necessary to retain one basic tenet of the classical heritage of political theory and to abandon another. A good constitution must be framed to direct both rulers and citizens to the life of domestic tranquility, prosperity and enlightenment which would constitute the happiness of the American people. The attempt must be made, however, without the classical equilibrium of an aristocracy balanced against the people. Even more important, the American republic was founded upon public opinion. The classical doctrine had been that most of mankind is incapable of attaining virtue, so that the corrupting passions must be held in check by fear manipulated by elites of superior capacities and attainments. To expect a popular and free government simultaneously was to set aside the wisdom of the ages. Yet, the Jeffersonians placed their faith in this idea which was as revolutionary as it was simple: extend and enlighten the electorate. "The influence over government must be shared among the people. . . . The government of Britain is corrupted because but one man in ten has the right to vote for members of parliament."[57] The republican goal of protecting liberty of conscience and speech would depend, as Madison repeatedly said, upon an appeal to the sense of the community which must be schooled in the maxims of free government. In "a government of opinion, like ours, the only effectual safeguard must be found in the soundness and stability of the general opinions on the subject."[58]

[56] Jefferson, *Notes on Virginia*, 114-115.
[57] *Ibid.*, 143; Jefferson, *Writings*, XV, 440.
[58] Madison, *Writings*, IX, 101.

From the contemporary perspective, it is particularly important to understand the significance of the Jeffersonians' conception of revolution as being political rather than social. It was, above all, neither a retreat from politics of the sort later preached by the Transcendentalists, nor was it an attempt to destroy the wide range of associations which commonly constitute social structure. It was not an effort to deny the necessity of civic virtue, but an attempt to expand it in order to include those whom de Tocqueville later called the coarser materials of which every society is abundantly composed. The Jeffersonian revolution was not a retreat into "individualism" defined as the privatization of life at the cost of civic participation. Neither did the Jeffersonians seek to liberate mankind by destroying traditional associations, not even the ecclesiastical, so long as they were voluntary. Their attack was confined to publicly ordained and supported religious establishments seen as enemies of the free mind. Experience with voluntary, and often extra-legal, associations created to further independence from Britain led Madison to argue, well in advance of de Tocqueville, that such groups must be freely organized to advance the first principle of republicanism: the free communication of ideas in public about the actions of government. Jeffersonians did not attack the family as a primary association. Primogeniture was denounced because it created an unnatural family structure by casting out all children but the eldest to subsist as best they could while the state supported with law the concentration of property and power in one child in the name of the family.

Nobody proclaimed the virtues of a free society more joyously. Society is not destroyed, but liberated, by a change of government. It consists naturally of an infinitely various web of associations and relations which men create to serve their needs without the coercive and centralizing force of the state and its destructive intervention. The Jeffersonians aimed to create a free society to exist with free, democratic government in a symbiotic relationship, serving the needs of the body politic and social. Their aim was liberation, not anomie.

A long life left Jefferson wiser and sadder about the relationship between revolution and public opinion, however. With Napoleon's final defeat behind them, he wrote to John Adams and expressed a thought which we can not dismiss lightly in our age. How, he asked, could The Enlightenment illuminate public opinion so brilliantly and, yet, allow France and England, "so distinguished by science and arts," to throw off all moral restraints and act unblushingly on the principle that power is right? "Your prophecies proved truer than mine . . . I did not in '89 believe that they [Europe's revolutions] would last so long and have cost so much blood."[59] On the other hand, it may be equally useful at this moment in history, when we are less sure where time has found us, to recall one Frenchman's generous estimate of the Jeffersonians' experiment in republican government. "Let us look to America," de Tocqueville urged Europeans, not to copy her institutions, "but to gain a clearer view of the polity that will be best for us" and for an understanding of those principles of balance and ordered liberty without which republics necessarily perish.[60]

[59] Jefferson, *Writings*, XIV, 394-395; see XV, 17-23, 32-44 on the subject of republicanism.

[60] Alexis de Tocqueville, *Democracy in America*, ed. Philips Bradley (2 vols.; New York: Knopf, 1945), I, cvii.

The Impact
of the
American Independence
and the
American Constitution: 1776-1848;
with a Brief Epilogue

Manning J. Dauer

At the time of the bicentennial it is fitting to examine some aspects of the early and later impact of American independence and constitution-making outside the United States. Was the early American experience largely confined to this country, with little effect beyond its borders; or did it exert a major influence on constitutional and other political developments abroad? If the American experience with self-government did have a substantial effect on other areas of the world, where were the influences most strongly felt and how direct was the impact of American independence and constitution-making on the events in these other places?

On this question of impact abroad there are two schools of thought which are strongly opposed. On the one hand there is that school which interprets the American tradition as being unique. This school has found increasing support of late among American historians and political scientists. Are they correct, or are they provincials who, in an age of increasing specialization, seek to magnify the importance of their own specialty, the United States? Are they so engrossed in their own country that they over-stress its differences, but do not know of broader scale forces, and do not know of the interaction of broader trends in ideas and in civilization at home and abroad?

To identify this first group who treat of the uniqueness of the American tradition, I find the most extreme examples among post-World War II American historians and political theorists. Among historians the outstanding example is Daniel Boorstin, starting with his *The Lost World of Thomas Jefferson* in 1948.[1] In this work he argues that the American Revolution was not a significant social movement; that it created minimal changes in this country; that it was not influential abroad. His *Genius of American Politics* continues this interpretation;[2] Chaper Five, for example, is entitled, "Revolution Without Dogma." Finally, his three-volume, *The Americans: The Colonial Experience*; the *National Experience*; and the *Democratic Experience*,[3] all emphasize those aspects of America which argue for a peculiarly American business dominated culture moulded by the North American continent. Part One of the last volume is entitled "The Go-Getters";[4] Part Six is "Mass Producing the Moment."[5] Book Three is entitled "The Thinner Life of Things."[6] There is no argument but that these are aspects of American development, but are they so paramount that they result in an interpretation that presents American development and American thought and culture as a virtual monolith?

Among writers on American thought, a similar interpretation to that of Boorstin is presented by Louis Hartz in his work entitled *The Liberal Tradition in America.*[7] Essentially, Hartz develops what he calls "the Lockian tradition in America." He feels that this is a middle-class, business tradition, which produces a political structure suited to and dominated by a bourgeois mentality. To begin with, this tradition springs from the absence, in the colonial period, of the class extremes: there are no serfs and no nobles. Thus America starts as a middle class community, breaks away from England on the issue of local (American) vs. empire control, and remains a middle class community. Moreover, America never

---

[1] (New York: Holt Co.).

[2] (Chicago: Univ. of Chicago Press, 1953).

[3] (New York: Random House, 1958, 1965, 1973). Also see *America and the Image of Europe* (Cleveland: World Publishing Co., 1960).

[4] *The Democratic Experience*, 3-244.

[5] *Ibid.*, 359-410.

[6] *Ibid.*, 411 ff.

[7] (New York: Harcourt, Brace, 1955).

experiences, except for the Civil War, sharp ideological or social conflicts. Somehow, even the conflict over slavery, emancipation, and later treatment of the blacks in America gets homogenized in Hartz, except for the Civil War flare-up. The same happens to conflict between farmers and industry, between labor and industry. Thus, once again the theme is that America is a middle class, Lockian monolith, and even the definition of Locke is given a peculiarly Hartzian series of definitions.

In contrast with these writers, I believe there is a pluralist tradition in America: that is, that in almost every period of American development, there are alternative ideologies, representing a spectrum of choices; also, that these ideologies are supported by opposing social strata who divide into differing political groups as reflected in differing political factions, coalescing in what are generally two political parties. Moreover, these ideologies and factions are often parts of a broader set of forces with counterparts in other countries going through a comparable period of development. On this basis the many aspects of American thought and culture are not unique. Developments elsewhere influence America, and often American developments influence comparable developments abroad. American ideas are most often a part of world movements.

To proceed specifically with the late eighteenth century, I agree that the background of the American Revolution can best be understood as a part of the movement for the enlightenment. Peter Gay in his work *The Enlightenment: An Interpretation,* and in his *Eighteenth Century Studies,*[8] correctly treats Thomas Jefferson and Benjamin Franklin as contributors to the ideas of this period along with Voltaire, Diderot, DuPont de Nemours, and others. Moreover, with the Europeans of this time Franklin and Jefferson, and to a lesser degree, Washington, exchanged correspondence, and Franklin, Adams and Jefferson were visitors to England or France and for a considerable time were residents abroad. Thus when the American Revolution occurred, the American movement was part of a world movement.

[8] (2 vols.; New York: Knopf, 1966, 1969); (Hanover: Univ. Press of New England, 1972). Also, see R. R. Palmer, *The Age of Democratic Revolution,* (2 vols.; Princeton: Princeton Univ. Press, 1959, 1964); and Jacques Godechot, *L'Europe et l'Amerique a L'Epoque Napoleonienne* (Paris: Presses Universitaires de France, 1967).

At this point we need to consider some of the main goals of the enlightenment as these goals were stated as ideology and as they became popular movements. In general they were based on the concept of improvement of human life on this earth. They argued for self-government, either Republicanism or limited monarchy. These were the concepts of the French, British, and other continental philosophers, and of their American counterparts. All of these supported free speech and free press. Some supported universal suffrage. Virtually all supported equality before the law, equality of economic opportunity, and the abolition of class privileges. Some supported the abolition of the nobility. While the middle class or bourgeoisie was in support of these concepts, and the idea of *laissez faire,* there also were other concepts supported by the masses. These included the abolition of slavery and serfdom and the institution of land distribution. In cities there was support for freeing labor from indentures and some supported workshop systems. Further, there was strong support for universal education, and many of the enlightenment school wanted tax supported education. Humane treatment of criminals, and reform of criminal law were supported. These reforms would help the poor, promote a fluid societal structure and limit social, political and cultural cleavages. A few of the more romantic believed that these reforms would lead to the perfectability of man. Most of the *philosophes,* however, thought this to be too optimistic.

The American Pluralist Experience and its Impact

Now turning to the American experience to specify what is the background, we start with a brief statement of the legacy from the colonial period, and present a view different from that of Boorstin and Hartz. This view supports the pluralist interpretation. In the colonial period there were extreme divisions between the large landholders, such as the patroons of New York, and the small farmers. In Virginia the small farmers staged Bacon's rebellion. Such events are examples of colonial movements based on opposing class divisions.[9]

Now we may turn to the American Revolution. I define a revolution as does Hannah Arendt in her work *On Revolution,*[10] as

[9] Bernard Bailyn, *The Origin of American Politics* (New York: Knopf, 1968).

[10] (New York: Viking Press, 1963).

including a shift of power in government structure which is achieved by force. It may or may not include a change in social structure. She, while recognizing the American Revolution, does regard it as primarily confined to a change in constitutional systems.[11] I agree that it was founded on a background of British principles, but I also agree with Lord Acton, who, in his *Lectures on the French Revolution*,[12] delivered Lecture II on "The Influence of America." He declared that the American Revolution carried British Whig principles of liberty and self-government to a much more advanced stage. A difference in degree was extended to become a difference in kind. He stated that the impact "surpassed in force all the speculation of Paris and Geneva."

In another sense, that of a transfer of both political and social power, the American Revolution was a true revolution. Drastic changes were introduced. For example, until 1775 the colonies had royal or proprietary governors who held an absolute veto over legislative acts. In many of the colonies there was an upper chamber of the legislature appointed by the governor or composed of narrow groups of aristocrats. The governor controlled the executive branch and often appointed the judges. The British Parliament in England could enact certain legislation for the entire Empire including the colonies, such as the Stamp Act, the Townsend Acts and other tax legislation. Colonial foreign policy was conducted by England. Colonial defense was under British control (with help from local militia), and royal armies were stationed in the colonies. Negotiations with Indians concerning Western territory were under the royal governors or the Crown. All of these provisions were changed by the Revolution.

Another dimension of the American Revolution is that at the time that there was a bitter war with England, lasting from 1775 until the Treaty of London granted independence in 1783, there also was a civil war in America between Whigs and Tories. One estimate places the number of Tories at 25% of the population numbering from 164,000 to 384,000.[13] The American State legislatures passed acts outlawing many of the Tories and making prop-

---

[11] *Ibid*, 258-270.

[12] (London: Macmillan, 1910), 20.

[13] John R. Alden, *A History of the American Revolution* (New York: Knopf, 1969), 252; Wallace Brown, *The King's Friends* (Providence: Brown University Press, 1965), 249-251.

erty confiscations. At the end of the war 60,000 to 100,000 Tories migrated, some to Canada, some back to England, some to Louisiana.[14]

The government structure and social structure of the colonies changed with the Revolution. The colonies became states with final legislative power, including power to tax. The colonial governors were supplanted by those chosen by the state legislatures or elected by the voters. These governors did not have absolute veto power. Foreign policy was under the Congress. Defense was joint between the continental army and the state militia. The aristocratic upper chambers of state legislatures were vastly changed. There thus was a sharp shift in political power.[15]

We also need to consider social aspects of change during the Revolution. In considering Jefferson as a revolutionary it also is necessary to weigh, even if briefly, how far the American Revolution changed social structure and set in motion forces which are of broader application in the world. Here there is argument. Jackson T. Main, in his book *The Social Structure of Revolutionary America*,[16] and A. M. Simons, *Social Forces in American History*,[17] take the view that there were broad social divisions in revolutionary America and that the Revolution had extensive impact outside the United States. Daniel Boorstin, in *The Lost World of Thomas Jefferson*, argues the opposite.[18] What then was advocated; what did Jefferson contribute; and what was the thrust of the Revolution? Turning to Jefferson's legislative measures as introduced in the Virginia Assembly, we find that the Virginia society of 1775 was stratified and highly structured. Much of the land was held in large estates. A change in the distribution of land was promoted by several new laws which Jefferson wrote and steered through the assembly. Prominent among these was the law abolishing primogeniture and entail. Under the old law no land from the entailed estate could be sold, and the inheritance of such land could not be

[14] Claude H. Van Tyne, *The Loyalists in the American Revolution* (N. Y.: P. Smith, 1929); R. R. Palmer, *The Age of the Democratic Revolution*, I, 188.

[15] Merrill Jensen, *The New Nation* (New York: Knopf, 1950).

[16] (Princeton: Princeton Univ. Press, 1965); "The Distribution of Property in Post Revolutionary Virginia," *Mississippi Valley Historical Review* (Sept., 1954), XLI, 241-258.

[17] (New York: The Macmillan Company, 1911).

[18] *op. cit.*

divided among the heirs. This naturally promoted concentration of property. Other legislation at this time provided for the confiscation of Tory estates. Then another important series of measures provided for the cession of Virginia's western lands to the central union and the opening up of this land into self-governing territories. Moreover, sale of western lands began to be routed through a land office and not through large scale land companies.[19] Jefferson even proposed, unsuccessfully, a system of homesteads for land distribution, a system which would not become reality until the administration of Abraham Lincoln. Furthermore, the land sales were limited at first as to availability of the offices and by the fact that large parcels were still sold undivided. Jefferson could not change this in the 1780's or 1790's, but he continually urged availability of land as a necessary step in creating equality of opportunity and breaking down social stratification. In 1800, before Jefferson took office a new federal land act was adopted. When he became President in 1801, he had his Secretary of the Treasury, Albert Gallatin, open up many branch land offices (sales also would be made on credit) and sales were made in small units.[20]

It also appears that Jefferson did not fear continual revolution in the United States. In 1786-87 Daniel Shay's rebellion took place in Massachusetts. In this movement debtor farmers, caught in a deflationary period after the end of the American Revolution, were badly hit. They could not keep up payments on their mortgages, and foreclosure procedures threatened. Thereupon the farmers of central and western Massachusetts moved to seize courthouses and to close the courts. This badly frightened many throughout the United States, and because the Massachusetts government failed to put down the revolt quickly, it was one of the factors leading to the calling of the Philadelphia Convention of 1787 for a stronger central government. But Jefferson responded differently. To James Madison he wrote on January 30, 1787: "I hold that a little rebellion now and then is a good thing. It is as necessary in the political world as storms in the physical. Unsuccessful rebellions indeed generally establish the encroachments on the rights

[19] Charles S. Sydnor, *Gentlemen Freeholders* (Chapel Hill: University of North Carolina Press, 1952); Merrill D. Peterson, *Thomas Jefferson and the New Nation* (New York: Oxford University Press, 1970), 113, 120, 278, 285.
[20] Benjamin Hibbard, *A History of the Public Land Policies* (N. Y.: The Macmillan Company, 1924).

of the people. . . ."[21] He noted the punishment for rebellion should be light, for severe punishments might discourage ardent opposition. A few months later, he wrote: "The tree of liberty must be refreshed from time to time with the blood of patriots and tyrants. It is natural manure . . . God forbid we should ever be 20 years without a rebellion."[22] He further noted that with 13 states independent and eleven years since Independence in 1776 there had been 11 x 13 years, with Shays' rebellion the first revolution since Independence. Thus there was only one outbreak in almost 150 years of self-governing states, a very conservative record. The rulers of a country cannot be reminded that "the people are not vigilant unless they are reminded from time to time by a rebellion."[23] Thus, the influence of Jefferson was on the side of continual change, periodic reassessment of laws, and even periodic forceful rebellion.

Other American Reforms

In another type of legislation, to break up stratification, Jefferson attacked the problem of the established Church of England. Under Virginia law, this was the state church and had state support. Jefferson was opposed to any but voluntary religious congregations. He wrote the bill to end the established church in Virginia, the Statute for Religious Freedom,[24] a measure which was generally followed as a model except in New England where the Congregational Church remained as the state church in many of the states until the 1820's and 1830's.

Jefferson also advocated reform of criminal laws and drafted in 1778, "A Bill for Proportioning Crimes and Punishments,"[25] which was introduced in the Virginia legislature but not adopted. It proposed a number of changes in the common law, and was ultimately influential in 19th century reform movements.

Jefferson likewise proposed elimination of the property franchise for voting. Such legislation was not enacted in the east until the Jacksonian period of the 1820's and later, but in the Western states

---

[21] From Paris, Worthington C. Ford, ed., *Writings of Thomas Jefferson* (New York: G. P. Putnam's, 1904) V, 256.

[22] Paris, Nov. 13, 1787, to Wm. Smith, *Writings* (Ford Federal Edition), V, 362.

[23] *Ibid.*

[24] *Writings* (Ford Federal Edition) II, 438, June 13, 1779.

[25] *Writings* (Ford Federal Edition) II, 393-414.

the property franchise ended. The total outcome was that leadership changed from the traditional aristocratic families, first to those like the George Clintons, who were a far cry from the aristocrats, and then to many of average social status.

Another aspect of developing social fluidity was the American development of public tax supported education. Here two trends came together. In New England the Puritan concept supported public education to enable the individual to read the Bible and to interpret it. Also in New England, in the Middle Atlantic States, and in the South, there was the tradition of the Enlightenment. This, then, led to Jefferson's introduction, during the Revolution, of a bill in the Virginia legislature for the public support of education, including scholarships for college support. In the Continental Congress he drafted legislation to dedicate lands in the northwest territory for public education. While Virginia did not enact his state plan, other states modified and followed it: New York in the field of common school education, Georgia and North Carolina in the case of state universities. Virginia finally followed in the 1820's. Jefferson also wrote, in his *Notes on Virginia,* which was published abroad, of the need for public education. Thus, once again there were common ideas among the European *philosophes* and their American counterparts. Also once again there was early action on a model plan in America, another evidence of implementing equality of opportunity.[26]

It next remains to examine what type of life Jefferson expected people to lead. Through the period of the *Notes on Virginia* in the 1780's he continued to hope that the United States would be an agrarian society of small independent farmers, and that manufactured goods should come from Europe. But soon he began to modify that view. He wrote to the DuPonts that the falls of the Delaware River in that state were excellent for a powder mill and that manufacturing had a future in America.[27] Thus he and the rest of his party eventually accepted commerce and manufacturing.

[26] "A bill for the General Diffusion of Knowledge," 1778. J. P. Boyd, ed., *The Papers of Thomas Jefferson,* II, 526; "A Bill for Amending the Constitution of the College of William and Mary, and Substituting more Certain Revenues for its Support," *Ibid.,* 535-543; James B. Conant, *Thomas Jefferson and the Development of American Education* (Berkeley: University of California Press, 1962).

[27] Gilbert Chinard, *Jefferson and DuPont de Nemours* (Baltimore and Paris: The Johns Hopkins Press, 1931), XXIV.

The Impact Abroad of the American Revolution

Looking at immediate influences on Europe from the American Revolution we may turn to the connection between Jefferson and Lafayette for certain examples, following the outbreak of the French Revolution in 1789. One of these points of impact was on the French Declaration of Rights, which in turn became influential on other European revolutions, such as those in Poland. In the case of the French Revolution, Jefferson and Thomas Paine were both involved.[28]

Thomas Paine was an Englishman who came to America in 1775 and was one of the most effective pamphleteers. His January, 1776 pamphlet *Common Sense* presented one of the first clear calls for independence. It was followed by an equally eloquent statement, *The Crisis*, which appeared in thirteen installments. At the close of the American Revolution he returned to Europe, visited France, and then returned to England. When Edmund Burke wrote his *Reflections on the French Revolution,* Paine replied in *The Rights of Man,* and sought to kindle revolutionary forces in England. Then in 1791 he went to France as an apostle of Republicanism. Returning to England he was outlawed in 1792, whereupon he was elected as a deputy from Calais to the French national convention. But as the French Revolution moved into the Jacobin dictatorship, Paine, a co-author of the Girondin version of a constitution for France, was suspect. Ultimately he was jailed in the Luxembourg Palace. With the overthrow of Robespierre, Paine with the support of the American Ambassador, James Monroe, was freed. He then wrote *The Age of Reason* (1795) which attacked organized religion and urged the doctrine of Deism. Finally with the rise of Napoleon he was ready to leave France. Jefferson offered transportation in 1801 on an American naval frigate lest England intercept a private vessel. But Paine ultimately sailed on a regular

---

[28] The best biographies of Thomas Paine are Moncure D. Conway, *The Life of Thomas Paine,* (2 vols.; New York: G. P. Putnam's Sons, 1892); and David F. Hawke, *Paine* (New York: Harper and Row, 1974); and Frank Smith, *Thomas Paine, Liberator* (New York: Frederick A. Stokes Co., 1938). The most complete edition of his works is William M. Van derWeyde, ed., *The Life and Works of Thomas Paine* (10 vols.; New Rochelle: Thomas Paine National Historical Association, 1925). There is also the Conway edition in four volumes, reprinted in 1967.

packet and arrived back in America on Oct. 30, 1802.[29] He was received by Jefferson and then went to his property, given by Congress, in New Rochelle, New York. He died in 1809 at the age of 72, and it might be thought that his revolutionary career and journeys were over. But not so. William Cobbett, another Englishman who moved back and forth between American and British careers, left America for the second time in 1819 to return to England. Cobbett aimed at parliamentary reform, religious reform, and fiscal reform. Regarding Paine as a symbol to rally support in England, Cobbett went to New Rochelle, hired gravediggers, dug up Paine and transported the remains secretly to England. It should be noted that in later years Cobbett became prominent in politics, history and literature as the author of *Rural Rides*, Cobbett's *Parliamentary History*, and became editor and publisher of *The Political Register*. Also, he was elected to Parliament. However, his theft of Paine's bones was not well received. Among others who commented on the bizarre affair, Lord Byron, with an eye on the anti-religious sentiments of Paine, wrote:

> In digging up your bones, Tom Paine,
> Will Cobbett has done well;
> You visit him on earth again,
> He'll visit you in hell.[30]

But in considering American impact on the French Revolution and other European revolutions, Paine was not alone. When the revolution broke out in France in 1789, Jefferson was Minister to France. He was sympathetic to the early stages of the revolution. Also, when the Bastille fell, Lafayette sent the key to George Washington, who displayed it above his mantle at Mount Vernon. Jefferson's role was more direct. Jefferson did suggest, in correspondence with the Marquis de Lafayette, who became leader in the French National Assembly, that the French had best proceed gradually, adopting a limited monarchy for the time being.[31]

[29] Dumas Malone, *Jefferson the President, First Term, 1801-1805* (Boston, Little, Brown, 1970), 196.

[30] Lewis Melville, *The Life and Times of William Cobbett in England and America* (London: John Lane, The Bodley Head, 1913), II, 116.

[31] Jefferson to Lafayette, Monticello, February 14, 1815, *Writings* (Washington, D. C.: Thomas Jefferson Association), XI, 246.

Proposed Declaration of Rights by Lafayette and Dr. Richard Gem, Jefferson to Madison, Paris, Jan. 12, 1789, *Papers of Jefferson* (Princeton: Princeton Univ. Press, 1950) (Boyd, ed.), XIV, 436-440. Jefferson to Lafayette and to

Until his departure from France, Jefferson worked actively in 1789 with the leaders of the French Revolution, especially with Lafayette, in the drafting of the French Declaration of Rights, in conferences concerning basic constitutional documents, and in an effort to have the King take the lead in granting a charter for a limited monarchy with a statement of the system of self government.

Another influence of the American Revolution was the creation of mass armies and citizen participation in them.[32] Prior to the American and French Revolutions armies were relatively small and were mercenary forces. The American state militia and the Continental Army were mass citizen armies which, with the aid of France, succeeded in defeating the British Forces. The French Revolution followed this model. The National Guard was organized first as a citizen's force, and then was incorporated into the regular army. These vastly increased forces were later available for conquest under Napoleon. All of this transformed the military basis of the Armed Forces in France first and then elsewhere in Europe.[33] The way was also prepared for the merger of the sentiment for nationalism and for popular identification with the military. Thus, the militia could be, as in America, the basis for limiting expenditures on defense and for limiting the role of the military. Or, under Napoleon, it could be the basis for large scale armies of conquest, armies numbering in hundreds of thousands.

At this point a general observation should be made regarding the basic position being taken as to the international impact of the American Revolution and the interaction with the French Revolution and other revolutionary movements in Europe and later in South America. R. R. Palmer[34] and Jacques Godechot have ob-

---

Rabaut de St. Etienne, Paris, June 3, 1789 (enclosing draft of a Charter of Rights), *Ibid.*, XV, 165-168; Lafayette to Jefferson, Versailles, July 6, 1789, *Ibid.*, XV, 249.

[32] Don Higginbotham, *The War of American Independence, Military Attitudes, Policies and Practice, 1763-1789* (New York: Macmillan, 1971).

[33] Higginbotham, *op. cit.*; Francois Furet and D. Richet, translated by Stephen Hardman, *The French Revolution* (London: Weidenfield and Nicholson, 1970), 77, 116; James Matthew Thompson, *The French Revolution* (Oxford: B. Blackwell, 1955), 395; Charles Comte, *Histoire de la Garde National de Paris* (Paris: A. Sautelet, 1827); Albert Mathiez, *The French Revolution* (New York: Grosset & Dunlop, 1969), 49.

[34] *The Age of Democratic Revolution*, II, 50-51.

served that even the historians of the French Revolution took a limited view of the impact of foreigners on the French Revolution. This topic was re-studied by Godechot in his *Le Grande Nation: l'expansion révolutionnaire de la France dans le monde, 1789 á 1799*, and also in his *L'Europe et L'Amerique*.[35] The position of these authors, with which I agree, is that there was a common climate of opinion among many of the leaders in America and in Europe and South America. A few individual leaders also went back and forth among countries. They corresponded; they exchanged documents and writings. The new laws were exchanged. Some, like the Jacobins, even sought to establish a world movement. Under Jacobin auspices, for example, French citizenship was extended to Paine, to Dr. Joseph Priestly, the British philosopher and scientist (who actually went to America rather than to France), to James Madison, to William Wilberforce, who led an international movement against slavery. However, there was never a formal international structure corresponding to the later Marxian first or second or third internationals. But there was interaction of individuals, ideas, and parallel developments in structure of bills of rights, laws, and some institutions.

A further illustration of how this exchange proceeded is found in the work of Thaddeus Kosciusko. Born in Poland in 1746, he served in the Polish Army as an engineering officer. In 1776 he came to America and offered his services to Washington, who was becoming reluctant to accept additional foreign officers. Kosciusko simply asked for a trial. Washington granted this, and found him so able that he commissioned Kosciusko as a Colonel. Thereupon, Kosciusko gained an excellent reputation at Bemis Heights, and in planning and installing the fortifications on the Hudson River at West Point. He concluded the war as a General and was granted lands in Ohio, returning to Poland where he became a Major-General. He led effective armed resistance against Russia and Austria and Hungary but the King made peace. Thereupon, in 1794, there was an uprising which established Kosciusko as General and head of the state. He issued a proclamation abolishing serfdom[36] and instituted other reforms. Eventually he was overwhelmed by the Russians, taken captive and imprisoned for two years in the fortress of Peter and Paul. Upon his release he re-

[35] (2 vols. Paris: Aubier, 1956 and 1967).
[36] Palmer, *op. cit.*, II, 152-153.

turned to America, and then went back to Europe. Napoleon offered to make him head of a puppet government of Poland, but he refused. Ultimately, he died in exile from Poland in 1817. This Polish uprising was unique in that others of the period took place in countries in which there were French armies.

THE INFLUENCE OF THE AMERICAN DECLARATION OF INDEPENDENCE, ARTICLES OF CONFEDERATION, THE CONSTITUTION AND THE BILL OF RIGHTS

The American Declaration of Independence was, of course, worldwide news and was immediately printed in the various newspapers in London, Dublin and elsewhere. A 1781 edition of American State Constitutions was printed in Philadelphia, and then in London and Dublin, and in Paris in 1783, after the Treaty of London recognizing Independence, this treaty was added. In Latin America the Constitution was printed in Lima in 1812 and in Mexico in 1823. A French printing appeared in Paris in 1792, and a German printing came in 1847. Jefferson's *Notes on Virginia* appeared in a Paris edition, translated into French, in 1786. Thus there was considerable circulation of these basic documents. The Federalist was reprinted in a French edition in Paris in 1791, and again in 1795.[37]

In Italy, as Napoleon established the Cisalpine Republic, the Pennsylvania State Constitution (in the drafting of which Franklin was the chief figure) was translated into Italian and published along with *Poor Richard's Almanac*. Other works of Franklin were translated and a history of America and of the American Revolution was published.[38]

As we move into the period of Latin American constitution-making, there was also interest in the American Constitution, along with interest in the Spanish Constitution of 1812 and 1820, and in French constitutions. The interest in the United States was especially great in those countries attempting or following a federal system: the Venezuelan Constitution of 1811, the Mexican of 1824, the Argentinian of 1853, and the Brazilian of 1891 are cases in

[37] Harold Syrett, ed., *The Papers of Alexander Hamilton* (New York: Columbia Univ. Press, 1962), IV, 290.

[38] Palmer, *op. cit.*, II, 299. A. Pace, *Benjamin Franklin and Italy* (Philadelphia, 1958). *Memoirs of the American Philosophical Society*, Vol. 47.

point.[39] The influence of the executive is greater in Latin America and there are many differences including the ability to suspend constitutional guarantees.

The American influence in Europe and other countries has continued. In 1830 and again in 1848 a wave of revolutions threatened monarchial regimes in Europe. Hungary had revolted in the period of the French Revolution, but the Austrian rule was restored. As early as 1829 the leaders of Hungarian nationalism looked to England and America. Stephen Szechenyi wrote in that year that America was "the land where the rights of mankind are the most equal [and] where the Constitution is the best." Finally, in 1848 Louis Kossuth was chosen Governor of Hungary by the Hungarian Parliament. Independence was declared, serfdom abolished, and land reforms were begun.[40] Austria was unable to restore rule, but Russia then joined against Kossuth, and in 1849 the Russians defeated Kossuth. He then fled to Turkey. Although Russia and Austria demanded the surrender of Kossuth, France, England and the United States supported him. Finally, Secretary of State Daniel Webster ordered an American frigate to Constantinople, and Kossuth and his family were transported to England. After a brief stay he came to the United States, landing in New York in December, 1851. Equally fluent in Hungarian and in English, his speeches in New York were attended by thousands. He then was invited to visit the President and to address a meeting of members of Congress. Next he toured the entire country, addressing many meetings in major cities and sessions of state legislatures. In all, he made over 200 speeches. His theme was the development of constitutional government, and how America served as a world model.[41] Hopefully, Kossuth might have brought about an American loan or diplomatic support for his government. This he did

---

[39] Russell Fitzgibbon, "Constitutional Developments in Latin America: A Synthesis," *American Political Science Review*, XXXIV (June 1945), 511-22. Lloyd Mecham, "Latin American Constitutions, Nominal and Real," *Journal of Politics*, XXI (May 1959), 258-275.

[40] George Barany, *Stephen Szechenyi and the Awakening of Hungarian Nationalism, 1791-1841* (Princeton: Princeton Univ. Press, 1968), 176. Erzsebet Andics, *Kossuth En Lutte Contre Les Enemis des Reformes et de la Revolution, Academia Scientiarum Hungaria, Studia Historica* (Budapest: Academia, 1956).

[41] P. C. Headley, *The Life of Louis Kossuth, Governor of Hungary* (Auburn, N.Y.: Derby and Miller, 1852).

not achieve, but he did arouse great enthusiasm for the further
spread of the concept of Republicanism and self-determination.

ALEXIS DE TOCQUEVILLE AND HIS *Democracy in America*

Alexis de Tocqueville and Gustave A. Beaumont, two young
Frenchmen, arrived in the United States in May, 1831 and departed
in February, 1832. Their commission was to survey the American
states' penal systems and make a report which might influence reform in France. Ultimately they made their report and eventually
it did influence such reform.[42] Their trip coincided with the first
administration of President Andrew Jackson. Of course the byproduct of the trip was de Tocqueville's *Democracy in America*,
the first volume of which appeared in 1835 and the second in 1840.[43]
The work is a classic. It treats not only of government but also
of the problems of mass society, and of standards in an egalitarian
nation. There are extensive criticisms in the final chapters of volume two. These have led some readers to view de Tocqueville
as essentially disenchanted with what he found. I think this is a
complete misinterpretation. De Tocqueville wrote, when preparing
his second volume, a letter to his English translator asking that his
intentions be more closely followed. He felt that in translation the
harsher English words were used, with the result that his judgments
appeared as more severe than in the French version. His intention
was to warn of dangers, and to speak frankly. But he was far from
expecting that the worst would happen. It also should be noted
that de Tocqueville was himself a member of the French Parliament and after the election of 1848, was a minister in the second
French Republic, and was imprisoned by Louis Napoleon when
Louis by a coup terminated the Republic and established the second Empire.

Be that as it may, in many respects *Democracy in America* is the
classic study of the trend toward equality which American republi-

[42] The best account of their trip is in George W. Pierson, *Tocqueville and
Beaumont in America* (New York: Oxford Univ. Press, 1938); and Pierson,
Tocqueville in America (New York: Doubleday and Co., 1959).

[43] J. P. Mayer, ed., *Alexis de Tocqueville Oeuvres Completes*, Vol. 1¹ and 1²,
de la Democratie en Amerique (Paris: Gallimard, 1960, 1961). There are
two translations, one by Henry Reeve as revised by Frances Bowen, and a
more recent one by George Lawrence and edited by J. P. Mayer (New York:
Harpers, 1966). The Mayer-Lawrence version is the better, but neither is
entirely satisfactory.

canism best exemplified when de Tocqueville wrote. De Tocqueville, while accepting the coming of equal opportunity and the development of universal suffrage, believed in the continued leadership of an adaptable, able group, such as the British aristocracy. Hence he admired the gradual adoption of reforms in England and, in his other great work, *L'ancien Regime et la Revolution,* which he published in 1856,[44] sharply criticizes the intransigent French aristocracy.

In terms of measuring the impact of American influence in France and in other countries, the work of de Tocqueville was influential but should be viewed as one of a series of works. In France there was the tendency to identify the Republican movement as "le parti Americaine" or l'ecole Americaine. In 1833 Charles A. Sainte-Beuve reviewed in his *Causeries de Lundi* of February 4, 1833, the work by L. P. Conseil entitled *Melanges politiques et philosophiques extraits de la correspondence de Thomas Jefferson, precedes d'un essai sur les principes de l'ecole Americaine et d'une traduction de la constitution des Etats-Unis. . . .*[45] Conseil's introduction states (my translation from the French):

> On the other side of the Atlantic there is a stable and peaceful nation which offers itself to men, for the last fifty years, for study and imitation. It gives an example of a republic organized on a design that furnishes a living answer to all the objections made by detractors of this form of government. They say a republic is not suitable for a populous nation—yet the United States counts thirteen to fourteen million inhabitants. They also say the republican form of government is not suitable for an extensive territory—yet the United States stretches over a great space estimated at about 295,000 square leagues. These critics also assert that republican government is completely incompatible with the morals and customs of our modern civilization—yet one finds in the United States, with morals and customs similar to ours, a search for wealth and an active business development which exceeds that shown by our European countries.
>
> Thus the United States of America and their institutions should become, from this day forward, the common tie holding together all contrary parties.

[44] J. P. Mayer, ed. (Paris: Gallimard, 1952). Other standard interpretations of de Tocqueville's concept of democracy are Marvin Zetterbaum, *Tocqueville and the Problem of Democracy* (Stanford: Stanford Univ. Press, 1967); Jack Lively, *The Social and Political Thought of Alexis de Tocqueville* (Oxford: Clarendon Press, 1962); Seymour Drescher, *Dilemmas of Democracy: Tocqueville and Modernization* (Pittsburgh: Univ. of Pittsburgh Press, 1965).

[45] (Paris, 1833). Cited in Gilbert Chinard, *Saint-Beuve, Thomas Jefferson, et Tocqueville* (Princeton: Princeton Univ. Press, 1943), 1.

One can give the name of l'ecole Americaine to those sages who have founded, directed, and consolidated the revolution in this country . . .

In this vein, when *Democracy in America* appeared, Sainte-Beuve also reviewed, in more balanced words than those of Conseil, the work of de Tocqueville.[46] Nor is the reception of the American model for dispersion of republicanism and extension of the suffrage confined to France. De Tocqueville stimulated Gladstone's anti-colonialist views in the Victorian era. Also, in the 1866-67 debates in England over suffrage extension, the American example and de Tocqueville were cited by John Stuart Mill, by Lords Elcho, Grey, Houghton, and Gregory. These named were ranged on both sides of the reform bill issue. At one point on two successive evenings in the debates there were four pro-and-con speeches based on de Tocqueville.[47]

Toward the end of the nineteenth century another work, *The American Commonwealth*, by Lord James Bryce, was published.[48] In his judgment on the American Constitution, Bryce wrote: "It [the American Constitution] ranks above every other constitution for the intrinsic excellence of its scheme, its adaptation to the circumstances of the people, the simplicity, brevity, and precision of its language, its judicious mixture of definitiveness in principle with elasticity in detail."[49] Thus again the American system was presented as a model. Certainly the Commonwealth arrangement adopted by the British reflected part of this judgment from the period after the American Revolution on into the twentieth century.

Summary and Conclusions

I have presented an interpretation which emphasizes the American ideology as a part of the trend toward the Enlightenment. I have emphasized first the interaction of America and Europe, and then of new developing areas such as the Hungarian uprising in southeastern Europe, and the Gladstone "little-England" movement. There were other American trends to be observed. Certainly, while America prided herself as a source for revolution in the 1790's, we might have dwelled on the fact that Washington

[46] *Causeries de Lundi*, 7 avril 1835.
[47] Seymour Drescher, *Tocqueville and England* (Cambridge: Harvard Univ. Press, 1964), 218-219.
[48] (New York: Macmillan and Co., 188). I have used the two volume edition of G. P. Putnam's Sons, 1959.
[49] *Ibid.*, I, 16.

rebuffed the attempts of the French minister, Genet, to draw America into the wars between France and England. He accepted the key to the Bastille, but also issued the first American proclamation of neutrality.

Further, while supporting the liberation of South America in the period of the 1820's, we launched on a war against Mexico in the 1840's for the annexation of Texas and to extend our boundaries to the Pacific. In the war with Spain we annexed Puerto Rico, and for a period placed the Philippines under tutelage. On the other hand, in World War I we sought to follow the concept of self-determination of nations. In World War II we also followed this policy, despite the strain produced between Franklin Roosevelt and Winston Churchill over Roosevelt's pressing for independence of India and of Arab countries in the Middle East. Thus, through World War II the American record, with departures, stood as one of supporting independence for developing countries, and the establishment of republican regimes.

Since World War II the symbol of America has been much less clear to developing countries. We first supported the French return to Indo-China, and then ourselves intervened in Vietnam. Our belief in a market economy is one reason, our fear of Communism another, our failure to understand twentieth century movements in developing countries is a third. It is indeed ironic that America, which stood at the forefront of popular movements from the Enlightenment until the end of World War II, should show limited comprehension of the twentieth century movements toward independence and popular control. It is possible that this lack of understanding can contribute, not to the check of dictatorship, whether of the left or the right, but to its increase.

At the same time, if post World War II interpreters of America find justification for interpreting America as exercising leadership through power, and this is the image of America in other areas, yet such interpreters should not rewrite the period of American Independence, or the period of the nineteenth and early twentieth century. To do this would be to rewrite the past in terms of the present. Moreover, it would ignore the pluralist tradition in America of competing ideologies and competing choices in American politics. It would also misinterpret the longer positive message of America to other countries and the interconnection of American ideas, culture and politics with world movements.

The American Contribution
to a
Theory of
Constitutional Choice

VINCENT OSTROM

T HE AMERICAN REVOLUTION was based upon a presumption that "government was instituted to promote the welfare of mankind, and ought to be administered for the attainment of that end."[1] The Declaration of Independence went on to assert:

That wherever any Form of Government becomes destructive of these ends, it is the Right of the People to alter and to abolish it, and to institute new Government, laying its foundation on such principles and organizing its powers in such form, as to them shall be most likely to effect their Safety and Happiness.[2]

This act of political revolution also implied a far-reaching intellectual revolution if the words of the Declaration of Independence were more than crude political rhetoric. First, it implied that people could develop criteria for assessing the performance of governments and determine limits to the legitimate exercise of authority by governments. Second, on the basis of such criteria, it implied that people can exercise a rightful prerogative to resist improper use of authority, alter and abolish an existing system of government and create a new system of government that would better advance their welfare. Third, the Declaration of Indepen-

---

[1] "Declaration of Causes and Necessity of Taking Up Arms, July 6, 1775" in U.S. Documents Illustrative of the Formation of the Union of the American States (Washington: Government Printing Office, 1927), 10.

[2] Ibid., 22.

dence implied that principles of government could be known so that men might institute a system of government by reference to certain forms that would yield effects likely to promote their welfare. By extension these implications might further suggest that a theory of constitutional choice could be used to alter and revise structures of government through extended periods of time.

These implications suggest that political systems can be designed on the basis of a calculated choice. Artisans in political design, presumably, can know what conditions will serve as the appropriate conditions or instrumentalities for realizing specifiable effects or consequences. On the basis of such knowledge, political systems can presumably be created that would be subject to limits and serve the ends that advance human welfare.

In exploring the American contribution to a theory of constitutional choice I shall examine three different approaches to the problem of constitutional choice. I shall turn first to Thomas Hobbes who concludes that the structures of political societies cannot be subject to limits. The prosperity of a people depends upon the obedience and the concord of those who are subject to the unlimited authority of the sovereign.

The American experiment in constitutional choice will then be examined to reveal the new intellectual horizons being pioneered by Americans. "The general theory of a limited Constitution,"[3] as Alexander Hamilton called it, was used to derive a radically different solution to the problem of constitutional choice from that which Hobbes has been able to derive.

The implication of these theories of constitutional choice is explored further in an examination of the Soviet experiment in constitutional choice. V. I. Lenin, in effect, returns to Hobbes' solution. The Leviathan rose from the ashes of a revolutionary movement to crush and destroy the power of the Czarist autocracy.

THOMAS HOBBES' THEORY OF CONSTITUTIONAL CHOICE

In reasoning through the problem inherent in the design and creation of a commonwealth as an "artifice," Thomas Hobbes demonstrates how men can use their power of reason to conceptualize rules of conduct which would enable them, if each man were to

---

[3] Alexander Hamilton, John Jay and James Madison, *The Federalist* (New York: The Modern Library, n.d.), 524.

act in accordance with such rules, to realize the advantages of a peaceful society. However, he recognizes that such an exercise in moral reasoning is not sufficient to constitute a peaceful and prosperous society. Rules of conduct cannot be given force and effect "without the terror of some power to cause them to be observed. . . ."[4] He emphasized that "covenants, without the sword, are but words. . . ."[5]

The design of a commonwealth depends upon the creation of a "commanding power" that can cause the covenants of law to be observed. A multitude of men can become a commonwealth only if some one body of men or some one man provides the multitude of men with a common voice to proclaim rules of law and a common army to wield the sword of justice. If a multitude of men are to enjoy the advantage of a common set of rules in organizing their relationships with one another there must be *one* system of law that provides that *common* set of rules. Any one system of law depends upon the existence of a single source of law. Thus the creation of a commonwealth for Hobbes can be attained in only one way: "To confer all their power and strength upon one man or upon one assembly of men, that may reduce all their wills, by plurality of voices, unto one will."[6]

Forms of government may vary, according to Hobbes, depending upon who is vested with the exercise of the supreme authority to govern. When sovereign prerogative is vested in one man the form of government is a monarchy. When vested in an assembly of select men it is an aristocracy. An assembly of all citizens, exercising supreme authority is a democracy or a popular commonwealth. In each case, ultimate authority to govern resides in one man or in one body of men.

The sovereign, whether one man or an assembly of men must, according to Hobbes, exercise supreme authority in the sense that such authority will prevail in the maintenance of ordered relationships among all those who are subject to the laws of a commonwealth. This supreme authority is unlimited. Those who exercise sovereign prerogatives have authority to use any means that are appropriate to realizing the peace and security of the common-

---

[4] Thomas Hobbes, *Leviathan*, Michael Oakeshott edition (Oxford: Basil Bladswell, 1960), 109.
[5] *Ibid.*
[6] *Ibid.*, 112.

wealth. These means include judging and censuring opinions. The well-governing of opinions, according to Hobbes, is conducive to the well-governing of men's actions. Those in sovereign authority are to decide what is fit to teach, which men are to be trusted to speak to the multitudes and what books are fit to print.

The ultimate authority to govern, according to Hobbes, must rest with a single center of authority that is unlimited, indivisible and unalterable. Only if there is a single center of authority can there be one law. Only if there is one law can a multitude of men share in the peace and security that derive from ordering their conduct in relation to a common set of rules.

Since those who exercise sovereign authority are the source of law, they cannot be held accountable to law. There can be no law that limits the authority of those who exercise the ultimate authority to govern. It is a logical absurdity, according to Hobbes, to suggest that those who exercise ultimate authority to govern can be limited by rules of law.

Since ultimate authority resides with those who govern, subjects cannot alter or change the form of government. Hobbes advises those who exercise sovereign authority that the people are to be taught, "first, that they ought not to be in love with any form of government they see in their neighbor nations, more than with their own, nor, whatsoever present prosperity they behold in nations that are otherwise governed than they, to desire change."[7] He goes on to assert that the prosperity of people derives not from the form of government but from the "obedience and concord of the subjects:"[8]

. . . nor do the people flourish in a monarchy because one man had the right to rule them, but because they obey him. Take away in any kind of state, the obedience, and consequently the concord of the people, and they shall not only not flourish, but in short time be dissolved. And they that go about by disobedience, to do no more than reform the commonwealth, shall find they do thereby destroy it.[9]

The sufficiency of Hobbes' solution depends upon the availability of benevolent and enlightened rulers who can identify their individual interests with the well-being of their subjects. The pre-

[7] *Ibid.*, 221.
[8] *Ibid.*, 221-222.
[9] *Ibid.*, 222.

sumption that those who exercise sovereign authority can judge what is fit to teach, and that prosperity derives from obedience and concord gives little consideration to problems of error and the consequences which follow from erroneous actions. Only in the conclusion to his discussion of the commonwealth does Hobbes warn of the dangers of error:

> There is no action of man in this life that is not the beginning of so long a chain of consequences, as no human providence is high enough, to give a man a prospect to the end. And in this chain, there are linked together both pleasing and unpleasing events; in such manner, as he that will do anything for his pleasure, must engage himself to suffer all the pains annexed to it; and these pains, are the natural punishments of those actions, which are the beginning of more harm than good. And thereby it comes to pass, that intemperance is naturally punished by diseases; rashness, with mischances; injustice, with the violence of enemies; pride, with ruin; cowardice, with oppression; negligent government of princes, with rebellion; and rebellion, with slaughter.[10]

If assumptions of benevolence and enlightenment are replaced by assumptions of fallibility and self-interest, there is no assurance that the interests of those who exercise sovereign prerogatives will coincide with the well-being of subjects. On the contrary, those who rule and those who act as favorites, counselors and agents of those who rule have an incentive to maintain and defend their special prerogatives as against those who are ruled. As Joseph Brodsky, the Russian poet, has observed, ". . . virtually every state sees its citizens either as slaves or as enemies."[11] The "state" stands above society and rules over society. The ruling class dominates the exercise of governmental authority; and, through that dominance, controls the allocation of values in a society. Obedience and concord give way to tyranny and alienation. Consent is lost; and oppression is gained. Oppression evokes resistance; and resistance, repression. The failure of those who govern gives way to those who seize control over the center of authority and proclaim themselves as the new sovereigns.

The iron law of oligarchy inherent in Hobbes' solution to the constitution of a commonwealth led Robert Michels to contemplate the following fate for mankind:

> The democratic currents of history resemble successive waves. They break ever on the same shoal. They are ever renewed. This enduring spectacle is

10 *Ibid.*, 240-241.
11 *New York Times Magazine*, October 1, 1972, 11, 78.

simultaneously encouraging and depressing. When democracies have gained a certain stage of development, they undergo a gradual transformation adopting the artistocratic spirit, and in many cases also the aristocratic forms, against which at the outset they struggled so fiercely. Now new accusers arise to denounce the traitors; after an era of glorious combats and of inglorious power, they end by fusing with the dominant class; whereupon once more they are in turn attacked by fresh opponents who appeal to the name of democracy. It is probable that this cruel game will continue without end.[12]

The prevalence of revolutions and coup d'etats in much of the contemporary world suggests that unitary constitutions ruled by fallible and self-interested men generate an antithesis of interests between rulers and the ruled. The antithesis evolves into a struggle and when a propitious opportunity arises new rulers are prepared to seize the reigns of authority. Governments are changed by accident and force rather than by reasoned choice. Those who seize power defend their prerogatives as unlimited, indivisible and unalterable. The integrity of "sovereignty" is maintained despite the succession of revolution, coup d'etats and political struggles.

THE AMERICAN EXPERIMENT IN CONSTITUTIONAL CHOICE

The Concept of Constitutional Government

The possibility of deriving an alternative solution to the problem of constitutional choice depends upon whether the language and structure of authority relationships can be extended to include reference to processes of constitutional decision making and to the formulation of constitutions as fundamental laws for the organization and conduct of government. The concept is ancient but the design of a system of government that would be capable of enforcing rules of constitutional law in relation to those who govern is of more recent origins. A solution to that problem was worked out by Americans in the course of the American Revolution. Alexander Hamilton explicitly stated the problem when he observed in the first paragraph of "Federalist No. 1.,"

. . . it seems to have been reserved to the people of this country, by their conduct and example, to decide the important question, whether societies of men are really capable or not of establishing good government from reflection and choice, or whether they are forever destined to depend for their political

[12] Robert Michels, *Political Parties* (New York: The Free Press, 1966), 371.

constitutions on accident and force. If there be any truth in the remarks, the crisis at which we are arrived may with propriety be regarded as the era in which that decision is to be made; and a wrong election of the part we shall act may, in this view, deserve to be considered as the great misfortune of mankind.[13]

Hamilton viewed the American effort in constitutional decision making as an experiment to determine whether men drawing upon "the general theory of a limited constitution" could design and create a system of government based upon reasoned choice.

Alexander Hamilton and James Madison provide the best explanation for that solution in *The Federalist*. Their explanation is an *a priori* analysis of the probable consequences which would follow from adopting a constitution formulated in the language of authority relationships. The power of their explanation is demonstrated by the circumstance that *The Federalist* is still, nearly two hundred years later, the major classic for understanding the operational characteristics of the American system of government.

The solution to the problem of constitutional choice as explained by Hamilton and Madison draws upon much the same intellectual foundations as Thomas Hobbes uses. They too recognize that words expressed on "paper parchments" will be no more than "advice or recommendation" if there is "no penalty annexed to disobedience."[14]

The task of conceptualizing a system of government which can be based upon a system of enforceable constitutional law arises only in a democratic society. If citizens are to conduct the affairs of government through open public deliberation and through officials who are their agents or public servants, then the community of citizens will be required to establish rules about the conduct of the community's business. If the citizenry meets in assembly to govern a society then rules specifying (1) the eligibility of those who are entitled to participate in assembly deliberations; (2) the time and place of meetings; (3) the procedures that apply to the conduct of business in an assembly; (4) the pluralities of votes that are required to make different types of decisions; and (5) the authority that is to be assigned to those who act as the officials and agents of an assembly, all become a part of the fundamental law in a simple democracy. These basic rules for the organization and con-

[13] Hamilton, *op. cit.*, 3.
[14] *Ibid.*, 91.

duct of an assembly are the primitive components for a constitution in a democratic society.

Montesquieu posed a basic paradox when he observed that democratic republics are vulnerable to internal imperfections if they become large, and vulnerable to external attack if they remain small.[15] The conduct of any assembly is subject to a technical constraint that only one speaker can be heard at a time. The larger the assembly the proportionately less voice each member can have in its deliberation and the greater reliance must be placed upon the officers of an assembly to set the agenda and control the deliberations. Thus, Madison observes that "In the ancient republics, where the whole body of the people assembled in person, a single orator, or an artful statesman, was generally seen to rule with as complete a sway as if a sceptre had been placed in his single hand."[16] An oligarchic tendency of a few to control the deliberations of the many, thus, reasserts itself in the constitution of a democratic assembly.

Montesquieu had conceptualized a confederation as offering the promise of reconciling the problems of internal imperfection and external defense. Retention of small size among constituent republics would reduce the dangers of oligarchy and the loss of voice so inimical to democratic institutions. Numerous small democratic republics could then join together to provide for their common defense and to deal with other matters of common concern in a confederation of democratic republics.

The American solution relied upon processes of constitutional decision making in formulating the fundamental law for constituting democratic republics. The process of constitutional choice was then reiterated to create a federal republic to take care of the common defense and matters of common concern to the Union as a whole. A "compound republic,"[17] as Madison called it, creates the basis for extending the principle of self-government to all political associations in a concurrent system of governments. By combining a number of key structural elements it was possible to formulate a

[15] Charles Louis de Secondat Montesquieu, *The Spirit of the Laws* (New York: Hafner Publishing Company, 1966), 126.

[16] Hamilton, *op. cit.* 382. See also chapter 5 in Vincent Ostrom, *The Political Theory of a Compound Republic* (Blacksburg, Virginia: Center for Study of Public Choice, Virginia Polytechnic Institute and State University, 1971) for a discussion of the size principle.

[17] *Ibid.*, 339.

system of government where the provisions of constitutional law could be enforced in relation to those who exercised the prerogatives of government.

Elements in the Design of Constitutional Government

Several basic elements in the structure of authority relationships are necessary for creating and maintaining a system of enforceable constitutional law. These include special attention to the legal status of constitutions and to the political status of processes for constitutional decision making. In addition, an enforceable system of constitutional law depends upon careful attention to specific types of provisions to be contained within a constitution. Maintaining the enforceability of a system of constitutional law, in turn, depends upon access to a theory of constitutional choice in deciding when and how to challenge the actions of governmental officials and how to alter the provisions of a constitution in light of changing conditions. We shall examine each of these factors in turn as they relate to the design of a system of constitutional government.

Special Status of Constitutions and Constitutional Decision Making. If citizens in a democratic society are to retain ultimate authority over the choice of decision-making rules that apply to the conduct of government, then the terms and conditions that apply to those rules need to be given separate legal and political standing. Madison distinguishes a "constitution" from a "law." A constitution is "established by the people" and is "unalterable by the government," while a law is "established by the government and is alterable by the government."[18] This distinction implies that the government in a constitutional republic does *not* have the prerogative of defining and altering its own authority. This prerogative is established through a distinct decision-making process identified as constitutional decision making.

If constitutional decision making is to be exercised by citizens in a constitutional republic, then arrangements need to exist where citizens can participate directly in efforts to formulate and revise the provisions of constitutions. Processes of constitutional deliberation can be conceptualized as involving a recommendatory process that is separate from a ratification process. Mechanisms such as constitutional initiatives where constitutional amendments are pro-

---

[18] *Ibid.,* 348.

posed by a petition of citizens, constitutional conventions and constitutional proposals advanced by recommendation of governmental authorities are among the methods used for proposing constitutional changes. The ratification process can be accomplished through constitutional referenda or other extraordinary processes which enable citizens to exercise control over ratification apart from those who discharge the ordinary governmental processes of determining, enforcing and altering ordinary legal relationships. The provisions of a constitution, thus, must be subject to formulation and alteration in accordance with decision-making processes that are unalterable by governmental authorities acting on their own initiative. Otherwise those governmental officials will be capable of modifying their own authority and would not be subject to enforceable limits established by the citizens in a democratic republic acting as constitutional decision makers.

Processes of constitutional decision making involve the choice of decision rules that apply to the conduct of government in a democratic republic. They do *not* involve the taking of *operational decisions* in the sense of selecting personnel, spending money, building public works, and managing public affairs. Since operational decisions are not taken as a part of the constitutional decision-making process, less urgency exists to take constitutional decisions quickly. Decision rules reflecting a higher level of consensus than simple plurality voting might also be used for processes of constitutional ratification when decisions lack immediate urgency but the costs of potential errors are extremely high.[19]

We can now conceptualize how "ultimate" authority to govern can be exercised by the citizenry in a democratic republic. Citizens must retain ultimate authority over the terms of constitutional law as well as the processes of constitutional decision making that establish the terms and conditions that apply to the conduct of governments. The terms of constitutional law are alterable by citizens acting collectively and are unalterable by governmental authorities acting alone. The task of maintaining and enforcing limits upon governmental authorities is essential in a constitutional republic. Establishing the special status of constitutions as fundamental law and the inviolability of popular control over processes

---

[19] James Buchanan and Gordon Tullock, *The Calculus of Consent* (Ann Arbor: University of Michigan Press, 1962).

of constitutional change are the first essential elements in creating
a system of constitutional government.

Constitutional Assignment of Authority to Govern. A constitutional government by definition involves limits upon those who
exercise governmental authority. In addition to the limits which
make a constitution unalterable by a government acting alone, the
general structure of a constitution is concerned with assigning decision-making capabilities for the conduct of government so that
no authority is unlimited and all authority is subject to limits. If
limited authority to govern is to be assigned among members of
a constitutional republic, that authority must be *distributed* among
diverse decision makers.

The first division of authority involves a reservation of constitutional authority to all persons functioning in a constitutional republic. A principle of equal right would apply to the reservation
of civil rights and individual prerogatives where each person would
reserve to himself such prerogatives as he would allow other men
to exercise in relation to him. Prerogatives reserved to individuals
as inalienable rights would imply correlative limitations upon officials who are assigned the special prerogatives of determining, enforcing and altering legal relationships.

An assignment of constitutional authority reserving to individuals
the authority to decide what is fit to learn and what can be com-
municated to fellow citizens is an essential prerogative if citizens
are to have free and reasoned discourse with one another and
exercise essential prerogatives of government in a democratic republic. Commensurate limitations would need to exist to prevent
governmental officials from interfering with these essential constitutional prerogatives of citizens.

Other constitutional prerogatives of citizens would include reference to the participation of citizens in various aspects of the political process. Eligibility to serve in public office should presumably
be broadly available to all citizens. Election to office should be
established on principles of representation that require officials to
be elected by their fellow citizens. Access of citizens to governmental decision-making processes and the obligation of officials to
consider citizen demands need specification in relation to authority
to petition for the redress of grievances, and constitutional entitle-
ment to due process of law and to equal protection of the law.
Provision for citizen participation in essential governmental proc-

esses including trial by jury, and citizen oversight of the discharge of public trust by governmental authorities through instrumentalities such as grand juries are among the basic constitution provisions that reserve essential prerogatives of government to citizens.

Finally constitutional prerogatives of citizens regarding the exercise of rights to property and the right to enter into contractual relationships are essential for the maintenances of social relationships and voluntary associations among persons in a democratic society. Property law and the law of contract establish the basis for most social relationships among individuals in a society. People in a democratic republic have a constitutional interest in property and contractual relationships if they are to govern their own affairs. These inalienable rights specify the residual authority retained by citizens in a democracy.

In addition to defining the constitutional prerogatives of individuals with correlative limitations upon the constitutional prerogatives of governmental officials, a constitution for a democratic society, if it is to serve as an enforceable system of constitutional law, will also depend upon an assignment of governmental prerogatives among diverse sets of officials so that each set of officials is subject to limits inherent in the prerogatives exercised by other officials. A system of enforceable constitutional law depends upon a separation of powers. Those who are responsible for rendering judgment in determining the application both of ordinary law and the provisions of constitutional law should do so with independence of those who are responsible for law making and for law enforcement. If the principle in equity, that no man is a fit judge of his own cause in relation to the interest of others, is to apply to the conduct of government, then those who exercise prerogatives of law making and law enforcement cannot be judges of their own causes of action in relation to citizens who are subject to law. An independent judiciary that is capable of rendering judgment in enforcing the claims of citizens in relation to their essential prerogatives as against officials who may usurp constitutional authority is an essential requisite for creating and maintaining an enforceable system of constitutional law.

If we assume that the behavioral implication of rules of law are publicly knowable and can be subject to common understanding by a community of individuals, then functions of law making can be separated from those of executing and enforcing law. If laws are publicly knowable and create grounds for action that are of essential interest to citizens, then citizens should be entitled to remedies that can mandate essential actions by executive authority or can enjoin improper actions by executive authorities. Laws creating public benefits should in a democratic society be subject to execution by actions of citizens as well as by actions of officials. Invocation of enforcement procedures by a citizen is a form of executive action in the broad sense of that term.

So long as laws are publicly knowable and subject to common understanding then processes of law making, law enforcement and adjudication of conflicts over law can be assigned to separate sets of authorities and still meet the condition of being one system of law that provides a common set of rules for ordering relationships among citizens in a democratic republic. Where laws are poorly formulated and based upon ambiguous terms such defects are more likely to be revealed where authority is limited. Individuals can contend more effectively about the meaning and ambiguities of law than where officials have unlimited authority and cannot be effectively challenged. Hobbes recognized that bad laws were traps for money that contributed to the corruption of political systems. However, he failed to see the importance of conflict and argumentation as providing bases for correcting the defects of legislation and improving the language of law.

The Actions of Citizens in Maintaining and Enforcing a System of Constitutional Law. Constitutions and processes of constitutional decision making are means for citizens to exercise fundamental prerogatives in participating as rulers in a democratic society. Each citizen is a ruler who can participate in processes of constitutional choice, in different processes of governmental decision-making, and is also subject to the rules of his own making. The effectiveness of a democratic constitution depends upon the capacity of citizens to enforce limits upon officials, and prevent officials from colluding to usurp the authority of government and transform a democratic constitution into an effective monarchy or aristocracy, to use Hobbes' terms. The facade of constitutional forms can be used to conduct plebiscites where people are asked to approve the exercise of unlimited constitutional authority by those who exercise governmental prerogatives. If any one individual possesses himself of unlimited authority and gains the consent of his fellow citizens in doing so he becomes a legitimate monarch in Hobbes' terms. "The death of the people" in a democratic society occurs when citizens can no longer exercise decisions which maintain effective limits upon the prerogatives of officials.[20] The viability of a democratic society thus depends, as Tocqueville has commented, upon a people reaching a level of civilization or a level of political consciousness where they can discern the causes of their misery and take appropriate remedial actions. If officials threaten to usurp constitutional authority, citizens must be sufficiently knowledgeable about the theory of constitutional choice to maintain effective limits upon those who exercise governmental prerogatives. In the final analysis, a system of enforceable constitutional law depends upon citizens who are prepared to pay the price of civil disobedience in being willing to challenge the constitutional validity of any official action and face punishment and official displeasure if their cause is not affirmed.

Key officials are relatively few in number and may find it in their interest to take actions which countervene constitutional limits to their authority. Yet official actions are presumed to be lawful until adjudged otherwise. In challenging the actions of officials that he considers to be constitutionally invalid, a citizen in a constitutional republic must assume the risk of defying authorities and of advancing his contention for consideration by other authorities and by his fellow citizens. A constitutional republic can be maintained only so long as citizens scrutinize the actions of officials and challenge those actions when they exceed the limits of constitutional authority. But such challenges must be based upon reasoned and non-violent contention—upon *civil* disobedience—if there is to be a basis for the exercise of reasoned choice in the governance of human societies.

Reiterating the Process of Constitutional Choice. The American Constitution of 1787 was based upon an assumption that peoples in different democratic republics can share a variety of common interests that require collective organization to deal with common problems. While any one community of interest will require a common set of rules for acting in relation to that community of interest, diverse communities of interest can be organized through the concurrent instrumentalities of different units of government. The process of constitutional decision making can be reiterated for

[20] Thomas Hobbes, *De Cive* (New York: Appleton-Century-Crofts, 1949), 97.

each different community of interest. Reiteration of the process of constitutional choice by creating concurrent units of government with overlapping jurisdictions is the basis for organizing federal systems of government.

Federal systems of government are ones where people have recourse to multiple units of government in organizing a system of government. If a federal system is one that is subject to effective constitutional limits then each unit of government will be subject to the provisions of constitutional law that define the prerogatives of citizens and officials so that no single set of officials is capable of exercising ultimate and unlimited authority in the governance of society. Different sets of officials are assigned prerogatives to determine, enforce and alter legal relationships subject to limitations. Those who are assigned prerogatives to function as officials are assigned an unequal authority where they can enforce rules of law in relation to all persons who are subject to those rules. But the persons who are subject to rules of law retain essential constitutional authority to establish the fundamental law that applies to those who govern. A symmetry of relationships is established. Citizens retain essential prerogatives to function as rulers in formulating and modifying the fundamental law. Citizens are also subject to the actions of officials who are assigned authority to determine and to enforce legal relationships subject to those rules of fundamental law.

Conclusion

Constitutional choice is not limited to an act of formulating an original constitution. Rather, constitutional choice is a continuing process through which structures of government can be revised and altered through time. A theory of constitutional choice includes that body of knowledge which enables communities of people to identify problems of institutional weakness and institutional failure and to formulate alternative arrangements that would continue to advance human welfare.

The basic elements in a theory of constitutional choice had been worked out in the course of the American experiment within approximately 15 years of the Declaration of Independence. The Articles of Confederation failed to provide a viable constitutional order. The lessons of that failure were taken into account in the development of a new constitution in 1787. The warrantability of the theory of constitutional choice used in the formulation of the Constitution of 1787 and the numerous state constitutions is subject to practical demonstration by whether or not those political experiments served as the basis for organizing political actions that yielded the intended effects.

THE SOVIET EXPERIMENT IN CONSTITUTIONAL CHOICE

The explicit theories of constitutional choice used by Thomas Hobbes in the *Leviathan* and by Alexander Hamilton and James Madison in *The Federalist* have not occupied a significant place in contemporary considerations of political development. Many of the discussions of political development turn, however, upon the exercise of governmental authority by some center of ultimate authority that can make authoritative decisions for a society as a whole. The problem of constitutional rule has received much less attention.

Yet, if these theories have merit they should help us to explain the consequences that follow from the efforts of different people to constitute systems of government. If we look at efforts to create systems of government as political experiments we can test the merit of ideas by whether or not they help us to understand the courses of actions and the consequences which have followed. We shall turn to the Soviet experiment to see whether these theories of constitutional choice help us to understand what occurred in the conduct of that experiment.

As one of the major experiments in constitutional choice, the Soviet experiment stands upon theoretical grounds that are at radical variance with the American experiment in constitutional government. In order to understand the relationship between theory and action it is necessary to turn to the explanation offered by those who exercised leadership in the Russian revolution. In doing so we shall draw upon the work of Vladimir Ilyich Lenin as he explains the basic elements of constitutional choice that are associated with the Russian revolution. The first element of constitutional choice involved the creation of the Communist Party as the instrument of a revolutionary movement. The second element involved seizure of state power and its exercise by the Communist Party as the dictatorship of the proletariat. The implications of this approach to the problem of constitutional choice needs to be considered on its own merits.

Constitution of a Revolutionary Movement

In the pamphlet *What Is To Be Done?*, Lenin formulates his basic thoughts about the practical problems of organizing a revolutionary movement.[21]   He sees the struggle as ultimately a military one that will be decided by a highly disciplined fighting organization.   The essential nucleus for that organization was to be created by the establishment of a revolutionary newspaper.   The network of agents to supply information for publication served as an extended intelligence gathering apparatus.   Frequency of publication and regularity of distribution provided evidence to others about the success of a revolutionary movement in establishing an organizational base for its activities.   Such an apparatus provided the essential command structure or "scaffolding" for a larger revolutionary movement.[22]

Lenin views "strict secrecy" as an essential requisite for a revolutionary organization.[23]   Mass organizations cannot hope to attain strict secrecy.   A revolutionary organization must be highly selective, composed of a limited number of trained professional revolutionists rather than broadly inclusive of all those opposed to a regime.   Lenin contends that the active participation of the masses will be increased tenfold to the extent that a small number of professional revolutionaries centralize the "secret work"[24]—essential decisions about revolutionary tactics —of the revolutionary movement.   Centralization of the secret command functions will give a unity to revolutionary efforts that will greatly increase its effectiveness.

Lenin also emphasizes the importance of the leadership to be exercised in a selective party of professional revolutionaries.   He indicates that "society" advances *very many* people who are "fit" for revolutionary work.[25]   They are the ones who have developed a consciousness of tyranny and oppression and are prepared to fight absolutism.   But these are just a multitude of individuals—they are not a "people" in the sense of being able to take collective action.[26]

[21] In V. I. Lenin, *Selected Works*, (New York: International Publishers, n.d.), vol. II.
[22] *Ibid.*, 21.
[23] *Ibid.*, 150.
[24] *Ibid.*, 140.
[25] *Ibid.*, 142.
[26] *Ibid.*

"Because we have no leaders, no political leaders, we have no talented organizers capable of organizing extensive and at the same time uniform and harmonious work that would give employment to all forces, even the most inconsiderable."[27] A unified leadership of a few professional revolutionaires is necessary "in order to unite all of these tiny fractions into one whole, in order, in breaking up functions, to avoid breaking up the movement, and in order to imbue those who carry out these minute functions with the conviction that their work is necessary and important. . . ."[28] Leadership is essential to effective teamwork in a revolutionary movement.

It is the concept of organizing the essential leadership function as a *separate* organization possessed of strict secrecy, specialized training, access to intelligence that makes it into "an army of omniscient people."[29] With extensive contacts capable of reaching out to larger multitudes of other people, a vanguard of professional revolutionaries can command a revolutionary movement. This separate organization of the leadership and command function is the embryo of a new sovereign of a new state.

Lenin quite explicitly rejects the application of "broad principles of democracy"[30] to the organization of a revolutionary movement. Broad principles of democracy presume for Lenin two conditions: (1) full publicity; and (2) reliance upon election in selecting leadership and in making decisions. Democracy requires full publicity in which the political arena is as open to public view as the stage in a theatre if every person is to decide for himself whom to elect to office. Full publicity, the principle of election and general control by voters leads to a process of "natural selection," Lenin observes, where each person will find "his proper place," do what he is "best fittted" to do, feel "the effects of his mistakes" and "prove before all the world his ability to recognize mistakes and to avoid them."[31]

But what application do these democratic principles have for a revolutionary struggle against the autocracy of Czarist Russia? In that circumstance Lenin contends that broad democracy is a "*useless and harmful toy.*"[32] Any attempt to practice *broad* democracy

[27] *Ibid.*
[28] *Ibid.*, 143.
[29] *Ibid.*, 164.
[30] *Ibid.*, 152.
[31] *Ibid.*, 153.
[32] *Ibid.*, 154.

will only facilitate the work of the secret police. Instead, "the only serious organizational principle the active workers of our movement can accept is strict secrecy, strict selection of members and the training of professional revolutionaries" to assume leadership of the revolutionary movement.[33]

The revolutionary apparatus proposed by Lenin involved a stable organization of leaders composed of a restricted membership of professional revolutionaries organized apart from the larger multitude of individuals in the working class and in other classes of society who form the mass of the revolutionary movement. The organization of the vanguard of professional revolutionaries depends upon strict secrecy, specialized training, centralization of authority and military discipline. It provides the essential intelligence, communication and command structure for a fighting force organized in accordance with principles of military organization.

At the strategic level of discussion, Lenin's analysis calls for a highly disciplined, centralized, military-type organization capable of capturing the fortress of the existing autocracy. Success would require the destruction of the existing state apparatus and the creation of a new structure of authority controlled by the revolutionary party as a highly disciplined, centralized, military-type organization. The revolutionary party had been fashioned as a command apparatus that was capable of engaging in a struggle against the command apparatus of the existing state on its own terms. In a sense the revolutionary party had been created as a mirror image of the autocracy it sought to destroy. Military discipline was required to combat forces organized by military discipline. The necessities of a revolutionary struggle against an unenlightened and oppressive Czar exercising the prerogatives of a Hobbesian sovereign required the creation of a new sovereign capable of realizing a revolutionary transformation of Soviet society. What, then, made the Russian Revolution such a radical departure in political organization and political development?

The Constitution of a Classless Society

Lenin's explanations for the tyrannical behavior of the Czarist regime in Imperial Russia turned on the theses advanced by Marx and Engels. They viewed the state as a product of society at a

[33] *Ibid.*, 155.

certain stage of development where that society is the subject of insoluble contradictions represented by irreconcilable class antagonisms. The state is created as an instrument of power which places itself above society and increasingly separates itself from society in order to repress conflict and keep order in society. Class antagonisms have their roots in private ownership of the modes of production in which the capitalist class uses its control of property to exploit the working class. The state is the organ of the capitalist class to maintain its domination over society. The bureaucracy, the standing army and the police are the principal instruments of state power organized for the suppression of the working class.

The institution of private property is viewed as the source of irreconcilable class conflict. The state is developed by the capitalist class as an instrument of domination over the working class. In Lenin's words, ". . . the state arises when, where and to the extent that the class antagonisms *cannot* be objectively reconciled. And, conversely, the existence of the state proves that the class antagonisms *are* irreconcilable."[34]

Given this explanation, the task of the revolutionist is to seize power and to crush and destroy the traditional apparatus of the state. Earlier revolutions had failed because they had concerned themselves with representative institutions of republican government and had failed to break up the executive apparatus of the state as reflected in bureaucratic and military organization. According to Marx, all revolutionary efforts in France prior to the revolution of 1848 had served only to bring the executive apparatus of the state to "greater perfection instead of breaking it up."[35]

On the eve of the October Revolution, Lenin urged that a successful revolution required that the revolutionists seize state power, crush and destroy the existing executive apparatus. A new apparatus of control would be created where the working class could exercise state power through the dictatorship of the proletariat. The oppressed majority would now eliminate the exploiters, and undertake the reconstruction of society by expropriating private property on behalf of all working people. With the elimination of private property the basis for class structure in society would be removed. A classless society would emerge. The state would wither away. Removing the basis for irreconcilable antagonism

[34] In V. I. Lenin *Selected Works*, vol. VII, 8.
[35] *Ibid.*, 25.

between classes would remove the need to rely upon the instrumentality of the state to moderate conflict and maintain order in the presence of irreconcilable antagonisms.

The radical thrust of the Soviet revolution lay in altering the basic structure of property rights. Private property was expropriated and eliminated as an instrument of exploitation. If the Marxian theory of social classes and class exploitation were correct, a classless society should arise and the state should wither away.

Milovan Djilas, a leading member of the Yugoslav Communist party, reviews the aftermath of the Communist revolutions and concludes that members of the revolutionary party had instead become the new ruling class in Communist countries.[36] Those who seized state power in effect became the new state. The members of the successful revolutionary party became the new ruling class capable of using the instruments of state power, and control over state ownership of property, to rule the masses of workers and peasants in Communist societies.

The new ruling class in Soviet society has all of the attributes that one might expect when fallible and self-interested rulers exercise the prerogatives of Hobbes' sovereign. Alterations in the structure of property rights have significantly modified the structure of social relationships in Soviet society. But the authority of those who are capable of determining, enforcing, and altering legal relationships is unlimited by any constraints of constitutional law. Rather, their authority is unlimitable and unalterable by those who were subject to Soviet rule. The fundamental structure of social classes, thus, arises from the relationships of rulers to the ruled and is grounded in the structure of authority relationships. The new ruling class, created as a highly disciplined military-type organization, became the new autocracy to replace the old.

The Fruits of the Soviet Revolution

The realization of a classless society and the withering away of the state have not been among the fruits of Communist revolutionary movement. The state apparatus persists but under the control of a new ruling class. Marxism did not supply a new theory of constitutional choice that would enable men to constitute a

---

[36] Milovan Djilas, *The New Class* (New York: Frederick A. Praeger, 1957).

classless society. Hobbes' theory of sovereignty is sufficient to account for the structure of government and the relationship of rulers to the ruled in Communist societies organized on the model of the Soviet experiment.

The theoretical implications of the Soviet experiment have been the subject of a rapidly growing literature on the part of critical and independent observers in the Soviet Union. Roy A. Medvedev in his study *Let History Judge* construes the oppressive measures of the Stalinist period as the usurpation of authority by a despotic person.[37] Andrei Sakharov sees freedom of thought and expression as essential means for correcting the error inherent in dogmatic policies of the party apparatus.[38] Andrei Amalrik sees the enforcement of legal limits upon the exercise of official discretion as a necessary condition for a lawful society and has appealed to Soviet courts in an effort to assert his rights under the Soviet constitution.[39] Realization of the aspirations of socialist societies would appear to depend upon a theory of constitutional choice whereby members of such societies can constrain the exercise of authority by officials through constitutional limitations.

The American solution to the problem of constitutional choice is only one approach to the creation of constitutional limitations upon the exercise of governmental authority. The separation of legislative action from executive functions in Parliamentary systems is an essential step in establishing legal limits upon executive action and in placing a constitutional constraint upon government. If executive action is constrained by standards of publicly enacted laws, citizens can have recourse to appropriate judicial or administrative remedies in placing some limits upon official discretion. If, on the other hand, the executive apparatus dominates the legislature, constitutional constraints become a meaningless facade, as Indira Gandhi has demonstrated.

The Marxian emphasis upon property rights, however, points to a critical variable in the organization of social relationships. Property rights involve a structure of authority relationships which

---

[37] Roy A. Medvedev, *Let History Judge* (New York: Alfred A. Knopf, 1972).

[38] Andrei Sakharov, *Progress, Coexistence and Intellectual Freedom* (New York: W. W. Norton Company, Inc., 1968).

[39] Andrei Amalrik, *Involuntary Journey to Siberia* (New York: Harcourt Brace Jovanovich, Inc., 1970).

assigns decision-making capabilities to individuals or collectivities of individuals to act in relation to events that are the object of property relationships. State control of property in the Soviet Union significantly increased the dominance of state authority and of the Communist party as the new ruling class.

CONCLUSION

Citizens in a democratic society can be their own governors, and engage in a process of self-government, only if they retain control over the ultimate prerogatives of constitutional decision making that establish the terms and conditions of government and are able to enforce those terms and conditions against those who serve as governmental officials. Otherwise, officials will advance their own interests by usurping constitutional prerogatives and make subjects of citizens.

Montesquieu had posed the basic paradox of democratic societies when he recognized that they are vulnerable to internal imperfections if they become large, and vulnerable to external attack if they remain small. Confederation, as Hamilton and Madison demonstrated, was an infeasible solution. A federal solution, in turn, depended upon a system of constitutional decision making and constitutional law whereby limits could be enforced in relation to all governmental officials and, thus, in relation to the exercise of all governmental prerogatives.

By developing a "general theory of the limited Constitution" and working out the solution to the problem of constitutional rule, the American revolution was able to realize its objective without devouring its own children. Demonstrating the theoretical feasibility of creating a system of constitutional rule is not sufficient unless those conditions are effectively maintained through all time. Unfortunately rhetoric about strict constructionism may conceal the secret intentions of those who pose the greatest threat to constitutional rule. A theory of constitutional choice is useful only as it informs the practice of self-government in human societies.

The Symbolism
of
Literary Alienation
in the
Revolutionary Age

Lewis P. Simpson

In *Mind in the Modern World*, Lionel Trilling points out that when Plato "undertook to say what the right conduct of mind should be, he found the paradigm in the just society." But in modern times the procedure has been reversed, and we find "the paradigm of the just society in the right conduct of mind." We evaluate governments in the ideal by "their intentionality, their impulse toward inclusiveness, by their striving toward coherence with due regard for the disparate elements they comprise, by the power of looking before and after."[1] A detailed comment on mind as the model of American society is not to Trilling's purposes in *Mind in the Modern World*. But in his discussion he makes an inference of the first importance for our understanding of the general cultural situation—and more particularly of the literary situation—in the age of our Revolution and early nationhood: the reversal of mind and society as paradigms of order was first fully defined in Thomas Jefferson's respect for mind as the model of government. Jefferson's attitude—or the attitude of the Enlightenment that found a cogent focus in Jefferson—had two drastic consequences. One of these is well known to us. We take it for granted as a fact of our existence. I mean the radical displacement of the traditional com-

[1] *Mind in the Modern World* (New York: Viking Press, 1972), 137-139.

munity—centered in Church and State, and in hierarchy, custom, and ritual—as the model of mind in America by the creation of public mind or public opinion as the model of society. In effect this occurrence relocated American society in the subjective realm of consciousness. The second consequence of the reversal of the paradigms of order in America stems from the first, but it is less discernible because it has been absorbed in the initial result—that is to say, in the subjectification of American society. I refer to the paradoxical, complex estrangement of American men of letters— of whom Jefferson, like Franklin and John Adams, was the very personification—from the Revolution and the new nation.

Never overt in the Revolutionary expression, this latter phenomenon is disclosed in a subtle and involved symbolism of cultural and literary displacement and alienation. I shall do no more here than attempt a brief examination of this symbolism in several representative works of the Revolutionary age—a period I conceive to extend from about the time of the first active agitation against England in the 1760's until the conclusion of the War of 1812, when American independence was finally secured. Within the broad signification of the term literature still prevailing in the eighteenth century, all the writings I shall refer to are literary works. They are the Declaration of Independence and *The Federalist*; selected poems of Philip Freneau; a novel, *Modern Chivalry* by H. M. Brackenridge; and a periodical essay, *The Rhapsodist*, and another novel, *Arthur Mervyn*, by Charles Brockden Brown.

I

The system of symbols governing the modern concept of the literary vocation came into existence with the articulation in Western Civilization of the order I have elsewhere called the Third Realm.[2] More commonly it is referred to as the Republic of Letters.

---

[2] Cf. Lewis P. Simpson ,"The Printer as Man of Letters: Franklin and the Symbolism of the Third Realm" in J. Leo Lemay, ed., *The Oldest Revolutionary* (Philadelphia: University of Pennsylvania Press, 1976). Also, cf. Simpson, "Federalism and the Crisis of Literary Order," *American Literature*, 32 (November 1960), 254-266; "Literary Ecumenicalism of the American Enlightenment," in Alfred Owen Aldridge, ed., *The Ibero-American Enlightenment* (Urbana: University of Illinois Press, 1971), 317-332; "The Southern Writer and the Great Literary Secession," in *The Man of Letters in New England and the South* (Baton Rouge: Louisiana State University Press, 1973),

As a realm additional to the realms of Church and State, the cosmopolitan Third Realm—comprehending all secular knowledge under the terms "letters," "literature," and "science"—inaugurated a great critique of the society based on the feudal concepts of custom and tradition, hierarchy and monarchy. By the eighteenth century the Great Critique—which embraced a cosmopolitan and crucial group of world historical men of letters from Francis Bacon to Thomas Jefferson, and which had as one powerful, if not entirely conscious, intention the moulding of government to the model of the human mind—had established the realm of Letters as a discrete dominion.

The differentiation of the Third Realm by the Great Critique was implemented—and at the same time shaped by—two world historical responses to mind's quest for power. One was the technological achievement of printing. The other was the Reformation. These events were dramatically and forcefully joined by the Puritan intellectuals (so large an influence on the American settlement), who insisted on the differentiation of mind from society. A classic statement is "Areopagitica" in which Milton opposes any imposition of authority by the Puritan commonwealth over the "commonwealth of letters and learning."[3] But the historical differentiation of the Third Realm did not reach fulfillment until the American Revolution, when a congress of colonials, led by a group of provincial intellectuals who achieved the status of world historical philosophes (notably Franklin, Jefferson, and John Adams), proclaimed the American Declaration of Independence. This document embodies the triumphant identity of the man of letters and the Third Realm. When the Declaration was proclaimed there no longer stood at the center of the world a king, a bishop, and a hierarchical society but the man of letters and his written declaration of mind's assumption of dominion and power. This dominion demanded full allegiance: "To preserve the freedom of the human mind . . . and freedom of the press, every spirit should be ready to devote itself to martyrdom. . . ."[4] Jefferson believed his rhetoric to be justified by the

---

229-255; "The Satiric Mode: The Early National Wits," in *The Comic Imagination in American Literature*, ed. Louis D. Rubin, Jr. (New Brunswick: Rutgers University Press, 1973), 49-61.

[3] See especially Michael Walzer, *The Revolution of the Saints: A Study in the Origins of Radical Politics* (New York: Atheneum, 1968), 124.

[4] Jefferson to William Green Mumford, June 18, 1789, in Adrienne Koch, ed., *The American Enlightenment* (New York: George Braziller, 1965), 341.

immutable truth of mind's authority. But if the basic American exemplification of the right conduct of mind as the paradigm of a just society is to be found in the Declaration of Independence, the Declaration also symbolizes—in a crucial if not absolute way—an attenuation of the authority of the Third Realm in modern history. Under the conditions of modern history as represented in the American microcosm, the Declaration forebodes a decline of the relation between the Republic of Letters and its citizen, the man of letters—between the man of letters and a political, economic, and social order which is emblematic of the order of rational, lettered minds, or the literary polity.

We may refer to the following elements in the Declaration: (1) its suggestion of the psychic expense attendant upon the loss of a traditional social order; (2) its suggestion of the loss of the classical-Christian sense of transcendent truth.

In the form in which it was accepted by the Continental Congress, the Declaration shows a certain inclination toward finding its climax not in the usurpation by the King of the "just powers" conferred on him by the "consent of the governed" but in a stern account of the crimes of a patriarch against the "brethren" of the colonies. In the version of the Declaration before amendment and deletion this tendency is more obvious. The King is something of a monster, albeit with the complicity of the people of the homeland, who "at this very time" are "permitting their chief magistrate to send over not only soldiers of our common blood, but Scotch & foreign mercenaries to invade & destroy us." It is "these facts" which "have given the last stab to agonizing affection," and that bid the "manly spirit" in us "to renounce forever these unfeeling brethren." In the denunciation of slavery Jefferson was more explicit in his depiction of the monstrous character of the King. He is said to have "waged war against human nature itself, violating its most sacred rights of life and liberty in the persons of a distant people who never offended him, captivating & carrying them into slavery in another hemisphere. . . . And that this assemblage of horrors might want no fact of distinguished die, he is now exciting those very people to rise in arms among us, and to purchase that liberty of which he has deprived them, by murdering the people on whom he also obtruded them: thus paying off former crimes committed against the LIBERTIES of one people, with crimes which he urges them to commit against the LIVES of another."

If the whole of the last section of charges drawn by Jefferson shapes a contrast (especially in the original version of the Declaration) between the rational and the irrational, and the King in his violation of the unalienable rights of man becomes a figure of barbarous irrationality, he is also a monarch who stands in violation of the unreasoning affections of kinship. A significant ambivalence of intention in the Declaration is inherent in its emotionality. The plain intention, to be sure, is to assert the right of revolution disclosed by the "laws of nature and of nature's God"; but this clear purpose is haunted by the expression of resentment against the corruption of a community founded not on rational hypothesis but in the ties of blood and the continuum of tradition.

A sense of doubt about intentionality in the Declaration, not mere deference to respect for the Deity, may be why the Congress amended the wording of the original version of the Declaration's conclusion *from* "We therefore the representatives of the United States of America in General Congress assembled do in the name & by the authority of the good people of these united colonies . . ." *to* "We therefore the representatives of the United States of America in General Congress assembled, *appealing to the supreme judge of the world for the rectitude of our intentions,* do in the name, & by the authority of the good people of these united colonies. . . ." The appeal "to the supreme judge of the world" to ratify the good intentions of the Revolutionists qualifies the equation between "nature's God" and the sovereignty of the "good people," and in fact introduces an unobtrusive but significant element of doubt into the Declaration about the rectitude of the people's intention as self-verifying or transcendently self-evident.[5] Indeed doubt of the existence of transcendent truth is a spectral presence in more than a little of the literature of the American Revolution. The acceptance of rational mind as the ideal model of a just society not only meant the rejection of constructs of perfect order existing in eternity—Plato's Republic, St. Augustine's heavenly city, Dante's community of hierarchy and degree—but meant too the rejection of the tradition of verifying the truth of order through contemplation. Contemplation depends on the acceptance of an infallible ideal of

[5] I quote from the text of the Declaration of Independence, conveniently presented with the excisions in parentheses, in Walter Blair, Theodore Hornberger, and Randall Stewart, eds., *The Literature of the United States* (Chicago: Scott, Foresman Company, 1953), I, 315-318.

order outside mind. From Descartes on mind became identified
with the introspective, unstructured functions of consciousness—
with the processes of cognition. Believing solely in its own existence, mind has no knowledge outside itself, and no reference for
action, outside its own functioning. Consciousness cannot transcend
consciousness.[6] Once the import of the loss of contemplative truth
was realized, the struggle to achieve a new mode of transcendence
became central to nineteenth-century romanticism, and a fateful
influence on modern history. But in the eighteenth century the
effective sense of rationality assumed the existence of the Third
Realm. If a transcendent republic outside mind did not exist, a
public order of rational, lettered mind—a public mind—conceived
by mind itself did. This order represented the right conduct of
mind as a truth verifiable in history by the man of letters.

In this connection, it is hardly too much to say, the most important fictional representation of the man of letters in the writings
of the Revolution and of the early American republic is Publius, the
composite mask of the authors of *The Federalist*. I have in mind at
this point the character of Publius as he speaks for Hamilton in the
first essay in the papers. In authoritative, measured eloquence he
presents his reasons for supporting the new Constitution, yet intimates the problematical quality of his support.

It has frequently been remarked that it seems to have been reserved to the
people of this country, by their conduct and example, to decide the important
question, whether societies of men are really capable or not of establishing
good government from reflection and choice, or whether they are forever
destined to depend for their political constitutions on accident and force. If
there be any truth in the remark, the crisis at which we are arrived may with
propriety be regarded as the era in which that decision is to be made; and
a wrong election of the part we shall act, may, in this view, deserve to be
considered as the general misfortune of mankind.[7]

It is not to be expected, Publius says, that philanthropy and pa-
triotism will insure a "judicious estimate of our true interests."
We expect "passions and prejudices little favorable to the discovery

6 See Hannah Arendt, *The Human Condition* (New York: Doubleday Anchor
Books, 1959), especially 249-297, for a discussion of thought in the modern
world to which I am indebted throughout this essay. I also have a general
indebtedness to Eric Voegelin, especially to *The New Science of Politics*
(Chicago: University of Chicago Press, 1952), 107-132.

7 Benjamin Fletcher Wright, ed., *The Federalist* (Cambridge: Harvard University Press, 1961), 89.

of truth" to arise from those who, secure in positions in the various
states, are fearful of a federal establishment, and from those who
want to profit from confusion and division. But Publius does not
dwell on this impediment to truth. He is more concerned with
those persons of "upright intentions" who may be "led astray by
preconceived jealousies and fears." Proponents of the Constitution
may be influenced by bad motives, there being no way to prevent
political factions involved in a "great national discussion" from
letting loose a "torrent of angry and malignant passions." Publius
wants to warn his fellow citizens against accepting "any impressions other than those which may result from the evidence of
truth." Saying he will offer his impressions frankly and solely on
the basis of his own deliberations, Publius enters a significant qualification of the evidence he has to present.

I will not amuse you with an appearance of deliberation when I have decided.
I frankly acknowledge to you my convictions, and I will freely lay before
you the reasons on which they are founded. The consciousness of good intentions disdains ambiguity. I shall not, however, multiply professions on
this head. My motives must remain in the depository of my own breast.
My arguments will be open to all, and may be judged by all. They shall at
least be offered in a spirit which will not disgrace the cause of truth.[8]

The reasons of Publius open to all but the motives for his reasons
hidden and locked away—this is the modified Hobbesian outlook
which informs the thinking of Hamilton, and which ramifies here
and there throughout "conservative" thought in the early Republic.
If, according to Hobbes, man is generically a creature of passions,
the objects of the passions are not a subject for philosophical inquiry. In Hobbes's version of society the motive of individual
passions replaces the ordering inspiration of a quest for the *sum-
mum bonum*. All that saves Publius from the Hobbesian bleakness
is his "consciousness of good intentions." I will not pretend that
I have an open mind on the Constitution, he says; I have finished
my deliberations upon it and concluded in its favor. My rational
intentions in presenting the case for the Constitution put me above
the ambiguity of human motives. What is at stake in the question
of the approval or disapproval of the Constitution is the representation to the world that by "their conduct and example" the American
people embody "reflection and choice" as the proper source of government. The underlying question, according to Publius, is not

8 *Ibid.*, 90-92.

whether the new nation embodies a unique nationhood but whether it represents the capacity of individuals in their collectivity as public mind or public opinion to act on the basis of good (rational) intentions. Publius symbolizes the constructive intentionality of public mind as a representation of the Third Realm. In Publius the eighteenth-century man of letters, the Third Realm is identified as the model of the emergent American Republic.

Even so Publius does not convince us of mind's propensity for good intentions. It is almost as though he is attempting, without success, to assume the sovereignty of good intentions over the truth he knows always to be darkly present in the processes of consciousness: the ambiguous connection between intention and motive. Publius is aware, we might say, of participating in an unprecedented internalization of history. Even as he urges upon Americans their historical opportunity to form a government based on reflection and choice, he implies the fear that public mind, or public opinion, will prove to be an insidious source of disorder, hiding both its intentions and motives in the breasts of thousands of persons and, as one young Federalist man of letters said, constantly exercising not a public but a "secret influence."[9] In spite of the fact that the press has become the education of everyman, public opinion, Publius intimates, is not an extension of but a threat to the Republic of Letters.

Yet if he anticipates a diminishing role for the man of letters as the representative of mind's authority in the novel American nation-state, Publius is the man of letters as eighteenth-century philosophe and Revolutionary statesman. He takes for granted his existence under the dispensation of the Third Realm, although he implicitly questions its efficacy. When we turn from the American man of letters in the role personified by Publius, to his role as poet and storyteller, we detect a more sensitive, and more distinct, awareness of the displacement of the man of letters in the early American nation-state. Freneau, Brackenridge, and Brown not only suggest in their writings that in the disparity between the golden intention of the Revolution—the establishment of a state based on rational, lettered mind—and the equivocal motivation of this purpose in the passions, there is a loss of literary authority. They self-consciously symbolize this loss in their depiction of the drama of the American

⁹ Joseph Stevens Buckminster, "On the Dangers and Duties of Men of Letters," *Monthly Anthology and Boston Review*, 7 (September 1809), 148.

poet, essayist, or novelist, who is presumptively engaged in hero-
ically imagining and proclaiming the new age being ushered in by
the Revolution yet is basically uncertain of his role. Even to the
extent of feeling himself somehow to be an outsider to the good
intentions of the Revolution.

II

Of all the Poets dead and gone,
I cannot recollect but ONE
    That throve by writing rhyme—
If *Pope* from *Homer* gained rewards,
Remember, statesmen, kings and lords
    Were poets, in his time.
A poet where there is no king,
Is but a disregarded thing
    An atom on the wheel;
A second *Iliad* could he write
His pockets would be very light,
    And beggarly his meal.[10]

The lament is not that of a distressed American Tory poet. It
is a retrospection on his own career by an aged Philip Freneau,
a major voice of the American Revolution and in his prime an
unrivalled denouncer of monarchy. *"Kings are the choicest curse
that man e'er knew!"* Freneau exclaimed in 1778, a conviction he reaffirmed in the 1790's, envisioning liberation from monarchy as the
key to the American future:

COLUMBIA, hail! immortal be thy reign:
Without a king, we till the smiling plain:
Without a king, we trace the unbounded sea,
And traffic round the globe, through each degree . . .
So shall our nation form'd on Virtue's plan,
Remain the guardian of the Rights of Man,
A vast Republic famed through every clime,
Without a king, see the end of time.[11]

Having once held such a view of kingship, how could Freneau, even
in satirical jest, allow himself later to conclude that in the destruc-

[10] "The City Poet" in Philip Freneau, *Last Poems*, ed. Lewis Leary (New
Brunswick: Rutgers University Press, 1945), 31-32.

[11] "America Independent; and Her Everlasting Deliverance from British
Tyranny and Oppression" in Freneau, *Poems*, ed. Harry Hayden Clark (New
York: Hafner Publishing Company, 1929), 25; "On Mr. Paine's Rights of
Man," *ibid.*, 125.

tion of a king lay the destruction of poetry and consequently the
sad lapse of his poetic career? The answer undoubtedly lies partly
in the neglect and penury Freneau endured in his long old age,
but fundamentally it seems to lie in his life-long suspicion that
rationality is not an inherent human capacity: that actually the
monster who is the king is born out of the monster in man. This
is the theme which emerges in Freneau's remarkable poem, "A
Picture of the Times, with Occasional Reflections" (1782):

> Cursed be the day, how bright so'er it shined
> That first made kings the masters of mankind;
> And cursed the wretch who first with regal pride
> Their equal rights to equal men denied;
> But cursed, o'er all, who first to slavery broke
> Submissive bowed and owned a monarch's yoke:
> Their servile souls his arrogance adored
> And basely owned a brother for a lord;
> Hence wrath, and blood, and feuds and wars began,
> And man turned monster to his fellow man.[12]

In contrast the poet pictures the pre-monarchical government conducted by "The hoary sage beneath his sylvan shade," who

> Imposed no laws but those which reason made;
> On peace, not war, on good, not ill intent,
> He judged his brethren by their own consent;
> Untaught to spurn those brethren to the dust;
> In virtue firm, and obstinately just, . . .[13]

Freneau discovers in the rise of monarchy a dispossession of man
from an original abode in a garden of reason and peace. But his
attitude toward the nature of this fall of man is uncertain. A king
would not seem to be as responsible for the abrogation of the rule
of reason as his subjects, who not only submit to a monarch but
adore his arrogance. Does a reverence of kingly authority answer
to profound, elusive motives of the human consciousness—to nameless terrors and tribulations of consciousness which reason cannot
respond to? Freneau does not pursue the problem he implies in
any certain way. In fact, he turns his poem toward a castigation
of King George, depicting his mind as possessed of and disordered
by the demon Ambition. But in its general implication Freneau's
"Picture of the Times" infers that the human mind itself is contra-

---

12 *Ibid.*, 85.
13 *Ibid.*, 85-86.

dictory and unreasoning and may be possessed by demonic motives. The poem virtually suggests an overpowering demonic
insurrection within mind against its original faculty of reason.
There are positive efforts in Freneau's poetry to represent the
American Revolution as a restoration of a pre-monarchical state of
reason, but all of his more complex poems about America indicate
a pessimistic outlook on, if not despair of, this prospect. Consider,
for instance, the well-known poem entitled "To An Author." This
has often been interpreted simply as a reflection on the transience
of literary effort in the sparse cultural environment of a provincial
world.

> Thrice happy Dryden, who could meet
> Some rival bard in every street![14]

But "To An Author" addresses itself not so much to the fate of the
individual poet in the barren American literary situation as to a
threatened deformation of the sensibility of reason, and the loss of
the poetic vision of America as a culture of reason.

> An age employed in edging steel
> Can no poetic raptures feel;
> No solitude's attracting power
> No leisure of the noon day hour,
> No shaded stream, no quiet grove
> Can this fantastic century move;
>
> The muse of love in no request—
> Go—try your fortune with the rest,
> One of the nine you should engage,
> To meet the follies of the age:—
> On one, we fear, your choice must fall—
> The least engaging of them all—
> Her visage stern—and angry style—
> A clouded brow—malicious smile—
> A mind on murdered victims placed—
> She, only she, can please the taste![15]

America, it would seem, finds in request neither Thalia, the muse
of pastoral poetry, nor Erato, the muse of erotic poetry, and summons only Melpomene, the forbidding muse of tragedy, whose sign
is a sword.

But, it is interesting to observe, the release of America from

[14] *Ibid.*, 353
[15] *Ibid.*, 353-354.

active warfare did not signify to Freneau a larger place for a poetry
of reason in the nation. On the contrary, by the end of the eighteenth century Freneau's vision of the role of the poet and his message in America became more despairing than it is in "To An
Author." In "The Americans of the United States," a poem devoted
to a characterization of the Republic near the end of its first decade,
Freneau finds no muse at all in request by America, seeing the
American future in an altogether antipoetic age of prose and commonsense:

> To seize some *features* from the faithless past;
> Be this our care—before the century close:
> The colours strong!—for, if we deem aright,
> The *coming age will be an age of prose*:
> When *sordid cares* will break the muses' dream,
> And COMMON SENSE be ranked in seat supreme,
>
> Go, now, dear book; once more expand your wings;
> Still to the cause of man *severely true*:
> Untaught to flatter *pride*, or fawn on kings.—
> Trogan, or Tyrian, *give them both their due.*—
> *When they are right, the cause of both we plead.*
> *And both will please us well,—if both will read.*[16]

"*If both will read.*" Freneau makes a gesture of resignation toward
the lapsing literary authority in America. Although he retains his
conviction of the poet's obligation to rebel against kings, he sees the
final destruction of the poetry of reason in the bourgeois mind. The
American republic will be dominated by "sordid cares" (which
are equated with "commonsense," meaning a devotion to the subjective motives of popular self-interest). An age of prose has issued
from an age of iron. Freneau recognizes his vision of the poet's
guidance in the restoration of an original republic of reason as a
poetic dream. When at the last he refers to the isolation of the
poet in a society without a king, he confirms the irony of his own
experience of rebellion against a king. A minor poet of the Great
Critique, an active citizen of the Third Realm, Freneau felt abandoned in a historical situation he had at once resisted and helped
to make.

The relationship of the man of letters to the early Republic is
explored both more explicitly and at greater length in Brackenridge's novel *Modern Chivalry* than it is in the writings of Freneau.

16 *Ibid.,* 150.

Loosely imitative of *Don Quixote,* this fulsome, discursive satire relates the adventures of Captain John Farrago and his Irish immigrant servant, Teague O'Regan, as they move about in the communities of an American frontier landscape, a world which mirrors that of western Pennsylvania, the home of Brackenridge and the scene of his comparatively small but emblematic career in American politics.

According to the author, the admonitory theme of *Modern Chivalry* (which was written over a period of twenty-five years, about half of the work being published in the 1790's and the whole not until 1815) is the danger of putting unqualified men in positions of trust and responsibility in a democratic society. But the comprehensive theme of the novel is the problematical role of the man of letters in a society, which, shaping itself in the protean image of public mind or public opinion, is incapable of defining its aims or recognizing its motives. *Modern Chivalry* describes a society given over to the vanity of equality. On the simplest level the theme of the fate of the man of letters in such a society is expressed in anecdotes about the aggressions of ignorance against letters. In one instance a candidate for office is accused of having been seen with a book in his hand. He protests:

I am innocent of letters as the child unborn. I am an illiterate man, God be praised, and free from the sin of learning, or any wicked art, as I hope to be saved; but here is a report raised up, that I have dealings in books, that I can read. O! the wickedness of this world! Is there no protection from slander, and bad report? God help me! Here I am, *an honest republican, a good citizen,* and yet it is reported of me that I read books. O! who can stop reproach? I am ruined; I am undone; I shall loose [sic] my election; and the good will of my neighbours, and the confidence of posterity.

Farrago reflects: "The time was, when learning would save a man's neck; but now it endangers it. The neck verse, is reversed. That is the effect of it. For the man that can read goes to the wall; not him that is ignorant. *But such are the revolutions of opinion.*"[17] In another incident which appears in *Modern Chivalry* a jury convicts a man of insanity because he admits of "being *addicted to books.*" In this instance a superior judge (in *Modern Chivalry,* it is to be noted, the lawyer and the judge often exemplify the man of letters) takes the case under advisement; and although

[17] Hugh Henry Brackenridge, *Modern Chivalry,* ed. Claude M. Newlin (New York: American Book Company, 1937), 419-420.

the outcome is not pursued in the novel, it would seem that the verdict will be overturned.

The major representation of Brackenridge's theme in *Modern Chivalry* occurs in Farrago's efforts to keep his illiterate servant from rising above the station he should occupy in the democratic republic. But the proper status of Teague is hard for his master to define. The whole society is pervaded by the vanity of equality, which binds not only the ignorant but the well educated to the bogtrotter's limitations. At one point, for instance, Teague is elected to membership in the American Philosophical Society. But the compelling influence of equality is dramatized most effectively in the impact it has on Farrago. His sensitivity to Teague's meaning in American society and the problems and vexations of his superintendence of Teague, a demanding and delicate task the Captain deems necessary to the welfare of the nation, become the substance of whatever plot *Modern Chivalry* has; and if the novel can be said to have a climax, this is reached when Farrago eventually realizes the nature of his vexatious role. He is the man of letters as democratic chevalier.

Democracy has its strength in strict integrity; in perfect delicacy; in elevation and dignity of mind. It is an unjust imputation, that it is rude in manners, and coarse in expression. This is the characteristic of slaves, in a despotism; not of democrats in a republic. Democracy embraces the idea of standing on virtue alone; unaided by wealth or the power of family. This makes 'the noble of nature' of whom Thomas Payne [sic] speaks. Shall this noble not know his nobility, and be behind the noble of aristocracy who piques himself upon his honour, and feels a stain upon his delicacy as he would a bodily wound? The democrat is the true chevalier, who, though he wears not crosses, or the emblazoned arms of heraldry, yet is ready to do right, and justice to everyone. All others are imposters, and do not belong to the order of democracy.[18]

Resisting the vanity of equality, the democratic chevalier invests democracy with a sense of the heroic. "Now the vote of the citizen takes the place of the sword of the adventurer," Brackenridge says. "Shall the knight of the Golden Cross be free from stain in his atchievements [sic]; and shall a republican prostitute his vote, or dishonor his standing in society, by bestowing it on the unworthy?"[19]

But if the proper role of the American man of letters is to be a democratic chevalier, Brackenridge does not see this as a self-

[18] *Ibid.*, 403-404.
[19] *Ibid.*

assured function. Shall the modern chevalier "complain of usurpation; of undue influence; or oppression and tyranny from ambitious persons; and not be jealous, at the same time of *democratic tyranny* in himself, which is the more pernicious, as it brings a slur upon the purest principles?" Brackenridge declares in Volume II, Part II, of *Modern Chivalry* that he "would make it a principal matter" of his novel to "form the heart to a *republican government.*" To this end he discusses the necessity of uprooting from the heart the "poison weed of ambition," this to be accomplished by translating the "ambition of doing good" into the *"pleasure* of doing good," which is the "greatest possible pleasure to a mind rightly informed."[20] The purification of the motives of the heart would bring rational intention and motive (head and heart) into a consonant relationship. The modern chevalier would make whole the Hamilitonian dichotomy of intention and motive in the American man of letters, and the man of letters would enter into a state of complete democratic sincerity. Yet Brackenridge remains doubtful about an idealistic reconciliation of the discrepancy between the intention of the Republic to be an emblem of rational mind and the motive of this aim. This is seen most graphically in his personal concern about a discrepancy between the overt intention of his authorship of *Modern Chivalry* and his inner motive in writing it. Is he writing primarily out of his hope to form the heart to a republican government? Or does he write out of his own heart's desire to pursue the pleasure and the power that are the artist's? Brackenridge confesses, *"There is a pleasure in writing, which only the man who writes knows."*[21] This, he acknowledges, is not the joy of doing good; it is the pleasure of self-love. And this, Brackenridge indicates, is related to a still deeper motive in writing his novel—the delight he takes in his power to "elevate small matters," to record the "freaks" of ordinary people, and thus to give the form of truth to the world immediately about him.

That is the very reason I assume this biography of Farrago. Any one can write the campaign of a great prince, because the subject sustains the narrative. But it is a greater praise to give a value to the rambles of private persons, or the dissensions of a borough town. One advantage is, that these transactions being in a narrow compass, the truth can be reached with more certainty, the want of which is a drawback upon histories of greater compass, most of

20 *Ibid.*, 481.
21 *Ibid.*, 492.

them being little better than the romance of the middle ages, or the modern novel.[22]

In his compounded ironies, including ironic comments on the genre in which he is writing, Brackenridge illuminates the status and meaning of the literary vocation in America by expressing the truth of his own life. *Modern Chivalry* is a highly self-conscious satirical fantasy about American democracy; at the same time it is an autobiographical history (in the guise of a biography of Captain Farrago) of an aspiring American man of letters—at once a revelation and a concealment of the author's career. Brackenridge began his career in a youthful self-recognition of his literary gifts and demonstrated these in his collaboration with Freneau in a patriotic poem, "The Rising Glory of America"; but later, suffering like Freneau from a sense of literary dislocation, he longed for the London community of writers. When he satirizes his literary capacities and mocks his ambition in the dissertation on style which introduces Volume III of *Modern Chivalry*, Brackenridge makes his covert conviction of a thwarted career all the more evident.

The fact is . . . I possess great versatility of stile, and vast compass of sentiment and imagination. Nature intended me for a writer, and it has always been my ambition. How often have I sighed for the garrets of London; when I have read histories, manners, and anecdotes of Otway, Dryden, and others, who have lived in the upper stories of buildings, writing paragraphs, or essays in prose and verse. I have lamented my hard fate that I was not one of these. Was I to go to London, of which I have sometimes thought, my first object would be to visit the aerial mansions of these divine inhabitants. There is not a garret where any of these have dwelt, or where any of their descendants now dwells, that I would not rummage to find papers, scraps and remains, of what may still be there. I would at any rate visit most of the present men who live by their wits, and converse with them, indulging that pleasure which one takes in a consimilarity of genius.[23]

But (again like Freneau) Brackenridge does not finally ascribe the frustration of the identity of the man of letters in America to the lack of literary community. In its total implication *Modern Chivalry* attributes this to the intangible dissolution of the public order of letters in the "convulsions of public opinion." The tension in Brackenridge's work between the high purpose of the man of letters—the democratic chevalier of good intentions—and the tyr-

[22] *Ibid.*
[23] *Ibid.*, 171.

anny of democracy is never resolved one way or the other. But
it is evident that if Captain Farrago cannot control Teague O'Regan, neither can his creator. Brackenridge, whose direct role in
the novel virtually replaces that of Farrago in the last five hundred
pages of the story, is unsuccessful in his advocacy of the principle
that the cobbler stick to his last. Teague, the symbol of public
opinion, subjects the master to the servant. Teague cannot be
repudiated by Farrago-Brackenridge, for the author's obligation to
democracy is to redeem Teague. Although in the democratic situation Teague owes nothing to the self-appointed chevalier, the chevalier is bound by the ties of his democratic idealism to the bogtrotter. As the adventures of Farrago-Brackenridge and Teague
come to an end in the days of the second war with England, the
author is wondering if Teague will become ambassador to England
when the hostilities end, and if this comes to pass, how he will
persuade the bogtrotter to dress "according to the customs of the
courts of Europe."[24]

Brackenridge likely would have added the European experiences
of Farrago and his servant to his mammoth record of their adventures had not death intervened in 1818. But, limited both
by his environment and his talent, he had probably exhausted his
apprehension of the drama of democracy and letters. While Brackenridge was composing his long, clumsy novel, a gifted and possibly
more advantaged writer had created a portrayal of the American
man of letters which is more complex than either Freneau's or
Brackenridge's. In the Philadelphian Charles Brockden Brown's
intuition of his age we find explicitly suggested the ironic subjection
of literary authority to pubic opinion that Brackenridge merely
intimates.

I venture to intrude myself upon the public, not in the fond expectation of
contributing a more than ordinary share of amusement or instruction to the
common stock. My ambition has already devoted me to the service of my
country, and the acquisition of true glory, but I am too well acquainted
with my own deficiencies, to hope for fame in this capacity. If my continual
struggles shall at length raise me to a level with mediocrity, and my readers
expect not the eccentric genius of a higher sphere, I shall be perfectly satisfied.
In the mean time I humbly bespeak their candour and indulgence to well
meant endeavours in their service. Every person who commits his writings
to the press has by that means voluntarily parted with his ancient liberty and
becomes the general vassal; If [sic] he brings to his new station spirit and

[24] *Ibid.*, 808.

vivacity sufficient to suit himself, at all times, and in every change of disposition, to the humours and caprice of his lord, he may perhaps, though a slave,
enjoy a state of splendid vassallage, and reflect with less uneasiness upon the
loss of freedom.   But if he possess neither abilities to please, nor industry to
attempt it, he may justly dread the consequences, and it is incumbent upon
him, as soon as possible, to imprecate the vengeance due to his rashness.   I
shall therefore, on my first appearance, very formally apologise to the good
company for the intrusion of so worthless a visitant: not that I suppose any
apology can vindicate dullness or inactivity in the eyes of the public.   It is
a voluntary obligation, which the writer enters into, and it is proper that the
intire [sic] performance of the condition be completed.   Satisfied that the
present circumstances of the writer if disclosed, would render his most glaring
deficiencies excusable, I am content to recommend myself as a candidate for
future approbation only.   An insatiable thirst for fame, is by no means incompatible either with a mean capacity or constitutional indolence.   Whenever
this heavenly spark is discovered, tho' surrounded by the wettest rubbish,
and smothered in the depth of rudeness, and obscurity, it is our duty to recall
it into being, to place it in a more favourable situation, and at length by care
and assiduity to raise it into life and action.   A genius for poetry and science
is little more than an inclination to excell in that particular department.   With
whatever defects of heart or understanding, therefore, it may be accompanied,
some indulgence should be allowed to the noblest infirmity of human minds.[25]

I have quoted from Brown's characterization of the Rhapsodist,
the periodical essayist he introduced to the public in 1789. Although the exact relation of Brown to the fiction of the Rhapsodist
can be no more than speculative, we are without doubt justified
in discerning the image of Brown's sensibility of vocation in his
inaugural work. The posture of the Rhapsodist is arresting. He
has come to Philadelphia from some remote western spot, where
(apparently after military service in the Revolution) he has cultivated the life of the man of letters in solitary independence. But
arriving in the city he immediately assumes the role of vassal to his
"lord," the reading public, voluntarily surrendering his freedom
of mind and yet appealing to the lord public to give whatever spark
of genius he may have a chance to burn. Displaying an inverted
pride—his gross flattery of his readers hiding his resentment, and
perhaps his disdain, of them—the Rhapsodist bows to the author's
dependence on the public in the age of printing and democracy.
But he counters his obeisance by expressing his self-knowledge of
the situation. In his calculated servility the Rhapsodist rules out
the possibility of the man of letters as a chevalier in the new Ameri-

---

[25] Charles Brockden Brown, *The Rhapsodist and Other Uncollected Writings*,
ed. Harry R. Warfel (New York: Scholars' Facsimiles and Reprints, 1943), 2-3.

can society. Farrago consciously saves what he can of order and decorum, of a past social and literary authority, by self-consciously investing himself in the symbolic role of democratic chevalier. The Rhapsodist has little regard for the role of author as moral perceptor. Proposing to "converse with his reader not as an author but as a man," he wants above all else to demonstrate that he is earnest and sincere.

Elaborating the theme of sincerity in modern literature, Lionel Trilling (in a learned and skillful study closely related to *Mind in the Modern World*) has shown how much the writer's desire for sincerity intensified with his discovery of the self's opposition to the falsity of modern society.[26] In America such a discovery was harder to come by than it was in Europe. Both the conservative consensus of the Federalists (which advocated the authority of social classification) and the liberal consensus of the Jeffersonians (which responded to the imperative of equality) inferred a suppression of self to society. The Rhapsodist would seem to be a case in point. Assuming the moral burden of instructing his readers about the ironic corruption of the ideal intentions of society by base motives does not seem to occur to him. To be sincere, he seems to say, is to be fully responsive to society's varied motives; to be the servant of its psychic needs. I am pressing hard on Brown's fragmentary conception of his periodical essayist. I do so because, for all his haste and awkwardness in composition, Brown is the craftiest and cleverest writer of the early Republic. He clearly invites us of the present age, who put so much store in literary subterfuge, to look beneath his surfaces. In the figure of the Rhapsodist, an American author who self-consciously assumes the guise of an ordinary man and subjects himself to the tastes of the private reader, Brown symbolizes the depletion of literary authority in the new nation.

A falling off from literary dominion is also a covert theme in Brown's best novel, *Arthur Mervyn*. It may be the novel's major theme. In the story Mervyn, a country lad (but less than the Rhapsodist your ordinary country boy, as the testimony of Mrs. Althorpe makes plain) takes over as narrator from Dr. Stevens, who, by virtue of the fact that he is a physician, is in the eighteenth-century sense an accredited man of letters. Mervyn employs a self-conscious and artful style which, as William Hedges says, "is

[26] *Sincerity and Authenticity* (Cambridge: Harvard University Press, 1972).

all palpitating sensibility embroidered with echoes of Sterne and
Shakespeare."[27] How he has acquired this manner—how this child
of obscure and ignorant parentage has learned to read, much less
to write so well—is a mystery, and it remains so. Mervyn's eccentric behavior before he comes to Philadelphia leads us to assume
that he has an artistic disposition and a penchant for letters and
learning. But Mrs. Althorpe, who gives Dr. Stevens an account
of the youth, cannot tell Stevens whence Mervyn "derived his love
of knowledge or his means of acquiring it."[28] The usual course
of the aspiring man of letters—study, apprenticeship to the discipline of writing, a developing consciousness of the polity of letters
and learning—is lacking in Mervyn's case. As in the case of the
Rhapsodist, Mervyn is a literary anomaly.

But he is more than this. He is a fantasy figure of the man of
letters. The symbolic import of Mervyn goes beyond his representation of the irregular literary situation in Brown's America.
Arthur Mervyn (his first name possibly is symbolic) tells his personal history in a style which defines his own consciousness as the
emblem of the conduct of his society.

The great aim of the modern chevalier in Brackenridge's novel
is to employ style, including satire on style, to demonstrate that the
good intentions of the rational society must be seen under the realistic aspect of the often perverse motives of the human heart. The
man of letters must give society a heart shaped by moral knowledge. Although he has intimations of the necessity of moral instruction as the basis of social action, Mervyn employs a rhetoric
accommodated to a society which in the vanity of equality has
begun to rationalize ignorance as innocence and to imagine its
history as a fable of innocence—a society of democratic public
opinion given to acting on the basis of its thoughtless and hence
incorruptible intentionality to do good. In one graphic scene in
his adventures, Mervyn goes in quest of the hapless Clemenza Lodi,
who has taken refuge in a Philadelphia brothel. At issue in this
episode of the novel is, as Mervyn puts it, "the rectitude of my intentions." He discusses the question in two or three amazing reflections on his self-assumed mission to invade the brothel. Here is

[27] "Charles Brockden Brown and the Culture of Contradictions," *Early
American Literature*, 9 (Fall 1974), 129.
[28] *Arthur Mervyn or Memoirs of the Year 1793*, ed. Warner Berthoff (New
York: Holt, Rinehart and Winston, Inc., 1962), 222-223.

Mervyn after being told by a servant girl that no one is present in the house:

Once more I reflected on the rectitude of my intentions, on the possibility that the servant girl's assertions might be true, on the benefits of expedition, and of gaining access to the object of my visit without interruption or delay. To these considerations was added a sort of charm, not easily explained, and by no means justifiable, produced by the very temerity and hazardness accompanying this attempt. I thought, with scornful emotions, on the bars and hindrances which pride and caprice, and delusive maxims of decorum, raise in the way of human intercourse. I spurned at these semblances and substitutes of honesty, and delighted to shake such fetters into air, and trample such impediments to dust. I wanted to see an human being, in order to promote her happiness.[29]

Here is Mervyn at the crucial stage of his invasion of the brothel, right before he opens the door upon Clemenza:

My behaviour, I well know, was ambiguous and hazardous, and perhaps wanting in discretion, but my motives were unquestionably pure. I aimed at nothing but the rescue of an human creature from distress and dishonour.

Mervyn adds:

I pretend not to the wisdom of experience and age; to the praise of forethought or subtlety. I chuse the obvious path, and pursue it with headlong expedition. Good intentions, unaided by knowledge, will, perhaps, produce more injury than benefit, and therefore, knowledge must be gained, but the acquisition is not momentary; is not bestowed unasked and untoil'd for: meanwhile, we must not be unactive because we are ignorant, whether our knowledge be greater or less.[30]

Is Arthur Mervyn a representation of the American storyteller and man of letters as an "innocent," or is he a representation of the American writer as a pretender to innocence—a free wheeling con man, who—in his dedication to life, liberty, and the pursuit of happiness—is always after the main chance; who mirrors the social and moral ambiguities of his society and uses them to his advantage? The evidence pointing toward an answer is uncertain, and we only complicate the uncertainty by trying to resolve it. Brown himself, we conclude, found the evidence to be equivocal. In Mervyn's mind we see the image of a rising, dynamic, egalitarian society which increasingly makes no distinction between intention and motive, ends and means. The ironic symbolic situation

[29] *Ibid.*, 303.
[30] *Ibid.*, 309.

in *Arthur Mervyn* suggests that the man of letters in American society, divorced from the moral authority of the realm of letters, has lost the ideal of his autonomy as a moral agent, and has in fact become identified with a rationalization of rational mind, public mind or public opinion. In his portrait of Arthur Mervyn, Brown suggests, the American man of letters—far from representing the authority of a rational formulation and refinement of American intentionality—symbolizes a cunning and frightening proverbial maxim: "The road to hell is paved with good intentions."

In the ironies of their self-conscious interpretation of the vocation of the American man of letters, Freneau, Brackenridge, and Brown reveal their discovery that the modern nation-state, divested of kings and priesthood and founded on the sovereignty of rational hypothesis, does not constitute a rational society. The modern state is not a rational mechanism like a watch, embodying the model of rational objective mind, but, in a direct and total way unknown before the reversal of society and mind as paradigms of order, the embodiment of the myriad, bewildering, subjective processes of human consciousness. In their differentiation of the role of the man of letters in the Revolution, Franklin, Jefferson, and John Adams had seemed more or less clearly to announce that the American man of letters would assert the inviolable independence of rational, lettered mind as the image of a new and just society. But as the dimensions of mind rapidly became ambiguous in America, this concept of the literary role lost its cogency. Freneau, Brackenridge, and Brown—whether we regard them as men of letters endeavoring to be Americans or as Americans trying to be men of letters—symbolize an isolation of the ideal of the literary vocation in the strange subjectivity of modern history.

British and European
Commentaries
on the
American Political
Experience

RENÉ DE VISME WILLIAMSON

THIS TOPIC is too vast for treatment in less than a book-length manuscript unless some arbitrary lines are set. One could consider current opinion as reflected in newspapers and magazines or analyze governmental reactions to the United States but, besides being unmanageable, these solutions are likely to be uninformed and transitory. It seems best to concentrate on scholars because their views are better informed and more enduring. There is also a time element involved, and it will be interesting to see what has changed and what has not. With these criteria in mind, I propose to concentrate on Hector St. John de Crevecoeur, Alexis de Tocqueville, Frances Trollope, and Harriet Martineau for earlier times. For contemporary authors, I propose to select Lord Bryce, Denis Brogan, Andre Siegfried, Raymond Aron, and Gunnar Myrdal.

When we first became an independent nation in 1776, we were regarded, as we regarded ourselves, as a unique revolutionary experiment. In those days, Europe was constructed very differently. President Monroe in his famous message referred to it as "their system" whose introduction in the Western Hemisphere would be contrary to our national interest. That system was characterized by absolute divine right monarchies, hereditary aristocracies, permanent bureaucracies, large standing armies, and established churches. Power was viewed as moving from the top down.

The United States, by comparison, was a federal republic in which there was no monarch, no hereditary aristocracy, no permanent bureaucracy, no large standing army, and no established church. Power was viewed as moving from the bottom up, according to the theory of popular sovereignty. These characteristics were very sharp and noted by every foreign observer. Some, like Tocqueville, were flattering and others were very hostile, e.g., Mrs. Trollope, but in general they agreed on the essentials.

One of the things which most impressed foreign observers was the strongly equalitarian nature of American society. This was much more than the total absence of titles of nobility. Said Harriet Martineau: "There is no class of hereditary rich or poor. Few are very wealthy; few are poor; and every man has a fair chance of being rich."[1] Crevecoeur made the same observation even before the American Revolution. Speaking of American society, he said:

It is not composed, as in Europe, of great lords who possess everything, and of a herd of people who have nothing. Here are no aristocratical families, no courts, no kings, no bishops, no ecclesiastical dominion, no invisible power giving to a few a very visible one; no great manufacturers employing thousands, no great refinements of luxury. The rich and the poor are not so far removed from each other as they are in Europe. Some few towns excepted, we are all tillers of the earth, from Nova Scotia to West Florida.[2]

This equality of condition was also noted by Tocqueville who attributed it in part to the law. British primogeniture and entailed estates were abolished with the result that there occurred a natural redistribution of wealth whenever a man died. All foreign observers are agreed that the westward movement played a part in this equalitarianism for, among pioneers, the only inequalities were those of ability and work. Some, like Mrs. Trollope, did not like it, finding American manners obnoxious and crude. Others had mixed feelings about it. Thus, Tocqueville found that equalitarianism is hostile to quality, a levelling influence so that "freedom of opinion does not exist in America."[3] Americans themselves were very proud of this feature of their life, even irritably so to many foreigners.

[1] Harriet Martineau, *Society in America* (Paris: A. & W. Galignani and Co., 1837), 15.

[2] Hector St. John de Crevecoeur, *Letters from An American Farmer* (New York: E. P. Dutton & Co., Inc., Everyman Edition, 1912), 40.

[3] Alexis de Tocqueville, *Democracy in America*, volume I (New York: Vintage Books, 1945), 275.

Another feature which struck early foreign observers was the importance of religion in American life. Religion in those days was overwhelmingly Protestant, of course, as Edmund Burke noted in the following passage:

If anything were wanting to this necessary operation of the form of government, religion would have given it a complete effect. Religion, always a principle of energy, in this new people is no way worn out or impaired; and their mode of professing it is also one main cause of this free spirit. The people are Protestants; and of that kind which is the most adverse to all implicit submission of mind and opinion. This is a persuasion not only favourable to liberty, but built upon it.[4]

Even in those days, however, religion in America had distinctively American features which were later to be emphasized by Andre Siegfried and Will Herberg. "I do not know whether all Americans," remarked Tocqueville, "have a sincere faith in their religion —for who can search the human heart?—but I am certain that they hold it to be indispensable to the maintenance of republican institutions."[5] Even before the American Revolution, there developed tendencies which made American Protestantism different from its European counterparts, tendencies leading toward what we now call civil religion. Crevecoeur described it thus:

The foolish vanity, or rather the fury of making Proselytes, is unknown here; they have not time, the seasons call for all their attention, and thus in a few years, this mixed neighbourhood will exhibit a strong religious medley, that will be neither pure Catholicism nor pure Calvinism. A very perceptible indifference even in the first generation, will become apparent; and it may happen the daughter of the Catholic will marry the son of the seceder, and settle by themselves at a distance from their parents. What religious education will they give their children? A very imperfect one.[6]

Mrs. Trollope found religion in America to be boorish and boisterous, but even she conceded its importance at least to the extent of recognizing in it the only variation in an otherwise drab existence.

A third characteristic of early America was the love of liberty. Edmund Burke commented on it thus: "In this character of the Americans, a love of freedom is the predominating feature which marks and distinguishes the whole. . . . They are therefore not only devoted to liberty, but to liberty according to English ideas and

[4] Edmund Burke, *Burke's Speech on Conciliation with America*, ed. F. G. Selby (London: Macmillan & Co., Ltd., 1961), 19.

[5] Tocqueville, *op. cit.*, 316.

[6] Crevecoeur, *op. cit.*, 50.

on English principles."[7] Much later, in the pre-Civil War period, the Frenchman Chateaubriand made the same point: "The most precious of the treasures that America held in her breast was liberty; each people is called upon to draw from this inexhaustible mine. The discovery of the representative republic in the United States is one of the greatest political events in the world."[8]

Not much was said by early foreign observers about political institutions and, in many cases, the situation has changed drastically. Take, for instance, federalism. Tocqueville makes much of the political decentralization of the country. Pointing out that the states antedate the federal government, he observes that "the Federal government, as I have just observed, is the exception; the government of the states is the rule."[9] The states, in turn, are also decentralized in that local governments are closest to the people and wield much power. The many elective offices and the short terms of appointive officials have the effect of making a professional bureaucracy practically non-existent: "I have shown that in the United States there is no centralized administration and no hierarchy of public functionaries."[10]

To the great themes of liberty and equality there was one glaring exception, namely the presence of Negro slavery. The early European observers all noticed it and commented upon it unfavorably, sometimes with considerable vehemence. But this slavery went much deeper than the legal status with which it is customarily associated. The answer to slavery in the Roman empire was the simple one of emancipation. But emancipation was not the solution to slavery in America because it was *Negro* slavery. As far back as 1837, Harriet Martineau spelled out the plight of the Negro in Connecticut—a free state—and her words have an astonishingly contemporary ring:

They are citizens. They stand as such in the law, and in the acknowledgment of every one who knows the law. They are citizens, yet their houses and schools are pulled down, and they can obtain no remedy at law. They are thrust out of offices, and excluded from the most honourable employments, and stripped of all the best benefits of society by their fellow-citizens who, once a year, solemnly lay their hands on their hearts, and declare that all

[7] Burke, *op. cit.*, 18.
[8] Chateaubriand, *Travels in America* (Lexington: University of Kentucky Press, 1969), 191.
[9] Tocqueville, *op. cit.*, 61.
[10] *Ibid.*, 91.

men are born free and equal, and that rulers derive their just powers from the consent of the governed.[11]

Tocqueville makes almost identical comments about the status of the Negro in the Northern free states during the Jacksonian period:

It is true that in the North of the Union marriages may be legally contracted between Negroes and whites; but public opinion would stigmatize as infamous a man who should connect himself with a Negress, and it would be difficult to cite a single instance of such a union. The electoral franchise has been conferred upon the Negroes in almost all the states in which slavery has been abolished, but if they come forward to vote, their lives are in danger. If oppressed, they may bring an action at law, but they will find none but whites among their judges; and although they may legally serve as jurors, prejudice repels them from that office.[12]

What the abolition of slavery in Connecticut did not accomplish, Lincoln's Emancipation Proclamation, the thirteenth, fourteenth, and fifteenth amendments did not accomplish either. The trouble is that the Negro has high visibility, a physical appearance which makes it impossible for him to "pass" unobserved, to be accepted in the same sense that European immigrants have been accepted. Some people call it racism. Others call it a fact of life.

Tocqueville opposed slavery, but he was nevertheless deeply pessimistic about the assimilation of the Negro people in American society. He argued that "the Negro transmits the eternal mark of his ignominy to all his descendants; and although the law may abolish slavery, God alone can obliterate the traces of its existence."[13] He further argues that "wherever the Negroes have been strongest, they have destroyed the whites; this has been the only balance that has ever taken place between the two races."[14] Only time can tell whether he correctly foresaw what would happen one hundred and fifty years later. What did he predict? "I do not believe that the white and black races will ever live in any country upon an equal footing."[15] Furthermore, "as they cannot become the equals of the whites, they will speedily show themselves as enemies."[16] They will seek liberty for themselves and, "if it be given, they will before long abuse it."[17] Tocqueville's pessimism

[11] Martineau, op. cit., 100.
[12] Tocqueville, op. cit., 373.
[13] Ibid., 372.
[14] Ibid., 373.
[15] Ibid., 388, 389.
[16] Ibid., 394.
[17] Ibid., 397.

with regard to race relations in the United States does not loom large in his book and is more like a footnote or excursus.

If we now move from the early period of American history to the present time, we find that British and European commentaries on the American political experience have changed greatly. From a revolutionary experiment to a bastion of conservatism is the essence of the change in British and European opinion of the United States. We have, of course, changed greatly from 1776 to 1976. But that does not explain this reversal of European opinion. The fact is that Europe has changed more than we have. Even if we leave the Communist countries out of consideration, it is undeniable that the rest of Europe is heavily and increasingly socialistic. As a consequence, if the economic system and not the constitutional political structure is the criterion by which a country is to be judged revolutionary or conservative (i.e., capitalistic), then the United States is indeed the outstanding conservative nation. With the exception of Lord Bryce and to some extent of Denis Brogan, British and European commentators have been most interested in the social and economic aspects of American life.

All of these writers have much to say about the effects of the immigration of Southern and Eastern Europeans on American politics and social life generally. They observe that, unlike the bulk of native Americans before 1890 who were overwhelmingly Protestant and Nordic, these new immigrants were Catholic in religion and either Latin or Slavic ethnically. Moreover, these immigrants were poor, often illiterate, and totally ignorant of democratic ways. Finally, instead of spreading themselves out over the countryside to open up the West, these immigrants concentrated in large cities, thus forming great chunks of people who assimilated slowly and brought into serious question the heretofore popular theory of the melting pot.

These developments were given special attention by the French scholar Andre Siegfried in his book *America Comes of Age* published in 1927 and another book, *America at Mid-Century*, published in 1955. They were also the object of Lord Bryce's attention, especially with respect to their effects on municipal and state politics. The great influx of immigrants since 1890 did much to accentuate bossism. The bosses welded these immigrants into solid blocs of votes by rendering essential services to them, both legal and illegal. By controlling the vote, the bosses reached out to the state in order to protect their municipal base, which otherwise might be eroded or destroyed by the state legislature.

The last phase of social evolution appeared with the rise of the civil rights movement. This movement is the offspring of the racial problem presented by the Negro in our midst. All commentators speak of it, but the most thorough, comprehensive, and exhaustive study of it was made by the Swedish author Gunnar Myrdal in his famous book *The American Dilemma*. Unfortunately this book was published in 1944 and therefore does not cover the important developments during the nineteen sixties and nineteen seventies. Even so, the essence of the problem was well grasped by Myrdal. He pointed out that our ideal pulls us one way and that our practice pulls us in the opposite direction. In one breath we stood by the Declaration of Independence and the Constitution with their emphasis on liberty, equality, and due process. In another breath we tolerated slavery and followed it with the segregation, exploitation, and oppression of the Negro. The tension became more and more acute as the Negro spread to the North, won court battles, took to the streets, and exerted pressure on the power structure.

The civil rights movement has had an enormous impact on American constitutionalism. It has made serious inroads into spheres previously entirely or predominantly state and local. This is most obvious in the field of education where, between court orders and insistent pressure from the federal department of Health, Education, and Welfare, control has passed in large measure to federal authorities. Tocqueville's remarks about the primacy of state and local governments are now obsolete. It has also made very serious inroads on the traditional right of private property. The hiring and firing of employees is now subject to a form of discrimination euphemistically known as Affirmative Action. The buying and selling of houses and the availability of restaurants are severely curtailed by federal regulations.

One of the points which early British and European observers made was that the United States was free of an administrative bureaucracy with a power of its own independent of the electorate. This point was also made by Myrdal as late as 1944, particularly as regards voting:

The vote would be of less importance to a group of citizens in this country if America had what it does not have, namely, *the tradition of an independent*

and law-abiding administration of local and national public affairs. By this we
mean a body of public officials who are independent in two directions: *personally,* as they are holding office under permanent tenure, being appointed
and promoted strictly according to merit, and, consequently, vested with
economic security and high social prestige; and *officially,* as they are trusted
with authority to put the laws into effect without political interference in
individual cases. . . . Such a governmental system is foreign to American
traditions.[18]

This gap in the American governmental structure, which was
noted from Tocqueville to Myrdal, has been remedied during the
nineteen sixties and nineteen seventies—if "remedied" is the right
word to describe an autocratic, unyielding, and increasingly all
pervasive bureaucracy. The effect of the Women's Liberation
Movement, with or without the ERA, can only accelerate the
bureaucratic trend because it enlarges the already expanding jurisdiction of the bureaucracy. Two Presidents, Richard Nixon and
Gerald Ford, have tried to check this trend, but to no avail. The
department of Health, Education, and Welfare goes right on with
its Affirmative Action program despite presidential disapproval and
there have been cases of outright disobedience by the bureaucracy
to direct presidential orders.

Europeans do not appear to be aware of this bureaucratic development in the United States. And they still think of us as a
haven for racism where Negroes do not get a fair shake. They
are either unaware of or unimpressed by the enormous progress of
the Negro race in the United States, a progress which has given
them a status unequalled by blacks anywhere else in the world.
The reason for this hostile attitude is partly due to a feeling of
jealousy and partly due to the spread of socialism in Europe. Moreover, the United States is one of the two great superpowers of the
world, and no country in that position has ever been popular.
Furthermore, the prevailing socialism automatically takes a dim
view of American capitalism because that capitalism weakens the
socialist claims by its industrial productivity, high standard of living, general acceptance, and political freedom.

When we speak of British and European commentaries on the
American political experience, it is interesting to note the shift of
emphasis. The great concern of many of these commentators is
not political mechanics or even capitalist economics, but American

[18] Gunnar Myrdal, *The American Dilemma* (New York, Evanston, and London: Harper & Row, Publishers, 1944), 432.

foreign policy. This shift of interest among the French is illustrated by the difference between Andre Siegfried and Raymond Aron. Siegfried is interested primarily in social and economic phenomena. The later work of Raymond Aron, *The Imperial Republic*, is concerned solely with foreign policy and takes up economic matters only in relation to it. Europeans have had mixed feelings about American foreign policy. America is now a superpower with all the responsibilities that go with such a position. Europeans have been afraid of American isolationism whereby the United States would refuse to accept these responsibilities. On the other hand, they have also feared that the United States would accept these responsibilities but would not know how to discharge them. Devoid of the centuries of experience the British have had, it was feared that the United States would bungle the job. This was particularly true of the Vietnam war which was almost universally condemned in Europe.

One of the best analyses of the American political experience in terms of foreign policy is by Denis Brogan. Brogan was, of course, a very distinguished scholar and an authority on almost every aspect of American life. His book, *America in the Modern World*, published in 1960, dealt with basic American traits more than with political structure or economic problems. He pointed to such traits as the illusion of omnipotence (the victor in two world wars found out how illusory this view of power was in Vietnam), and ineradicable belief in progress, not only in America but everywhere, the confidence that foreign countries would adopt American values and institutions. Institutional matters are not always assets, says Brogan, pointing to the irresponsibility of American political parties, the dangers of separation of powers, the influence of federalism in eliminating able men from national politics because they live in the "wrong" state, the defects of the seniority rule in Congress. Nevertheless, these defects are not fatal and can be lived with successfully. The basic trouble, according to Brogan, is a matter of the American spirit which finds it difficult to live in a world it did not make. Therein lies the greatest challenge to the American people as they face the world after two hundred years of national existence.

Towards the Restoration
of the
American
Political Tradition

GEORGE W. CAREY

JAMES McCLELLAN

STUDENTS OF THE AMERICAN POLITICAL TRADITION have continually asked and attempted to answer certain basic questions about the nature and purpose of the American Political System: What are our commitments as a people? What are our abiding beliefs and values? What are our goals as a people united for action in history? In sum, what is the American political tradition?

While certain contemporary behavioralists might argue that such questions embroil us in a needless metaphysical exercise that has little or no bearing on the "real" world, some theorists would counter that it is inherent in the processes of human inquiry, be they individual or collective, that these questions should be posed and answered in some manner. An introspective individual at some point in his life asks similar fundamental questions: Who am I? Where am I? What is my place in the order of being? But, if these questions seem obtuse to some, we need only point out that 1976 presumably marks our 200th birthday as a nation. It is a collective birthday, so to speak, so that in one form or another, consciously or not, we as a people are critically examining ourselves. In our public discourses, albeit in variant form, we are asking of ourselves as a people: What do we stand for? What are our orgins? To what have we committed ourselves? Where do we stand in light of our goals and ends? And it is well that we raise these questions, the more so as we are at this point in history a giant in the world. Woe unto us, to paraphrase the late John Courtney Murray, if we behave as a lumbering giant who knows not where he is going because he knows not where he has been.[1]

In our endeavors to "find" ourselves and the meaning of our tradition, there has been an understandable tendency to focus on what can appropriately be termed the founding period of our nation, that period running from shortly before 1776 to 1789, from the pre-Declaration of Independence period to the ratification of the Constitution.[2] For our part, we find this area of focus to be reasonable, for by using the founding period as a standard or guide, we have some basis for determining the practices and thoughts of the colonial period which were instrumental in shaping our political structures. Likewise, with the founding period as our guide, we are in a better position to measure the extent to which our political tradition has changed, as well as the degree to which certain principles of that era have become an unquestioned or assumed part of our tradition.

This fundamental agreement about where to look (or, at least, where to begin to look) for our roots would certainly seem to hold out great promise that further consensus would be forthcoming regarding the substance of our tradition. Indeed, other circumstances would also suggest that the task of self-appraisal to which we have referred could readily be accomplished without major differences of opinion arising concerning the core meaning of our tradition. For one thing, still today, we are only 200 years from the beginning of the founding period—a long time, to be sure, but not so long when viewed in the broader historical context. Put otherwise, the number of intervening generations between then and now has not been so great as to preclude transmission of the basic values and beliefs of that era.[3] Moreover, there is a con-

[1] *We Hold These Truths* (New York: Sheed and Ward, 1960). See, in particular, "Part One: The American Promise."

[2] Among the more prominent works of recent time which reflect this approach are Clinton Rossiter's, *Seedtime of the Republic* (New York: Harcourt, Brace, 1953); Bernard Bailyn's, *The Ideological Origins of the American Revolution* (Cambridge: Harvard University Press, 1967); and Gordon Wood's *The Creation of the American Republic, 1776-1787* (Chapel Hill: University of North Carolina Press, 1969).

[3] The period covers less than ten generations and less than three not too lengthy life spans.

tinuity to the American experience. Unlike many of our European counterparts, as Daniel Boorstin has noted,[4] we do not have around us the ruins of past regimes or empires which serve as visual evidence of the discontinuity of tradition. Nor have we been conquered and subjugated by foreign armies, suggesting that our tradition has not been distorted by alien influences. And to these considerations, we may add the following: we are not bereft of the kinds of documentary evidence that can help us to understand and comprehend the tradition. We have official documents (e.g., the Declaration of Independence and the Constitution), pamphlets, recorded debates, personal correspondence of the principal actors, and newspapers. There is an abundance of material along these lines from which to reconstruct the ideals of the founding era. What is more, the principal events of the era, our independence and the adoption of the Constitution, were deliberate undertakings, a fact which would seem to render them, as well as their purposes and the circumstances surrounding them, well suited for dispassionate and scholarly investigation.

For us, what is remarkable, in light of the foregoing, is that no consensus has emerged concerning the meaning of our tradition. What is even more astonishing is that the controversy and confusion surrounding the founding period and its meaning have grown, so it would seem, in direct proportion to the amount of scholarly investigation of it. Over the years, for example, the "all men are created equal" clause of the Declaration has been given an almost endless variety of meanings, far too numerous for us even to attempt to catalogue.[5] These meanings, in turn, have been used as the measure of the extent to which we have achieved our goals and how far we still have to go. The Constitution, itself, in many particulars has been the subject of controversy, so much so that we can say our tradition does not present us with unambiguous answers on many vital matters concerning how we are to govern ourselves according to its provisions. Such issues as federalism, separation of powers, and judicial review most certainly would rank among these.

We grant that, for a variety of reasons, these and similar elements of our tradition were found to lead to honest differences of

[4] *The Genius of American Politics* (Chicago: University of Chicago Press, 1953).

[5] For one partial attempt, see *A Casebook on the Declaration of Independence*, ed. Robert Ginsberg (New York: Thomas Y. Crowell, 1967).

opinion. But the controversies and differences concerning our tradition which are of concern to us are broader and far more basic. Richard F. Gibbs, formerly Director of the North Carolina Bicentennial Commission, states a concern shared by many reflective students of the American tradition. In the statement which follows, he highlights a basic and often ignored problem relative to the status of the Declaration and the Constitution.

By proclaiming July 4, 1976 as the 200th anniversary of the nation, it (the American Revolution Bicentennial Commision) reinforces a liberal interpretation of American history that obscures, often even eclipses, the very concept of the Republic, the founding principles of which lie at the heart of conservatism. The effect of this interpretation is to excise the process of forming the Republic under and by the Constitution from the history of the American Revolution and to create the impression—false, of course—of a basic antagonism between the Declaration of Independence and the Constitution.

Such an interpretation has tended to dominate the teaching of American history for most of this century, and its general public acceptance has been a significant factor in the long train of liberal successes. Centering on Charles Beard's economic interpretation of the Constitution, advanced in 1913 as a mere hypothesis (which never proved out), it became buttressed by J. Franklin Jameson's hypothesis (also never proven) of the Revolution as a social movement, and Vernon Parrington's beautifully written, but avowedly prejudiced, *Main Currents in American Thought*. The Declaration is portrayed as the ultimate expression of Revolutionary ideals, to wit, egalitarianism, popular majority rule, and human rights; the Constitution is cast in the role of counter-revolutionary reaction in support of monied privilege, minority rule, and property rights. Through the instrumentality of this interpretation, the Constitution has been repeatedly attacked and perverted in a number of its most vital and fundamental areas.[6]

Gibbs is quite correct. Since the second decade of this century, through the diligent efforts of numerous academics and intellectuals, a wedge has indeed been driven between the Declaration and the Constitution. He is also correct in observing that the Constitution—and we should add the theory underlying it, the so-called "Madisonian model"—have been depicted as reactionary,[7] as a deliberate effort to dampen or thwart the true revolutionary ideals expressed in the Declaration. Thus, the two documents have come

---

[6] "The Spirit of '89: Conservatism and Bicentenary," *The University Bookman*, Vol. 14 (Spring, 1974), 54.

[7] See Chapter One of Robert Dahl's *Preface to Democratic Theory* (Chicago: University of Chicago Press, 1956).

to be viewed not merely as incompatible with one another but as embodying antagonistic principles.[8]

If these observations are not startling, their implications most certainly are. Boldly stated, they come to this: Is July 4, 1776 our real birthday? What is it, apart from our declared intent to separate from Great Britain that we should be celebrating? Why shouldn't we look upon the Declaration simply as prologue, or a necessary step in the advancement to nationhood, which culminated in the ratification of the Constitution? Why shouldn't we mark our beginnings as a nation in 1789, rather than 1776, for the fact is we only became a nation in the fullest sense of that word with the adoption of the Constitution?

While these are important questions, and we shall treat certain aspects of them later, it is important that we first delve into the matter of how this current state of affairs came about; for this will put us in a better position to understand the nature of our present perplexity.

Since the 1930's, if not earlier, there has been a definite correlation between the meaning attached to our tradition and the central elements of the so-called liberal view. This could well have been the result of the ascendance of liberalism in our academic institutions, as well as its acceptance in the more general political arena. Nevertheless, this development necessitated some alterations in the way in which our founding period was viewed. First, the Declaration had to assume a central place in our tradition, principally because, as Gibbs intimates, it lends itself to a variety of interpretations, most of which are compatible with the doctrines of contemporary liberalism and some of which are supportive of that doctrine. Second, the Constitution, on the face of it, presents very special problems which cannot, as we shall see, be reconciled with certain core liberal tenets. And these two factors taken together provide us with the major reason why the Declaration is accorded primacy in our system, even to the extent that the Constitution is to be evaluated in terms of the presumed principles embedded in

---

[8] The extent to which this thesis was accepted and incorporated into history texts is traced by Robert E. Brown, *Charles A. Beard and the Constitution* (Princeton: Princeton University Press, 1956), 3-22. On the extent to which this theme permeates certain leading American government textbooks, see George W. Carey, "Introductory Textbooks to American Government," *The Political Science Reviewer*, Vol. I (Fall, 1971), 154-183.

the Declaration. To see this more clearly, we must move back in time to the intellectual origins of modern liberalism.[9]

The principal elements of the liberal interpretation to which we have referred are to be found in the Progressive theories of the earlier part of this century. In this regard, we can do no better than briefly examine the writings of the eminent and influential Herbert Croly; for his works are indispensable to a complete understanding of contemporary liberalism.[10] Indeed, Croly's thoughts so closely parallel modern liberalism that Croly may justifiably be regarded as having laid the basic foundations of contemporary political thought among liberal intelligentsia.

Croly's concerns were manifold but one of his major theses was that our "National Promise" could be realized only through a new and expanded conception of democracy. Democracy was not, according to Croly, "merely government by the people, or majority rule, or universal suffrage."[11] Neither was it a matter "exclusively of individual rights" nor of "equal rights."[12] Important as these were, "the salutary and formative democratic purpose consists in using the democratic organization for the joint benefit of individual distinction and social improvement."[13] Thus, democracy and the "National Promise" involved ends above and beyond those normally associated with democracy as a political process or the protection of minority "rights." The importance of this, in light of subsequent developments, was Croly's tendency to view democracy as the equivalent of liberalism, and not as a means to higher goals of the polity.

What ends did Croly envision? They were broad in scope and dealt with major facets of our social and economic system. His general aim, however, seemed to be the attainment of a "higher type of associated life."[14] In Croly's view, this involved fairly drastic "reform" of the economic system. The "traditional American con-

---

[9] We shall concentrate here on his most comprehensive work, *The Promise of American Life* (New York: The MacMillan Co., 1911).

[10] Contemporary liberalism's debt to early "progressivism" and Croly, in particular, is great. See Samuel H. Beer, "Liberalism and the National Idea," in *Left, Right and Center,* ed. Robert A. Goldwin (Chicago: Rand McNally and Co., 1965), 142-169.

[11] *Op. cit.,* 207.

[12] *Ibid.*

[13] *Ibid.*

[14] *Ibid.,* 208.

fidence in individual freedom," he wrote, "had resulted in a morally and socially undesirable distribution of wealth."[15]   The existing concentration of wealth he held to be "inimical to democracy, because it tends to erect political abuses and social inequalities into a system."[16]   The basic cause of these social and economic inequities, Croly maintained, was directly attributable to "the chaotic individualism of our political and economic organization,"[17] an individualism fostered by the dominant American tradition of that day.   Thus, one of his principal ends was to seek a fundamental alteration in what had become part of the American way of life, namely, self-acquisitiveness.   To accomplish this, he argued, there was a need "for the subordination of the individual to the demand of a dominant and constructive national purpose. . . ."[18]   This meant that the government, with the tools available to it, must "diminish the undesirable competition and encourage the desirable competition," by minimizing the "mercenary motive" and placing a premium on "excellence of work."[19]   Men could be "made permanently unselfish," in conformity with Croly's enlightened democracy, "only by being helped to become disinterested in their individual purpose. . . ."[20]

The foregoing, involving as it does wide scale regulation of the economy and the placing of government in the role of using its authority to alter basic value patterns and practices, obviously necessitates a strong national government.   And throughout his work, Croly constantly emphasizes this fact; the ends he sought could only be achieved through a government which possessed sufficient powers to implement them.   For this reason, he was highly critical of the American system which embodied the principles of federalism and separation of powers.   In his words,

Founded as the national government is, partly on a distrust of the American democracy, it has always tended to make the democracy somewhat suspicious of the national government.   This mutual suspicion, while it has been limited in scope and diminished by the action of time, constitutes a manifest impediment to the efficient action of the American political system.[21]

[15] *Ibid.*, 22.
[16] *Ibid.*, 23.
[17] *Ibid.*
[18] *Ibid.*
[19] *Ibid.*, 415.
[20] *Ibid.*, 418.
[21] *Ibid.*, 33.

Moreover, in Croly's view, the Constitution was the "bulwark of individual and local rights" which tended to protect the economically privileged. As such, it constituted, in still another way, an impediment to the realization of the "National Promise."[22] Croly was under no illusion that the transformation which he sought would come about easily. Far from it. Throughout his writings, he shows an awareness of a widely accepted American tradition that in most particulars would have to be abandoned before the "National Promise" would have any chance of success. The "existing constitution," he wrote, is regarded with a "superstituous awe" and most people "shrink with horror from modifying it even in the smallest detail."[23] The "great bondage of the American spirit" is this "superstitious fear" which deters the people from organizing "their political, economic, and social life in the service of comprehensive, lofty, and far-reaching democratic purpose."[24] Likewise, he realized that the emancipation of the individual from the pursuit of selfish objectives and his subordination to a broader national purpose would not be an easy task. In sum, he acknowledged that he was calling for "a radical transformation of the traditional national policy and democratic creed."[25] For all of this, however, there is a healthy strain of determinism in Croly's theory: the traditional American system was showing definite signs of breaking down because of the social and economic inequities it had produced.

The extent to which Croly's perspective and general theory have been accepted in most respects by modern liberal academics probably needs no elaboration here. But the extent to which they have become the unquestioned national goals of our tradition is remarkable.[26] We need look no farther than the *Report of the*

---

[22] *Ibid.*, 35.

[23] *Ibid.*, 278.

[24] *Ibid.*

[25] *Ibid.*, 25.

[26] No doubt Roosevelt and his "brain trust" had a good deal to do with this. See Alpheus T. Mason's introduction to Chapter XIX, *Free Government in the Making*, (3rd ed.; New York: Oxford University Press, 1965), 764-767. See also Franklin D. Roosevelt's campaign address to the Commonwealth Club in San Francisco, 23 September, 1932, reprinted in this volume, at pp. 767-775. This was one of the first efforts to link the goals of contemporary liberalism to the Declaration of Independence. Note the similarity between Roosevelt's thinking and Croly's, as expressed in *The Promise of American Life*.

President's Commission on National Goals (1960), wherein we find Clinton Rossiter writing:

Democracy, let us remember, has a fundamental commitment to equality, in the best and most realistic senses of that word: to equality before the law, equality of political voice, equality in constitutional rights, equality of opportunity, and equality of consideration. Somehow we must push farther and faster than we have in the past—through education, persuasion, example, and where clearly necessary, force of law—to honor this commitment. Somehow we must eliminate the sordid or timid techniques of unequal treatment that still leave millions outside the circle of first-class citizenship in which most Americans are privileged to go about their affairs. While America is not a guaranty of success, it is a promise of opportunity; and we have no more pressing task in the decade before us than to see that the promise is made in good faith to all who live among us.[27]

Our tradition, in large part, comes down to advancing the democratic (i.e., liberal) creed which, in turn, commits us to the advancement of equality through positive governmental action. And Rossiter even parallels Croly's sense of inevitability concerning the advancement of these goals. The "democratic spirit," much like Croly's "American spirit," simply impels us in this direction, suggests Rossiter:

If this means that some men must renounce old privileges in order that other men may enjoy new liberties, then that is the way the knife of democratic aspirations will have to cut. It would be happier for all, to be sure, and far healthier for American democracy, if those who now deny other men their rights and opportunities as Americans could be persuaded to suppress their fears and to let democracy take its natural course. One way or another, however, the goals of the next decade, and of every decade after that, must be conceived and pursued as goals for all Americans.[28]

Henry M. Wriston, the Commission Chairman, put the matter in broader context in his introductory essay to the report. According to Wriston, "The ideology of the Declaration and the Bill of Rights shaped our History. It set in train forces that moved, inexorably,

[27] "The Democratic Process," in *Goals for Americans* (Washington, D.C.; Prentice-Hall, Inc., 1960), 74. The "Introduction" to the Commission Report opens with these words: "The paramount goal of the United States was set long ago. It is to guard the rights of the individual, to ensure his development, and to enlarge his opportunity. It is set forth in the Declaration of Independence drafted by Thomas Jefferson and adopted by the Continental Congress on July 4, 1776. The goals we here identify are within the framework of the original plan and are calculated to bring to fruition the dreams of the men who laid *the* foundation of this country." (Emphasis supplied).

[28] *Ibid.*, 75.

toward democracy"—a "democracy," as his article clearly reveals, patterned after Rossiter's democracy and Croly's "National Promise."[29] What Croly advanced and acknowledged to be a radical departure from our traditional values (e.g., self-reliance, individual initiative, rugged individualism) has now been accepted by many leading academics as *the* tradition, as if the older tradition to which Croly alluded had never existed. What is clear, however, is that any linkage between this newer tradition and the values, commitments, and goals articulated during our "formative" years must be derived from the Declaration of Independence. How else, for example, is it possible for the moderns to speak in such terms as national "commitment" or "promise" when referring to such goals as equality? Certainly they could not be referring to the Constitution. As we shall see, the Constitution, and the operation of government under its form, present difficulties for the adherents of this newer liberal tradition. So much was acknowledged in the earlier writings of Beard,[30] Smith,[31] and Croly.[32] As Croly put it, "The deification of our undemocratic Constitution was the work of a democracy which failed to understand the proper relation between popular political power and popular economic and social policy."[33] In his judgment, it was the work of "undemocratic" or, at best, "semi-democratic" elements.[34]

But using the Declaration as the reference point for our tradition and the source of our commitments as a people is not without difficulties which, when taken together, pose insurmountable ob-

---

[29] "The Individual," *Ibid.*, 37.

[30] *An Economic Interpretation of the Constitution* (New York: The MacMillan Co., 1913).

[31] James Allen Smith, *The Spirit of American Government* (New York: The MacMillan Co., 1907).

[32] *Op. cit.*

[33] *Progressive Democracy* (New York: The MacMillan Co., 1915), 51.

[34] *Ibid.* This interpretation has been discredited by the research of Robert E. Brown, *op. cit.*; Chilton Williamson, *American Suffrage from Property to Democracy* (Princeton: Princeton University Press, 1960); and Forrest McDonald, *We the People* (Chicago: University of Chicago Press, 1958). See also, John P. Roche, "The Founding Fathers: A Reform Caucus in Action," *American Political Science Review*, Vol. 55 (December, 1961), 799-816; and Martin Diamond, "Democracy and the Federalist: A Reconsideration of the Framers' Intent," *American Political Science Review*, Vol. 53 (March, 1959), 52-68.

stacles to rendering our tradition at all coherent. The first of these
is definitional or conceptual in nature. What, for example, is one
to make of equality of opportunity, which is but one among many
differentiations of the Declaration's equality clause? Its narrow
meaning involves freedom from laws and regulations which dis-
criminate against certain individuals or groups in an arbitrary and
capricious manner, while bestowing advantages on others. In
this sense, it would involve a neutrality on the part of government
toward individuals which comprise the society, so that each would
be unhindered in the development of his potential. Of course, even
in this narrow conception, government would play a role, not unlike that of a referee in competitive sports, to see that the participants abide by the "rules of the game." For this reason, among
others, formulation of equality of opportunity even in a limited and
narrow sense is not without difficulty.[35] What seems clear, however,
is that equality of opportunity takes on a broader and far less definite meaning in the context of the newer liberal interpretation of
the tradition: one of the obligations of government is to take
positive measures to insure that each individual, in so far as possible, begins the competitive race in life from approximately the
same starting point.[36]   In this context, then, equality of opportunity
becomes a rather open ended goal which, off at the end, could
justify a totally egalitarian and even totalitarian society, the more
so as each generation feels compelled in honoring our national
commitment to take upon itself the task of fully realizing this goal.[37]
In any event, one is left to his own imagination in picturing the
general conditions that would prevail in a society which closely
approximated this goal.

A second difficulty, which is related to the first, concerns the fact
that the goals derived from the Declaration, especially those deal-

[35] A view of equality of opportunity, very similar to this, was held by
Herbert Hoover.   See his American Individualism (Garden City: Doubleday,
Page, 1922).

[36] Equality of opportunity has come in some quarters to mean "equality of
result." See Friedrich Hayek, The Constitution of Liberty (Chicago: University of Chicago Press, 1960), 91-93; and Yves R. Simon, The Philosophy of
Democratic Government (Chicago: University of Chicago Press, 1951), 222-
230.

[37] For a trenchant discussion of this point, see Robert Nisbet's review essay,
"The Pursuit of Equality," on John Rawl's A Theory of Justice in Public
Interest, Vol. 35 (Spring, 1974), 103-120.

ing with equality, are goals intended for all the people. This logically means that if they are to be advanced or achieved, (a) the national government will have to serve as the instrumentality; and (b) the national government will have to possess sufficient powers for this purpose. This consideration alone accounts for the liberal assaults upon our Constitution, its structures and operations. We can, for instance, cast the liberals' hostility toward the Supreme Court during the first third of the century, and their subsequent *volte face*, in a light different from what is customary. Quite obviously, there was displeasure with the substance of the Court's decisions before 1937, particularly because they were viewed as protecting vested property rights and economic inequality. Yet, a more basic difficulty with the Court, from a theoretical point of view, was that its decisions strengthened the centrifugal elements of the constitutional fabric, principally by acknowledging a wide sphere of state sovereignty which precluded effective national action in critical areas. Of course, the Court (and a point overlooked by some of its liberal critics of the past),[38] armed with the "higher law" argument, always possessed the potential of becoming the nationalizing force that it has now become. Indeed, from the perspective of the liberal tradition, few developments of this century could be more gratifying than to see the Court interpreting the Fourteenth Amendment so broadly and in such a way as to nationalize not only the Bill of Rights but also so many of the goals inherent in their interpretation of the Declaration.[39]

While the issues of federalism and the Court may no longer pose difficulties for the new traditionalists, other elements of our political order most assuredly do. In recent decades our political parties have come under sustained attack as undisciplined organizations, frequently unresponsive to the popular will. Because of their de-

[38] Henry Commager, for one, advocated abandonment of the "higher law" principle because he viewed it as a barrier to the realization of liberal goals. See his "Constitutional History and the Higher Law" in *The Constitution Reconsidered*, ed. Conyers Read (New York: Harper and Row, 1968), 223-245.

[39] Thus Rossiter could write in 1960, "Despite the crossfire in which it finds itself today, the federal judiciary is probably the best prepared of all our institutions to meet the challenges of the next decade. *Op. cit.*, 68. See also, Louis Henkin, "Some Reflections on Current Constitutional Controversy" in Conyers Read, ed., *op. cit.*, 351-380; and Eugene V. Rostow, *The Sovereign Prerogative: The Supreme Court and the Quest for Law* (New Haven: Yale University Press, 1962), especially Chapter 4.

centralized nature and diffuse power (both of which are the direct
outgrowth of our federal structure), there is no way by which
national majorities can hold them responsible or accountable for
their behavior.[40] More than this, parties in their present state are
not suitable instruments for the formulation of coherent and far-
reaching national policies; they are utterly incapable of affording
programmatic choices which would convert elections into a meaningful democratic exercise. And what makes matters worse, as
those familiar with the reformist literature know too well, the constitutional provisions for separation of powers and bicameralism
often produce deadlock, delay, or unprincipled compromises on
vital public policy matters.[41] Our Presidents, who normally see
our national purposes clearly and who speak the authentic voice
of the American people,[42] are frequently crippled in their efforts
to lead. James McGregor Burns summarizes the discontent with
the present system in terms that are quite understandable in light
of what we have said: "We cannot define our national purpose
and mobilize our strength to move vigorously against the problems
that beset us at home and abroad."[43]

The foregoing merely indicates that broad dimensions of the
seemingly immovable constitutional road blocks to the achievement
of our national commitments and goals, given the liberal reading
of the Declaration. Yet it leads us to what we consider to be the
decisive objective to those who view our tradition in terms of the
liberal interpretation of the Declaration. Simply put, such a view
of the tradition can only explain our collective behavior by "Ptole-
mizing," that is by constructing elaborate and somewhat tenuous
theories to explain away that which does not accord with their
conception of the tradition. They do so, moreover, in the face of

40 For a comprehensive appraisal of the major literature on responsible two-
party proposals, see Evron Kirkpatrick, "Toward a More Responsible Two-
Party System: Political Science, Policy Science, or Psuedo Science?" American
Political Science Review, Vol. 65, (December, 1971), 975-990.

41 One of the more comprehensive books dealing with this "problem" at the
formal institutional level is Herman Finer's The Presidency: Crisis and Regen-
eration (Chicago: University of Chicago Press, 1960). This work also contains a comprehensive summary of past institutional proposals designed to
overcome legislative-executive friction. See, in particular, Appendix A.

42 At least the "strong" Presidents who advance the goals of liberalism. See
Clinton Rossiter, The American Presidency (rev. ed., New York: Mentor, 1962).

43 The Deadlock of Democracy (Englewood Cliffs, N. J.: Prentice-Hall,
1963), 325.

another, simpler, and more commonsensical view of the tradition, which does serve to put the events of our founding period in a meaningful context.

The root issue we may state as follows: the proponents of the liberal view of our tradition, from Croly through Burns, would have us believe that the Framers consciously constructed a system which would make the task of achieving our revolutionary ideals difficult, if not impossible. In regard to this, two observations are called for. First, assuming, *arguendo*, that goals and commitments can be read into the Declaration, it is far from certain that they were intended to possess the meaning attributed to them by modern liberals. In sum, it might well be that the modern liberal is misreading the Declaration by reading back into it his own egalitarian prejudices. And this contention takes on added force because the American Revolution, as revolutions go, must certainly be viewed as one of the more conservative.[44] Sobriety, save possibly for the rhetorical extravagances in describing the acts of King George III, is the dominant characteristic of the Declaration.[45]

Second, in dealing with the alleged antagonism between the Declaration and the Constitution, we must recognize the obvious: we are dealing with documents of a different order or status, that is, documents with fundamentally different purposes. The Declaration of Independence is just what it says it is, a document in which the colonies "dissolve the political bonds" that had united them with Great Britain. The Constitution is clearly an ordering document which specifies in some detail the structure and rules of government, as well as its general purposes. This is not to say there is no inter-relationship between the two documents. The Declaration in no uncertain terms anticipates, so to speak, the relationship that has come about. The colonists, it declares, are free "to institute new Government, laying its foundation on such principles and organizing its power in such form, as to them shall seem most likely to effect their Safety and Happiness." This alone reinforces the distinction

[44] Russell Kirk, *Roots of American Order* (La Salle, Ill.: Open Court, 1975), Chapters 9, 10, and 11.

[45] For an interesting comparison of the French with the American revolutions which illustrates our point, see Friedrich Gentz, "French and American Revolutions Compared" in *Three Revolutions*, ed. Stephan Possony (Chicago, Henry Regnery, 1969). This analysis originally appeared during the reign of Napoleon. John Quincy Adams translated it into English and introduced it to Americans in 1800.

we have drawn between the two documents. Moreover, the sequence of events in our history shows a continuity between them,
not irresolvable conflict. The fact is that there was no perceived
conflict between the Declaration and the Constitution until the
1830's, when "abolitionists such as William Ellery Channing and
William Lloyd Garrison denounced the Constitution, arguing that
the 'self-evident truths' of natural rights in the Declaration were
the supreme law of the land."[46]   And this view, as we have noted,
did not really gain currency until well into the twentieth century.

It is understandable why modern liberalism would like to touch
base with the American tradition at one of its critical junctures,
since this would lend legitimacy and "force" of tradition to its
ideology. We cannot help but note, however, the paradoxical consequence of this, namely, the manifest inability of the ideology to
give meaning to our past. Perhaps this is why Croly in his *Promise
of American Life* made no effort to link his program to the Declaration. While we could attribute his failure to do so to a number of
reasons (not the least of which might be that the Declaration sets
forth unalienable rights which could be construed as limiting the
powers of government to achieve our "National Promise"), we do
know that he did perceive the difficulties inherent in any such
linkage.[47] Thus, he can most appropriately be viewed as setting
forth the outlines of a new and distinct tradition which he hoped
would take hold and supersede the old. Whether this is so or not,
it is the modern attempt to fuse the two which has created our
present and somewhat confused situation.

If liberal efforts to weld their ideology to the tradition have
caused confusion, they have also served to bring into clearer focus
certain enduring elements of our tradition, elements which have
over the years successfully withstood attacks by those who would
like to transform our system. The most important of these relate
to the values, assumptions, and goals which were brought to bear
in structuring our form of government; to those areas, that is,

[46] James McClellan, *Joseph Story and the American Constitution* (Norman:
University of Oklahoma Press, 1971), 101-102.

[47] Croly, it should be noted, was wary of the Declaration and the Bill of
Rights because they could be interpreted to restrict the powers of the national
government and impede the realization of the "National Promise." In this
regard, he differs from the modern liberal who normally views the Bill of
Rights as an extension of the Declaration, and considers both to be at the
heart of our tradition.

where the conflict between liberalism and the tradition bequeathed to us by our Founders is most severe. While we cannot treat all of them here at length, a few deserve our attention.

First, the Framers did exhibit an hostility toward direct, or as we might put it today, plebiscitary democracy. Madison's arguments at the Convention and in *The Federalist* seem to be reflective of the general sentiment on this score. In pure democracies or small republics wherein the people make decisions directly, there can be "no cure for the mischiefs of faction."[48] The extended republic, on the other hand, did provide such a cure. One of the chief advantages of an extended republic was perceived to be the need for representatives—"a chosen body of citizens, whose wisdom may best discern the true interests of their country"[49]—to meet and deliberate on the affairs of state. Moreover, the multiplicity of varied interests stretched out across the republic would make the process of the majority formation a slow, deliberate one, in which factions would stand little chance of success. The concern to provide for deliberation by worthy and knowledgeable members of the community even extended to provision for a second legislative assembly. "What bitter anguish," Madison asked rhetorically, "would not the people of Athens have often escaped if their government had contained so provident a safeguard against the tyranny of their own passions?"[50]

So a fundamental part of our tradition, we may safely say, places great stress on achieving unity out of diversity through deliberative processes, of attempting to find the deliberate will of a heterogeneous people. Understandably enough, those who presume to know *a priori* our national goals, national problems and the like, or those who, from year to year and decade to decade, see new national crises and problems, are simply bound to feel a sense of frustration with a political system designed to produce a deliberate consensus. Certainly this applies with equal force to those who see transcendent goals or visions of another and drastically different social order.[51]

[48] *The Federalist* (New York: Modern Library, n.d.), Federalist 10, 58.
[49] *Ibid.*, 59. See also (on the role of representatives) Federalist papers 55, 56, and 57.
[50] *Ibid.*, Federalist 63, 410.
[51] Consider, for example, such radical left groups as the People's Bicentennial Commission.

Second, it is also true that the Framers, almost to a man, possessed a carefully reasoned distrust of government. To be sure, they wanted a far stronger national government but they recognized that its powers could be used by those in authority for their own purposes; that the wielders of power could betray their public trust. Preventing the abuses of government, while simultaneously insuring that the national government would possess powers sufficient for its objectives, was one of their major concerns. Their answer to this problem was to divide legislative, executive, and judicial functions because they accepted as axiomatic the proposition that a union of these functions constituted "the very definition of tyranny."[52] And that is why many reformist proposals, directed at centralizing governmental power in order to achieve more rapidly our presumed ideals to meet the demands of the time, are totally inimical to the tradition of the founding period. Only those who follow the proponents of the new tradition, for instance, can derive much pleasure from the notable aggrandizement of power by the Presidency or the Courts in recent years. Yet, for all of this, a division of powers is fixed into our constitutional structure, along with provisions (as we have recently been reminded) by which imbalances can be remedied. As long as this is the case, we cannot stray too far from one of our most fundamental principles of government.

Finally, and in our view most important, our tradition is one that recognizes the diversities and differences among men. As Madison put it, "In all civilized societies, distinctions are various and unavoidable."[53] And while they were well aware of the dangers inherent in republican government, they certainly did not accept the view that the function of government is to alter or change the nature of man. Quite the contrary. For Madison, at least, this was an impossibility; for "the latent causes of faction are . . . sown in the nature of man."[54] Only "theoretic politicians," to use his expression, presumed otherwise.[55] Thus, they realized that men could be short-sighted, selfish, evil, mean, wicked, and cruel. But, happily, in their estimation, men were capable, given the proper

[52] Federalist 47, *op. cit.*, 313.
[53] *The Complete Madison*, ed. Saul K. Padover (New York: Harper and Bros., 1953), 41.
[54] Federalist 10, *op. cit.*, 55.
[55] *Ibid.*, 54.

circumstances and institutions, of that amount of virtue necessary for self-government with justice.[56]

These are, then, certain enduring principles of the American political system which have retained their vitality, despite efforts to revise our political tradition in order to bring it into line, so to speak, with modern ideologies and partisan aspirations. Such revisionism has only produced a distorted picture of our constitutional order which, in turn, has served to justify "reforms" that run counter to the basic elements and assumptions upon which the system was built. To an alarming degree, American political scientists, by revising the tradition to fit the times, are guilty of this practice.

As a prolegomena toward a better understanding of our political tradition, we must come to the realization that it is not the exclusive domain of any ideology or modern political creed. As simple and obvious as this point may seem, its acknowledgement would serve to dispel much of the confusion surrounding our system and its operations. More than this, such a realization would better enable us to determine the wisdom and propriety of current policies and practices in light of the basic assumptions which underlie those political institutions that have served us so well for nearly two centuries.

---

[56] See Federalist papers 55 and 76. Madison's comments on June 20, 1788 in the Virginia Ratifying Convention are revealing on this point: "But I go on this great republican principle, that the people will have virtue and intelligence to select men of virtue and wisdom. Is there no virtue among us? If there be not, we are in a wretched situation. No theoretical checks, no form of government, can render us secure. To suppose that any form of government will secure liberty or happiness without any virtue in the people, is a chimerical idea. If there be sufficient virtue and intelligence in the community, it will be exercised in the selection of these men; so that we do not depend on their virtue, or put confidence in our rulers, but in the people who are to choose them." *Debates on the Adoption of the Federal Constitution,* ed. Jonathan Elliott (New York: Burt Franklin, 1888), Vol. III, 536-537. This stands in sharp contrast to the usual depiction of the Framers' view of man. See, for example, Richard Hofstadter, *The American Political Tradition* (New York: Vintage Books, 1948), Chapter One.

Bicentennial
Reflections
on
Party Government

JASPER B. SHANNON

ALL INSTITUTIONS are currently in crisis. Certainly, this is a commonplace commentary in the media and the press, the pulpit, and the forum. Representative government is in greater danger a generation after waging a successful war of survival to destroy totalitarian dictatorship than at any time in two hundred years. Victory has its hazards no less than defeat. In the immediate flush of triumph, the United States with its new source of power, the fission of the atom, appeared to have an unlimited imperial mission to spread the gospel of representative democracy with political parties as the instrument of conversion. The Marshall Plan reinvigorated faltering democratic institutions in the West while the substitute Mikado, General MacArthur, gave the Japanese the new tablets of stone from a battleship instead of from Mount Sinai.

Today the United States struggles to survive in the midst of technological quicksands undreamed of in the halcyon days following Japanese surrender. Everywhere democratic government is under attack and retreat is on the border of catastrophe. It is not the strength of its foreign adversaries so much as internal lack of cohesion that endangers what is called representative democracy.

Party government may be approached in many fashions. It has been studied historically, socially, economically, and recently, statistically and psychologically. For a Bicentennial celebration major attention needs to be given to the genetic and evolutionary aspects.

American political parties are still young. The long history of man is an account of violence, of inhumanity and fraud. One need not be a Calvinist to recognize the existence of sin in the world either original or acquired. St. Augustine's admonition that government deals only with the second best and not the ideally best was an early foresight of Watergate and Richard M. Nixon. After all, the Christian Father had seen and heard much of Rome.

Representative government was not discovered until fifteen hundred years of blundering had brought Christianity to the brink of disaster. In the midst of the violence of searching for the true faith, England stumbled upon a kind of representative and monarchical mixture that emerged after civil war, dictatorship, and restoration. The by–product of civil disorder and a period when life was "short, nasty and brutish," a new world was discovered, explored, and partly settled. An ideology of self-government emerged and a promise of a new way of life appeared. Later it was to become the last best hope of man on earth. This belief has always been endangered by cynicism and despair. Thus, a review of its growth is appropriate at the end of two centuries. Perhaps the owl of Minerva will take its flight in the twilight. . . .

Popular government and its offspring, party government in the United States, was born two centuries ago in the afterglow of the Age of Reason. A century later the overwhelming triumph of democracy was widely predicted. Out of the ideas of Locke and the experience of the Bloodless Revolution in England in 1689 developed a widely held belief in peaceful domestic change. The king was a powerless symbol designed to perform the sentimental tasks of government while behind the façade was the real governmental operation based upon policies hammered out in discussion, debate and within a form of logic. Always there was the possibility of appealing periodically to the body of a nation composed primarily of the landed gentry and the principal shopkeepers who comprised the base of British society. The arguments were directed to a people—male, property owners who composed a narrow élite—termed the electorate. To persuade this body of middle-class enfranchised citizens to vote many devices were employed.

Sometimes "treating" was open and a covert bribery, through campaign literature and oratory induced partisan decision. Increasingly a group of professional organizers and persuaders influenced apathetic and lethargic middle-class men to exercise their political rights or, more correctly speaking, privileges. Heads were counted after oral choices were made. One more than half of those voting selected the members of the House of Commons. Party organizations adopted names such as Tory, meaning supporters of the ruling monarchy, or Whigs, those who opposed centralized and absolute powers. Slowly two governments appeared— one that was official, exercising governmental power, and the other a potential government later called "the shadow cabinet," criticizing and eroding confidence in incumbent officials who "advised" the monarch on policies. When "confidence" was lost, the Opposition asked that Parliament be dissolved and the voters permitted to make a decision.

The myth of rationality in man existed widely for about a century from the genesis of the Industrial Revolution until Darwin's *Origin of the Species* was published. The American Civil War put to a test the innocent faith in man's reasonable nature. Locke's effort to reconcile the conflicting demands for liberty and property resulted in a kind of "muddling through" in England. Frenchmen relied upon logic but Englishmen depended upon experience. Parties were growths of the "Topsy" kind, not logical formulae. Final truth was too elusive to be grasped by ordinary men. Like Machiavelli, politicians saw men in the unflattering light of reality, not in the bright Platonic aura of eternal verities.

However, in Germany, Hegel's effort to find universal laws in human behavior was applied in a rigidly absolutist fashion by Karl Marx who, with Darwin, contributed so much to the corrosion of the rational myth. Where Hobbes found the only cure for anarchistic chaos in absolute violence in the hands of an autocrat, Locke found the remedy in counting heads regardless of their contents. Even here, mathematically, the odd head determined the outcome. Locke put property beyond the limits of government, even one based upon the consent of the governed. Madison and Jefferson, in the Bill of Rights and the Kentucky and Virginia Resolutions, asserted the right of nullification or even secession when the government assumed authority over the expression of thought in speech and press. When a majority accepted the Madison-Jefferson position, the Federalist minority lived with the result, though reluctantly, and only after a modification in Jefferson's first Inaugural that the majority will to govern had to be "rightful"— that is, non-violent, morally acceptable.

In the Constitution, compromise rather than abstract principle governed. However, the relationship of master to servant or em-

ployer to employee was a property right excluded from governmental power and left to economic power. Slavery by pragmatic
necessity remained under local control. The lamb of liberty lay
down with the wolf of property. Slavery was to be open to modification in twenty years when the slave trade must cease. Change
was acceptable though it must be peaceful, that is, by persuasion,
not by coercion.

The contest between moral imperatives and the necessity of expediency, or compromise, between different views and contrasting
cultures was papered over in the American Constitution by the
three-fifths compromise and by providing for extinction of the slave
trade in twenty years (1808). Advocates of national policies who
approved of industrial and urban growth competed with friends
of continued agrarian dominance, but a kind of *modus vivendi*
allowed the coexistence of mutually hostile principles. As the
frontier expanded and immigration increased, population grew
rapidly. From three million to 30 million within four decades increased the difficulties of adjustment even though the vast expanse
of territory allowed for wide diversity among the heterogeneous
elements in the national complex. Rigid adherence to the widely
proclaimed doctrine of equality in the Declaration of Independence
clashed with the insistence upon cultural diversity by the defenders
of southern uniqueness based upon the leisure class views of John
Calhoun.

The origins of party owed as much to a difference of view over
foreign policy as over national and local allegiances. One group
held to the gradual change by elections and the other was friendly
to revolutionary action. The "Revolution of 1800" led to slow and
regulated change. Jefferson founded a party that governed under
his guidance for a quarter century. Neither John Adams nor his
son, John Quincy Adams, believed in parties. New parties were
born in the West, each allied to the East, one with Massachusetts,
the other with New York.

Nowhere was the struggle more evident than in the new Western states of Tennessee and Kentucky. Both states adhered to the
rhetoric of Jeffersonian democracy but in one the leadership came
from a militant, warlike, unsophisticated soldier, Andrew Jackson,
and the other from a lawyer, Henry Clay, trained and indoctri-
nated in the liberal Lockian views of Chancellor Wythe.

Clay spent a lifetime advocating gradual, peaceful change, with
a slow emancipation of slaves. By a narrow vote in the Constitu-

tional Convention of 1792, slavery was introduced into Kentucky. The pattern of sectional alignment was set in a state of nature where a new civil government was created. The youthful and freshly migrated Clay in 1799 fought fiercely for the acceptance of gradual emancipation but the slaveholders in his local community won. The franchise was curtailed to white males.

Fifty years later, Clay, now "the Sage of Ashland," was even less successful in achieving any modification of slavery while one of his own partisans succeeded in including property in slaves as a natural right beyond governmental control in the Kentucky Constitution of 1850. This was barely fifteen years before violent and coercive emancipation came through the thirteenth amendment. Henry Clay founded and controlled a political party which died with him. Whigs tried in vain to find a formula by which gradual social change could eradicate or diminish the ills of slavery. Clay's Whig successor and spiritual protégé, a reluctant Republican, Abraham Lincoln, was compelled to fight a fierce Civil War to establish the right of the majority or plurality to govern. Lincoln's first inaugural is the clearest statement of the doctrine of majority or party government.

The central idea of secession is the essence of anarchy. A majority, held in restraint by constitutional checks and limitations, and always changing easily, with deliberate changes of popular opinions, is the only true sovereign of a free people. Whoever rejects it does, of necessity, fly to anarchy or to despotism. Unanimity is impossible. The rule of a minority as a permanent arrangement, is wholly inadmissable [sic]. Thus, rejecting the majority principle, anarchy or despotism in some form is all that is left.[1]

Rejection of this principle led to four years of bloody warfare. Abandonment of party government was the most costly blunder in two hundred years of American experience. Lincoln's warning was applicable in the 1960's as in the 1860's. The results of visceral reactions to public questions can be disastrous in any age or time. In order to maintain the supremacy of political due process government had to invoke force with deadly results.

In so doing, Lincoln assumed arbitrary powers to suppress civil liberties and to confiscate millions of dollars in private property. His assassination attested to the ultimate power of violence over reason. In establishing the principle of majority rule, a heritage of

---

[1] Roy P. Basler, ed., *The Collected Works of Abraham Lincoln.* The Abraham Lincoln Association (New Brunswick, New Jersey: Rutgers University Press, 1953) Vol. IV, 268.

hate and racial conflict developed which continued for a century. The ashes smoldered and threatened to ignite again to destroy the very foundation of consensus and government by the consent of the governed. The Democratic party had to start over in 1866 and face a new Republican party that governed virtually six decades. During this period the entire nation changed from agricultural to industrial. The emotions aroused during civil war and reconstruction were the deepest impulses of human nature. In the continued emotional clash over forced school busing there is a constant endangerment of the entire concept of government by reason and rational decision. An apparent majority seeks to destroy a culture of separation by color that existed not in one section alone but in every region of the country while the minority now approaches a population equal to that of the entire country in 1860. Today, the minority is nearly ten times the total population when the experiment in self-government began two centuries ago.

Can a system of government developed among a body of people all of whom had inherited the tradition of the Judeo-Christian respect for civility, survive in the midst of a pluralistic, secular, alienated, urban, industrialized society? If the much-criticized Puritan ethic of hard work and self-reliance is dead, then what ethic succeeds it? Can the bitch goddess of success supplant the Virgin as the overall value code of a viable political system. Can the dynamo supply not only the physical energy for survival but also the élan vital for a civil and spiritual dynamic under which the residual institutions of representative government operate?

Representative government and toleration are devices of relatively recent discovery. If the Conciliar movement had succeeded in the Middle Ages, the Protestant Revolt might well have been avoided. In the two centuries before American independence England hammered out a crude doctrine of live-and-let-live in a religiously pluralistic society. Even a French monarch declared a throne to be worth many a Mass.

Toleration—different from tolerance—was an outgrowth of a balance of internal power reached when there was no firm majority and repeated efforts at a political religion had failed in the colonies. The Constitution of the United States was the result of a spirit of toleration both in religion and in politics. Slave and free states reached an accommodation, a kind of domestic *détente*. Small states and large states harmonized their differences in a bicameral representative system that recognized both equality and majority principles. Finally, an indirectly chosen energetic executive was made a coequal with a majority of the legislature. An aristocratic life-appointed judiciary assumed the authority to say what the sacred covenant meant. Fear of all government underlay the Constitution. The founding fathers distrusted the one, the few, or the many, as John Adams trenchantly expressed it. All governments are operated by men who are alike afflicted with sin or the lust for power. The paradox of one man's power including property in another human being haunted American ideology. One man's liberty was another man's deprivation. No one could be trusted with another's liberty. The absolute was that no man was a fair judge in his own case. Men were alienated from government in 1776 and 1787 no less than in 1975-76. How does leadership gain the confidence of the led? The Constitution framers shaped the presidency to fit their presiding officer and former military chief, George Washington. His prestige and fame finally assured the ratification of the Constitution, especially in his native Virginia, whose inclusion was essential for the establishment of the new Federal government itself.

From Washington to Eisenhower leaders in military life, successful achievers in the manipulation of violence have been the favorite leaders in Executive Office. Success in man's most primitive activity, namely, destruction of his fellow man by strategy and violence, has been the chief qualification for leadership in domestic and foreign policy. Bellicosity instead of statesmanship has been the outstanding trait of popularly-elected presidential leaders. John Adams and Thomas Jefferson were equally opposed to a military élite such as Hamilton sought to impose by the organization of the Cincinnati—a body of Revolutionary war officers with a pretension for hereditary nobility. Jefferson, the symbol of statesmanship by reasonable men, created the first opposition to the incumbent administration of George Washington.

Factionalism grew as Madison had predicted in Federalist No. 10. Division developed out of policies of taxation as well as over the succession. Personal ambition and the lure of power divides all bodies where power may be exercised. Policies frequently are the rationalization of personal ambitions. Hamilton personified the policy wishes of a developing industrial élite (tariffs), a creditor commercial class (national bank), and a military and naval group (soldiers). Jefferson, however, symbolized the interests of plantation owners and the primitive earth hunger of yeomen who were anxious to acquire land from the natives (Indians) by force or treachery or both. Since farmers and their spokesmen represented the numerical majority they were able to defeat John Adams though the Machiavellian Burr used a credit device—an indirectly chartered bank—to intimidate merchant voters even as Hamilton did.

Similarly, the cunning Burr invented in New York City a method of making voters out of members in social clubs as property owners—a prerequisite to voting in New York. With the oral vote and a "dirty tricks" infiltration into the ranks of faction-ridden Federalists, a majority in urban New York gave Jefferson the presidency in 1800. Success was made possible by the combination of plantation, agrarian Virginia and the growing metropolis of Manhattan, locally controlled by the "Pig Pen," an incipient development of Tammany Hall, that ultimately has made the vast metropolis a more solid Gibraltar for the Democratic Party than the much vaunted solid south. Thirty years later behind the façade of an Indian fighter, a Van Buren-Jackson combination gave dominion to Jacksonian democracy with the ascendancy for a generation of this alleged farmer-labor alliance. At no time did the "Jacksonian persuasion" offer any hope to the southern slaves or the conquered Indians.

When the Federalists succeeded in self-destruction during the first two decades of the 19th century the old party alignment had fallen into disarray. A new cult of personality arose around sectional or regional interests, personified by John Quincy Adams and Daniel Webster from New England, William Crawford of Georgia and John Calhoun of South Carolina. Henry Clay and Andrew Jackson contended for the leadership of the west in Kentucky and Tennessee. The militant Jackson more nearly represented the virtues and vices of the acquisitive frontier while Clay, following geographic determinism, illustrated the more civilized drift of the second—and legal—frontier. Because of the limitation to three candidates, Clay as number four, but as the influential Speaker of the House, had to choose between the staid New Englander with whom he had disagreed and even quarrelled, John Quincy Adams, and Andrew Jackson, the nearly professional duelist, executioner of British soldiers, and charismatic Indian warrior. A third possible selection, William H. Crawford, victim of a paralytic stroke, was in effect not eligible. Compelled because of Crawford's bad health to choose between a statesman and a warrior, both his political

rivals, Clay made the fatal political mistake of choosing the statesman.

When Clay joined the Adams administration he was accused of
engaging in a corrupt bargain. Clay and Adams did what Jefferson and Burr had done earlier and Jackson and Van Buren were
to do almost immediately. Jackson had a group of camp followers,
especially Blair and Kendall, who with the indirect bribery of the
public printing kept up a steady claque of newspaper propaganda
against the "bargain" and in adulation of the Old Hero. The one
chance to avoid the Civil War was probably thwarted by the defeat of Clay, the pacificator and compromiser, who advocated an
end to slavery extension and a gradual movement toward ultimate
emancipation. Instead a series of weak presidents, Van Buren,
Harrison, Tyler, Polk, Taylor, Fillmore, Pierce and Buchanan either
failed to bridge the gap or arrived at Buchanan's futile conclusion
that states had no right to secede but, at the same time, the Federal
government had no right to stop them. There was no consensus
upon a perpetual union, notwithstanding the famous toast of Jackson. Calhoun, like the Adamses, never believed in parties but in
the pluralism of regional coalitions and dual executives.

After southerners in 1844 destroyed Van Buren's expectation of
a second term by the institution of the two-thirds rule for nomination in the Democratic Party, a minority exercised a veto power.
Paradoxically enough, in 1848, Van Buren led a hopeless contest for
a new third party of Free Soilers. He was joined in this effort
by the son of John Quincy Adams, whose administration Van Buren
had done so much to destroy.

By 1830, the party system had become a natural method of
choosing the succession to the presidency. The original electoral
college was dead and the party nominating convention became its
successor by selecting alternative candidates. Increasingly large
numbers of citizens (male, white adults) were permitted to make
a choice, frequently the rather dubious one of rejection of the
lesser evil. Obtaining the nomination was the first step and the
selection of a nominee was made on the basis of who would be
least offensive to large groups of voters, hence least likely to offend
any considerable segment of the electorate. The election of a
popular Indian fighter and amateur warrior, as a Democrat, in 1828,
set a precedent that was adopted in 1840 by the Whigs with the
nomination of another warrior, William Henry Harrison, to be the
successful candidate.

A byproduct of Jacksonian democracy was the ascendancy of the spoils system, partly as an outgrowth of the increasing size of the electorate. As property and religious qualifications fell, the necessity for organizing and getting voters to the polls grew. Few people had the inclination or leisure to devote full time to the manufacture and processing of the consent of the governed. Self-interest needed to be motivated. Office was the reward for political action. Since taxes were necessary even for the least government, the reward of a tax collector's job was a principal incentive for intense party performance. By the time Abraham Lincoln became president, Horace Greeley declared the collector of port in New York combined with the Navy Yard employees to be sufficient in number to select the delegates of the New York state delegation. In turn, the large New York delegation could almost determine the nominee. In fact, President Lincoln found his Cabinet torn between his Secretary of the Treasury who nominally controlled the New York port patronage and his Secretary of State, a member of the old Whig Weed organization, who wanted to pass out offices. Later, through an unsophisticated soldier, U. S. Grant, Senator Conkling headed the New York Republican machine that almost nominated Grant for a third term. Conkling defeated confirmation of the Reformer, President Hayes' nominee, Theodore Roosevelt, senior, for the collector's job. His father's death, perhaps from anxiety in this struggle, was a powerful factor in setting Theodore Roosevelt, Jr., on a Civil Service reform career. Chester Alan Arthur, the spoilsman collector of port, elected Vice President in 1880, succeeded to the presidency after Garfield's assassination and signed into law the first Civil Service Reform Act.

The Republican Party actually came into existence when two great patronage organizations merged in 1855; namely, the Whig machine started by Thurlow Weed, when the state chairman, Morgan, joined the Republicans in Albany. Linked to the body of Democratic professionals headed by the Blair family, especially Francis Preston, Sr., a winning coalition was established. The one-time impecunious newspaperman from Kentucky whose debtor status led Blair to desert Clay and join Jackson had made a modest fortune out of the public printing. Ironically, Abraham Lincoln nationalized governmental printing by making it a public business like the post office. By expedient disposition of the patronage, the political genius of Lincoln created a viable political party that governed the nation from 1861 until 1932 with only two intervals under

Democratic presidents—Cleveland and Wilson—neither of whom had popular majorities. By welding the Whig merchants, bankers and industrialists, and the old Hamiltonian *entente*, to the body of emancipation idealists and rural free land beneficiaries, Lincoln fused a winning combination that made secure his hold on the federal government. He confiscated the slave property of the ruling class and established a protective tariff subsidy to industry at the expense of agriculture which led ultimately to the liquidation of the agricultural foundation of the nation's economy. By granting free land to former soldiers and a growing body of North European immigrants, Lincoln unwittingly set the pattern for a technological and scientific order governed by centralized capitalism.

The effort to create a Civil Service independent of party consideration enormously complicated the governmental bureaucracy by recruiting personnel with no policy or ideological motivation. The result clothed the exercise of public interest purposes with red tape and built-in inefficiency. Deprived of the party activity of avid seekers of political jobs, the dynamic force of manipulating the electorate fell upon propaganda and the agencies of influencing opinion.

At first, the press, then later radio and television furnished the stereotypes that governed the action of politicians. As the press ceased to be partisan and became primarily "just another business" whose principal purpose was making a profit, the cost of organizing and propagandizing voters greatly increased. The necessity of collecting funds for parties and candidates tended to dominate policy. During the Civil War, one set of bankers (the Rothschilds) controlled the Democratic party and another (the Cooks) financed the war and first, Republican Chase, and later Grant. As economic nationalism grew in importance the Republican party turned to tariff beneficiaries under the great Philadelphia merchant, John Wanamaker, later succeeded by the industrial genius and political manipulator from Ohio, Mark Hanna. He effectively destroyed the chances of a neo-Jeffersonian-Jacksonian agrarian, William Jennings Bryan, from staying the sweeping development of finance capitalism. When Theodore Roosevelt pulled down the Republican temple in 1912, he still kept close alliance with George W. Perkins, the Wall Street banker, who had control of the Progressive National Committee. Because Roosevelt was a practical man he saw the necessity for public financing of parties and politicians. While still president, Roosevelt publicly declared that the hope of democracy depended upon the financing of parties from taxes. Six decades elapsed before positive steps led to the enactment of subsidy legislation. The creation of the dollar tax check-off later enlarged into reform legislation, was enacted in 1974 as a way of generally strengthening the political process.

In the meantime an attack had been made both locally and nationally on the convention or representative system of nominating candidates. Tammany Hall had produced a systematized means of organizing politics on a non-doctrinal, non-policy basis with office grabbing and public jobs as a means of motivating voters. Finally, the abuses of the nominating process handed control of public policy to a narrow élite of professional politicians and powerful interests. The nominating convention of 1912 demonstrated how an incumbent administration could dictate its renomination over a popular former president with wide personal support. In Wisconsin, "old Bob" LaFollette introduced the direct primary as a method of allowing voters to participate in nominating candidates. The direct primary was regarded by its followers as a panacea for the evils of democracy by having more democracy. The Wisconsin primary was "open" to all voters regardless of party affiliation. Its advocates believed the "good people" would always vote right.

The primary was a byproduct of the emphasis on the intellectual capacity and interests of voters. It failed to take into account the limited mental interests and attention span of a constantly enlarging electorate. Doubled in number by the enfranchisement of women in 1920, the electorate has been further expanded by enfranchising 18-year-olds—under the faulty logic that if 18-year-old males are old enough to fight, this is justification for giving the franchise to 18-year-old females. Much evidence indicates that the younger voters do not exercise the franchise and many are alienated from the voting process. In the meantime what James Bryce years ago described as the "fatalism of the multitude" has grown with the vast expansion of the voter potential. Furthermore, a very narrow understanding of the nature of parties taught by civics teachers in the public schools has discouraged party participation and involvement because somehow "parties" and politicians are wicked and "dirty."

Parties have been voluntary associations of citizens with no power to raise revenue. Informal coalitions from their birth, they have been weakly structured except in local loyalties and interests. In competition with multinational corporations, international brother-

ment. Emotion had displaced reason and the whole future of the
democratic experiment is in doubt. Can a nation survive the fears
of white and black of each other? At the same time, the non-
rational forces of racism and class have extended themselves over
the globe and the existence of world government has been put
in jeopardy. Even the future of man himself is in a perilous state.

Clearly party government has neither solved man's inherent
problems nor furnished a remedy for an imperfect human nature.
Some people gloat over the eclipse of parties as viable institutions
for the prevention of violence, and they resort to bullets again in
substitution for ballots. Some political scientists have pronounced
the two-party system dead. Demagogues on the right such as
Joseph McCarthy and the John Birchers have produced fiascos
such as the Goldwater disaster for the Republicans in 1964. In
1968, the Minnesota dilettante, Eugene McCarthy, led the modern
children's crusade that climaxed in the Chicago convention of 1968
and the temporary rescue of Richard M. Nixon from oblivion.

The continuation of the "new politics" of disruption and crowd
demonstrations linked with a crude attempt to impose proportional
representation upon moderate Democrats produced the party catastrophe of 1972 and the national landslide for Richard Nixon. His
overwhelming reelection was overthrown since his methods of campaigning and administration resulted in the Watergate debacle and
the unprecedented resignation of both a President and a Vice
President. The brainless elements of both Right and Left are in
positions to capture the nominations of the two old parties. A
semi-martyred former perennial candidate poses a potential threat
to the two-party tradition, so that the friends of representative
government despair of the consequences of polarization and alienation simultaneously. Now that the alienated exceed the number
of those claiming to be Republican, the prospect in 1976 is dismal
indeed.

What primaries and quota representation have not accomplished,
television and current civic education may achieve. As social problems grow more complex and unsolvable except by some kind of
compromise that satisfies none of the apostles of perfection, faith
in government by the consent of the governed diminishes, and
may ultimately be destroyed. With the death of confidence in self-
government, cynicism and despair grow. When nihilism, or the
lack of faith in ideals or traditions arrives, it is easy for legendary
personalities such as the Kennedys to displace institutions.

hoods of workers as well as numerous professional associations, political parties have lacked funds and specialized personnel. It is small wonder that parties have developed no fixed ideology or ideals that are enduring.

At first, Federalists nominally favored a stronger central government founded upon the self-interests of creditors, bankers, industrialists, and moneyed interests in general. The Democratic party started as an opposition group whose declared purposes were to restrain the growth of centralized power either military, economic or social. Local government was the center of Republican (Democratic) institutions to defend the liberties of citizens from centralized encroachment upon freedom of thought and action.

Property in human beings proved to be the rock upon which both old parties splintered, rending them finally asunder. In 1852, using the façade of a quasi-military figure, the Whigs fielded their last presidential candidate, the obese Winfield Scott. With the record of the Compromise of 1850 the last achievement of their fast-dying longtime leader, Henry Clay, the Whigs satisfied neither the Abolitionists of the North and West nor the apologists for slavery in the South who had come to regard slavery as a positive good that could develop a significant civilization along Aristotelian lines. The Whig party carried only Massachusetts and Kentucky, the original Whig states of John Quincy Adams and Henry Clay. In 1856, Kentucky voted for a Democrat and Massachusetts for a Republican, while the Whig residue voted for Millard Fillmore, now leading an intolerant American party.

Four years later, Lincoln, co-opted by the Republicans, joined with Hannibal Hamlin, a former Democrat, to obtain scarcely 40% of the popular vote but a majority of the electoral college to win the presidency. The Democrats divided between the Douglas "squatter sovereignty" majority and the Buchanan-Breckinridge minority. The two-thirds rule prevented anyone from obtaining the nomination. With four parties in the field only an electoral college made possible the election of a president at all. A substantial portion of the Union (eleven states) refused to acknowledge a plurality choice and thus a onetime consensus broke down.

The price of abandoning two party government was a fearful one. The bloody result was a half-million casualties, the destruction of hundreds of millions of dollars in property, as well as a legacy from the war of military government and racial hatreds which still haunts regional politics and prevents rational representative govern-

Two hundred years is a brief period in the long history of man. In an environment of scarcity and deprivation those people most keenly sensitized to fear and flight—the impulses which beget hatred of one's fellows—frustration leads to aggression and the creation of the heroes of violence, the Hitlers, the Stalins, and the Mao Tse Tungs. Such persons abhor criticism and opposition. In Watergate, a glimpse appeared of the power-oriented individual who sets up enemies lists and becomes wedded to the belief that the end justifies the means. These devices destroy dissent, privacy, and ultimately all civic freedom.

In 1975-1976, violent clashes in the Near East between Jews and Arabs, Moslems and Christians; in Portugal, between Catholics and Communists; and in Ireland, the revival of ancient hatreds between Catholics and Protestants alarm serious students of government. Coercive school busing exacerbates animosities between majorities and minorities in the United States. The frightening prospect of internal dissolution and ensuing chaos with dictatorship creates a threat hanging over the future of man. Nuclear weapons can be in the possession of individuals, cabals, and gangs. Terrorism feeds on itself. Violence is daily fare in the media, television, radio, the press and the movies, accompanied by growing vandalism. Theft, murder, and mayhem undermine confidence in the rationality of man. A resort to self-help and private security systems fosters a new feudalism not unlike that which ensued for a thousand years after the Roman rule of law was eliminated by internal conflict and barbarian invasions.

Those who insist upon "rights,"—which are really privileges— such as the right to dissent, the right to jobs, and the right to education may disappear in the senseless use of bombs and arson as a means of achieving their "rights." With the advent of television, its ever-sovereign camera nervously focusing on the behavior of men, the "demonstration" has taken on national and even international proportions. In fact, the camera went on the moonflights and even precedes man in interstellar missions. The crowd or mob once primarily a phenomenon of urban conflicts may now become a factor in national party conflicts. The camera dramatized the bitter fight at the Democratic nominating convention in 1968. It continued to wield a tremendous influence in 1972 when the pictures from Miami Beach presented militant spectacles with urban and minority stereotypes much too evident. The reelection of Richard Nixon was virtually assured. A later version of the quiet and harmonious

Republicans meeting in Miami Beach only sealed the fate of the Left extremists who captured the Democrats in 1972 as the Right extremists had been exposed in their seizure of the Republican party in 1964. Lyndon Johnson and Richard Nixon need not have campaigned at all. Nor did they need to have gone to such lengths of promising too much as Johnson did in 1964 and of violating the political and legal mores as Nixon did in 1972.

The current (1976) unpopularity of all politicians is partly the result of the rising tide of popular expectations highlighted by Adlai Stevenson a few years ago. *Can party institution based upon small town organization and agrarian beliefs extend itself to a new politics of the urban masses?* Issue discussion is more likely to produce conflict than consensus, and reason falls before the onslaught of emotion as crowds become mobs and personality cults succeed due process as a means of achieving decisions. A mobile, restless and rootless electorate rearranging preferences (classified as prejudices by opponents) may well lead to the emergence of more coercion instead of consent or consensus.

Representative government through political parties confronts the dilemma of all organizations; namely, the respective roles of the leader and the led. Unable to rely upon birth or inheritance for an ethic acceptable to the led, the democratic politician must constantly be persuading by word or deed the approval of people with all the hazards this imposes. If politicians are often accused of chameleon traits frequently castigated as hypocrisy by critics, it is the result of the volatility of public opinion, at best, a very slippery concept. Franklin D. Roosevelt was denounced as a warmonger when he proposed a quarantine of aggressors in 1937. Later he was bitterly attacked as an aggressor when he pushed for rearmament and finally succeeded, with Willkie's support, in persuading Congress to adopt conscription. Four years later the same man was as intensely criticized after Pearl Harbor for not preparing the nation against potential attack. After China succumbed to Communism in 1949, the Republican party accused Democrats of twenty years of treason and built up a successful slogan of "communism, Korea and corruption" in 1952. When Cuba fell to Castro, the Democrats accused Republicans of negligence and inadequate preparedness, especially after the Russians launched Sputnik into outer space. When the Bay of Pigs episode rebounded to the discredit of the Kennedy Administration, the young President took an intransigent stand in the missile crisis of 1962. Undoubtedly a principal factor in the Kennedy-Johnson administration's handling of Vietnam was the fear of an assault upon the "ins" for being responsible for another one hundred million people falling under Chinese or Russian control if an Indochinese debacle occurred. When the Johnson administration undertook to end the Vietnamese conflict by victory, the attack upon Johnson and Humphrey was intense enough to destroy their 1964 overwhelming triumph and to influence the victor of 1964 not to run in 1968. War opponents defeated Hubert Humphrey and paved the way for the Nixon triumph. He, in turn, had to negotiate a dubious peace agreement with defeat the general result. Nixon meanwhile began dismantling the program for domestic reform in welfare, full employment, and civil rights which was the Democratic response in 1964 to the popular demand for change. In consequence many of the disillusioned were alienated and many pseudo-intellectuals led a senseless attack upon all political leaders.

During its first century the two party approach broke down once with disastrous results. At the close of the second century, the outlook for its survival is grave. Political science gave the two party idea a fairly careful study in 1950, but adolescent political scientists have been attempting to discredit it ever since. If the adversary method is dropped in political due process, will it long survive in the legal realm? For more than a decade hedonism appears to have triumphed in the philosophical and literary world. Pseudo-intellectuals such as Arthur Miller and Gore Vidal have popularized the gutter design. Freud and Marx are now the deities of the secular religion that dominates what were once regarded as educational institutions. These organizations appear more interested in brawn than brains. As institutions of higher learning they furnish circuses for mindless entertainment. Rational discourse is crowded out and the hope of an intellectually disciplined leadership falls aside.

If universities devoted a tenth as much of their energies to the discovery and training of political talent as they do to athletic prowess as recruiting agents for professional football and basketball, the prospects for the future of politics might be much brighter.

Perhaps a renewal of Jefferson's pertinent inquiry needs to be revived.

Sometimes it is said that man can not be trusted with the government of himself. Can he, then, be trusted with the government of others? Or have we found angels in the forms of kings to govern him? Let history answer this question.[2]

Occasionally the reported comment of pessimistic old John Adams arises. "Perhaps this world is the lunatic asylum of the universe." His observation that men are "fools, ambitious and greedy" is demonstrated daily on the camera for the benefit of those who have ignored Graham Wallas' sage conclusion about the over-intellectualized premise as fundamental in human nature.[3]

Political science may need to reconsider its preoccupation with trivia and concern itself with the problem of *cohesion,* the essential nature of which requires a reexamination of political parties which have given a semblance of unity to a constitutional straitjacket with its theological trinity of judiciary, executive and legislative. If two hundred and twenty million people are to have descendants to celebrate a tricentennial, a more thoughtful approach must be given to the continued existence of "the last best hope of man on earth."

[2] Thomas Jefferson, *First Inaugural Address,* March 4, 1801.
[3] Graham Wallas, *Human Nature in Politics,* 1st edition, 1906.

Revitalization and Decay: Looking Toward the Third Century of American Electoral Politics

WALTER DEAN BURNHAM

As the calendar points toward the bicentennial of American independence, the United States finds itself in the grip of a pervasive and remarkably long-lived political crisis. Signs of this crisis are everywhere to be seen. They have appeared in a variety of forms: in George Wallace's campaigns, in and out of the Democratic party, since the spring of 1964; in Barry Goldwater's nomination by the Republicans that year; in the assassinations, riots and protest demonstrations of 1967-1972; in the failure of the Democratic conventions of 1968 and 1972 to achieve either legitimacy or consensus; in Richard Nixon's rise from the politically dead in 1968, and in his richly deserved reinterment in 1974; and in much else besides. So far from being exhaustive, such a list of pathological symptoms could be extended almost indefinitely. They add up to a syndrome; and it seems very likely that 1976 will make its own contributions to that list.

Conventional wisdom, such as it now exists, stresses the importance of two chief proximate causes of this state of affairs: the Vietnam disaster in foreign policy and the mix of poverty and civil-rights programs in the domestic arena. One implication of this argument is that, with Vietnam now in the past and with a general discrediting in public and elite opinion of the kind of experiment in positive federal action associated with the "Great Society," things will return to normal in the near future. This is in fact the chief hope of some of the neo-conservatives who have contributed to the bicentennial issue of *The Public Interest*.[1] It seems that there has been an "excess of democracy" in the recent past, that too many individuals and groups have developed a notion that they are "entitled" to things from government. Obviously, a reduction in politically organized demand on the system is one specific remedy for the crisis of political legitimacy which is everywhere in view. Moreover, such reductions in demand have been brought about before in our history, and highly successfully—most conspicuously, in the period 1900-1915. Nevertheless, there appears to be some deep fear among the authors of this symposium that things will not be quite so well or neatly arranged this time, and the fear is probably justified. It would seem certain that the removal of Vietnam from the agenda and the growing consensus that the Great Society was a Bad Thing will be of major short-term influence in determining the agenda and personnel of the 1976 election. But the general crisis of the American political system remains a cardinal reality of our time, even if students no longer protest over the war and ghetto riots do not typically occur in the mid-1970s as they did in 1967-1968.

One of the most interesting and suggestive features of this crisis has been the re-emergence of concern, by academics, journalists and the brighter political operatives alike, about the prospects for a critical realignment in the United States. Rather often—as with Kevin Phillips' *The Emerging Republican Majority*,[2] or as in a *New York Times* editorial of November 30, 1975—this preoccupation becomes a kind of thirst for the event, a kind of waiting for Godot. There are fundamental reasons why both the awareness of such events and the yearning for them should be so acute in our time, and reflected in the writings of people who otherwise agree rarely enough about American politics. From an *analytic* point of view, the periodically-recurring critical realignment sequence discloses the foundations of American politics, and of the adaptive capacities of the political system to the consequences of sweeping change in economy and society. Analysis of such events brings relationships to light which are rarely if ever seen in any other context. This

---

[1] No. 41, Fall 1975. See especially Samuel P. Huntington, "The Democratic Distemper," 9-38; Seymour M. Lipset, "The Paradox of American Politics," 142-165; and Robert Nisbet, "Public Opinion versus Popular Opinion," 166-192.

[2] New Rochelle: Arlington House, 1969.

analysis permits—if it does not require—a reordering of many received truths about the way in which the political machinery and its
elite role-holders cope with pressures for major change.

From an *operational* point of view the contribution of critical
realignments has been no less fundamental. In the past, such events
have arisen out of a growing—and inherent—dissynchronization
between the capacities, routines and official ideologies of political
elites and the organizable political effects at the mass base of relatively uncontrolled change in a capitalist society. They are the
ultimate empirical demonstration of two propositions about American electoral politics. First, once established, a dominant political
alignment, its associated elites and their activities will continue to
function in a routinized way indefinitely unless acted upon by some
overwhelming external force. Second, the adjustments of policy
outputs and interest representation which American pluralists have
celebrated in our parties and other institutions operate within
strictly limited areas at the margins. No established political elite
is prepared to incorporate demands the effective realization of which
is incompatible with its fundamental interests or with the existing
rules of the game. Where changes which are more than at the
margins of an existing political game are concerned, every elite
actor will tend to respond as an extremist, however much he prides
himself on his pragmatism or however much he extols the virtues
of incremental change.

But some vehicle of adaptation, some mechanism by which political agendas can be redefined in terms of the organized needs of
today rather than those of 35 years ago, is functionally necessary.
Some means must be found by which an inherently static steering
mechanism—the political order—is to be brought back into phase
with economy and society. Political stability depends upon this.
So do other important political goods, such as specific and generalized legitimacy, the restoration of the "two-party system" as
mythic symbol of national integration scarcely less important than
the Constitution, and the accumulation of sufficient power resources
in the hands of the winners to produce minimal coherence of policy.
This vehicle has historically been the critical realignment. It has
historically provided an essential means by which all these goods
have been furnished. In the current crisis, these goods are manifestly in short supply. It is hardly surprising that so many of us
have waited for another critical realignment to extricate us from
our difficulties.

The thesis of this article may be stated in a few propositions. (1) Critical realignments have historically been induced by the political system's incapacity to undergo more than marginal incremental change. They have been America's surrogate for revolution.

(2) Critical realignments are phenomena which are dramatic, sudden changes with characteristics which are relatively easy to measure and document. But underlying the numbers are primordial qualitative issues. Each of them has been an integral part of the process by which a dominant American value system has been brought up to date, or revitalized, without breaking down or dissolving in the process. Ultimately, then, the periodic historical rhythms of disruption, realignment and restabilization in electoral politics are more than measurable behavioral phenomena. They are fundamentally manifestations of constitution-making and remaking, of applied political theory in general and of Lockian political theory in particular.

(3) There are excellent reasons for supposing that critical-realignment processes as historically understood have ceased to exist. For the analytical literature dealing with these phenomena has always either stated or assumed a necessary and intimate connection between them and the political parties as mobilizing and channeling organizations. It is precisely this partisan link which has been cumulatively dissolved. The post-1963 era in American politics has many of the most essential ingredients of critical realignment: a wavelike spread of protest, including a third-party movement and direct-action activity of many kinds; a tremendous increase in the volatility of electoral coalitions; a severe decline in the legitimacy and effectiveness of official elites and the policies they attempt to make; and a disruption of rules of the game once accepted as "natural" and "satisfactory." Yet if it is another in our periodic upheavals, this crisis sequence has worked athwart parties, and has worked to their dissolution rather than to their revitalization. As I have remarked elsewhere, the post-1963 era appears best described as a "critical realignment to end all critical realignments," that is, it is a sequence which has already produced major and perhaps irreversible changes in the way people vote and in the distribution of power in American politics, but at the expense of parties in the political system.[3]

[3] Walter Dean Burnham, "American Politics in the 1970s: Beyond Party?"

(4) To the extent that this is so, it raises issues far broader than those of interest to electoral-politics specialists alone. The "two-party system" has been an essential constituent element in American politics as a whole: it has channeled, moderated and made predictable the effects of multiple pluralist demands upon policy-makers. It has also been of periodically vital importance in revitalizing, by "modernizing," the operational side of the American belief system. To speak of its abolition, or even of its vitiation, is to argue three related propositions:

(a) The erosion of "party-in-the-electorate" is both effect and cause of a breakdown, graver than at any time in the previous history of the country, in its basic value symbolisms.

(b) The disappearance of the critical-realignment sequence as a mechanism for revitalization and for allocating priorities among issue claimants entails the proposition that there is no available mechanism for the political reintegration of the United States of any traditional kind.

(c) The United States, in its bicentennial years, is in an historical *caesura*, a fundamental transition from what it has been as a polity since its foundation and toward something else.

Let us turn to each of these in the space which remains to us.

II

It is a commonplace of recent comparative scholarship that America as a polity is fundamentally "different" from other nations which have passed through and beyond industrial-capitalist economic and social development. Primordially, this difference is to be found in the dominant value-system—what Gaetano Mosca has called the "political formula"—as that value-system was institutionalized through political structure and expectations, and supported by uniquely favorable demographic, resource and external (or international) variables. An enormous amount of scholarly effort in the past generation has gone into the analysis of all three components: values, institutions and contexts. From the value-analytic school has come a view of the United States as essentially a polity bound together by a Lockian-liberal (or bourgeois-individualist)

---

in William N. Chambers and Walter Dean Burnham, eds., *The American Party Systems*, 2nd ed. (New York: Oxford, 1975), 308-357.

political formula.[4] Institutionalists such as Samuel Huntington have stressed the archaic, nondevelopmental and internally nonsovereign nature of the political system, going so far as referring to it as a "Tudor polity."[5] Contextualists have emphasized the temporal and spatial implications of the "fragment culture" experience, the continental size of the country and the extraordinary heterogeneity of the racial, ethnic and cultural groups which populate it, the uniquely favorable historical balance between population and exploitable economic resources, and the also uniquely favorable isolation of the country through most of its independent existence from credible external threats to that existence.

The composite view of the American political system which these studies give us is a compelling one. It is the picture of a political system founded upon primordial value-axioms which can be summarized as a consensus on *self-regulation* for individuals, groups and subcultures. This self-regulation may be viewed as implying certain things about political struggle and the role of the state in the political economy; it also may be viewed as requiring for its existence the maintenance of certain essential boundary conditions separating politics on one side from the socio-economic system on the other.

The dominance of self-regulation as the primordial value consensus bespeaks, of course, the ascendancy of the "absolute bourgeois" to an extent unthinkable in any other advanced industrial country. It presupposes a dense network of socialization mechanisms, economic interests and shared premises among political elites which are uniquely favorable to the self-transforming dynamic of capitalist development. It likewise presupposes, as both Hartz and Huntington have stressed, a lack of antecedent structures in either the cultural or the economic system which could offer serious long-

---

[4] The *locus classicus* of this view is, of course, Louis Hartz, *The Liberal Tradition in America* (New York: Harcourt, Brace, 1955). See also Louis Hartz, ed., *The Founding of New Societies* (New York: Harcourt, Brace, 1964), especially Part I; and, for a quantitatively-based statement Donald J. Devine, *The Political Culture of the United States* (Boston: Little, Brown, 1972).

[5] Samuel P. Huntington, *Political Order in Changing Societies* (New Haven: Yale University Press, 1968), 93-139. As Huntington points out, such great institutionalist scholars of an earlier generation as A. F. Pollard and Charles H. McIlwain were also keenly aware of this neo-medieval structure of American politics.

term resistance to the unfolding of that dynamic, or serious long-term challenge to its ascendancy either in the moral or the operational realm. It follows—one is tempted to say, almost inexorably—that political conflict among diverse groups will tend in such a system to be extensive but normally fragmented and confined to the margins of their social existence, where they come into politically-organizable tangential relationships with each other. But such conflict has not been organized in terms of a mass-based assault whose purpose is the capture of the state in order to bring about transformations in society and economy; or to resist such capture. In short, no feudalism, no socialism.

As there has been no long-term, sustained effort to use politics to modernize society in the United States, so both the self-regulation value premise and the ingeniously complicated institutional mechanism created by the Constitution have worked to give us a dominant historical experience: that of the internally nonsovereign state, in which the "hard-state" consolidation and its conversion from absolutist to democratic principles of legitimacy have never occurred. Seriously to assert, as Huntington does, that the American political system is a "Tudor polity" is also necessarily to assert that neither external nor internal stimuli have come into being to produce political development. Such a formulation necessarily asserts that American political history has an enormous built-in tendency toward stasis, in the sharpest possible contrast with the "permanent revolution" in the autonomously developing socio-economic system. Put another way, there is always an "old politics" in every generation, and its practitioners—as Lowi and others have shown—have little or no incentive to innovate.[6]

Clearly, such a model suggests a major contradiction: strong longitudinal tendency toward stasis in the political steering mechanism versus an unparalleled dynamism of development elsewhere. For one cardinal aspect of the American political formula is a powerful normative encouragement of political participation on an egalitarian basis. Moreover, one universal fact of life in modern society has been that major changes in the relations of production and in the organization of the political economy have profoundly disrupted the expectations and lives of large numbers of people.

    [6] See Theodore Lowi, "Toward Functionalism in Political Science: The Case of Innovation in Party Systems," *American Political Science Review*, Vol. 57, 570-583 (1963).

Such people, as the pluralists have taught us correctly, gravitate toward government and politics to redress the balance. In the United States they do so in Lockian-liberal terms: in his Cross-of-Gold speech in 1896, Bryan did not call for socialist revolution or the dictatorship of the proletariat, but for expanding the concept of "businessman" to include his small farmers and shopkeepers in the allocation of benefits. But they gravitate nevertheless, and they typically find that the celebrated incrementalism and pluralism of the existing political elite tend to work only for already-acknowledged players in the current game of politics. The result is not in the main revolution, but the American surrogate for revolution— the critical realignment and the exceptional phenomena associated with it.

It has always been recognized impressionistically that these convulsions involve not only major changes in major-party electoral coalitions and equally major transformations of both public policy outputs and the locus of power among competing political institutions. They also involve conflicts over basic political values within the overarching American self-regulation framework. A 1973 study by Zvi Namenwirth has evaluated the configurations of value-change by means of content analysis of party platforms.[7] Namenwirth is able to identify a dominant long-term cyclical pattern in value change, with the modal wavelength among his value-item categories of 152 years, and with peaks in these waves occurring precisely where historical realignment crises have been at their maximum: 1856, 1894, and 1932.[8] Analysis of the content of these maxima in value-concerns suggests a fourfold classification across time, as well as a prediction that the first classification pattern will reappear about a century and a half after its first appearance. In Namenwirth's scheme, these are, in order:

(a) the expressive phase, dominated by problems of defining the nature and boundaries of the sociopolitical system and by absolutist moral claims of right and wrong (e.g., 1856 and the civil-war alignment);

(b) the adaptive phase, in which conflicts over legal powers to act and over the structure of governmental steering mechanisms

---

[7] J. Zvi Namenwirth, "Wheels of Time and the Interdependence of Value Change in America," *Journal of Interdisciplinary History,* Vol. 3, No. 4, 649-684 (Spring 1973).

[8] *Ibid.,* 661.

tend to predominate (e.g., the realignment of the 1890s and its aftermath, with the impetus toward constitutional and legal aspects of allocation problems being provided by the revolutionary impact of industrial concentration upon legal and political machinery and norms established in a pre-industrial era);

(c) the instrumental phase, in which key issues of allocation involving economic means and objectives tend to predominate with emphasis on "production," "accomplishment" and the like (e.g., 1932 and the New Deal's completion of the building of the corporate state);

(d) the integrative phase, dominated by proliferation of diverse groups whose members tend increasingly to act on the belief that they are being illegitimately deprived of leverage on the political system, that—compared with "the others"—they are suffering from fraternal relative deprivation.[9]

Namenwirth himself is careful to insist that this effort represents a first effort in the longitudinal analysis of value-configurations in American politics, and that neither his modal wave patterns nor his interpretations ought to be viewed mechanistically or deterministically.[10] Nevertheless, the temporal congruence of his long-term peaks in value-change with disruptive change in mass voting behavior and other characteristics of the political system is extraordinarily close. It corresponds also to the more qualitative findings of historians of the political formula in the United States. Thus, it is not surprising to find that historians of Jacksonian-era politics find it necessary to begin with the "integrative" conflicts over enfranchisement in the 1818-1821 period and move on to discuss the crucial importance of the Anti-Masonic movement—America's first third party—in the evolution of mass politics in the Northeast.[11] Similarly, historians of the Civil War/Reconstruction era have stressed—especially recently—the rigidity and absolutism

[9] This latter phase has a peak, according to Namenwirth, occurring in or around 1970; according to our analysis, in a crisis sequence which has not been marked by critical realignment, at least in its traditional form.

[10] Namenwirth, op. cit., 683.

[11] The best single treatment of these conflicts for a single important state remains Lee Benson, The Concept of Jacksonian Democracy: New York as a Test Case (Princeton: Princeton University Press, 1961), especially 1-46. See also Ronald P. Formisano, "Deferential-Participant Politics: The Early Republic's Political Culture, 1789-1840," American Political Science Review, Vol. 68, 473-487 (1974).

of value-polarizations and the corresponding psychic energy released, great enough to create and sustain for a generation a national system of mass political mobilization never seen before or
since, and to sustain a Southern political tradition which has survived even to the present day.

One may oversimplify the dominant agendas of national politics
as follows. The revolutionary struggle in the 1770s dealt with the
issue of creating an independent political entity. The conflicts of
the proto-Jacksonian era involved the emergence of mass democracy
and its partisan structures, which—in an agrarian context—meant
a dispersal of power over the political economy of the country from
the center to the peripheries. The critical-realignment sequence
of 1854-1860 inaugurated a chain of events which overthrew a
social system, were fundamental to a nation-building breakthrough
in the United States, and organized values in terms of the axioms
of free labor, "enterprise" and national unity. The disruptions of
the 1890s regenerated a majority for a Republican party which was
unambiguously in favor of economic development and "modernization" under the only organizable auspices of the time—industrially
concentrated private enterprise. Out of this realignment sequence
came the dominant political image of elites during the next generation—the business corporation as a model of efficiency, rationality
and progress for the whole political order.[12] Operationally, major
strides—not without conflicts and heartburnings—were made toward
the establishment of corporatist structures of negotiation and accommodation between politics and the dominant structures of the
industrial economy. This movement was enormously accelerated
by the collapse of the market economy in 1929. Out of this immense dislocation, the ascendancy of interest-group liberalism—
the operational conversion of Locke's individual into Locke's group
—was consolidated and broadened to incorporate organized labor
and, increasingly, government agencies as interest groups in their
own right. Yet, as Lowi has pointed out, this conversion in turn
generated accumulating problems of integration and legitimation.[13]

[12] The corporate ideal comes out very clearly in the "bible of Progressivism,"
Herbert Croly's *The Promise of American Life* (New York: Macmillan, 1909).
It is of course not surprising that Republican platforms stress the archaic,
provincial and incompetent character of the Democratic coalition and leadership continuously from 1896 through the 1920s.

[13] Theodore Lowi, *The End of Liberalism* (New York: Norton, 1969),
especially 68-97.

By the late 1960s and 1970s new waves of demand for participation
—polarization around Namenwirth's integrative value-dimension—
broke through the barriers of the "old politics," and the stage
seemed set for a new critical realignment.

Certainly, it may be said that down through the 1940s at any
rate, these upheavals were directly associated with successful revitalizations of the American self-regulation value norm: broaden-
ing the base of participatory inclusion in politics, redefining the
nature of the union and the political economy, adapting to the
organizational imperatives of industrial capitalism, and converting
self-regulation from the normative level of the individual to that
of the group. These revitalizations, to people living through the
times in which they occurred, were in every sense problematic.
They arose out of acute decay, of manifest dissynchronization between traditionally-held, generationally-conditioned beliefs and
major events which produced widespread anxiety and, in the words
of the social psychologists, cognitive dissonance. The regularity
with which third-party uprisings and other forms of protest broke
into the open in the early stages of these crises reflected not only
the overt unwillingness or capacity of established party and governmental leadership to cope with urgent demands. They also reflected, negatively, upon the great constituent importance of the
two major parties, and of the two-party system, in the American
governmental scheme. The resolution of these crises was, correspondingly, associated with the disappearance of these movements
and protests, and an effectively unchallenged resumption of the
two-party system's hegemony over electoral politics and elite recruit-
ment. Much has been written, and accurately enough, on the importance of institutional factors—for example, the indivisible, separately elected executive and the first-past-the-post electoral regime
—in contributing to the suppression of third-party movements. But
the durable historic hegemony of the two-party system ultimately
rested upon two more central factors. In the first place, it was
possible to achieve an operational consensus, accepted by the large
majority of the electorate, on the new agendas and priorities of
politics which were laid down in the wake of a revitalized self-
regulation norm structure. Secondly, the transition from mass politics to interest-group politics was greatly assisted after 1900 by an
enormous decline in participation and a wide-spread liquidation of
party competition. This was partly the result of outright force (as
in the South), partly the consequence of restrictive legislation set-

ting up hurdles for would-be voters, and partly a "pure," if complex and controverted, behavioral phenomenon.[14]   Partisan linkages which did not fit this new semi-elitist dispensation tended to evaporate; the business consensus of the "system of 1896" thus rested upon an *organizable* electorate, and upon *organizable* political issues.   The result was an electorate which was proportionately much smaller, and skewed much more toward the upper end of the class structure, than it had been since the participation controversies of the 1820s.   Nevertheless, if at some considerable price, the agendas of the new model of self-regulation did achieve consensus and legitimacy, as did the model which replaced it in the 1930s.

The processes involved here, at least viewed very broadly at the macro level, have striking similarities with processes of revolutionary change sketched by Chalmers Johnson,[15] and—for the specialized world of scientific research communities—by Thomas R. Kuhn.[16]   Each of these authors suggests a five-stage model of decay and restabilization.   Kuhn's model is by now well known to political scientists: scientific revolutions arise from the very dynamics of the enterprise and the finite limitedness of any given paradigm within which research is carried on.   Beginning with a "normal science" situation, with its attendant puzzle-solvings and textbooks, we proceed to a stage in which anomalies are discovered; then to a situation where anomalies pile up to the point where the credibility of the paradigm is undermined and a "scientific crisis"— complete with manifest signs of individual cognitive dissonance among researchers—develops.   This crisis deepens until, in a condition of acute and widespread intellectual contradiction, a scientific revolution, a reintegration of the conceptual map of the field, takes

---

[14] One of the most recent examinations of the issues involved in this demobilization is to be found in the colloquy between the present author and Professors Philip E. Converse and Jerrold G. Rusk. See Philip E. Converse, "Change in the American Electorate," in Angus Campbell and Philip E. Converse, eds., *The Human Meaning of Social Change* (New York: Russell Sage Foundation, 1972), especially 263-337; Walter Dean Burnham, "Theory and Voting Research: Some Reflections on Converse's 'Change in the American Electorate,'" *American Political Science Review*, Vol. 68, 1002-1023 (1974); and Jerrold G. Rusk, "Comment: The American Electoral Universe: Speculation and Evidence," *ibid.*, 1028-1049.

[15] Chalmers Johnson, *Revolutionary Change* (Boston: Little, Brown, 1966), especially 59-118.

[16] Thomas R. Kuhn, *The Structure of Scientific Revolutions*, 2nd ed. (Chicago: University of Chicago Press, 1970).

place under the aegis of a single individual of outstanding genius. The revolution, if it occurs at all and if it succeeds, leads to a new integrative paradigm. Researchers can then go happily back to the laboratory to resume their puzzle-solving as a new "normal science" comes into being.[17]

Chalmers Johnson, borrowing from the anthropologist Anthony Wallace's work on the Iroquois Indians, finds a very similar pattern of upheaval.[18] The key concepts here are those of "mazeways" and "revitalization." Any social system has institutions of socialization out of which individuals acquire a patterned set of beliefs and expectations about their society and their place in it. Presuming that these mazeways provide relevant and accurate cues by which individuals can achieve their objectives in society, a "steady state" exists. In this steady state, the legitimacy of key social and political institutions is high—often taken for granted—and deviant behavior, anomic or criminal, is limited. But this steady state can be disrupted either by the unevenly-distributed effects of endogenous socio-economic development or by massive shocks created by exogenous stimuli. A leading example of the former is the impaction of industrialization upon a society (conspicuously, upon its agrarian sectors). Examples of the latter would include defeat in war or the effects of neocolonialist economic penetration of traditional societies by economically developed countries. If the resultant crisis is sufficiently pervasive, the society (and a growing number of individuals in it) will move into a condition of increased stress, and thence into a state of cultural distortion. At this stage, the traditional mazeways disintegrate, with a severe contradiction between the cues given by the older norms and the setting of social action to which the individual attempts to apply them. Increasing numbers of individuals, finding the dissonance psychologically intolerable, respond in three primary ways: by criminal deviance,

---

[17] Kuhn also makes the point that older-generation scientists committed to the original paradigm are rarely converted to the new one. The revolution succeeds as it is internalized by the young in the field, who have much less to lose, and as the old die off. A very similar generational pattern seems to exist in critical realignments, including that of the 1930s for which limited retrospective survey information is available. See Angus Campbell, Philip E. Converse, Warren E. Miller and Donald E. Stokes, *The American Voter* (New York: Wiley, 1960), 154. One infers the existence of a phenomenon which in the world of politics might be called "political desocialization."

[18] Johnson, *op. cit.*, especially 108-112.

by withdrawal into passive anomie, and by joining protest-oriented mass movements. Measurable indicators of these "pathologies" will show strong tendencies to increase.

At this stage, assuming that the governing elite cannot or will not cope effectively with this accumulated stress, it is likely to be confronted with a situation of power deflation—a loss of control through previously customary means associated with a decline in its political legitimacy. Assuming that the society does not disintegrate altogether under the stress, the response (typically, though not always, led by a successful counterelite) will be the development of a *revitalization movement* led by a charismatic leader. At the center of this movement's success is its leadership's ability to propose and enforce a radically new ideology and, through it, to define new mazeways of right belief and right action through which the personality of the individual-in-society can be reintegrated. Presuming the success of such a movement in achieving hegemony over the society at large, and the success of its value-transformations in reshaping the basic institutions and norms of the society, the revolution will become institutionalized and routinized; a new steady state will evolve out of it.

The Johnson-Wallace theory of transformational change makes, as it should, ample allowance for the disruptive effect of externally-generated pressures. But both of the models discussed here focus heavily upon internal processes and growing internal contradictions as basic motive forces. In the case of American politics, we have suggested that there are several primordial realities which have influenced it across its history: the self-regulation axiom, the autonomy of socio-economic development from more than marginal political constraints in the normal case, and the tendency toward stasis in the political or steering mechanism. The historic American critical-realignment sequence emerged in a context where threatening external pressures were essentially non-existent. It was a dialectical process, involving a nonincremental eruption, the end product of which was the resynchronization of a dynamic socio-economic system and a static polity, a recovery of steering capacity, a revitalization (or "bringing up to date") of the operational and normative aspects of self-regulation and, hence, the relegitimation and restabilization of the political economy.

The parallelism between the stable-state/realignment dynamic which has so marked American political history and the models of revolutionary change suggested above is consequently not fortuitous.

It arises from the basic principles of action in a "Tudor polity" dominated by an enduring normative hostility to the public sector and most ranges of collective action. The dialectic involved here, not so paradoxically, has worked so clearly because both Marxists and pluralists have been wrong in their assessments and predictions: the Marxists because, for reasons Hartz and others have stressed, the sociological bases for enduring, effectively organized radical political action have not existed in the United States; and the pluralists since, if the political system and its established elites were at any given time as receptive to emerging demand as their analysis claims, the periodic critical realignment sequence as such would probably never have come into being at all.

III

There seems abundant empirical evidence to support two propositions which bear on the present and probable near future of American politics, and which vitally relate to critical realignment and the party system. The first of these is that the United States is currently involved in a crisis of the value system which is at least as profound as any of its predecessors, and very possibly more so. Out of this crisis has arisen the problem of what Samuel P. Huntington, with some whimsy, calls a "democratic distemper,"[19] associated with a serious loss of steering capacity at the center and a major decline in public-opinion support for the leading political and economic institutions of the society. The second argument is that the critical-realignment sequence—at least as historically understood—has ceased to exist and, so far as one can tell, no adequate substitute mechanism for adapting political action to the effects of change in society and economy has even appeared on the horizon as yet. The two phenomena seem interrelated: the nature of the crises, conflicts and antagonistic mobilizations of recent years has been such as to destroy electoral coalitions which are capable of giving leadership broad-based support across divided institutional boundaries. The loss of such capabilities in turn stimulates a

[19] Huntington, "The Democratic Distemper," op. cit. The analysis which he and a number of his colleagues offer can be assimilated to the Johnson-Wallace model with astonishing ease. Their overwhelming preoccupation with authority and with maintenance of a status quo elite which is nowhere subject to serious criticism for its contributions to the state of affairs they deplore defines, it seems to me, where analysis ends and ideology begins.

spread of popular distrust of politics, politicians and parties. So far, the cycle has been feeding upon itself.

The ultimate causes for this collapse of the party system's role in the American political process are immensely complex, and they go back to the supplanting of mass politics by interest-group and technocratic politics in the first decade of this century. More proximately, however, we can point to two overwhelming changes in the context of American politics, changes which in effect destroyed two implicit boundary conditions within which the traditional constitutional structure had functioned.[20] The first of these was the final collapse of relatively unregulated market capitalism in 1929, and the overthrow of the preceding, dominantly laissez-faire, value synthesis. This was replaced by a consolidation of interest-group liberalism both as an operational code for public-policy formation and as a logic of justification among academic political scientists. The second of these boundary conditions to be destroyed was, of course, that of isolation from credible external threat to national security. In its place, historically, almost in the twinkling of an eye, emerged an imperial military-bureaucratic structure under the control of a President who was essentially liberated from any domestic checks and balances. And the end product of this was the Vietnam war. These two fundamental changes in the contexts of American politics, were of course reinforced by an ongoing technological revolution and by the tendency of the dominant sectors of the political economy to grow into multinational scope and complexity. They have created an intolerable stress between the autonomist voluntarism of the traditional American political and social code and the "real world" which Americans experience in their daily lives.

The state in the contemporary political economy is responsible for doing two primary things: promoting capital accumulation at home and preventing as far as possible the emergence of threats to capital abroad; and maintaining social harmony. In the empirical world of American politics from 1945 through the early 1960s, both

[20] Another old-time institutionalist was the first to develop this point in a systematic way as it related to presidential power, and as long ago as 1941. See E. S. Corwin, "Some Aspects of the Presidency," *The Annals*, Nov. 1941, 122-131. Reprinted as "The Aggrandizement of Presidential Power," in Robert S. Hirschfield, ed., *The Power of the Presidency*, 2nd ed. (Chicago: Aldine, 1973), 245-258.

objectives were more or less successfully accomplished—at home through pluralist policies which were the outcome of negotiations and conflicts among organized peak groups over a circumscribed range of regulatory and allocation issues; and abroad through the anti-Communist consensus.

To an overwhelming extent, this accomplishment rested upon two negative bases. First, in the real world of pluralist politics the effective working of a complex and non-sovereign political system depends upon excluding from the game segments of the population whose entry would require a major change in the play. Second, chiefly in foreign policy issues, success in maintaining harmony is dependent upon an elite consensus extending across institutional boundaries, upon excluding foreign policy from serious debate as a partisan issue, and upon the skill of elites in avoiding diastrous and culturally indefensible mistakes. Both of these negative conditions were shredded away during the 1960s, as the federal government moved into a much broader range of domestic policy intervention and into the disastrous Vietnam adventure.

This power implosion or deflation was an extremely complicated thing. It has given rise to an immense literature of analysis and explanation. A good deal of it tends to confuse symptoms or consequences (the New Left uprising in the universities for example) with underlying causes. As to the identity of the latter, the literature appears to speak with the tongues of Babel. What might these causes be? Three lines of analysis might prove fruitful in dealing with this question.

(1) The stakes in maintaining social harmony through public policy were systematically raised after about 1960, and at the same time the efforts to achieve it were systematically distorted and undermined by the practical workings of interest-group liberalism. The raising of the stakes is associated chiefly with the changes in the international and domestic contexts of black Americans, and with the cumulative collapse of the legitimacy of the "racial settlement" which had been consolidated early in the twentieth century. From the initial civil-rights struggles radiated waves of basic challenges to the traditional American political way of doing business. The courts acted, first in the field of school segregation, subsequently in apportionment and voting-rights cases and further afield, in response to the paralysis which gripped the elected policymaking branches of government. This, and subsequent congressional legislation, destroyed the Southern home rule which had been a cardi-

nal part of all preceding American politics since 1877 (emphatically including the New Deal). This had devastating consequences for the Democratic presidential coalition and volatilized the Southern "periphery" into hostility against the "center."

Apart from this major change in official evaluation of constitutional rights, poverty was "discovered" in the early 1960s. This reflected growing liberal concern with the reality that the United States has, in Gunnar Myrdal's phrase, the largest, most disorganized social infrastructure to be found anywhere in the western world. But this poverty has become increasingly identified since World War II with the inhabitants of cities, the nerve centers of the political economy; and in particular with black and Spanish-speaking minorities suffering from multiple deprivations. Categorical programs undertaken to deal with these poverty issues developed *pari passu* with, and in response to, the rise of militancy and group pressure on the political process among black urbanites.

Once again, interest-group liberalism functions as it typically has in the past. It responds with policy to meet the demands of organized groups, but it does so by ignoring the countervailing claims of other people not as effectively organized and with one crucial limitation. Since the basic structures of power, status and ownership in the society are not to be significantly changed to meet the demands of low-status people, the response to such claims will tend to be rhetorically sweeping but operationally quite limited and even within that range—for vital structural reasons—inadequate and disappointing in its actual effects. The result of this is that low-status people who do not qualify on economic or racial criteria for largesse will believe themselves to be the victims of illegitimate discrimination. They will believe as well—with excellent reason—that liberal intellectual and political elites are making them bear the lion's share of the social costs of change. Low-status people who do qualify, on the other hand, will find that rhetoric far outstrips real performance and that their basic poverty problems are virtually as intractable as ever. In such a context, the extension of the scope of public-sector activity for the sake of promoting social harmony will have the effect of multiplying group conflicts, of cumulatively eroding the political base for liberal-activist initiatives, and of eroding belief in the justice and efficacy of public-sector activity as such.

(2) It is a commonplace to observe that a peculiar mob psychology tends to emerge among businessmen and the public generally

during a protracted economic boom.[21] People come to believe that prosperity can last forever; the psychology involved tends to move toward "go-go," with the increasing acceptance of the proposition that money is a quasi-free good and that all sorts of infinite possibilities exist for achieving wealth on a mass basis and in the near term. Typically, when this boom is followed by a bust, conservative principles are recalled, the money-changers and the gamblers are condemned and a kind of retrenchment hangover dominates the public mood. During the post-1929 hangover, business, banking and Wall Street were the villains of the morality play, in rough proportion as they and the political elites who supported them had claimed in the earlier boom to be the sole creators and managers of perpetual prosperity.

Between 1945 and 1969—and particularly in the 1961-1969 period —the United States had a uniquely sustained boom. There was a major difference with the experience of forty years earlier: *This time, the state and the public sector were much more heavily involved in the boom.* Domestic expenditures on social capital and social expenses in welfare, education and other programs underwent an enormous expansion after 1961. Of course, much of this expenditure was "wasteful"; so were gambling on the stock market and the lending practices of the country's largest banks. But granted the axiomatic acceptance of free enterprise in the political culture and a parallel distrust of governmental expenditures, the post-1969 retrenchment hangover involved a major and growing public reaction against public-sector extravagance, and a growing belief that political institutions and the men who work them cannot cope with the problems of the political economy. The theory of interest-group liberalism has no capacity to develop a serious critique of the mixed state-private capitalist system. Hence there is in this political formula no capacity to develop a coherent program for sustained management or planning with some general interest in mind. So it has also happened that liberals have largely accepted the bankruptcy of government activism and, in the mid-1970s, frequently reveal themselves to have perspectives on policy which are nearly indistinguishable from those of conservatives.

[21] The best recent popular discussions of this mood are found in John K. Galbraith, *The Great Crash 1929* (Boston: Houghton Mifflin, 3rd ed., 1972) and, for the post-1961 boom, John Brooks, *The Go-Go Years* (New York: Weybright and Talley, 1973).

(3) It is also by now a commonplace to observe that the United States was led into the Vietnam quagmire by activist liberals, led by presidents who relied upon a small elite of "the best and the brightest." The moral debacle which this war generated is difficult to overestimate either in terms of its intensity or its longer-range effects. As protest mounted, the protestors found that this part of the American political system was stoutly resistant to their demands for their claims that the extent of death and destruction which the United States inflicted on Vietnam vastly outweighed any legitimate assertion of the country's national interest. The radicalization which ensued was confined in its most extreme forms to a small minority of the population; but that minority was strategically concentrated in the academic and professional communities. The resulting disruptions, mobilizations and countermobilizations were enormous. The defeat of the peace movement and the nomination of Hubert Humphrey in 1968 by the Democrats in Chicago was so laced with illegitimacy that it was not only possible to elect Richard Nixon but to transform radically the selection procedures of the Democratic party and to pave the way for the further disruption of the Democratic presidential coalition in 1972.

Perhaps the most important constituent element which has been thrown into the melting-pot of liquidation is the party system itself. The practical consequences of interest-group liberalism in its activist phase have been the jamming up of the system through a wavelike proliferation of intense group demands for (or against) change through public policy and a demonstration of true limits of "pluralism" in representing the public at large. Where the parties have not been actual promoters of official activities regarded widely, and for different reasons, as illegitimate, they have been seen to be irrelevant to what actually happens. Federal judges are seen to displace elected officials and take charge of school systems. A consortium of bankers, business executives and budget experts is seen to depose the elected officials of the country's largest city. A president is seen to stage his re-election wholly outside of his party and to abuse his authority to the point where he is restrained not at all by his party but by a Congress very reluctantly performing its constitutional duty.

The situation in 1976 can be summarized quite briefly. The present structure of public opinion concerning the chief institutions of the political economy reveals the lowest level of trust in and support of such institutions and the men who run them ever recorded in the history of surveys. It is exaggerating only slightly to say that as of early 1976 modal support exists within the electorate for the following propositions.[22] The United States, politically, is a plutocracy. It is governed conspiratorially by a closely interconnected political and economic power elite. The objective of this elite is to promote the welfare of the haves at the expense of the have-nots. This elite's rule is maintained by hypocrisy and by systematic lying to the people. The government is both confused and incompetent; it spends money to buy off vocal groups, but the money simply fuels inflation without solving the problems involved.[23]

Very obviously, it is easy to overstate both the extent and intensity of this alienation, and in particular to draw a picture of public opinion which suggests it to be much more clear and structured than in fact it is. It is also vitally important in any analysis of this opinion to recall two other points. In the first place, surveys continue regularly to show that the large bulk of the population continues its support for the governmental system as system, expressing hope that it can be made to work well somehow and

[22] The most recent evidence for this is contained in two articles, one by Christopher Lydon in The New York Times, February 1, 1976, 1, 35, and the other by Norman Miller in The Wall Street Journal, February 2, 1976, 1, 13. Items from pollsters in the latter article include the following: 65% believe that "most politicians don't really care about me" (Caddell); 58% believe that "people with power are out to take advantage of me" (Harris); 49% believe that "quite a few of the people running the government are a little crooked" (Market Opinion Research); 68% believe that "over the last 10 years, this country's leaders have consistently lied to the American people" (Caddell); 57% believe that "both the Democratic and Republican parties are in favor of big business rather than the average worker" (Hart). It is obvious that such levels of alienated response are of recent origin. See, e.g. the time series for 1966-1973 in the Louis Harris survey for the U. S. Senate, Confidence and Concern: Citizens View American Government (Committee on Government Operations, U. S. Senate, 93rd Cong., 1st Sess. [Dec. 3, 1973]), especially Part 1, 28-35.

[23] " 'A substantial 69% believe that government spending is a major cause of inflation,' Louis Harris says. Most people fear that 'simply legislating new programs that employ more people and spend more money may not in the end solve anything and will create a bloated, seemingly permanently in-place bureaucracy.' " Miller, op. cit., 13. Caddell finds that, in 1974, 12% of the voting-age population believed that their vote mattered and actually went out and voted; for another 25%, voting was a "spectator sport," and 63% did not vote at all—the lowest off-year turnout since 1942 and, outside the South, the second lowest off-year turnout of all time.

at some time. Second, a crucially important point made by Chalmers Johnson should be borne in mind. A political system may be in a condition of severe disequilibrium or even "cultural distortion" without revitalization necessarily occurring. People cannot and will not fully repudiate their existing regime and norms associated with it unless a structured alternative, a counter-ideology developed by counter-elites and entrepreneurs, is available. People in the main will not take leaps into the dark, more or less regardless of how unsatisfactory the present may seem to them. To the extent that the consensus theorists are correct in their assessments of American political culture, it would follow that no structured alternative to one or another possible variant of a self-regulation ground norm can exist. Perhaps more accurately, no such alternative can exist until some indeterminate point is reached at which the contradictions between socio-economic development and cultural axioms are so acute and so anxiety-conducive that Americans are impelled to look elsewhere than to self-regulation as their universalistic ground norm.

There is scant reason, so far as the evidence of surveys tells us, to assume that mass opinion has arrived anywhere near such a point. On the other hand, the literature of malaise among American intellectuals is now becoming extensive, and is increasingly oriented to the precise problem of the political and social formula, the *Grundnorm*. Books are written on the decline of authority, political ungovernability, the end of the party system and the dissolution of the melting pot by the interaction of its human ingredients.[24] Secretaries of State give speeches which could well have been ghost-written by Oswald Spengler. Professor Lowi defines *The End of Liberalism,* i.e., the dissolution of the *Grundnorm*. George Cabot Lodge, a prominent figure in the Republican party and a professor at Harvard Business School, argues that Lockian liberalism is manifestly dead as a political formula, that neither business nor any other institution in the political economy can now function successfully because they lack an adequate normative context, and that a "new American ideology" is called for.[25]

[24] See, *e.g.,* Robert Nisbet, *Twilight of Authority* (New York: Oxford, 1975); David Broder, *The Party's Over* (New York: Harper & Row, 1972); Nathan Glazer and Daniel P. Moynihan, *Beyond the Melting Pot,* 2nd edition (Cambridge: MIT Press, 1970), "Introduction: New York City in 1970."

[25] George Cabot Lodge, *The New American Ideology* (New York: Knopf, 1975).

Professor Daniel Bell argues, in a vein very reminiscent of Joseph Schumpeter, that the normative integuments which support the system are being dissolved by its (and their) internal contradictions.[26] Perhaps the most remarkable aspect of this spate of literature is that it has come overwhelmingly from a conservative, order- and authority-preoccupied intellectual elite, a great many of whose members began their careers on the left end of the American political spectrum. One looks in vain for a comparable literature of trenchant defense of interest-group liberalism, its practitioners and its programs.

IV

Decay in the binding force of a *Grundnorm* entails—at least under conditions of continuing pluralism and democratic consent —decay in the performance of key political institutions. We have argued here and elsewhere that the periodically-recurring critical-realignment sequence was, historically, the chief means by which an essentially static politics could be re-integrated with an enormously dynamic socio-economic system. It depended for its existence, as did the major political parties in their traditional form, upon the possibility for revitalizing the basic self-regulation axiom. This was done by operationally redefining its main terms in such a way as to restore its apparent relevance to the new conditions in society and economy produced by long-term dynamic change. Thus, premises which were regarded as liberating and energizing in the Jacksonian era came, in the industrial America of the post-1896 period, to be regarded as reflecting the interests of a reactionary and provincial agrarian-colonial sector in the new political economy. It was, ultimately, this capacity for normative revitalization which made possible the agreement upon agenda priorities—and the disagreement between parties over the policies to be followed in dealing with those priorities—on which critical realignments and the conflicts between parties rested.

In all probability, we have now reached a point where the critical-realignment sequence in its traditional form must be relegated to the history books. If this assessment is correct, it means that a vital instrument by which the steering mechanism adapts to change while maintaining the uneasy coexistence between democracy and state-

[26] Daniel Bell, *The Cultural Contradictions of Capitalism* (New York: Basic Books, 1976.)

private capitalism has probably disappeared. Any such view rests upon several assumptions. First, the interest-group-liberal variant of the self-regulation axiom has definitively exhausted itself. Second, no earlier variant—say, the neo-laissez-faire which is preached by some candidates and some scholars in 1976—can cope with the objective allocation problems of this political economy at its present level of development. Third, no creative renewal of the self-regulation *Grundnorm* is likely to occur. It is my own view that the first two assumptions are almost certainly valid, and the third is probably valid as well. To the extent that this assessment of the situation is correct, it follows that the political parties and the electoral process have lost the normative underpinnings on which they and the electorate's constituent (*i.e.*, constitution-redefining) role in the political process historically rested.

In a context such as this, certain essential ingredients of the current American electoral puzzle fall into a coherent pattern. For example, one of the most significant elements in this puzzle has been the growth of the far right in political influence and power since the great Goldwater breakthrough of 1964. This has been associated, chronologically and otherwise, with the breakup of the Democratic presidential coalition, and the ineffectiveness among candidates on the party's left which was so conspicuous as the 1976 presidential season got under way. Moreover, the 1968 candidacy of George Wallace represents the first significant third-party protest since the Civil War to emerge from the right rather than the left end of the American political spectrum.

A point which is frequently made by students of cultures under stress is that "revitalization movements"—analogous to Toynbee's "savior with a time machine"—may be either archaistic or futuristic according to the specific historical and cultural situaton in which they take root. Flight into an hypostasized past appears particularly to appeal to members of a threatened middle class under modern conditions of stress, involving as this stress does the threat of total loss of traditional socio-economic status and of essential cultural values.[27] Revolutionary-futuristic revitalization, on the

[27] The literature on the rise of fascism and Nazism in the 1930s has long stressed this point. See William S. Allen, *The Nazi Seizure of Power* (Chicago: Quadrangle, 1965). For another discussion, see Walter Dean Burnham, "Political Immunization and Political Confessionalism: The United States and Weimar Germany," *Journal of Interdisciplinary History*, Vol. 3, 1-30 (Summer 1972).

other hand, is a particularly remote possibility in a culture whose basic axioms have been perennially hostile to mass collective action. One can imagine a radical breakthrough in consciousness as the self-regulation axiom reaches exhaustion in a political economy which is empirically collectivized; but this would necessarily be limited to a very small group of intellectuals and activists. Entrepreneurs—both academic and political—whose rhetoric calls the anxious and the threatened to join in a crusade for the restoration of ancient political and economic truths would seem to have an overwhelming advantage over such contenders in appealing to mass opinion. Whether they will have a decisive advantage over the moderate liberals and moderate conservatives who defend the status quo remains to be seen. But in broad outline, one could suspect that the immediate prospect for American politics is an oscillation back and forth between interest-group liberalism and more archaic variants of the self-regulation axiom. This implies that the authority problem which so concerns Professor Huntington and his associates will remain a problem. And it would be reasonable to suppose that at some point authoritarians might propose definitive solutions to it, and that an apathetic and shrunken electorate might endorse those solutions.

There is one central aspect of the American *Grundnorm* which must not be lost sight of. The self-regulation axiom has been the only indigenous formula for preserving both concentrated bigness in government and political economy on one hand and political democracy on the other. As many observers of American politics have pointed out, the basic axiom of the political culture—in whatever generational variant—has insisted upon the cardinal proposition that capitalism and political democracy are compatible with each other, and both are equally necessary.[28] But empirically, the

---

[28] This is well set forth, so far as business ideology is concerned, in Francis X. Sutton *et al.*, *The American Business Creed* (Cambridge: Harvard University Press, 1956), especially 19-52. The argument continues to be made by intellectuals virtually *in haec verba*: see Irving Kristol, "On Corporate Capitalism in America," *The Public Interest*, No. 41 (Fall 1975), 124-141. But the argument cuts both ways. Precisely this linkage in our conventional norm structure has historically worked to prevent certain possible, more authoritarian resolutions of the tensions between the concentration of economic power and the potential threat to it which the existence of political democracy incorporates. The survival of this nexus in the normative structure is one of the most problematic questions confronting American politics in the last quarter of the century.

transformations in American political economy after the 1890s entailed, as we have suggested, a long-term movement toward redefining democracy in ever more elitist terms and in skewing the responses of the political system toward the organized-producer end of the social structure. The demands of empire abroad and concentrated, interpenetrated bigness of organization at home have made the democratic element in the system still more problematic. These demands can be expected both to continue and to intensify.

The collapse of the self-regulation axiom as consensual norm necessarily involves not only the decay of institutional performance and the authority crisis of which we have heard so much. It also involves a decay in support, particularly among executive elites and neo-conservative intellectuals, for traditional democratic values in the political system. For the latter, the key questions are those of accumulating enough power resources to carry through policies designed to protect and promote the interests of the basic institutions of the political economy at home and abroad. The chief adversaries who stand in the way of this quest are those discontented elements of the public who mobilize in opposition to these policies, whose opposition tends to defeat the effort to accumulate power. Lost to view in all this is the equally important point that the present crisis is also a crisis of democratic values and practices. This aspect of the crisis cannot be resolved without a thoroughgoing transformation of the structures of electoral politics, and a remobilization of the more than half of the citizenry who are outside the universe of active citizenship. In turn, such a transformation must depend upon an effective revitalization of the political culture, one which achieves an effective reintegration of democratic and egalitarian values.

Without such a revitalization—without, if one will, a new kind of critical realignment which gives genuine constituent force to the electorate's role in the political system—two political alternatives are very likely to present themselves. These are the continuation of electorally-reinforced institutional deadlock, with incoherent and unstable policy initiatives and implementations; or a resumption of the thrust toward authoritarian executive-bureaucratic control which culminated in the Nixon presidency. And the neo-conservatives are almost certainly right in their belief that the former of these alternatives is too fundamentally defective to be viable for very long in the world of concentrated power and steering needs in which we now live. If the restoration of authority cannot be brought about through a renewal of democracy in a post self-regulation age, it will be brought about in some other fashion.   In such case, one need not expect that the traditional instrumentalities of electoral politics will have much part of play or, perhaps, that any organized successors will come into being.

The future of political democracy in the United States is thus bound up with the conclusion which Louis Hartz reached twenty years ago: "What is at stake is nothing less that a new level of consciousness, a transcending of irrational Lockianism, in which an understanding of self and an understanding of others go hand in hand."[29]   In the two decades which have passed since these words were written, much has happened to dissolve the binding force of this irrational Lockianism on American culture and on American politics, with consequences which we have explored here.   Whether transcendence or new levels of consciousness are being achieved is a much more doubtful proposition.   What is clear is that, as the United States celebrates its bicentennial, it is passing through one of the great transitions in its political history.   The wresting of as much freedom and individual self-realization as possible from the grip of necessity remains as problematic and as essential a human activity as it has ever been in the course of that history.

---

[29] Louis Hartz, *The Liberal Tradition in America, op. cit.,* 308.

Judicial Review:
Vagaries and Varieties

RORERT J. HARRIS

WHEN ALEXANDER HAMILTON in the seventy-eighth number of the Federalist[1] and John Marshall in *Marbury v. Madison*[2] founded judicial review upon the solid rock of popular sovereignty in order to curb popular government they performed an ingenious and prodigious feat. After comparing the people and Congress with principal and agent to affirm the supremacy of the Constitution over a statute, Hamilton confidently observed that this conclusion did not "by any means suppose a superiority of the judicial to the legislative power. It only supposes that the power of the people is superior to both." Reflecting generally after the manner of men of principle and substance of the time, he proceeded further to justify judicial review as a protection against the "ill humours which the arts of designing men . . . sometimes disseminate among the people themselves," and as a guard against the "cabals of a representative body." Popular sovereignty for Hamilton was a useful argumentative artifice, but in other ways Hamilton's enthusiasm for it was carefully restrained. Like Hamilton, Marshall based judicial review upon the supremacy of the people and the Constitution which was a product of their will. Thus he emphasized the "original right" of the people to establish such principles as "shall most conduce to their own hap-

---

[1] Jacob E. Cooke, ed., *The Federalist* (Middletown, Connecticut: Wesleyan University Press, 1961), 525, 527.

[2] 1 Cr. 137, 175-180 (1803). The view that the Constitution was ordained and established by the whole people of the United States is a recurring theme in some of Marshall's greatest opinions. See especially *McCulloch v. Maryland*, 4 Wheat. 316 (1819); *Cohens v. Virginia*, 6 Wheat. 424 (1821); and *Gibbons v. Ogden*, 9 Wheat. 1 (1824).

piness" and through this "original and supreme will" to organize the
government and assign powers to its departments. To be sure,
Hamilton and Marshall were not the first to use popular sovereignty
as a device for curbing its exercise. The advocates of constitutional
reform in 1786 and 1787 skillfully exploited the concept after Shays'
Rebellion to correct the deficiencies of the Articles of Confederation, calm "the unsteadiness of the people," curb the excesses of
state legislatures and majorities generally, and thereby protect "the
worthy against the licentious."[3]

Unlike Hamilton and other protagonists of constitutional revision
Marshall made no invidious comments about the "ill humours" of
designing men, "the unsteadiness of the people," or "the cabals of
representative bodies," at least in his official opinions. As a corollary to the fiction that the Supreme Court is the supreme people
speaking, he created the fiction that "Judicial power as contradis-
tinguished from the power of the laws has no existence. Courts
are the mere instruments of the law, and can will nothing."[4] Accordingly, judicial power can act only when a question is submitted in a case, and a case arises only when a party asserts his
rights "in a form prescribed by law."[5] Justice George Sutherland
extended this idea to declare:

> From the authority to ascertain and determine the law in a given case, there
> necessarily results, in case of conflict, the duty to declare and enforce the
> supreme law and reject that of an inferior act of legislation which, transcend-
> ing the Constitution, is of no effect and binding upon no one. This is not
> the exercise of a substantive power to review and nullify acts of Congress, for
> no such substantive power exists. It is simply the necessary concomitant to
> the power to hear and dispose of a case or controversy properly before the
> court, to the determination of which must be brought the test and the measure
> of law.[6]

In a less sophisticated approach, Justice Owen J. Roberts reiterated
the same principle and proceeded to make judicial review a very
simple exercise. When an act of Congress is challenged as being
unconstitutional, he declared, "The judicial branch of the government has only one duty,—to lay the article of the Constitution

---

[3] Gordon S. Wood, *The Creation of the American Republic*, 1776-1787
(Chapel Hill: University of North Carolina Press, 1961), Chs. IX, XII, and
XIII, especially pages 532-536.
[4] *Osborn v. Bank of the United States*, 9 Wheat. 738, 866 (1824).
[5] *Ibid.*, 819.
[6] *Adkins v. Children's Hospital*, 261 U. S. 525, 544 (1923).

which is invoked beside the statute which is challenged and to decide whether the latter squares with the former." In so doing the Court's only power is "the power of judgment," and the Court "neither approves nor condemns any legislative policy."[7]

The fiction that courts are the mere instruments of the law without will or discretion encounters some difficulties in the interpretation of the Constitution according to its *true* meaning. Is the Constitution to be interpreted to meet changing conditions, or is it a static document, immutable and inviolable until amended as prescribed by Article V? There have been two answers to this question. Marshall saw the Constitution as being meant to endure for "ages to come, and consequently to be adapted to the various crises of human affairs."[8] To a similar effect is Justice Oliver Wendell Holmes' observation that the words of the Constitution "have called into life a being the development of which could not have been foreseen completely by the most gifted of its begeters. It was enough for them to realize or to hope that they had created an organism; it has taken a century and has cost their successors much sweat and blood to prove that they created a nation. The case before us must be considered in the light of our whole experience and not merely in that of what was said a hundred years ago."[9] It is rather obvious that the Marshall-Holmes view of a changing Constitution under judicial adaptation, whatever may be its conceded merits, is hardly consistent with the proposition that courts act without will or discretion.

The other answer propounded by Chief Justice Roger B. Taney and others, despite many disadvantages, is consistent with courts acting as automatons. In *Dred Scott v. Sandford*,[10] Chief Justice Taney regarded the Court's task as construing the Constitution "as it was understood at the time of its adoption" speaking "not only the same in words, but the same in meaning and intent" as when it came from the Framers. "Any other rule of construction would abrogate the judicial character of this court, and make it the mere reflex of the popular opinion or passion of the day." Similarly, Justice David J. Brewer could find that constitutional questions "are

---

[7] *United States v. Butler*, 297 U. S. 1, 62-63 (1936).

[8] *McCulloch v. Maryland*, 4 Wheat. 316, 407 (1819).

[9] *Missouri v. Holland*, 252 U. S. 416, 433-434 (1920). See also Justice William O. Douglas' opinion for the Court in *Harper v. Virginia Board of Elections*, 383 U. S. 663 (1966).

[10] 19 How. 393, 427 (1857).

not settled by even a consensus of present public opinion, for it is the peculiar value of a written constitution that it places in unchanging form limitations upon legislative action, and thus gives a permanence and stability to popular government which otherwise would be lacking."[11]   Thus Brewer not only affirmed his faith in an unchanging Constitution, but he echoed his precursors who feared the "unsteadiness of the people" and the "ill humours" of designing and artful men.   Indeed, Justice Brewer was more open in his expressions of fear of the mob than any other judge with the possible exception of his uncle, Justice Stephen J. Field.   He raised the spectre of "the black flag of anarchism, flaunting destruction of property" and "the red flag of socialism, inviting the redistribution of property."   He cited, too, "the danger from the multitude," and against these evils his remedy was to "strengthen the judiciary."[12]

An inevitable concomitant of the premise that the judges know the law and apply it without will or discretion is that judicial review has operated to create the further fiction that judicial decisions interpreting the Constitution are the authoritative Constitution. The Court itself has never expressly propagated this doctrine but has equated judicial decisions with the supreme law of the land,[13] an entirely different matter.   Indeed, given the number and frequency of reversals of precedents which began in Chief Justice Taney's term, the Court has never been in a position to assert such a dogma.[14]   It has been useful to persons and groups with a strong vested interest in a particular rule of decision.   The slavery interests used the fiction as a sanction for slavery.   Later, vested economic interests employed it to criticize the Court for massive reversals of earlier pro-business decisions from 1937 into the 1940s, as did the segregationists in 1954 and later to condemn the Court for departing from the Constitution which they identified with *Plessy v. Ferguson.*[15]

[11] *Muller v. Oregon,* 208 U. S. 412, 420 (1908).

[12] Address to the New York Bar Association (January, 1893), quoted in Alpheus T. Mason, *The Supreme Court from Taft to Warren* (rev. ed., Baton Rouge: Louisiana State University Press, 1968), 25-26.

[13] *United States v. Peters,* 5 Cr. 115 (1809); *Cooper v. Aaron,* 358 U. S. 1 (1958).

[14] For lists of overruled decisions see Justice Louis D. Brandeis' dissent in *Burnet v. Coronado Oil and Gas Co.,* 285 U. S. 393, 405-411 (1932); and the opinions of the Court in *Helvering v. Griffiths,* 318 U. S. 371, 401 (1943); and *Smith v. Allwright,* 321 U. S. 649 (1944).

[15] 163 U. S. 537 (1896).

One of the results of judicial revew is to invest private litigants and the federal courts with great power to control public policy and condemn federal and state legislation. Although the federal or state governments are parties in a majority of the suits challenging the validity of legislation, a significant number of these suits in other years involved only private litigants. In *Pollock v. Farmers' Loan & Trust Company*[16] a stockholder's suit challenged the income tax of 1894 in a petition for an injunction to restrain the company of which he was a stockholder from paying the tax. By leave of the Court, the United States filed a brief in support of the tax. In *Carter v. Carter Coal Co.*[17] an amicable family disagreement resulted in a suit for an injunction by a litigant against the company of which he was president to restrain the company from complying with the Bituminous Coal Act. The government appeared as a party only because it was joined as such in companion suits. In both instances the legislation challenged was invalidated. In *Fletcher v. Peck*,[18] the *Dartmouth College Case*,[19] and *Fairfax's Devisee v. Hunter's Lessee*[20] the Court rendered important constitutional decisions in purely private litigation. Another anomaly is that the states, for whose benefit the Tenth Amendment was presumably proposed and ratified, are in a less favorable position to challenge legislation as an invasion of their reserved powers than are private litigants.[21] In the Carter Coal case attorneys general or their representatives from the coal producing states filed briefs as *amici curiae* to defend the constitutionality of the law. The Court was more interested in the plea of the Carters than in the interests of the states most directly affected. *Ashton v. Cameron County Water Improvement District*[22] is an extreme example of the perversion of the Tenth Amendment to protect private rights at the expense of state interests. Here the Court in a five-to-four decision invalidated the Municipal Bankruptcy Act of 1934 which permitted local units of government to file bankruptcy proceedings, but only

---

[16] 157 U. S. 429 (1895).

[17] 298 U. S. 238 (1936). In suits challenging acts of Congress in private litigation the Judiciary Act of 1937 joins the United States as a party.

[18] 6 Cr. 87 (1810).

[19] *Trustees of Dartmouth College v. Woodward*, 4 Wheat. 518 (1819).

[20] 7 Cr. 603 (1813).

[21] *Massachusetts v. Mellon*, 262 U. S. 447, 484-485 (1923); see, however, *Missouri v. Holland*, 252 U. S. 416 (1920).

[22] 298 U. S. 513, 531 (1936).

with the consent of the state of which the local unit was a subdivi-
sion. After emphasizing the states as essential to the Union, Justice
James C. McReynolds declared that "Neither consent nor submission by the States can enlarge the power of Congress"; and that
"The sovereignty of the State essential to its proper functioning
under the Federal Constitution cannot be surrendered; it cannot
be taken away by any form of legislation." The Court also regarded state consent to such proceedings as an impairment of the
obligations of contract.

Such mysteries of judicial review, which are comparable to those
of theology, are not always so obvious in their actual exercise.
Between 1789 and 1976 the Court invalidated 105 acts of Congress
or provisions or applications thereof in 108 cases. In the same
period it invalidated more than 900 state statutes and local ordinances or sections or applications thereof. Neither in frequency,
nor incidence, nor importance has the course of judicial review
been even, but has been subject occasionally to abrupt fluctuations.
Roughly, the Court's invalidation of statutes falls into five periods:
(1) from 1789 to 1865, when the Court struck down only two acts
of Congress and 60 acts of state legislatures; (2) 1865-1888, when
sixteen acts of Congress and a larger number of state laws were
found bad; (3) 1888-1937, when the number of invalidations of
federal legislation increased by 54 to a total of 73 or 78, depending
upon the mode of counting, and 401 state or local invalidations;
(4) 1937-1953 when only three federal statutes were found defective and 95 state statutes fell; and (5) 1953-1976 when the Court
declared 25 provisions of acts of Congress invalid in 32 cases, and
when state invalidations approached 1000.[23] In contrast to these
data are the thousands of cases in which federal and state legislation was found constitutional. Even so, judicial review is essentially a destructive enterprise, for the Court can only veto or uphold,
it cannot legislate positively.

[23] For listings in whole or part of cases invalidating federal legislation, see
Edward S. Corwin, ed., The Constitution of the United States: Analysis and
Interpretation (Washington: Government Printing Office, 1953), 1241-1254;
Henry J. Abraham, The Judicial Process (rev. ed., New York: Oxford University Press, 1975), 288-293; William F. Swindler, Court and Constitution in
the 20th Century: The Old Legality, 1889-1932 (Indianapolis: Bobbs-Merrill
Co., 1969), 344-345. See also Benjamin F. Wright, The Growth of Constitutional Law (New York: Reynal & Hitchcock, 1942), passim for classifications
of many invalidations.

The two findings of statutory unconstitutionality prior to 1865 were totally unnecessary. In *Marbury v. Madison*,[24] Marshall deliberately distorted the thirteenth section of the Judiciary Act of 1789 to bring it into conflict with Article III of the Constitution and to hold that the Court had no jurisdiction of the suit after having decided its issues on their merits. This enterprise did provide him with the opportunity to lay down the justification of judicial review, although it had already been exercised in *Hylton v. United States*[25] where the Court reviewed the validity of an excise tax on carriages and sustained the tax on its merits. Similarly, Taney, as spokesman of the Court in the Dred Scott[26] case, held invalid that part of the Missouri Compromise which excluded slavery from designated territories of the United States, and made broad pronouncements that Negroes were not and could not, under the Constitution, be citizens of the United States or any state, only to conclude that the Court had no jurisdiction. With respect to state legislative power Marshall construed the prohibition against the impairment of contracts broadly and removed it from its historical context by extending it to include public as well as private contracts so as to give protection to legislative grants and corporate charters.[27] Thereafter, despite some relaxation of the rigors of the contracts clause by the Taney Court, it became one of the more prolific sources of judicial review of state legislation until the Twentieth Century.[28] Unlike Marshall, Taney and some of his coadjutors wrote occasional opinions which revealed their acute awareness of the distinction between the better and baser sorts of persons, especially immigrants. Thus, Justice Philip P. Barbour, in an immigration case, could affirm the power of a state "to provide precautionary measures against the moral pestilence of paupers, vagabonds, and possibly convicts" just as it could guard against "the physical pestilence" of infectious articles and persons.[29] Taney

---

24 1 Cr. 137 (1803).

25 3 Dall. 171 (1795).

26 *Dred Scott v. Sandford*, 19 How. 393 (1857). The case could have been decided on the authority of *Strader v. Graham*, 10 How. 82 (1850), without reaching the constitutional issues raised here.

27 *Fletcher v. Peck*, 6 Cr. 87 (1910); *Dartmouth College v. Woodward*, 4 Wheat. 518.

28 Wright, *Growth of Constitutional Law*, passim.

29 *Mayor of New York v. Miln*, 11 Pet. 102, 142 (1837).

was no less emphatic in his dissent in the *Passenger Cases*[30] in an effort to save a New York law seriously burdening the admission of aliens. He referred to the worst and most dangerous elements of the population and invoked the spectre of a "mass of pauperism and vice" flooding a state with tenants from their almshouses, or felons from their jails."[31]

With the end of the Civil War and Reconstruction judicial abstention after the pattern of the Marshall and Taney periods came to an end. Some of the more serious constitutional issues of the War never reached the Court and those that did were concerned primarily with presidential action.[31] The Court in one way or another avoided passing upon the constitutionality of congressional Reconstruction and wilted in the fierce heat of the fires kindled by War and Reconstruction.[32] Otherwise, judicial review underwent dramatic acceleration. For 23 years, between 1865 and 1888, the Court was finding its way, and its work was characterized neither by activism nor by extreme restraint. Of the 16 acts of Congress found invalid, the more important were the Test Oath Act of 1864,[33] the legal tender clauses in an act of 1862 in a case reversed soon afterwards,[34] the Enforcement Act of 1870 protecting the rights of Negroes to vote,[35] provisions of the Second Enforcement or Ku Klux Act of 1871 designed to enforce the guarantee of the equal protection of the laws,[36] and the Civil Rights Act of 1875[37] which required equal accommodations in inns, theatres, and transportation facilities.

The invalidation of the test oath was a reaffirmation of colonial and early American antipathy to bills of attainder and ex post facto laws as well as a confirmation of the absolute effect of a presidential pardon. The first legal tender decision was in the interest of creditors and contained seeds of substantive due process. In addition

[30] 7 How. 283, 467 (1849).

[31] *The Prize Cases*, 2 Bl. 635 (1863); *Ex parte Milligan*, 4 Wall. 2 (1866).

[32] *Mississippi v. Johnson*, 4 Wall. 475 (1867); *Georgia v. Stanton*, 6 Wall. 501 (1868); *Ex parte McCardle*, 7 Wall. 506 (1869).

[33] *Ex parte Garland*, 4 Wall. 333 (1867). For a similar state invalidation see *Cummings v. Missouri*, 4 Wall. 277 (1867).

[34] *Hepburn v. Griswold*, 8 Wall. 603 (1870), reversed in the *Legal Tender Cases*, 12 Wall. 457 (1871).

[35] *United States v. Reese*, 92 U. S. 214 (1876).

[36] *United States v. Harris*, 106 U. S. 629 (1883).

[37] *Civil Rights Cases*, 109 U. S. 3 (1883).

it reverted to the fears of some of the Framers for the sanctity of contracts, even though there is no contracts clause to limit the federal government. The decisions adverse to legislation designed for the protection of the rights of Negroes were based upon an extremely narrow view of state action and seriously limited the power of Congress to enforce the Civil War Amendments as clearly stated in their last sections.

The years between 1865 and 1888 were also a period of transition in constitutional law and judicial review as applied to state legislation. The Court wavered between deference to legislatures under a narrow but historically correct interpretation of due process of law and strict judicial scrutiny of legislation affecting economic liberty as vigorously advocated by Justices Stephen J. Field and Joseph P. Bradley in especially trenchant dissents.[38] In 1877 the Court emphatically rejected substantive as distinguished from procedural due process and insisted, after granting that all power may be abused, that "for protection against abuses by state legislatures the people must resort to the polls, not to the courts."[39] Such judicial forbearance was temporary. In 1884 Justice Stanley Mathews intoned magisterially that "arbitrary power, enforcing its edicts to the injury of the persons and property of its subjects, is not law, whether manifested as the decree of a personal monarch or of an impersonal multitude,"[40] and that the enforcement of constitutional limitations by judicial process is "the device of self-governing communities to protect the rights of individuals and minorities . . . against the power of numbers" and "the violence of public agents transcending the limits of lawful authority. . . ." Three years later the Court formally wrote substantive due process into the Fourteenth Amendment while sustaining a Kansas prohibition statute[41] and no longer was the Court forced to rely upon those limitations on governmental power "which grow out of the essential nature of all free governments . . . without which the social compact could not exist."[42] A new era of judicial review was on its way.

In the twenty-two years when Chief Justice Fuller presided over

[38] *Slaughter House Cases,* 16 Wall. 36 (1877).
[39] *Munn v. Illinois,* 94 U. S. 113, 134 (1877); see also *Davidson v. New Orleans,* 96 U. S. 97 (1878).
[40] *Hurtado v. California,* 110 U. S. 516 (1884).
[41] *Mugler v. Kansas,* 123 U. S. 623 (1887).
[42] *Savings & Loan Association v. Topeka,* 20 Wall. 655, 663 (1875).

the Court 14 acts of Congress were invalidated. Some of these
seriously crippled the power to govern. The most important statute
to be nullified was the income tax provision in the Tariff Act of
1894 where the Court, responding to the plea of Joseph H.
Choate, "corrected" a "century of error" and ignored a significant number
of precedents to conclude that an income tax derived from land
or other property is a direct tax and hence unconstitutional as not
being apportioned among the states according to population.[43]
The cumulative effect of a number of decisions delimiting the scope
of the commerce clause contributed further to weakening national
power. In the *Employers' Liability Cases*[44] the Court annulled a
workmen's compensation law as applied to all employees of carriers
engaged in interstate commerce because it extended coverage to
wholly intrastate activities and could not be saved by interpretation.
The Court contributed to further erosion of the commerce power
in *Adair v. United States*[45] where it held unconstitutional an act of
Congress prohibiting interstate carriers from discharging or threatening to discharge employees because of membership in a labor
union as an abridgment of freedom of contract under the due
process clause of the Fifth Amendment and the lack of any connection between interstate commerce and union membership.

Far more devastating to the commerce power was *United States
v. E. C. Knight Co.*[46] where the Court, without annulling the Sherman Anti-Trust Act, narrowly restricted its application and contri-
tributed thereby to the diminution of national power. Employing
technical concepts used in cases involving state regulation affecting
commerce as a measure of national power, the Court ruled that a
98% monopoly of the sugar refining industry was not a violation
of the Sherman Act because the statute applied and implicitly could
apply only to interstate commerce. The Court distinguished between manufacturing and commerce, regarded commerce as movement across state lines with a distinct beginning and an end, and
found that a monopoly in manufacturing had at best an indirect
and remote effect upon commerce as distinguished from a direct
effect. Thus without invalidating a statute the Court expanded

[43] *Pollock v. Farmers' Loan & Trust Co.* 157 U. S. 429, 158 U. S. 601
(1895).
[44] 207 U. S. 463 (1908).
[45] 208 U. S. 261 (1908).
[46] 156 U. S. 1 (1895).

judicial review and laid the foundations for invalidations which were to come.

The Supreme Court has always been more active in the invalidation of state legislation than of congressional statutes, and from 1888 to 1910 the Court liberally employed due process clause to the Fourteenth Amendment to invalidate statutes governing maximum hours[47] and prohibiting "yellow-dog" contracts[48] under the rubric, freedom of contract, which had been written into the due process clause earlier.[49] In the same period the Court assumed a supervisory control of state legislatures and public utility commissions in fixing rates for public utilities by converting the concept of a fair return upon a fair value[50] into a judicial question and enunciating a formula of valuation for rate-making purposes which rendered the tasks of rate-making bodies very difficult and further enhanced judicial review.[51] In this period, too, the Court began to take a closer scrutiny of the power of the states to tax property allegedly outside their jurisdiction.[52] Significantly, as invalidations on grounds of substantive due process arose, those void as impairments of the obligations of contracts declined. Due process relieved the contracts clause of much of its burden. State legislation affecting interstate commerce contributed a significant amount of litigation, but the Court on the whole was tolerant of such legislation. By all accounts, the Court had converted judicial review into an absolute veto of federal and state legislation without exercising it as frequently as it was to do in future years when the Court, using the concepts and doctrines formulated under Chief Justice Fuller, brought judicial review from maturity to its golden age.

The tempo of judicial findings of unconstitutionality increased during the ten years of Chief Justice Edward Douglass White's and Chief Justice William H. Taft's tenure of nine years. Twelve acts of Congress or provisions thereof were found unconstitutional in

---

[47] *Lochner v. New York*, 198 U. S. 45 (1905).

[48] *Coppage v. Kansas*, 236 U. S. 1 (1915).

[49] *Allgeyer v. Louisiana*, 165 U. S. 578 (1897).

[50] *Reagan v. Farmers' Loan & Trust Co.*, 154 U. S. 362 (1895), where the Court asserted its power over rate-making without annulling rates prescribed by the legislature. See also *Railroad Commission Cases*, 116 U. S. 307 (1886), and, more important, *Chicago M. & St. Paul R. Co.*, 134 U. S. 418 (1890), with its dual themes of procedure and substance.

[51] *Smyth v. Ames*, 169 U. S. 466 (1898).

[52] *Union Refrigerator Transit Co. v. Kentucky*, 199 U. S. 194 (1905).

thirteen cases in the White period and 19 in the Taft years, or 31 in 20 years.

The seeds which Chief Justice Fuller planted in the Sugar Trust case bore a bountiful harvest in *Hammer v. Dagenhart*[53] where Justice William R. Day reaffirmed the distinctions between manufacturing and commerce and direct and indirect effects to write the five-to-four opinion invalidating a rather modest child labor act and in effect amended the Tenth Amendment by qualifying "all powers not delegated" to "all powers not expressly delegated." He thereby achieved what the states rights protagonists had not been able to achieve in the First Congress in 1789. Although the Court was tolerant of regulations of interstate commerce in the 1920s to the point of being benign,[54] it invoked the Tenth Amendment to invalidate a clumsily drawn tax on the products of child labor[55] and a tax on trading in grain futures.[56] The most important invalidation occurred in *Adkins v. Children's Hospital*[57] where the Court revived freedom of contract to annul a minimum wage statute for the District of Columbia. Writing for the Court, Justice Sutherland elevated freedom of contract into a preferred position and reversed the usual presumption of validity in favor of a statute into one of invalidity on the principle that freedom of contract is the rule, regulation the exception. Finally, not to be overlooked, is *Myers v. United States*[58] which invalidated a statute requiring the Senate's advice and consent to presidential removals of first, second, and third class postmasters.

It was upon state legislation that the sharp judicial cleaver fell most heavily and most often from 1921 to 1935 when the Court struck down more than 325 statutes, according to one count, including eighteen municipal ordinances.[59] The overwhelming majority of these rulings were for the protection of economic interests. Even a superficial analysis of all these cases would require a volume and an enumeration of them would partake of the prolixity and variety of a catalog. Some representative examples are worthy of

[53] 247 U. S. 251 (1918).
[54] *Brooks v. United States*, 267 U. S. 43 (1925); *Stafford v. Wallace*, 258 U. S. 495 (1922).
[55] *Bailey v. Drexel Furniture Co.*, 259 U. S. 20 (1922).
[56] *Hill v. Wallace*, 259 U. S. 44 (1922).
[57] 261 U. S. 525 (1923).
[58] 272 U. S. 52 (1926).
[59] Swindler, *Court and Constitution*, 345.

notice. The concept of business clothed with a public interest which Chief Justice Waite devised in 1877 to justify the constitutionality for rate or price fixing of goods or services was converted into a limitation upon such legislation to invalidate a type of compulsory arbitration law for the settlement of labor disputes in a limited number of industries,[60] laws fixing the resale prices of theater tickets,[61] the price of gasoline sold from the wagon,[62] and the fees charged by employment exchanges.[63] In *New State Ice Co. v. Liebmann*[64] the Court applied the same concept to invalidate an Oklahoma statute restricting entry into the ice business by requiring a certificate of convenience and necessity. Both qualitatively and quantitatively the Court accelerated its strict review of rate orders of public service commissions and rendered effective rate regulation very difficult because of lengthy delays caused by litigation and the complexities of the criteria it required commissions to apply in making valuations for rate-making purposes. Following the rule which required independent judicial review of commision findings, both as to law and fact, in rate-making proceedings in the earlier Ben Avon case,[65] the Court in effect became a national public service commission for rate-making purposes. In a succession of cases the Court substituted its judgment for that of a commission without, of course, fixing a rate and reduced commissions to little more than advisory bodies, submitting recommendations to the federal courts.[66] The Court also subjected double taxation to closer judicial scrutiny by reversing an earlier decision[67] to condemn double taxation on movable property[68] and to give rise to the

[60] *Wolff Packing Co. v. Court of Industrial Relations*, 262 U. S. 522 (1923).

[61] *Tyson & Bros. v. Banton*, 272 U. S. 418 (1927).

[62] *Williams v. Standard Oil Co.*, 278 U. S. 235 (1929).

[63] *Ribnik v. McBride*, 277 U. S. 350 (1928).

[64] 285 U. S. 262 (1932).

[65] *Ohio Valley Water Co. v. Ben Avon Borough*, 253 U. S. 287, 293-294 (1920).

[66] *Missouri ex. rel. Southwestern Bell Telephone Co. v. Public Service Commission*, 262 U. S. 276 (1923); *Bluefield Waterworks and Improvement Co. v. Public Service Commission*, 262 U. S. 679 (1923); *McCardle v. Indianapolis Water Co.*, 272 U. S. 400 (1926). These cases and their progenitor, *Smyth v. Ames*, 169 U. S. 466 (1898), were reversed in *Federal Power Commission v. Hope Natural Gas Co.*, 32 U. S. 591 (1944), but the Court did not abdicate review of rates as a possible deprivation of property without due process of law.

[67] *Blackstone v. Miller*, 188 U. S. 189 (1903).

[68] *Farmers' Loan & Trust Co. v. Minnesota*, 280 U. S. 204 (1930). See also *Baldwin v. Missouri*, 281 U. S. 586 (1930).

later rule that only the state of domicile could tax intangible property.[69]

In an equally far-reaching opinion in *Truax v. Corrigan*,[70] by a vote of five to four, the Court invalidated an Arizona statute rigidly limiting the power of the State's courts to issue injunctions in labor disputes. Combining the due process and equal protection clauses, Chief Justice Taft asserted that due process of law secures "equality of law in the sense that it makes a required minimum of protection for everyone's right of life, liberty, and property, which the Congress or the legislature may not withhold." He regarded the equal protection clause as a guarantee of protection against the granting of an immunity to one class as against another.[71] Here a restaurant was held to have a property right in the conduct of its business and to be entitled to an injunction to restrain a strike and a secondary boycott as the minimum of protection required even though other remedies were available. The decision evoked a fairly familiar lament from Justice Holmes against the use of the Fourteenth Amendment "beyond the absolute compulsion of its words to prevent the making of social experiments that an important part of the community desires, in the insulated chambers afforded by the several states, even though the experiments may seem futile and even noxious. . . ."[72] Finally, in *Morehead v. New York ex rel. Tipaldo*,[73] the Court invalidated a state minimum wage law on the authority of the Adkins case and thereby rendered minimum wage legislation impossible by any government.

In striking contrast to the amount of economic legislation invalidated are the few decisions sustaining civil rights against adverse legislation. Two state laws curbing freedom of expression were annulled in 1931 for the first time in history,[74] although the Court in an earlier decision of great importance[75] had written freedom of expression into that liberty protected by the Fourteenth Amendment. In 1936 freedom of the press was the beneficiary of further

---

[69] *First National Bank of Boston v. Maine*, 284 U. S. 312 (1932), reversed in *State Tax Commission v. Aldrich*, 316 U. S. 374 (1942).

[70] 257 U S. 312 (1921).

[71] *Ibid.*, 332, 333.

[72] *Ibid.*, 344.

[73] 298 U. S. 587 (1936).

[74] *Stromberg v. California*, 283 U. S. 359; *Near v. Minnesota*, 283 U. S. 697.

[75] *Gitlow v. New York*, 268 U. S. 652 (1925).

protection against a state punitive tax.[76] In 1923 the Court sustained on due process grounds the right of a private language teacher to follow his profession and annulled a state law prohibiting the teaching of foreign languages to children under a given age.[77] In the same year it invalidated an Oregon statute requiring children to attend public schools to the exclusion of private schools[78] and thereby sustained the right of parents to supervise the education of their children as a part of that liberty protected by due process of law. In general, protection of civil rights against state action prior to 1935 is found largely in cases reversing convictions by state courts as denials of equal protection of the laws or deprivations of due process of law.[79] These observations are not meant to imply that the Court was grossly indifferent to so-called "human rights." The cases concerning them rarely arose and rights had not undergone their inflation which came after 1953.

By 1930, when Charles E. Hughes became Chief Justice, the Court had accumulated a full arsenal of weapons with which to strike legislation inconsistent with economic or political laissez-faire, and the New Deal provided an ample hunting ground for judicial marksmen. Between 1930 and 1937 the Court invalidated fifteen acts of Congress or sections thereof, and eleven of these fell in 1935 and 1936, over a span of less than seventeen months. Liberally employing and expanding technical conceptions of commerce developed earlier, but in more emphatic and comprehensive language, the Court annulled the National Industrial Recovery Act,[80] the Railroad Retirement Act,[81] and the first Bituminous Coal Act[82] as invasions of the reserved powers of the states under the Tenth Amendment. A complicated tax and spending plan for the control of agricultural production under the first Agricultural Adjustment Act was also held to violate the Tenth Amendment.[83] The dogma

[76] Grosjean v. American Press Co., 297 U. S. 233.

[77] Meyer v. Nebraska, 262 U. S. 390 (1923).

[78] Pierce v. Society of Sisters, 268 U. S. 510 (1925).

[79] Norris v. Alabama, 294 U. S. 587 (1935); and Powell v. Alabama, 287 U. S. 45 (1932), respectively, are notable exceptions.

[80] Schechter Poultry Corp. v. United States, 295 U. S. 495 (1935). Also invalid as unconstitutional delegation of legislative power.

[81] Railroad Retirement Bd. v. Alton R. Co., 295 U. S. 330 (1935).

[82] Carter v. Carter Coal Co., 298 U. S. 338 (1936). Also an invalid delegation of legislative power.

[83] United States v. Butler, 297 U. S. 1 (1936).

of state sovereignty was invoked to dispose of the Municipal Bankruptcy Act[84] and the due process clause of the Fifth Amendment
to nullify the Farm Bankruptcy Act.[85] As though the invalidations
of the Recovery and Coal Acts on grounds of the Tenth Amendment
were insufficient, the Court made sure by finding them to be unconstitutional delegations of legislative power, and for the first time
invalidated a statutory provision on this ground. By any reckoning
the Court had become extremely "activist" in protecting the right
of a corporate collectivism to be free from regulation by both the
federal and state governments, and it had used language and reasoning which rendered effective government in a complex industrial
society difficult to the point of being impossible. Furthermore,
judicial activism from 1921 to 1935 was unrestrained either by
precedent or by such self-effacing restraints as presumption in favor
of the validity of statutes and the oft repeated rule that the Court
is concerned only with the constitutionality of a statute, never its
wisdom.

In this impasse between the judiciary and the political branches
of the government something had to yield, and under the impetus
of President Franklin D. Roosevelt's proposal to enlarge the Court
by as many as six members, the Court made a hasty and strategic
retreat even without a single change in its membership. In the
words of the late Senator Henry Ashurst, the Court, "if it did not
see the light, felt the heat," and thereby demonstrated that it is
better to make a good run than take a bad stand. The retreat began
in the spring of 1937 when, aided by the switch of Justice Owen J.
Roberts, the Court by a five-to-four vote reversed earlier decisions
to sustain a state minimum wage law in a case which socialized
liberty and subjected it to the restraints of due process of law in a
social organization.[86] Not long afterwards the Court, without reversing any previous decisions, sustained by a five-to-four vote the
National Labor Relations Act of 1935 on reasoning which could
have readily been used to uphold the Recovery and Coal Acts,
even though it paid some deference to the concept of direct and
indirect effects.[87] Finally, during the same spring, again without

[84] *Ashton v. Cameron County Water & Improvement Dist.*, 298 U. S. 513
(1936).
[85] *Louisville Joint Stock Land Bank v. Radford*, 295 U. S. 555 (1935).
[86] *West Coast Hotel Co. v. Parrish*, 300 U. S. 379 (1937).
[87] *National Labor Relations Board v. Jones & Loughlin Steel Co.*, 301 U. S.
1 (1937).

any change in the personnel of the Court, the Justices by a vote of five to four sustained the provisions of the Social Security Act of 1935[88] which contained a tax designed to induce the states to enact unemployment compensation laws to meet Social Security standards. By any standard the tax was far more coercive than that of the Agricultural Adjustment Act and was intended to induce state and not private action. Justice Benjamin N. Cardozo, in perhaps his greatest opinion, distinguished temptation from coercion and wrote into constitutional law a theme as ancient as Eden and effectively withdrew the Tenth Amendment as a limit to the power to tax. In all these cases the four horsemen of conservative reaction, Willis Van Devanter, James C. McReynolds, George Sutherland, and Pierce Butler, dissented.

With subsequent changes in the composition of the Court all the concepts and dogmas employed prior to 1937 disappeared. The Tenth Amendment was reduced to a truism.[89] The power of Congress to regulate commerce became as broad as the needs of the economy, and the power to tax came to be limited only by the express terms of the Constitution except for a few vestiges of state immunity from federal taxation. Due process of law as a protection of economic interests became a relic in the museum of rejected precedents, which increased in number in the 1940s. Edward S. Corwin correctly viewed these developments as a constitutional revolution[90] which restored to the federal and state governments those powers conferred by the text of the Constitution and thereby ushered in the decline of judicial review for sixteen years. From 1937 through 1953 only three statutory provisions of federal legislation were held unconstitutional, the least in any comparable period since 1865. In 1943 the Court invalidated a section of the Federal Firearms Act, which created a presumption that firearms possessed by a person convicted of a violent crime were transported in interstate commerce, as creating an unconstitutional presumption of guilt and violating procedural due process.[91] Three years later the Court invalidated, as a bill of attainder, a rider to the Urgent Deficiency Appropriation Act of 1943 which prohibited payment of

---

[88] *Steward Machine Co. v. Davis*, 301 U. S. 548 (1937).

[89] *United States v. Darby Lumber Co.*, 312 U. S. 100 (1941).

[90] *Constitutional Revolution, Ltd.* (Claremont: Claremont College, Calif., 1941).

[91] *Tot v. United States*, 319 U. S. 463 (1943).

compensation to three designated federal employees except for military service or jury duty on a charge by the House Un-American
Activities Committee.[92] The Court thereby construed punishment
to include penalties other than those inflicted by courts after conviction, somewhat unnecessarily, because it could have reached
the same result by ruling that the provision was an unconstitutional
usurpation of the President's removal power. Finally, in 1952 the
Court held unconstitutional on grounds of vagueness a section of the
Pure Food Drug and Cosmetic Act of 1938 which made consent
of the operator of a factory a condition for entry for inspection and
made refusal to consent a crime.[93]

During the same period there was no decline in the number of
annulments of state legislation, but there was a vast difference from
earlier cases in the kinds of statutes invalidated. Ninety-five state
laws, local ordinances and regulations, or applications of them were
found void. Due process of law accounted for 31, the First Amendment for 26, the commerce clause and conflicts between federal and
state law for 22, and equal protection for 13. There were two invalidations each under the Thirteenth Amendment and the contracts clause, and one each under the ex post facto clause, the
prohibition against taxes on imports or exports; the Fifteenth
Amendment, and the privileges and immunities clause. Although
a few of the due process and equal protection cases involved economic rights, nearly all of the latter and many of the former were
concerned with rights other than property. The significant increase
in so-called "human" rights was a portent of things to come. In a
number of the equal protection cases the Court was examining with
greater scrutiny racial discrimination by state and local governments and requiring that separate facilities be in fact equal, in language that made separate facilities impossible.[94] There was great
activity in the areas of freedom of expression and religion, and these
and other cases concerned with vagueness of statutes inhibiting
publication or the showing of motion pictures. By 1945 freedom of
speech was exalted into a preferred position and the usual presumption of the validity of statutes was reversed into one of invalidity.
By 1941 the Court had almost completely abandoned the protection

[92] *United States v. Lovett,* 328 U. S. 303 (1946).
[93] *United States v. Cardiff,* 344 U. S. 174 (1952).
[94] *Sweatt v. Painter,* 339 U. S. 629 (1950); *McLaurin v. Oklahoma Bd. of
Regents,* 339 U. S. 637 (1950).

of economic interests[95] and in 1949 Justice Hugo L. Black could somewhat exuberantly refer to the rejection of the "Allgeyer—Lochner—Adair—Coppage doctrine."[96]

Far more important than the raw statistics can indicate are important shifts in doctrine. A notable shift occurred in *United States v. Carolene Products Co.*[97] which demonstrates how from trivial cases great principles grow, and how a formula, despite its lowly origins in a footnote, can become a dogma. Although Justice Harlan F. Stone in the text of the opinion of the Court retained some judicial supervision of economic legislation under the rational basis test, that part of his opinion has been ignored or rejected, and his famous footnote has endured with the usual distortion which concepts and principles undergo in subsequent constitutional interpretation. "There may be," he wrote, "a narrower scope for operation of the presumption of constitutionality when legislation appears on its face to be within a specific prohibition of the Constitution, such as those of the first ten amendments, which are deemed equally specific when held to be embraced within the Fourteenth." Justice Stone certainly did not intend that the judiciary abandon all scrutiny of economic legislation, nor did he intend to adopt a presumption of invalidity of legislation affecting the Bill of Rights.[98] Although noting that it was unnecessary to inquire whether legislation restricting political processes, the right to vote, dissemination of information, activities of political organizations, freedom of assembly and religion would require stricter judicial scrutiny, he settled the issue by raising it. Finally, he referred to the question of "whether prejudice against discrete and insular minorities which tends seriously to curtail the operation of those political processes ordinarily to be relied upon to protect minorities, and which may call for a correspondingly more searching judicial inquiry."[99] Whatever Justice Stone may have meant in these tentative and even speculative formulations, he provided the doctrinal justification of the "double standard" in judicial review and the intellectual rationalization for much of what the Court has done since 1938.

Accordingly, constitutional adjudication has been well prepared

[95] *Olsen v. Nebraska*, 313 U. S. 236 (1941).

[96] *Lincoln Federal Labor Union v. Northwestern Co.*, 335 U. S. 525, 535 (1949).

[97] 304 U. S. 144, 152 (1938).

[98] Mason, *The Supreme Court*, 158-160.

[99] 304 U. S. 144, 153.

for the advent of the "new" judicial review and for judicial resurgence after some period of decline. From 1954 through 1974
the Court found 32 provisions of acts of Congress constitutionally
infirm and more than 300 provisions of state statutes or local ordinances. More important than the bare statistics of increased
annulments of federal statutes from 1953 to 1975 are the developments in specific cases. The most important of these is *Bolling v.
Sharpe*[100] where the Court held that the due process clause of the
Fifth Amendment prohibited racially segregated schools in the District of Columbia. While conceding that the Fifth Amendment
contains no equal protection clause, Chief Justice Earl Warren
asserted that due process and equal protection are not mutually
exclusive, since each is derived from the "American concept of fairness." The Court held due process less explicit than equal protection and refused to imply that the two are "mutually interchange-
able," but "discrimination may be so unjustifiable as to be violative
of due process." Accordingly, said the Court, "Classifications based
solely upon races must be scrutinized with particular care, since
they are contrary to our traditions and hence constitutionally suspect." Finally, as an echo of *Allgeyer v. Louisiana*, the Court
asserted that liberty "is not confined to mere freedom from bodily
restraint" and "cannot be restricted except for a proper governmental objective."[101] With equal protection written into the Fifth
Amendment for some purposes, the Court in subsequent decisions
applied concepts of equal protection to prohibit statutory distinctions between native-born and naturalized citizens so as to expatriate
the latter if they returned to their land of birth and continuously
resided there for three years,[102] legitimate and illegitimate children
whereby the latter received a smaller share of social security benefits,[103] households whose members were all related and those not
for purposes of a household's eligibility to receive food stamps, and
between illegitimate children born or conceived before their father's
disability and those afterwards for purposes of receiving social
security benefits.[104] Finally, the Court held void a provision of the

[100] 347 U. S. 497 (1954).
[101] *Ibid.,* 499-500.
[102] *Schneider v. Rusk* 377 U. S. 163 (1964).
[103] *Richardson v. Davis,* 409 U. S. 1069 (1972). See also 342 Fed. Supp.
588.
[104] *United States Dept. of Agriculture v. Moreno,* 413 U. S. 528 (1973); and
Jiminez v. Weinberger, 417 U. S. 628 (1974), respectively.

United States Code which required a service woman to prove that her spouse was dependent upon her support in order to obtain dependency allowance while routinely granting them to men without proof of dependency. Justice William J. Brennan, Jr., speaking for three other justices, averred that arbitrary classifications based on sex are suspect in the same way as those based on race, alienage, and national origin and therefore subject to strict judicial scrutiny. Justice Potter Stewart's concurrence in the judgment on grounds of invidious discrimination implies that a majority of the Court had written the whole of the equal protection clause and interpretations of it.[105] Justice Lewis F. Powell, Jr., in a concurrence in which Chief Justice Warren E. Burger joined, was unwilling to equate classifications on the basis of sex with those of race, alienage, or national origin. In *Oregon v. Mitchell*[106] a coalition of conflicting minorities joined to invalidate a section of the Voting Rights Act of 1970 lowering the voting age in state elections as unauthorized by the equal protection and enforcement provisions of the Fourteenth Amendment. In all of constitutional history the reading of the equal protection clause of the Fourteenth Amendment into the due process clause of the Fifth was one of the more remarkable feats of judicial thaumaturgy, because it converted the due process clause of the Fifth into something substantially more than the same clause in the Fourteenth and thereby created the anomaly that the same thing is not really itself.

A number of statutory provisions of the Nationality Act of 1940 and the Immigration and Nationality Act of 1952 met judicial disapproval partly on the assumption that citizenship is inalienable unless formally renounced and that forced expatriation is cruel and unusual punishment in a rather distended view of that term. The void provisions were those which provided for forfeiture of citizenship of service men dishonorably discharged for war-time desertion,[107] of those persons who left or remained outside the country

---

[105] *Frontiero v. Richardson*, 411 U. S. 667 (1973). In *Johnson v. Robison*, 415 U. S. 361 (1974), the Court expressly stated that anything invalid under the equal protection clause of the Fourteenth Amendment is invalid under the due process clause of the Fifth, but sustained denial of educational benefits to conscientious objectors as no violation of equal protection. The Court also repeated the formula that legislation affecting discrete and insular minorities is subject to strict judicial scrutiny.

[106] 400 U. S. 112 (1970).

[107] *Trop v. Dulles*, 356 U. S. 86 (1958).

to evade military service, without indictment, trial or conviction,[108] of those citizens who voted in a foreign election,[109] and expatriation of naturalized citizens continuously residing in the country of their origin for three years.[110] Similarly, the Court looked unfavorably upon trials by military courts of dependents of military personnel stationed abroad for both capital and noncapital offenses,[111] of civilian employees for offenses committed abroad,[112] and of a discharged service man for an offense committed while serving in the armed forces.[113]

Just as the Court in other years had made a fetish of freedom of contract as a part of that liberty protected by due process of law, it wrote into the due process clauses of the Fifth and Fourteenth Amendments the right to travel to invalidate two federal statutory provisions. A section of the Subversive Activities Control Act made it unlawful for any member of a Communist organization either registered under the Act or under final order to register to apply for a passport or its renewal, or to use or attempt to use it. In *Aptheker v. Secretary of State*,[114] the Court, speaking by Justice Arthur Goldberg, found the provision void on the dual grounds of the right to travel under the Fifth Amendment and freedom of association under the First, and further as creating an unrebuttable presumption that members of such organizations, if given passports, will engage in activities inimical to the United States. Citing and quoting *Kent v. Dulles*,[115] the Court reiterated the view that the right to travel abroad is "an important aspect of the citizen's 'liberty'" guaranteed by the Fifth Amendment of which the citizen cannot be deprived.[116] In *Washington v. Legrant*[117] the Court invalidated a section of the District of Columbia Code denying welfare assistance to persons with less than one year of residence as

[108] *Kennedy v. Mendoza-Martinez*, 372 U. S. 144 (1963).
[109] *Afroyim v. Rusk*, 387 U. S. 253 (1967).
[110] *Schneider v. Rusk*, 377 U. S. 110 (1964).
[111] *Reid v. Covert*, 354 U. S. 1 (1957); *Kinsella v. Singleton*, 361 U. S. 234 (1960).
[112] *Grisham v. Hagan*, 361 U. S. 278 (1960); *McElroy v. United States*, 361 U. S. 281 (1960).
[113] *United States ex rel. Toth v. Quarles*, 350 U. S. 11 (1955).
[114] 378 U. S. 500 (1964).
[115] 357 U. S. 116 (1958).
[116] 378 U. S. 500, 506.
[117] 394 U. S. 618 (1969).

an interference with the right to travel without ascribing it to any particular constitutional provision. Citing and quoting from *United States v. Guest*[118] to the effect that the right to travel from one state to another "occupies a position fundamental to the concept of our Federal Union," Justice Brennan went on to find that the residence requirement had a "chilling effect" upon the exercise of a constitutional right.[119]

The First Amendment played a part in three invalidations. A section of the United States Code making it an offense for anyone except actors in theatrical productions to wear the uniform of the armed forces so long as the portrayal does not discredit the military service was held to be a violation of free speech as applied to a kind of guerilla theatricals in a street demonstration on the ground that actors like all others enjoy free speech.[120] In *Blount v. Rizzi*[121] the Court annulled a section of the Postal Reorganization Act which authorized the Postmaster General after hearings to halt the use of the mails and postal money orders for commercial distribution of allegedly obscene material and to detain such materials pending the outcome of proceedings. The section also failed to meet what the Court thought were adequate procedural safeguards. The inclusion of the use of the mails in freedom of speech in an earlier decision led to the invalidation of an act of Congress requiring a request in writing by a prospective recipient to receive unsealed mail from abroad if it contained Communist propaganda.[122] Finally, on grounds of vagueness the Court affirmed without opinion a lower court decision which held void a section of a law of the District of Columbia of 1882 which prohibited unauthorized demonstrations on capital grounds.[123]

The Court employed freedom of association to condemn a provision of the Subversive Activities Control Act which prohibited the employment in a defense facility of any one knowingly a member of a Communist action organization under a final order of the

[118] 383 U. S. 745 (1966).
[119] 394 U. S. 630.
[120] *Schacht v. United States*, 398 U. S. 58 (1970).
[121] 400 U. S. 410 (1971).
[122] *Lamont v. Postmaster General*, 381 U. S. 301 (1965). The *Lamont, Schacht,* and *Blount* cases were the only instances of invalidation of federal legislation as abridgements of freedom of speech prior to 1976; but see following note.
[123] *Chief of Police v. Jeannette Rankin Brigade*, 409 U. S. 972 (1972).

Subversive Activities Control Board to register.[124] A similar fate befell a section of the Labor-Management Disclosure Act of 1959 which made it a crime for a member of the Communist Party to serve as an officer or employee of a labor union on the ground that the provision was a bill of attainder under a broad and distorted view of that concept and of punishment.[125] Other decisions invalidating federal legislation are of less than cosmic importance. Sections of the Wagering Tax Act, the National Firearms Act, and the Marijuana Tax Act[126] ran afoul of the guarantee against self-incrimination. Sections of two statutes, one criminal and one civil, fell under the weight of irrebuttable presumptions as denials of due process of law.[127] A section of the Federal Kidnapping Act was found unfair in authorizing only the jury to impose the death penalty as an impermissible burden on the right under the Fifth Amendment not to plead guilty and the right to a jury trial under the Sixth.[128] Finally, the Court found a section of the Higher Education Facilities Act void, because it limited for only 20 years the use of facilities constructed under federal grants to secular education and thereby established a religion.[129]

Aside from reading the equal protection clause into the Fifth Amendment, emphasizing travel as a fundamental right, and broadly interpreting the Bill of Rights, these cases break no new frontiers. Certainly, they are not comparable to the decisions of invalidity from 1895 to 1937. The Court's obsession for rights generally obviously impaired governmental power to protect defense plants against subversives, to preserve order in the streets, to regulate labor unions which the Government subsidizes under the National Labor Relations Act, and to control eligibility for welfare benefits. With the exception of *Bolling v. Sharpe*, no fundamental rights would have been seriously impaired if contrary decisions had been made. It is notable that except for the welfare and food stamp cases none involved economic rights. It is worth more than casual

[124] *United States v. Robel*, 389 U. S. 258 (1967).

[125] *United States v. Brown*, 381 U. S. 437 (1965).

[126] *Marchetti v. United States*, 390 U. S. 39 (1968); *Haynes v. United States*, 390 U. S. 85 (1968); and *Leary v. United States*, 395 U. S. 6 (1969), respectively.

[127] *United States v. Romano*, 382 U. S. 136 (1965); and *United States Department of Agriculture v. Murry*, 413 U. S. 528 (1973).

[128] *United States v. Jackson*, 390 U. S. 56 (1968).

[129] *Tilton v. Richardson*, 403 U. S. 672 (1971).

attention to note that ten of these cases were decided after Richard
M. Nixon and John N. Mitchell had brought four "strict construc-
tionists" to the Court as compared with twenty-one invalidations
over a period of fifteen years.

As it has been from the beginning of judicial review, the Court's
activity has been much more pronounced in the sphere of state
legislation. To give a detailed analysis of almost four hundred
invalidations of state laws and local ordinances since 1953 would
require a treatise on constitutional law. It will suffice, therefore, to
note the major areas of judicial activity and the concepts employed
by a libertarian and egalitarian court to find state and local legislation infirm. A major and perhaps the most important theme of the
Court since 1953 has been equality in terms of equality before the
law or equality in rights as regards discrimination because of race,
alienage, or national origin; political equality, as regards representation and the suffrage, and an approach to equality of condition
with respect to the operation of otherwise valid laws upon the poor.
A second major theme has concentrated upon the substantive free-
doms of the First Amendment, primarily freedom of expression and
the guarantee against an establishment of religion. A third major
theme centers around procedural rights of criminal defendants.
The work of the Court in this area consists mainly of review of
criminal convictions rather than review of state laws, though not to
their total exclusion. It is enough to note that by the gradual nationalization of most of the Bill of Rights the Court has in effect
formulated a uniform criminal code of procedure consisting of
minimum standards with which the states must conform and to this
extent it has assumed a supervisory role over the administration of
criminal justice in the states.

In race relations the Court has wrought a constitutional revolution, but by 1976 had not succeeded either in consolidating its
results or in controlling its consequences. The decision of the
Court in *Brown v. Board of Education*[130] reached a great result in
one of the least satisfactory opinions ever written. The opinion
of the Chief Justice reversed earlier decisions, not because they
were wrong when made, as it could easily have done, and left open
the issue of whether the equal protection clause merely condemns
segregation by law or requires compulsory integration. Hence, it
has led to the controversy over busing and has converted federal

[130] 347 U. S. 483 (1954).

district judges all over the country into school administrators.   In
the leading case, *Swann v. Charlotte-Mecklenburg County Board
of Education,*[131] the Court sustained an order of a district court
directing extensive busing, but denied that schools had to reflect
population patterns by race and that busing could be ordered to
achieve racial balance.   Nevertheless, racial imbalances could be
taken into account by federal district courts.   Chief Justice Burger,
speaking for the Court, went on to say that "racially neutral" assignment plans submitted by a school board to a district court "may be
inadequate" because such plans fail to counteract the continuing
effects of past school segregation.   Consequently, "affirmative action in the form of remedial attendance zones is proper" in dismantling a dual school system.   In other words school boards and
courts must not be "color blind."   Thereby, the Court violated
one of its frequently repeated rules that there can be no discrimination because of race and that racial classifications are invidious and
unconstitutional.[132]   Busing of pupils to achieve racial integration
does and must by its intrinsic nature classify pupils according to
race.

Despite reiterations that racial classifications are invidious, the
Court has sustained a program for preferential treatment of qualified American Indians for employment in the Bureau of Indian
Affairs on the ground that the classification was "political rather
than racial in nature" and was consistent with "Congress' unique
obligation toward the Indians" who are members of federally recognized tribes.   This decision and federal "affirmative action" programs raise serious questions concerning preferential treatment for
minority groups with past and present disadvantages, "compensa-
tory" equality, benign quotas or goals, and discrimination in reverse.   To the contrary is *Loving v. Virginia*[133] where the Court
struck down Virginia's anti-miscegenation law and rejected the idea
that equal application of a criminal statute to both races is enough
"to remove the Fourteenth Amendment's proscription of all invidious racial discrimination" or to immunize it "from the very heavy
burden of justification which the Fourteenth Amendment has traditionally required of state statutes drawn according to race."

When Justice Holmes called the equal protection clause "the last

[131] 402 U. S. 1 (1971).
[132] *Morton v. Mancari,* 417 U. S. 535 (1974).
[133] 388 U. S. 1 (1967).

refuge of constitutional arguments,"[134] no one could have forecast these developments and others including the blurring of the ancient distinction between legitimacy and illegitimacy, an approach to economic equality, or the use of the clause by some judges to question the validity of capital punishment. In a per curiam opinion in *Furman v. Georgia*[135] the Court held that the imposition and carrying out of the death penalty in the circumstances of these cases constituted cruel and unusual punishment in violation of the Eighth and Fourteenth Amendments. Justice William O. Douglas adduced data to demonstrate that capital punishment bears most heavily upon the black, the poor, the helpless, and the despised and found that the administration of capital punishment had an aspect of caste and was applied in such a way as to deny equal protection of the laws. Justice Brennan looked upon the Eighth Amendment as prohibiting punishment so "severe as to be degrading to the dignity of human beings,"[136] and found capital punishment in these cases degrading to human dignity and so arbitrarily imposed as to constitute cruel and unusual punishment.[137] Justice Stewart rejected arguments of racial discrimination posed by Justices Douglas and Marshall, but found that the death penalty could not in these cases "be so wantonly and freakishly imposed." Justices Brennan and Thurgood Marshall thought capital punishment in any circumstances unconstitutional and adduced arguments and data more appropriate for consideration by a legislature than a court. Chief Justice Burger, Justices Harry Blackmun, Powell, and William H. Rehnquist dissented. The separate and multiple opinions of the majority and the close division of the Court held the status of capital punishment in doubt. Certainly, the suggestions by Justices Brennan and Marshall that capital punishment was being rejected by society proved false insofar as 34 states adopted revised laws on the subject following this decision.

A second major contribution of the Court to the development of the law of equality is the extension of the equal protection clause to political equality in the reapportionment and suffrage cases in which the Court has invalidated scores of statutes and has permitted district courts to impose upon the states reapportionment

[134] *Buck v. Bell*, 274 U. S. 200 (1927).
[135] 408 U. S. 238 (1972).
[136] *Ibid.*, 271.
[137] *Ibid.*, 293.

plans for purposes of representation. The leading case in reapportionment is *Reynolds v. Sims*[138] where the Court enunciated its formula of one man, one vote and made it applicable to both houses of a state legislature as a requirement of the equal protection clause. Relying upon *Gray v. Sanders*[139] which completed the process begun in earlier cases by converting the suffrage from a privilege to a fundamental right and invoking among other things the Declaration of Independence and the Gettysburg Address, Chief Justice Warren concluded that the right to vote "is of the very essence of a democratic society" and debasement or dilution of the weight of a vote is equivalent to denial of the franchise. Because the right to vote "in a free and unimpaired manner is preservative of other basic civil and political rights, any alleged infringement of the right of citizens to vote must be carefully and meticulously scrutinized."[140]

From these premises it was a short step to close judicial scrutiny of state voting requirements generally. Typical cases are *Harper v. Virginia Board of Elections*[141] and *Dunn v. Blumstein*[142] where the Court invalidated the Virginia poll tax for state elections and Tennessee's requirement of one year of residence to qualify for the suffrage. In the poll tax case Justice Douglas, over dissents by Justices Black, John M. Harlan and Stewart, repeated the theme that voting is a fundamental right and restrictions upon it must undergo close judicial scrutiny. Accordingly, a state denies equal protection when it makes affluence or the payment of a tax a qualification for voting. More significantly he candidly declared that the "Equal Protection Clause is not shackled to the political theory of a particular era" and the Court is not confined "to historic notions of equality . . . Notions of what constitutes equal treatment for purposes of the Equal Protection Clause *do* change."[143] Although residential qualifications for voting are prescribed by all of the states and are among the oldest, the Court in the Tennessee case was not deterred in its approach. Justice Marshall contributed further to the distortion and distention of the equal protection

[138] 377 U. S. 533 (1964).
[139] 372 U. S. 368 (1963); 377 U. S. 533, 555.
[140] 377 U. S. 533, 562.
[141] 383 U. S. 663 (1966).
[142] 405 U. S. 330 (1972).
[143] 383 U. S. 663, 669.

clause by placing fundamental rights and compelling state interests
in irreconcilable conflict and requiring the law to meet close judicial
scrutiny. To do this he linked the fundamental right to travel with
that of voting, although it is difficult to see any connection between
the two, and found the residence requirement to penalize the right
to travel. Two fundamental rights against the lack of any compelling state interests equalled unconstitutionality.

The deficiencies of these opinions and portions of that in *Reynolds
v. Sims* are serious. First, the text of the Constitution clearly and
emphatically leaves suffrage requirements to the states subject only
to the prohibitions of the Fifteenth, Nineteenth, and Twenty-sixth
Amendments. If the interpretations of equal protection in these
and other cases are binding, the Fifteenth and Nineteenth Amendments have become superfluous. Second, the congressional history
of the Fourteenth Amendment provides conclusive evidence that the
equal protection clause in no way controlled suffrage requirements.
Many of the Radical Republicans who were responsible for the
submission of the Fourteenth Amendment desired a provision for
Negro suffrage, but abandoned plans for it because they knew they
lacked the votes for it.[144] Hence, they settled upon an indirect
suffrage provision in Section 2 whereby the number of a state's
representatives in Congress could be reduced in proportion to the
disqualification of male voters of twenty-one years of age except for
participation in rebellion or other crime. Third, many of the Radi-
cals who participated in the submission of the Fourteenth Amendment were active leaders in the Fortieth Congress which submitted
the Fifteenth Amendment. Judicial changes in the text of the
Constitution are not new but *Dunn v. Blumstein, Harper v. Board
of Elections,* and *Oregon v. Mitchell* which invalidated state requirements of more than eighteen years of age rank among the more
blatant examples.[145]

In a number of cases the Court has displayed a tender solicitude
for what Justice Barbour once called the "moral pestilence" of
paupers by invalidating state laws believed to conflict with the

[144] For a defense of equal protection as a guarantee against discrimination
in the suffrage, see William W. Van Alstyne, "The Fourteenth Amendment, the
'Right to Vote,' and the Thirty-Ninth Congress," *The Supreme Court Review,*
1965, 53-86.

[145] On the congressional history of the Fourteenth Amendment see J. B.
James, *The Framing of the Fourteenth Amendment* (Urbana, Illinois: University of Illinois Press, 1956).

rights of indigents. The leading case is *Shapiro v. Thompson*[146] where the Court applied substantive equal protection to hold void two state statutes imposing a requirement of one year's residence to qualify for welfare benefits. Here again the Court confused governmental power with compelling state interests to find that the statutes placed an unconstitutional burden upon the right to travel. With the possible exception of this case with its concepts of fundamental rights and compelling state interests, the Court has refused to place distinctions on the basis of wealth or poverty into the category of intrinsically suspect classifications. The most important case is *San Antonio Independent School District v. Rodriguez*[147] where the Court sustained the general property tax as a major source of revenue for public schools in the face of the argument that this plan of financing public schools discriminated against the poor. Justice Powell as spokesman of the Court avoided the clash of fundamental rights and compelling state interests by holding that education is not a constitutional right. Justice Brennan dissented separately, Justice White joined by Justices Douglas and Brennan dissented, and Justice Marshall joined by Justice Douglas dissented.

Along with the equal protection clause the guarantees of the First Amendment as carried over into the Fourteenth have been a fruitful source of invalidations of state laws and local ordinances. Some of the cases like those invalidating prayers or scripture readings in public schools and public aid to parochial schools[148] pose no serious threat to the power to govern even though they raise questions concerning the definition of a religious establishment. In applying the guarantee of freedom of religion, the Court has occasionally erected a monument to freedom, as in the second flag salute case where Justice Jackson, speaking for the Court, put freedom of religion and the right of the children of Jehovah's Witnesses to remain silent above the votes of majorities in eloquence worthy of

---

[146] 394 U. S. 618 (1969), a companion case to *Washington v. Legrant*, same citation.

[147] 411 U. S. 1 (1973). After the spring of 1954 equal protection cases veritably exploded. At that time equal protection questions had been raised or resolved in approximately 550 cases. From the October 1954 term through the October 1973 term, equal protection issues, excluding federal cases, were resolved in 175 decisions with a majority decided unfavorably against the states.

[148] *Engel v. Vitale*, 37 U. S. 421 (1962); *School Dist. of Abington Township v. Schempp*, 374 U. S. 203 (1963); *Lemon v. Kurtzman*, 403 U. S. 602 (1971), respectively, among others.

Jefferson, Madison, and other devotees of freedom of conscience,[149] but for the most part, during the late 1930s and 1940s it protected the right of religious groups to make squalid nuisances of themselves and to blast men's sleep in order to save their souls.[150] Decisions affecting freedom of the press have rendered the law of libel largely ineffective and have erected the rule against previous restraint into a near absolute except for motion pictures.[151] Although the Court still clings to the rule that obscenity is not protected by the First Amendment, its comical efforts to define obscenity have, in effect, converted it into a national board of censors reviewing books, periodicals, paintings, and motion pictures to ascertain whether in law or in fact they are obscene. The spectacle of the highest court in the land reviewing all these objects of bad taste to ascertain whether their content, taken as a whole, predominantly appeals to prurient interests, is patently offensive to prevailing community standards, and is without "serious literary, artistic, or scientific value," transforms fantasy into reality and is hardly consistent with the earlier conceptions of judicial review.[152]

Far more serious than any of these decisions to the power of the states to govern is the inflation of freedom of speech to confuse speech with conduct and to include the right of a draft resister to wear in public a jacket with an offensive and obscene word printed upon it, notwithstanding Justice Harlan's bland assurance "that one man's vulgarity is another's lyric";[153] the rights of persons to address policemen with the foulest of epithets on the basis of overbreadth of the ordinances as distinguished from their specific application;[154] and the right of a witness in a trial to call his alleged assailant a foul name in open court, because it was not directed at the judge or any court officer.[155] By 1976 such decisions had ceased to be uncommon. Aside from overbreadth and what the Court has called a "chilling effect" on the exercise of constitutional rights, the ra-

---

[149] *West Virginia Board of Education v. Barnette,* 319 U. S. 628 (1943).

[150] *Saia v. New York,* 334 U. S. 558 (1948). See also *Kunz v. New York,* 340 U. S. 290 (1951).

[151] *New York Times v. Sullivan,* 376 U. S. 254 (1969); *New York Times v. United States,* 403 U. S. 713 (1971), respectively.

[152] *Miller v. California,* 413 U. S. 15 (1973).

[153] *Cohen v. California,* 403 U. S. 15 (1971).

[154] *Gooding v. Wilson,* 405 U. S. 518 (1972); *Lewis v. New Orleans,* 415 U. S. 130 (1974).

[155] *Eaton v. Tulsa,* 415 U. S. 697 (1974).

tionale of condoning such behavior was well expressed by Justice Harlan in *Cohen v. California* where he regarded the protection of the use of an expletive as coming under "the usual rule that governmental bodies may not prescribe the form or content of individual expression." If to many the consequence of this freedom appears to be "only verbal tumult, discord, and even offensive utterance," it produces side effects of the "broader enduring values which the process of open debate permits us to achieve. That the air may at times seem filled with verbal cacophony is, in this sense, not a sign of weakness but of strength."[156]

The late 1960s and early 1970s were a period of turbulence generated by opposition to the Vietnam War. The streets and other public places became a forum for sundry disorders after the manner of some civil rights demonstrations in the early sixties with the difference that most of the civil rights demonstrators were peaceful and non-violent in contrast to the behavior of their antagonists. The Court's handling of disorders by war resisters was uneven. A number of local ordinances were found void for vagueness or overbreadth.[157] In the area of symbolic speech the Court sustained the right of high school pupils to wear black armbands in class in opposition to the Vietnam War at the expense of school discipline[158] and of others to burn the United States flag.[159] Decisions in these two areas presented once again speech intermingled with conduct and raised serious questions concerning the place and manner at and by which expression is constitutionally protected. Certainly, the Court's decisions on freedom of expression since 1953 hardly comport with the Jeffersonian-Madisonian view of free expression as a discussion of public policy and criticism of governmental administration free from previous restraint or the threat of prosecution for seditious libel.

Building upon the First and other amendments and glosses upon them, the Court created a masterpiece of judicial innovation in *Griswold v. Connecticut*[160] where the Connecticut anti-contraceptive

---

[156] 403 U. S. 15, 24025.

[157] *Coates v. City of Cincinnati*, 402 U. S. 611 (1971); *Bachellar v. Maryland*, 397 U. S. 564 (1970), but contrast with *Colten v. Kentucky*, 407 U. S. 104 (1972), and *Grayned v. City of Rockford*, 408 U. S. 104 (1972).

[158] *Tinker v. Des Moines School Dist.*, 393 U. S. 503 (1969).

[159] *Street v. New York*, 394 U. S. 576 (1969).

[160] 381 U. S. 479 (1965). One of definitions of penumbra in Webster's *Third International Dictionary* is "A marginal region or borderland of partial

law was found void. Eschewing substantive due process as something which was offensive, Justice Douglas, in his peculiarly imaginative way, invoked specific constitutional guarantees and penumbras emanating therefrom to find that the statute unconstitutionally abridged the right of privacy. First, he cited the guarantee of freedom of speech which yields a peripheral right of freedom of association contained in the penumbra of the First Amendment. Next came the guarantees of the Third, Fourth, and Fifth Amendments against the quartering of troops in people's homes, unreasonable searches and seizures, and self-incrimination, and, finally, the almost forgotten Ninth Amendment to enable the Court to find in their mysterious interstices a penumbra of the right of privacy in the sanctity of the marital relationship. It is small wonder that Justice Black complained that the Court was restoring a discredited line of cases applying substantive due process to invalidate economic legislation and writing the personal predilections of the individual judges into the Constitution on the basis of fundamental principles of justice and the traditions and conscience of the people. Eight years later Justice Blackmun, as spokesman for the majority, employed the same rationale to find a state abortion law an invalid invasion of privacy which, as a fundamental right, could be justified only by a compelling state interest.[161] Justice White's complaint that "as a raw exercise of judicial power" the Court had authority to decide as it did, but that the judgment was an "improvident and extravagant exercise of the power of judicial review" was not amiss.[162] Regardless of the merits of anti-contraceptive and anti-abortion laws, there is nothing in the text of the Constitution which forbids them.

Just as the Court has bestowed welfare benefits upon transients and voting rights upon the uprooted, it has figuratively given handouts to vagabonds. In *Papachristou v. City of Jacksonville*[163] Justice Douglas, speaking for a unanimous Court, cited and quoted such jurisconsults as Henry D. Thoreau, Vachel Lindsay, and Charles Reich on the joys of the open road, nightwalking and star gazing to hold void a comprehensive city ordinance making va-

---

obscurity, or of some blighting influence, as of doubt or chagrin." Justice Douglas' opinion fits this definition in a number of respects.

[161] *Roe v. Wade*, 410 U. S. 113 (1973).

[162] *Ibid.*, 222.

[163] 405 U. S. 156, 164 (1972).

grancy a crime on grounds of vagueness. The ordinance, with its specifications of the components of vagrancy, cut a very wide swath, but the language of the Court was equally broad and cast doubts concerning the validity of any vagrancy law however carefully drawn. Thus the Court appeared to reject a concept of English and American criminal law sanctioned by antiquity and common practice since the Statutes of Labourers enacted in 1349 in the reign of Edward III and contrary to a decision of 1953.[164] The increased incidence of judicial review since 1953 is attributable to a number of factors: (1) the nationalization of most of the Bill of Rights and the preferred position accorded to the rights of the First Amendment; (2) the advent of substantive or the "new" equal protection with its confusing and mischievous dichotomy of fundamental rights and compelling state interests; (3) the distortion to the point of perversion of Justice Stone's famous footnote in the Carolene Products Case; and (4) the relaxation of the Court's own rules governing judicial review such as the requirement of standing of parties in cases or controversies, the avoidance of constitutional issues whenever the case can be decided on other grounds, the refusal to decide political questions and moot cases, and the presumption of the validity of statutes. The fourth factor needs further attention. Pursuant to its obsession for the First Amendment, the Court has accorded standing to taxpayers to challenge expenditures of funds from the general treasury where the guarantees of the First Amendment are involved.[165] In many situations instead of avoiding constitutional issues the Court has rushed to meet them, particularly in the cases involving overbreadth.[166] The concepts, political questions and mootness have been substantially, and perhaps in some instances, salutarily narrowed.[167] Worst of all, perhaps, is the abandonment of the presumption of the validity of statutes in favor of invalidity when issues arise under the First Amendment and the "new" equal protection.

[164] *Edelman v. California*, 344 U. S. 357 (1953).

[165] *Flast v. Cohen*, 392 U. S. 83 (1968).

[166] *United States v. Robel*, 389 U. S. 258 (1957); *Gooding v. Wilson*, 405 U. S. 518 (1972), but contrast *Younger v. Harris*, 401 U. S. 37 (1971), and *Broadrick v. Oklahoma*, 413 U. S. 601 (1973).

[167] *Baker v. Carr*, 369 U. S. 186 (1962); *Gilligan v. Morgan*, 413 U. S. 1 (1973); *Powell v. McCormack*, 395 U. S. 486 (1969); on mootness note also *Powell v. McCormack, Roe v. Wade, supra; Doe v. Bolton*, 410 U. S. 179 (1973).

Whatever the reasons, the "new" judicial review is far different from the "old," but the two have one element in common, namely, judicial supremacy. Whereas under the "old" judicial review the Court was an activist guardian of entrenched wealth and of corporations in protecting their freedom of contract and property broadly defined after 1895, under the "new" judicial review it has become the equally active guardian of the lowly, the submerged, and the despised of the earth and has undertaken the task of defending and promoting democracy, equality broadly defined, and fundamental traditions of fairness and justice. After 1895 the "old" judicial review was based upon the premise of a static Constitution, immutable and inviolable. The "new" judicial review, based as it is upon unnatural fusion of Realist Jurisprudence and natural law, presupposes an ever changing Constitution, especially as regards constitutional rights. The "old" judicial review, especially after 1890, lagged behind Congress, the President, and state governments. The "new" judicial review has been far ahead of each and has had a substantial influence in stimulating the political branches of government to catch up as well as to work considerable changes in public opinion.

The "new" judicial review extended the frontiers of freedom and equality, and the desegregation and the earlier reapportionment decisions are in the great tradition of early American political thought and fit neatly into Justice Stone's formula for judicial protection of discrete and insular minorities when the ordinary political processes fail. Surely, it is no disparagement of these attainments to suggest that the Court may have gone too far and that many of its opinions lack that craftsmanship which was characteristic of the great opinions of Marshall, Taney, Holmes, and Stone. Reforms in government are frequently overdue and just as frequently overdone.

The "old" judicial review produced laissez-faire in economics to create a sector where no government could enter. The "new" has gone far toward producing laissez-faire in the behavioral and cultural sectors. Each in separate ways affected the federal system, but the "new" judicial review has more significantly altered it by creating a government of almost unrestrained powers in economic matters at the expense of state power under the supremacy clause and, in turn, seriously limiting the power of the states to govern in matters other than economic. The "old" review was Hamiltonian after 1890 and was aimed at curbing the distempers and passions of legislative bodies and the ill humours of the people exploited by artful and designing men. The "new" judicial review is decidedly not in the tradition of Hamilton, Marshall, or Taney. Indeed, to men like Taney and Barbour it would appear to be too solicitous of the "moral pestilence of paupers, vagabonds, and possibly convicts." To the dour John Adams and some of his contemporaries it would appear to destroy that virtue which they regarded as the essential foundation of a republic, and to the constitutional reformers of the 1780s it would appear to be a device to protect the licentious against the worthy.

Congress:
Retrospect
and
Prospect

N INETEEN SEVENTY-SIX is the bicentennial of the Nation; whether it also celebrates 200 years of the Congress of the United States depends upon a point of view. Is the Continental Congress, which was more or less the government of the revolutionary coalition, a part of the history of Congress? Or was it a prologue? If it were the latter, it was a necessary and productive one. Because the experience of that revolutionary body provided the negatives which were necessary to make effectiveness possible for its successor. A numerous body can *not* govern without an executive. A legislature can *not* solve problems without adequate powers. A representative assembly can *not* work unless factions are reasonably controlled and some semblance of consensus is obtained. A political appendage can *not* succeed until it is incorporated into some centralized structure.

The Continental Congress, with its own President who could only preside, turned to what would be its successor Congress's chosen instrument—the committee.[1] But there were to be too many of them—so many that members could not legislate for attending committee meetings. John Adams, for example, sat in committees from four in the morning until ten at night. He was a member of 90 recorded committees. Moreover, the committees were not

[1] A good summary is found in Louis Fisher, *President and Congress* (New York: Praeger Publishers, 1972), 1-16.

peopled with members known to have abilities suited to their as-
signments. There were no merchants on Foreign Affairs, no military men on the War Board. Inevitably, competent chairmen came
to do all the work. The tireless Franklin handled a multitude of
jobs. The need for executive direction led to the creation of what
were to become departments of the executive under the Constitution—Foreign Affairs, Finance, War, Marine, Attorney General.
By the time of the Constitutional Convention, the need for separated
branches of government, with overlapping jurisdictions, seemed
plain to most who were participants in it.

Two fundamental concepts, built into the Constitution (with
qualifications), have had most to do with the evolution of the modern Congress. They are federalism and the separation of powers.

Federalism, as almost everyone knows, is the distribution of
powers between centralized and state (or provincial) governments
in a constitutional system in which the allocation cannot formally
be changed without the participation of both levels. In the American system, powers are relegated to the national level, the remain-
ing powers going to the states or the people. But while powers
have been reallocated formally only infrequently, changes by actions of the branches of government are constantly occurring in a
dynamic society. This makes a federal system most difficult to
make work. The "line of federalism" constantly must be drawn
and re-drawn. Public education, for example, was firmly in the
possession of the states until the middle of the 20th century. But
federal aid to returning veterans of World War II who wanted to
go to college, support of research to meet the challenge of Sputnik,
money to build facilities for the student boom in higher education
in the 1960's—all brought the federal government into direct intervention so massive that it is impossible now to draw the line between what is appropriate to state and federal levels. Again, a
presidential candidate campaigned recently on the issue of "law
and order." But what most citizens think of when that phrase is
evoked is safety—safe streets, parks, and neighborhoods. A president has little control over such safety—though that, too, can
change.

Why then did the Constitution-makers choose a system so difficult
to work? History shows that federalism was about as much central-
ism as the people would stand. The power and the glory then belonged to the states. Before the Declaration, individual states en-

gaged in their own separate resistances to the King were reluctant to proceed together. They were, in many cases, slow to join the new Union, which began its life on March 3, 1789, with only 11 member states. For many years more, the states' prestige far exceeded that of the national government. Many Americans had never seen a federal employee besides the postman. High office-holders in the Nation sometimes resigned to take similar positions in a state. The location of the national capital in the artificially created Washington, D. C., which had little to attract citizens to visit it, added to the disparity in the pride and affection they showed for their respective governments.[2]

Federalism, translated into the life of the practicing politician, is localism. Throughout much of the history of Congress, the member spent only part of his time in the capital—about half a year for the "long" session, and four months for the "short," or lame-duck" session. The remainder of his time he lived in his state (and district, for representatives) where he made a living, like other men. He was, therefore, a "representative" in the psychological, as well as the political, meaning of the term. He was "like his folks." He understood them, shared their hopes and expectations, their biases and strengths. Congress mirrored in its personnel the diversities of the Nation.

Now, even with the "professionalization" of a Congress which has come to require almost full-time service of its members, localism persists, enhanced by the decline of the parties. Local organizations seldom impose barriers between members and their constituents.

So the congressman has come to be almost entirely a self-selected leader with his life-line to the constituency. It is he (or she) who decides that he is a statesman, needed by the public, and sets out to convince the public. While the constituency supports the member, blessed security is assured. But when the constituents suspect that his heart may be elsewhere, his political life is in hazard; who lives by the sword, dies by the sword. The examples are many: Scott Lucas and Ernest McFarland, Senate Democratic Majority Leaders; Fred Harris, Wayne Morse, J. William Fulbright. Careers, both successful and still promising, come to an end far from

[2] James Sterling Young, *The Washington Community, 1800-1828* (New York: Harcourt, Brace and World, Inc., Harbinger Books, 1966), Ch. 1.

the Nation's capital. And there is no way they can be recouped—
no "safe districts," as in England, to which they can repair.

So members of Congress concentrate on constituencies—successfully it seems, as average tenure lengthens steadily and turnover
decreases. This is crucial to the nature and operations of Congress:
a member secure in his home base need fear no other political
threat. And that security is a basic element of the independence
of Congress.

The historic liberal concept of separation of powers is the second
fundamental which has had much to do with shaping the American
system.

Its pedigree is impressive. John Locke believed that separation
had preserved England from the tyranny which generally oppressed
the nations of the continent. Montesquieu, the French philosopher
who wrote the celebrated *The Spirit of the Laws*, accepted Locke's
thesis (although his famous statement on separation is a small part
of a very large book). Blackstone, the English lawyer who was
read by so many Americans, took it as received doctrine.

But the Americans were not doctrinaire, even in the application
of their doctrines. They were used to a governor appointed by
the king, an upper house similarly chosen, and a lower house
elected by the people. A cabinet government was an idea far in
the future, but the colonial government had some of its seeds. Their
governor was an executive who also had a strong legislative hand.
The upper house counseled the governor, sat as a judicial court,
and was part of the legislature. The lower house, usually estranged
from the king's men, were legislators only. But the powers were
not confused; they were exercised separately. The Founding
Fathers separated the institutions, but in providing "checks and
balances" they commingled the exercise of the distinct kinds of
powers among the institutions. They apparently accepted Madison's dictum that all Montesquieu meant was "that where the whole
power of one department is exercised by the same hands which
possess the whole power of another department, the fundamental
principles of a free constitution are subverted."[3]

So the legislative power rests not just with Congress, but with a
president who espouses a wide array of programs and is judged by
his legislative "box score," and also with a judiciary whose decisions
may be more important legislation than Congress's (e.g., the School

[3] Fisher, *President*, 23.

Desegregation Cases in 1954 and Baker v. Carr, "one-man, one-vote" ruling in 1962). The executive power is shared by a Congress which must acquiesce if a president is even to reorganize the executive department. The courts take on administrative tasks of breath-taking scope but are confined in jurisdiction by congressional and presidential legislation.

But the people, the institutions, are separated. No officer may serve in more than one branch simultaneously. This has had profound effect on Congress since the beginning. A parliamentary body may take its information and directions from the executive because the ministry is also the leadership of the principal legislative body. No so with a Congress to whom the executive branch must be "they." So each house established committees early on to test information and recommendation. Special committees gave way to standing, and standing committees gained specialized jurisdiction. In time the committees gained virtual control over subjects in their jurisdiction. In 1884, Woodrow Wilson said, "Congress in session is Congress on public exhibition, whilst Congress in its committee rooms is Congress at work."[4]

The two concepts together insure the freedom of Congress from control by the executive. The local base of the individual member frees him from domination by *any* party leader, in his body or in the White House. His principal work is performed on one or more committees, the chairmen of which ascend to the preeminent positions through seniority. Whether one likes it or not, a seniority chairman, answerable only to his own constituency, cannot be coerced by party leaders in his body nor in the presidential establishment. He is, to use an old east Texas phrase, "as independent as a hog on ice."

Specialized jurisdictions make the committee system a system of power. The full powers of the parent body are parceled out among the committee chairmen, who must further parcel them out among subcommittee chairmen. A power-minded chairman may try to thwart his lieutenants in the exercise of their rightful power, but he is seldom successful. A feudal system is a tempting analogy and helpful within limits.

Paradoxically, the committee system also gives a member a chance to slip the bonds of localism. He can build subject-matter

---

[4] *Congressional Government*, 15th printing (New York: Meridian Books, 1958), 69.

competence as he gains seniority and so come to have a nation-wide constituency among those who are concerned by that subject matter, who court the member more assiduously than his home constituents do. One thinks of John Fogarty and Lister Hill in health; Wayne Morse, Carl Perkins and Edith Green in education; Mendel Rivers in armed services, and a host of others.

We begin then with a Congress which, more from political necessity than design, has achieved a large measure of independence from the other branches of the government and is the partner the Constitution intended it to be. That has its strengths and weaknesses, which can best be considered after an examination of the party leadership within Congress and the leadership of the President of the United States.

PARTY LEADERSHIP OF THE TWO HOUSES

The principal leader of the House of Representatives is the Speaker. He has no counterpart in the Senate, where the most important leadership position is that of the Majority Leader.

The Speakership is historically rooted in the Speaker of the House of Commons in England, but our office has taken significant departures from its model. Like the English, our Speaker is the "House's man"; his principal glory is that he is wed to his House. A Speaker of the British House once told King Charles I, in answer to a royal question, "I have neither eyes to see, nor tongue to speak in this place, but as the House is pleased to direct me, whose servant I am here. . . ," and disked imprisonment and perhaps his head thereby.[5]

The British Speaker today is primarily a fair presiding officer. He is a member of Commons, elected by and "representing" a district, which usually returns him without challenge; but upon election he forswears partisanship, even ceasing to frequent places where he is likely to meet politicians. The rulings from the chair of the principal officer of the House of Commons must not be tainted by politics.

The American Speaker likewise is supposed to be, in the main, a fair presiding officer. But Speaker Cannon once remarked, "I am as fair as I can be, given the exigencies of American politics." So

[5] Arthur Irwin Dasent, *The Speakers of the House of Commons* (London: John Lane the Bodley Head, 1916), 193.

the ambiguity of contradictory roles complicates the American Speaker's job. The partisan dimension was introduced by Henry Clay and the Speaker today is recognized primarily by his success in advancing his party's interests. Sam Rayburn demonstrated the primacy of this role in 1941 when, on the eve of war, he declared a vote at an end when a bill to extend the services of draftees was one vote ahead. Perfect fairness was deemed not as important.

The American Speaker has yet another role: he is elected in and represents a congressional district. Often the Speaker has little to worry about, but automatic reelection is no part of our custom. Mr. Rayburn again illustrates the point: he successfully carried the burden of the New Deal and Fair Deal—and always had opposition in his conservative northeast Texas district.

The Speaker is the chief officer of the House of Representatives itself; he is elected by the whole body to an office established in the rules. Not so the Majority Leader of the Senate, who is strictly a party officer. The office of "leader," majority and minority, was created by the Democrats in 1920, and by the Republicans in 1925, but the function was recognized before that. Aldrich dominated the Senate in the T. Roosevelt-Taft era and Kern was Wilson's highly successful leader.

What shall we say about these offices? What kind of person holds them and what does he do?

If one were to look to the incumbent Speaker, Carl Albert, one would say that the office is, on the whole, rather passive, with the Speaker occasionally making a strong speech on national policy and reputedly exercising influence on critical issues. With his demonstrated knowledge of the House and its ways, he doubtless does much more, but he is not a public performer.

But this does not tell us much about what the office has been in other times and circumstances, and might be again. The magnetic Henry Clay was the first to use the full powers of the office. He was elected Speaker his first term. He resigned his House seat twice and was promptly re-elected on his return. He represented the new nationalism, resenting England and proposing an invasion of Canada. He appointed "war hawks" chairmen of the committees. In a word, he put the stamp of his personality and passions on a willing House.

At the end of the century, "Czar" Reed and "Uncle Joe" Cannon were virtual dictators of the House. A confluence of propitious

rules and iron wills made this possible. Cannon appointed committees and their chairmen, was chairman of the Rules Committee,
controlled the timing, content and character of the debate of bills,
and had unlimited power over the recognition of speakers ("For
what purpose does the gentlemen rise?"). No bill could reach the
floor without a rule. The Rules Committee members were three
Republicans, two Democrats. The latter were ignored and quit
attending meetings. The Republicans' three were controlled by a
"majority." As Cannon put it, "Me and one other."

This arrangement offered responsible party government by a dictator. But the dictator was not responsible to the tides that ran in
the country or in the Republican majority. Inevitable revolution,
by a bipartisan coalition, trimmed the office to size.

Sam Rayburn held the office longest and is considered by many
the greatest of the Speakers. Unmarried most of his life, Rayburn's bride was the House of Representatives. He knew its moods
and its habits. His great principle was accommodation ("You have
to go along to get along.") but he would put his carefully nourished
prestige and influence on the line in order to preserve it. For example, he won a very close vote to enlarge the membership of the
Rules Committee to end the dominance of the conservative chairman, "Judge" Howard Smith. His chief strength was his personification of the House of Representatives.

The same variability in role and performance can be found in the
leadership in the Senate. If the present Majority Leader, Mike
Mansfield, were the norm, we could say the Leader is a kind of
chairman, seeking to help the Democrats achieve what they want,
personally and collectively. He seeks no power, even claiming that
"I have less power than any other Senator." He has said that
"Johnson was the greatest leader the Senate ever had," but he has
no desire to be like Johnson. He does not attempt to round up
votes. He believes that "Senators are grown men and can make up
their own minds." Although he has held his leadership post longer
than any other senator, he keeps in close touch with the needs and
opinions of his Montana constituents and will put them ahead of
almost any other business.[6]

Leaders, whatever their personalities, often are products of the

---

[6] Andrew J. Glass, "Mike Mansfield, Majority Leader," in Norman J. Ornstein,
ed., *Congress in Change* (New York: Praeger Publishers, 1975), 142-154.

situation in which they find themselves.[7] Examples are found in two very dissimilar men who found themselves in quite similar circumstances—John Worth Kern and Joseph T. Robinson, leaders for Woodrow Wilson's New Freedom and Franklin D .Roosevelt's New Deal, respectively. Kern, a freshman senator, was a sweet man, persuasive, patient, conciliatory, quick to turn away wrath. Employing a daily caucus to rally the Senate Democrats, Kern obtained a majority on every bill Wilson wanted but one. His situation was special. The Democrats had been in the minority for many years and welcomed leadership. Moreover, the dammed-up desires of a large majority in the country, Democrats, Republicans, and Progressives, demanded legislative action. Much the same situation spelled opportunity for Robinson in 1933. But what a different man! Robinson was a two-fisted boss who loved a fight. He used a bulldozer, not a wand. He stepped on toes willingly, perhaps gladly. No ideologist, he followed the Democratic party line wherever it took him.

Lyndon Johnson, too, had a special situation—a Republican president and a shattered party in the Senate.[8] He carefully put the party back together and used it—and always some Republicans —to achieve a remarkable mastery of the Senate. He said "the only power available to a leader is the power of persuasion," but in his hands persuasion was a many-edged tool. He used his superiority in information, control of communications, rewards and punishments, to line up the votes. He usually had the compromises and the majority before he went to the floor. Mansfield has correctly stated that he and Johnson were "different personalities," with wholly different conceptions of the office.

So the party leadership positions have been many things at different times. The roles chosen by committee chairmen have varied as widely (though the job remains the same; the differences seem to be personal *rather* than situational) but they do not represent national party concerns, as the leaders do—or may. It is significant at this juncture of history that party leadership seems to concern itself almost wholly with what happens to bills after they come out of committee. On the substance of the laws, the feudal barons prevail.

[7] Ralph K. Huitt, "The Internal Distribution of Influence: The Senate," in David B. Truman, ed., *The Congress and America's Future* (Englewood Cliffs, N. J.: Prentice-Hall, Inc., 1965), 77-101.

[8] *Ibid.,* "Democratic Party Leadership in the Senate," *The American Political Science Review,* LV. (June, 1961), 331-344.

PRESIDENT AND CONGRESS: THE HISTORY

To write about Congress alone is to separate the inseparable. The partnership of President and Congress, the rivalry of President and Congress, have provided much of the drama and tension of the national story. Authors and editors today have a habit of pitching their analyses in terms of Congress *against* the President, and in this putative continuous conflict conventional wisdom has the President winning hands down, with Congress becoming a kind of vestigial figment of the founders' grand scheme.

The analysis properly begins with Jefferson, with the surfacing of parties and the relinquishing of the fiction that a president could lead the whole Congress and "factions" could be avoided.[9] Jefferson was an extreme Whig; he could and did speak of the "Supreme legislative power." He could well afford to do so; he was himself a supreme legislative leader, guiding Congress through lieutenants who could exercise persuasion for him. He made good use of the party caucus, and had yeoman service from Albert Gallatin, his Secretary of the Treasury, who had great influence with Congress. Jefferson's successors, moreover, were nominated by the congressional caucus, which preserved his strong legislative position for 24 years—through the administrations of Madison and Monroe. The case is easy to make that this was a presidential era.

Jackson, too, was strong. He rode into power on the crest of a genuine popular revolution, the builder of a grass-roots party. Jackson did not perceive his role as that of an initiator; but he used the veto unsparingly, and he did not hesitate to appeal to the people over the heads of Congress (on the United States bank issue). Moreover, he confidently proclaimed his capability of making his own constitutional interpretations.

But this presidential preeminence was not to last. The committee system made leadership difficult. More important, slavery was the dominant issue for the next two decades. It could not be solved but peace could be prolonged through compromise, a task for a "numerous" institution, not a singular executive. Certainly, the presidents of this era were not distinguished. Lord Bryce, the English authority of *The American Commonwealth*, believed they

---

[9] The historical section is based largely on Edward S. Corwin, *The President: Office and Powers,* 4th Edition (New York: New York University Press, 1957), Ch. 1.

were the most mediocre presidents in American history. "They were intellectual pygmies beside the real leaders of that generation —Clay, Calhoun, and Webster." And again, "Who now knows or cares to know about the character of James K. Polk or Franklin Pierce?"[10] Who, indeed?

Lincoln's strength needs no testimonial but he did not exercise it through Congress. He relied on the "war powers," on his position as "Commander-in-Chief." He left Congress mostly to his secretaries. But this was indubitably a presidential era, with Lincoln exercising as near dictatorial powers as any executive in the country's history.

But his successor came as close to being ousted from his job by Congress as was possible. One senatorial vote saved him. There is no need to approve congressional policies of that time to recognize that Congress was in the saddle.

There followed then a period which Bryce thought had somewhat better presidents than in the pre-Civil War period. Perhaps so, but it was in 1888 that Bryce published his famous chapter, "Why Great Men are not Chosen Presidents."[11] One reason he gave was that "four-fifths of his work is the same in kind as that which devolves on the chairman of a commercial company or the manager of a railway. . . ," a judgment probably based on the incumbents of that period.[12] It is true that Congress deserves no plaudits either. It was a sad time, with the brains and aggression going into building and plundering the country, with government having to settle for second-best.

Theodore Roosevelt, the first modern president, recognized the great power of moral leadership; the White House, he said, was a "bully pulpit." He tried to capture the people's imagination with releases designed to hit the news-hungry Monday papers and his personal style was dynamic and dramatic. Nevertheless, his administration could not be called a presidential era. The tyrannical Cannon, his jaw set against the future and even his own time, gave Roosevelt little to gloat over. He and Senator Aldrich, not the president, said what was to be.

Woodrow Wilson's first term marked one of the great periods of presidential leadership of Congress in this century. His first 18

---

[10] (New York: Macmillan Company, 1912 edition), 83.
[11] *Ibid.*, 77.
[12] *Ibid.*

months saw the passage of great acts of legislation—Clayton Anti-Trust Act, Federal Trade Commission Act, Federal Reserve Act, Underwood Tariff, to name a few. And it was he who stormed against a filibuster which would give him authority to arm merchant ships—which he did anyway—and prompted passage of the first cloture act. But in the end he made mistakes with Congress—calling for a Democratic Congress in 1918 in defiance of bi-partisanship and negotiating the Versailles Treaty without the help of senators. It was the Senate which finally pulled him down.

Franklin D. Roosevelt returned charisma to the presidency. Like Wilson, he had a period of enormous legislative productivity. But he hurt himself terribly with the 1937 court-packing plan, only to have his authority reinstated by World War II. By the time of his death toward the end of the war, he had lost much support again. His career seems clearly to support the "law of ebb and flow." In twelve years there were distinctly presidential and congressional periods.

No successor until Lyndon B. Johnson had firm leadership of Congress. Immediately after Kennedy's death, and with his landslide victory over Goldwater, he had scope to exercise his superb legislative skills and the third period of enormous legislative output in this century was achieved by the President and Congress.

The rest is too recent to need recounting.

PRESIDENT AND CONGRESS: A BALANCE

The conventional wisdom of our time holds that Congress is the weak sister in the national triune and must be propped up and reformed. Congress is weak and the President strong, so it goes, and the imbalance is becoming progressively more grave. The argument is supported by a Janus-like logic which, in its way, is unanswerable: if a flood of major legislation is passed it is because Congress is weak and compliant; if legislation does not move it is because Congress is weak and obstructive. A national preoccupation among the system pundits, therefore, is diagnosis of the congressional malaise and prescriptions for it. It is not a new game; Woodrow Wilson initiated the long unrequited love affair of many American political scientists with the British parliamentary system almost a century ago. Today an array of reformers make some part of their living telling Congress what it ought to be and do.

Even some members of Congress have joined the chorus, but it is obvious that Congress itself, in its institutional life, has not got the word. It summons executive officers just short of the President to come to the Hill to advise or to account for their performance. Ignorant of its impotence, Congress pigeon-holes or re-writes Administration bills, reenacts vetoed appropriations, and sometimes overrides vetoes. The Senate refuses confirmation of Supreme Court nominees. Members introduce bills of their own as if that were their right and often see all or part of their ideas incorporated into law.

The history of Congress is a curious story of failure indeed when viewed in the context of its historical counterparts. Since the time when Congress was established in the first article of the Constitutions, England has seen its monarch—a real chief executive then—become a bored civil servant, its upper house lose all its power to the lower, which in turn has succumbed to a ministry which runs the Commons and the bureaucracy both. France has run through two kingdoms, two empires, five republics and one Charles de Gaulle. The list could go on but this should do. Congress has changed with the times within its original constitutional structure and mandate. It is today without question the most powerful national legislature in the world. The powers and prerogatives of its individual members are the envy of their brethren in the most prestigious of parliaments.

What is the relative strength of the executive and Congress?

One is confronted at once with the lack of an adequate measure of political power. Equally ambiguous is the matter of which performs better the shared functions of governance for the system. Perhaps this is the place to begin—with a summary analysis of the way each goes about the tasks of representation, legislation and controlling the government of the United States.

Whatever its deficiencies, Congress is a representative body (which may be why the Americans see its flaws so clearly). Its members, as we have said, literally are never wholly safe with the electorate. Most keep in touch with constituents, some obsessively, through visits home, newsletters, TV and radio tapes, and a variety of other tactics. Almost any citizen can have some degree of access through his representative because no member of Congress is impotent and some are influential indeed. Interest groups need not work their way into the inner sanctum of a ministry; multiple points

of access are offered by members of appropriate committees. The
marvelous flexibility of committee hearings lends itself to a variety
of representational roles. Information and public education on
new problems—say, radiation fallout—can be had from the best
faculty the country affords. Causes which cannot win can be given
their day in court. Explosive issues can be slowly deflated through
progressively duller and more technical witnesses. Morality plays
can be staged. The permutations are almost endless.

It is safe to say the executive branch cannot match the warmth
and versatility of Congress's representational performance. But
who can strike a balance between that and the grand role of the
President as chief of state, symbol of unity, spokesman for America?
The founding fathers knew the Nation needed a king and gave it
one. The endless difficulties caused by this unhappy mixture are
well known, especially to a presidential candidate running against
an incumbent. Nevertheless, the combination provides assets too.
In a time of crisis no committee can equal the grandeur of the
single leader.

The division of labor in the legislative function is not so easy to
delineate. Congress is pleased to consider the President the initiator; his bills and messages are the points of departure, at least, for
what the committees do. But congressmen initiate too, often well
before a proposal has caught on with the public. When it does the
Administration appropriates it as it pleases, seldom giving credit.
The specialized committees probably give an individual measure
as good consideration as it could get. They are in continuous communication with the interest groups which are themselves part of
the representational system. But the executive agencies are, in
effect, interest groups as well. Their help is invaluable in bringing
to bear the vast resources of the bureaucracy. It is useful to think,
not of a legislative policy system but of many, each made up of
congressmen, bureaucrats, interest groups, and concerned publics,
all of which are involved in a policy issue.

But one distinction may be made sharply: only the President so
far can set priorities. Strengths have their costs: the decentralized
power structure of Congress which is proof against presidential
domination precludes the kind of party leadership which can make
national programs. The congressional system has respected its
inner logic, rejecting devices which might exercise control over the
whole body, just as the English parliamentary system has rejected

whatever might dilute the perfect and responsible concentration of power in the Prime Minister and his colleagues. We shall discuss later the attempt of Congress to set priorities through a reformed budget process.

What of control of the government? In his justly famous *Considerations on Representative Government*, published in 1861, John Stuart Mill said, "Instead of the function of governing, for which it is radically unfit, the proper office of a representative assembly is to watch and control the government. . . ."[13] This the House of Commons tries to do by holding the ministry, which is its own leadership, responsible for all the acts of government. Congress requires in its rules that each specialized committee shall oversee the work of the agencies which administer the programs in the committee's jurisdiction. It is safe to say congressional oversight is not very effective. Congress can and does perform well as ombudsmen for constituents who think they find the bureaucracy unresponsive. But the important task is seeing that legislation is carried out as its authors intend in hearings and reports, floor debate and conference reports. There is no way that congressional committees can make sure that those who write regulations and supply details will read the record.

In fairness, it should be said that the President probably does not do much better. Two million civil servants spread across a continent-wide nation are hardly susceptible of control by a thin overlay of temporary political appointees. What makes the bureaucracy generally a productive and responsive partner in governance is not political control, it is likely, but professional integrity and a commitment to the democratic ideals which most of us share.

If the foregoing truncated assessments are fair, we have not offered much help in measuring the respective strengths of executive and Congress. Perhaps it will be better to put the question more crudely: to what extent can the President get his own way? More than before?

In foreign policy, everyone knows the answer: the President is dominant; Congress is reduced pretty much to scolding. Not so in domestic affairs. The power of the President vis-a-vis Congress has shifted and continues to shift, over time and within single administrations. The only interpretation of this history which seems

[13] *On Liberty and Considerations on Representative Government* (Oxford: Basil Blackwell, 1948), 172.

convincing is found in the "law of ebb and flow." The presidents have not grown at the expense of Congress; some great periods have been shared and some have been alternated. The presidency may be "imperial" today, but the incumbent cannot afford to be imperious. The partnership goes on, with relative power ambiguous, as always.

A similarly ambiguous answer is suggested by the record of the respective branches in protecting their own turfs. Each has committed aggressions on the other; both have avoided constitutional showdowns. Roland Young states in his *Congressional Politics in the Second World War* that both President and Congress clearly crossed the boundary into the other's domain several times; when the outcome was satisfactory neither complained. This suggests that pragmatic common sense has had much to do with the success of the partnership.[14]

In any event, "partnership" is the key word. The evidence does not show that either partner can attain a lasting primacy over the other.

AN ATTEMPT AT ASSESSMENT

The entire focus of this essay has been on Congress as an institution of government, a part of the American political system. No attempt has been made to itemize substantive actions for success or failure. For one thing, it is not possible to isolate what was distinctly congressional from what was contributed by other operational sectors in the system. Again, actions have unintended and unanticipated consequences; what seems achievement today may be perceived as disaster later. But it is possible to suggest what Congress as a legislative body and representative assembly can and cannot do.

Congress almost never can address itself to whole questions affecting the whole system. It is organized to deal piecemeal with problems. Jurisdictions assigned and jealously guarded see to this. One remembers the late 1960's when the House Subcommittee on Postsecondary Education held hearings for amendments to the higher education legislation. The most crucial question facing higher education then was what would be done to the draft law. Mrs. Green, who chaired the Subcommittee, was bitterly frustrated;

[14] (New York: Columbia University Press, 1956), *passim.*

the witnesses could not discuss that. The subject belonged to the Armed Services Committee, In 1976, problems of energy and the economy are in like circumstance.

A second disadvantage is that committees and subcommittees have such close ties with interest groups, which are an integral part of their world, that the subcommittee may come in effect to represent the interests. One thinks especially of the House Agriculture Committee, six of whose subcommittees were for many years organized along *commodity* lines, a frank admission that the job of the subcommittee is to protect the interests of those who produce that commodity. When the administrative agencies which carry out the programs are added, the circle is complete. There are differences among these parties to be sure, and they are not conspirators against the public interest, but there still is a parochialism and narrowness in their outlook.

What cannot be gainsaid is that the Congress cannot be held politically responsible for its overall performance. Congress is two houses, separate and distinct, with differing modes of operation. Congress is two parties, unable to hold party lines, not organized to take party positions. Congress is 40 standing committees, many more special committees, task forces, etc., each with a piece of the job. Congress is 535 individual members, each catering to his own district or state and depending on his own resources to retain his seat. Nowhere is there a handle with which to take hold of the whole Congress. The President must face the whole people but he truly leads Congress only occasionally and for short periods. He can go down in utter ruin without necessarily affecting the fortunes of a single member of Congress.

Weaknesses and strengths often are opposite sides of the same coin. The glory of Congress is that it is an independent national legislature, truly the last of that kind. It can oppose the President, override his veto, and hold him to account. There should be great national pride in that.

To the citizens it offers multiple points of access. No individual nor group need penetrate to a ministry; one's own congressman or a committee member will be available and frequently can be effective help. Frequent trips home by most members assure that the opinions of the great Nation are pretty accurately reflected on Capitol Hill. Not so with the President. Given the vastness of his domain and the necessary shield between him and people, he is apt to fall prisoner to the views of the world held by his staff. Needless to say, their lives tend to be cabined and confined as well.

If Congress is, as it is argued here, a highly successful political institution and a durable partner in the grand alliance, how can we account for the widespread clamor for its reform and reorganization?

The reasons doubtless are many—including always the possibility that the critics' assessment might be right. But this may be suggested: the operations of Congress are far and away more open and public than those of the President and the appellate courts. Congress, its committees and members, are on almost continuous display. We know its faults because we can see them—over and over again.

The President, who begins with the advantage of the inherent drama of his office, can with modern technology stage-manage almost every appearance he makes before the public. He is becoming increasingly remote from the American people. The internal life of his office is not open to systematic scrutiny by anyone. The decision-making processes of the administrative agencies are likewise secure from public view. It is easy therefore to believe that they are more rational and based on better knowledge than the untidy procedures of Congress. Experienced persons say they are not.

The Supreme Court enjoys even more nearly complete privacy. Blackrobed justices render decisions of far-reaching political import and explain how they arrived at them mostly in legalisms.

But the congressional "image" is not nearly so important as the political education of the people which comes from openness to the public. Members of Congress recognize this and are moving toward more, not less, open actions. Recorded votes in committee of the whole in the House, public mark-ups and even some open conferences, are examples. The House of Representatives is even considering televising some of its proceedings.

An intriguing aspect of the congressional image, noticed again and again by scholars, is the paradox of a poor opinion of Congress coupled with high marks for the district's own congressman. Traveling around their home districts with 10 representatives, Richard Fenno found that, "Invariably, the representative I was with—young or old, liberal or conservative, Northerner, Southerner, Easterner or Westerner, Democrat or Republican—was described as 'the best congressman in the United States."[15] At the same time, polls show only about a quarter of respondents speaking favorably of *Congress*. He suggests several reasons, one of which is that members work harder at their own than institutional public relations. This surely is true, even to the extent of running "against" the institution—i.e., blaming the structures and procedures of Congress for preventing his carrying out many of his own promises.

Congress, in the 1970's, was in a mood for reform. Several steps had been taken, the most important being the Congressional Budget Act of 1974.[16] This legislation established a budget committee in each house and a joint Congressional Budget Office. It requires two resolutions a year, one in the spring and another in the fall, which will control the most important elements of taxing and spending, overall and by individual appropriations. The future of the legislation remains to be determined but if it succeeds it will repair the largest undeniable defect in the operations of Congress, its inability to set priorities.

Reforms are hindered by the uncertainty of what *is* a reform. Today's evil often is yesterday's reform. The tyrannical Rules Committee against which Speaker Rayburn fought was one of the reforms imposed on tyrannical Speaker Cannon. Seniority as a selector of chairmen is a reform over selection by a Speaker who exacted detailed promises of legislation as a price, and of election by the whole body preceded by several months of log-rolling. Structural and procedural devices give little assurance of permanent rectitude.

The same is true with the questions of why Congress is slow, and why Congress does not pass legislation that solves our problems. There is no proof that hurrying legislation makes it better nor that anyone knows what legislation will solve problems. In its 200 years of life the Nation has endured travail and made much progress. Today we face bright opportunities and threatening crises. Like the people who create it biennially and sustain it, Congress must do the best it can.

---

[15] "If, as Ralph Nader Says, Congress is 'the Broken Branch,' How Come We Love Our Congressmen So Much?" In Ornstein, *Congress*, 277-287.

[16] Allen Schick, "The Battle of the Budget," in Harvey C. Mansfield, Sr., ed., *Congress Against the President* (New York: The Academy of Political Science, 1975), 51-70.

The Presidency in 1976:
Focal Point
of
Political Unity?

GEORGE E. REEDY

ANY ANALYSIS of the current state of the Presidency must begin with the realization that the office is the focal point of our national life. It cannot be understood if it is regarded solely as the apex of an administrative structure. In fact, the managerial functions are secondary to the political roles of leadership and unification. The fundamental question is not how well a president meets a payroll but how well he meets the problems of his time.

In the political realm, problem solving takes on dimensions that go far beyond quantitative analysis and syllogistic conclusions. "Right" answers alone are not enough. Programs are not self-operating. They must be put into effect by leaders in whom the people have confidence. Ultimately, this means leadership with whom constituents can identify and, in the American system, that means the person who occupies the Presidency. There is no other office through which united action is possible.

The Congress, of course, can debate broad policy issues and achieve a form of unity. Basically, however, this is a consensus reached by rubbing off rough edges and ignoring issues which cannot be resolved. The Courts can consider specific disputes and issue findings which are binding and frequently have political repercussions throughout our society. But these are likely to be in the form of prohibitions rather than initiatives. And both the Congress and the courts must look to the Presidency to translate their agreements into effective action. The Executive is the "do something" branch of our government.

This is the factor which infuses any analysis of the Presidency with a tinge of anxiety. There are far too many respects in which the state of the Presidency can be regarded as the state of the nation for any sentient person to regard the office dispassionately. We are committed to the presidential concept in a manner which leaves us virtually incapable of thinking of the United States in other terms.

Often the terms "nation" and "president" are used interchangeably without any awareness of the fact. When we say that "the nation" is doing something we usually mean that it is acting in accord with presidential directives. When we say that "a new national policy has been declared" we mean that it has been declared by the President. When we speak of a "buoyant, confident" nation, our mental image is usually that of a buoyant, confident president. Conversely, when we speak of a "strong" president, we mean one who has mobilized the nation in his behalf and when we speak of a "weak" president, we mean one who is presiding over a divided nation.

Under these circumstances, many of the current proposals to limit the powers of the Presidency must be regarded with considerable skepticism. It is doubtful whether those powers can be limited without limiting the powers of the nation itself—unless we are willing to make very fundamental changes in the entire governing structure and not just in the Presidency. There is no evidence that the American people, as of this writing, are in a mood for anything so drastic as a parliamentary system or some version of committee government. We have probably gone as far as we are going in the direction of limitation with the War Powers Act.

It is highly probable that legal "limitations" would have little effect upon the office anyway—other than to spur some future "activist" president to greater heights of ingenuity. The history of the Presidency has made it rather clear that the only workable limitations on power are those which presidents have imposed upon themselves or which have been imposed upon them by political circumstances. There is very little that can stop a Chief Executive who has the voters with him as did Franklin Delano Roosevelt during his first two terms in office.

These are all thoughts which must be borne in mind when assessing the state of the Presidency in this bicentennial year. It is tempting to assume that the institution has suffered a severe setback. The shock of Viet Nam and Watergate is still affecting our view of government. Congressional committees continue to reveal examples of presidential misuse of such agencies as the FBI and the CIA. The private lives of many recent Chief Executives are being spread on the record and it is difficult to regard them as models of propriety. It is an understatement to assert that voters have lost their awe of the men who hold the office.

To use these factors as the basis for a prediction that the Presidency will be downgraded, or drastically altered, however, is a long, intellectual leap. It may well be that the occupant of the office will never again enjoy the automatic sanctity that went with the position for so many years. But the fact still remains that our nation can express its will only through a president. The institution is central to our political and social system and we cannot cripple it without crippling ourselves.

Actually, it would be very difficult to cripple the office under any circumstances. The concept that presidential conduct can be restricted by passing some laws is quite naive. There is a power inherent in the nature of the Presidency that goes far beyond anything that has ever been granted to him by Congress and which cannot be taken away by legislative action. It lies in the capacity for initiative that is inseparable from control over the action arm of the American government. As long as the President has the confidence of the American people, he can always precipitate situations to which both Congress and the courts must react.

At the moment, this power does not appear to be very great. But this fact is due to the current disillusionment with American institutions generally. It has nothing to do with formal structure or the laws. It is doubtful whether Congress could prevent a "caretaker" or any other president from committing troops to overseas action. The problem is how the troops would behave and how the American people would react. It is true that Congress made it clear that it would not support American intervention in Angola. What is significant, however, is not the Congressional determination but the fact that the Congressional determination was based upon clear cut evidence of popular disinclination to embark upon the project. A few years earlier, it would have been relatively simple for the President just to "go in."

To assume that this disinclination means a decline in the Presidency, however, is to view the situation in a false perspective. What seems more likely is that the American people are evolving a new perception of the role of the United States in the world. The shape of that image is not altogether clear. But certainly, it does not include a continuing effort to keep other countries out of the communist orbit at all costs.

What this perception means is that for the time being, presidents will lack the human resources to play the role of Harry S Truman in Korea or John F. Kennedy and Lyndon B. Johnson in Viet Nam. We have a tendency to forget that both those ventures were essentially extensions of policies which had solid, public backing. By every indication, the American people were agreeable to drawing lines on the globe over which the Soviet Union and Communist China could not step without retaliation. It was no less clear that they approved highly of many of the clandestine CIA and FBI activities which now draw so much condemnation. Of course, they assumed these activities would be directed against "them" and not against "us."

There is nothing new in presidential inability to act because the country will not support the action. It has happened many times in our history. This is a function of time, place and the context of the action.

What may be new, however, is that future presidents may be held to stricter accountability than they have in the past. It is entirely possible that the walls which shielded presidents from the rough and tumble of political conflict may have been broken down. If so, it is a development that has tremendous potentialities. Whatever else we may have learned from Viet Nam and Watergate, it is obvious that in both instances the Chief Executive was far too insulated from the main stream of American thought.

It is doubtful whether stricter accountability would manifest itself in new structures. Legally, Congress cannot assume any controls over the Presidency that it does not have already (such as the power of the purse) without violating the Separation of Powers doctrine. Healthy as it might be, we are unlikely to enjoy the spectacle of a president appearing before the House of Representatives once a week, or even once a month, to answer questions. This is not in the cards.

The nature of political reality is such, however, that it need not necessarily take on structure. Political leaders absorb lessons of conduct which have a remarkable persistence. Thus, when I first went to Washington in 1938, the Teapot Dome scandal of 1924 was still a fairly common topic of conversation. There could be little doubt that the memory of it kept some people reasonably honest who might otherwise have been tempted to stray. Even more astonishing to me was the fact that the Committee on the Conduct of the War—a group set up during the Civil War—was discussed with equal familiarity whenever some legislator proposed an investigation of defense activities. It was regarded as the ideal example of an enterprise to be avoided.

It could well be that similar roles will be played by the memory of the Democratic National Convention of 1968 and the Senate Watergate hearings of 1973. The outburst of savage violence at Chicago in 1968 was a direct reaction to a President who persisted in a war which large segments of our youth were unwilling to fight. The humiliation of once-powerful men before the Senate Committee was a direct result of an atmosphere in which a president had come to regard himself as somehow outside the rules of conduct that governed ordinary men. It will be many decades before the pictures of either the violence or the humiliation fade.

Obviously, these are factors which loom large in the thinking of the incumbent, Gerald Ford. Whatever else may be said about the man, he has exhibited a remarkable ability to avoid the traps of isolation in which his predecessors were ensnared. However, this is not conclusive. He is, after all, a "caretaker" in the full sense of the word—the first appointed president in our history. It could well be that the election process—which is akin to sanctification in many respects—could alter his thinking.

The odds are against it. The specifics of the Chicago convention and the Watergate hearings will fade rapidly. But basic concepts will remain fresh for decades. One is that even in the United States, people can take to the streets and render orderly processes impossible. The other is that Congress does have some ultimate powers with which any President who has lost touch with reality can be broken. Future White Houses (to personalize the mansion) will know that there are others who must be taken into account.

This, of course, was the principal factor in the isolation of the modern presidency—the feeling that other human beings did not have to be taken into account, except for manipulative purposes.

Presidents had developed a number of techniques for by-passing Congress in the field of foreign affairs and they really did not care too much about anything else. Therefore, White House planning became almost exclusively a matter of adding up physical resources. It was assumed that people would go along anyway.

There were formal obeisances to the principle of consultation with the Congress but the consultation produced little more than formal certificates of little meaning. Lyndon B. Johnson was the master at producing such certificates; his outstanding achievement in this respect was the Tonkin Gulf resolution. The method was simple. All he had to do was to place the country in a position where it was threatened, or seemed to be threatened, and then ask the Congress to back him in meeting the threat. It was impossible not to comply.

Only a very foolhardy president would care to try that technique at the present time. It would be disastrous. What is more important, however, is that even in the future, when the nation will presumably be in a more acquiescent mood, presidents will be somewhat uneasy about foreign adventures. They will know that there is something that Congress can do about such things and therefore it is prudent to take Congress into account early. In this respect, the War Powers Act is probably more potent than analysts will concede. The machinery it establishes is faulty and appears to be of only minor account. But there is potency in a Congressional *assertion* of power, no matter how vague the assertion. In this instance, Congress has *asserted* its determination to bring limited wars under control. In the proper context, it will find a means to make good on the assertion.

It is interesting to speculate on what would have happened had the War Powers Act been in effect before the American involvement in Viet Nam became major. It is difficult to believe that the machinery would have kept us out of the conflict. But it is not at all difficult to believe that it might have been used by Congress to extricate the United States from the war sometime in 1968. In other words, it offers Congress an opportunity to throw a president off stride but it is unlikely that the opportunity will be seized until there is sufficient public dissension to goad the House and the Senate into action. Laws like this are workable.

Incidentally, in this respect it should not be forgotten that presidents might welcome Congressional action in such affairs. One of the problems of the Vietnamese type war is that presidents, once they are committed to intervention, have no graceful way of putting an end to it except by victory or defeat. Once the initiative has been taken, the results are inexorable. Eventually American soldiers will be killed, confronting the President with the problem of either telling himself that those men died because of his poor judgment or deciding that the cause for which they died was so important that it must be won at all costs. The choice that presidents will make under such circumstances is obvious—they will send more men to vindicate the deaths of the first group. When some of these men are killed, the psychological forces for vindication become even more binding and more men are sent. The commitment becomes stronger and more irrevocable with each casualty.

In a parliamentary government, it is possible to handle such matters through the traditional vote-of-no-confidence route. This means the replacement of the Prime Minister with someone who can direct the necessary pull-out. There is no similar machinery in the American system. In the past, there has been nothing we could do to repeal a disastrous commitment except to wait for the next election. It is conceivable that the War Powers Act could serve us very well in that respect.

The War Powers Act, however, does not solve what has been revealed, to my way of thinking, as the gravest problem of the presidential structure. It is that we lack a graceful way of replacing a president when he becomes incapable of governing the nation. When we contract with a man to run our affairs for a four-year period, we are stuck with that man, short of death or misconduct of the grossest sort. It does not matter whether we are headed for immediate and apparent disaster. There is nothing we can do but go down with the ship of state.

Arthur Schlesinger has argued that the Founding Fathers intended the impeachment power to be equivalent to a vote of no-confidence. Personally, I cannot read anything in the Federalist papers to that effect. But in this instance, the intention of the Founding Fathers is irrelevant. It is evident to anyone who has been close to the Congress of the United States that impeachment will be invoked only in situations in which presidential *wrongdoing* has eliminated all other alternatives. It will *not* come into play over issues of politics or incompetence. The Andrew Johnson story will not be repeated.

Mr. Nixon had reached the stage where he could no longer govern the country. The income tax episode alone cost him so much in terms of public confidence that he became ineffective. But he could have become just as ineffective and still avoided impeachment by minor alterations in his relations with Congress. He made the mistake of persisting too long in a course of conduct which Congress would not accept and eventually found resignation to be the only path open to him that did not lead to impeachment.

The point becomes clearer when it is applied to other men who lost the confidence of their constituencies. Both Lyndon B. Johnson and Harry S. Truman presided over gravely weakened presidencies when they left office. Herbert Hoover found himself virtually powerless during his last two years and incapable of securing adoption of economic recovery programs which his successor extracted from Congress with ease. Buchanan was a totally ineffective president and, even though the Civil War was probably inevitable at that point, one cannot help speculate as to whether a stronger man might have made a difference.

In all of the instances cited in the preceding paragraph, important issues were at stake. The nation was in bad need of strong leadership and there was no manner in which it could be made available. None of the men had committed offenses which justified impeachment and even had they done so, the outcome would have been their replacement by vice presidents who could probably have done little other than to warm the presidential chair for the balance of the term.

These are the circumstances which tempt analysts to recommend an American transition to parliamentary government. It would seem to hold forth a very simple solution. When a man loses his political grip, a mere vote of no-confidence removes him and someone else is put in his place. It seems to be as easy as removing a pitcher who has just walked in three runs and sending him to the showers while the left-hander with the outcurve takes over the mound.

Unfortunately for the parliamentary political scientists, it is NOT that simple. Parliamentary government outside of Germany has not usually worked well except in nations where there was an hereditary monarchy to take over the Chief-of-State role and insure continuity. Parliamentary government requires participation by disciplined political parties. The United States does not qualify on either count. We have no governing monarchy or aristocracy and our political parties, despite periodic efforts to infuse them with ideologies, are basically coalition nominating mechanisms that are unlikely to change.

There have been some suggestions that we institute a vote-of-no-confidence procedure and call a new election in the event that such a vote goes against a president. The difficulties here are even more staggering than a transition to parliamentarianism. Who would run the nation in the interval between repudiation of the President and the election of a new one? What kind of machinery would be established for the nomination of the candidates? Could the nation afford the social disruption of an extra presidential election between those that are customary and anticipated? It is difficult to take such proposals seriously and they are cited here only to make a point—that we are probably not going to make any basic change in the office of the Presidency.

As a general rule, occasions such as this are used to examine an institution to determine whether it has served us well and then to seek remedies for deficiencies. In the case of the Presidency, the question is probably irrelevant. The office is so central to our entire way of life that our political structures have accommodated themselves to the Presidency rather than the other way around. The White House is an institution that cannot be changed in a basic sense without affecting every corner of American politics.

The nature of our political parties is a case in point. They owe their character to the nature of the Presidency. From an executive standpoint we have put all our eggs in the Presidential basket. There is no conceivable method of establishing a coalition government under our Constitutional system. Therefore, of necessity we have established political parties that are coalition nominating machines. We did not plan it that way. It was just that there were no alternatives as long as the capture of the White House was the long-range objective of political warfare.

Similar points will emerge from an examination of our Federal-State system or the relations between the executive and legislative branches of the government. It quickly becomes clear that there are no simple "one-shot" changes that will solve our problems.

In short, we must ask ourselves *how* we will live with the Presidency, not *whether* we will live with it. Probably this statement should be made even stronger. The question is more likely how we will live with an *even stronger*, rather than a weaker, Presidency. The current fad for advocating "smaller" government is bringing a strong response from those who sigh for "the good old days." It is hardly in keeping with the realities of our times, however. Every sign points to more governmental action, barring a catastrophe equivalent to the fall of the Roman Empire, and in American terms that means more presidential action. The world has become too complicated and too interdependent for anything else.

Once we adjust to the realities, we will probably get along fairly well with an even stronger Presidency. We will, perhaps, be forced to concede that there are simply no answers to many of the problems with which we are presented. It is doubtful, for example, whether we will ever find a graceful way to make a transition when an incumbent becomes ineffective. But most problems are solved "by main strength and awkwardness" anyway and this problem will just have to go in that category. We have survived up to this point and when we weigh the risks of continuing an ineffective incumbent in office against the risks of securing an effective remedy, it is probably best to leave well enough alone.

Furthermore, a more powerful president need not be less accountable. The factors we have discussed already—the memories of The 1968 Democratic Convention and the Watergate hearings—will be potent in persuading future presidents to a higher degree of Congressional consultation. This may not lead to *wiser* decisions (there is no guarantee of wisdom in Congress or in any other body), but it will lead to decisions that are in closer accord with political reality. This, in turn, means a restoration of stability—an atmosphere in which there is a chance of making some wise decisions.

It should be stressed, however, that there is probably more to the current problems of the Presidency than Viet Nam and Watergate. These are merely aspects which are the most amenable to discussion. It may well be that for the time being we are passing through a stage of social transition in which the constituencies that make for strong presidencies do not exist—a period in which the old values have been seriously weakened and nothing has come along in their place. Such times are always difficult for political leaders.

Throughout most of our history, American politicians have dealt with issues that are essentially economic. In effect, they have been resource brokers who know how to split up the economic pie among competing economic groups. This has been especially true since the advent of the New Deal. Majorities have been forged by bringing together farmers, workers, small businessmen, professionals, educators and others through a series of compromises that left each one reasonably quiet, if not happy. All of a sudden, technology has outmoded the classic pattern.

Of course, every issue has economic implications. But many of the most troublesome issues we face today are social, rather than economic. The Women's Lib movement is far more than a demand for "equal pay for equal work." Of necessity it is bringing about deep changes in the relationships between men and women. The rise of the minority groups has become far more than a demand for "equal opportunity." It has become a drive for integration into a society which, up to the last few years, has rejected them. Brokerage politics will no longer do and politicians are reduced to such language as "Chairperson" and to having a black assistant campaign manager on every election staff.

These, of course, are only two of the issues which a political candidate must face. Sooner or later, he or she will be confronted by the Gay-Liberation movement; the Right to Life movement; the environmentalists and Common Cause. It will be impossible for him or her to find the common denominators out of which majorities were forged in the past. They simply do not exist.

It is obvious that our society is going through some basic changes which have spawned such movements. Eventually they will coalesce into something with which political leaders can work. The coalition has yet to take form and until that happens, all of our politics will be confused. The Presidency cannot be exempted from this process. Lacking true majorities in our population, we will probably go through a period of "accidental" presidents—men who just happened to be standing in the right place at the right time. It is noteworthy that the current crop of candidates appears to be men who have applied for the job, rather than nominees who have been produced by the mysterious process under which leaders and followers come together.

This period will come to an end. Somewhere along the line, leaders will arise who can articulate the desires of the new constituencies and bring them together in a common purpose. And when this happens, it is a virtual certainty that the process will take place through the classic, presidential process.

The South
and
Sectionalism
in
American Politics

Numan V. Bartley

The late David M. Potter in an essay aptly titled "The Enigma of the South" pointed out that "for more than half a century the South has been a kind of sphinx on the American land."[1] The South was the "Sahara of the Bozart," a region about which, William Faulkner observed, northerners were eager to believe anything "not even provided it be derogatory but merely bizarre enough and strange enough."[2] In very recent times, these stereotypes have faded. The consensus historians have made their point that southerners have been Americans more than anything else. Whether Americanism denotes entrepreneurial values and democratic impulses or whether the South harbors in extreme form the "racist, violent, hypocritically pious, xenophobic, false in its elevation of women, nationalistic, conservative," and other values allegedly common to American civilization generally is yet to be finally determined.[3] In any case the new regional synthesis is admirably cap-

---

[1] David M. Potter, "The Enigma of the South," *Yale Review*, 51 (October 1961), 143.

[2] William Faulkner, *Intruder in the Dust* (New York: Random House, 1948), 153.

[3] Howard Zinn, *The Southern Mystique* (New York: Simon and Schuster, 1964), 262, and, from a more favorable perspective, Grady McWhiney, *Southerners and Other Americans* (New York: Basic Books, 1973).

tured in the title of a recent book about the South, *The Americanization of Dixie; The Southernization of America.*[4]

Politically, the South's longstanding reputation for demagoguery
and bizarre behavior has not been because its citizens were notice-
ably united on salient issues. The contention between lowland
plantations and upland farms, city and countryside, haves and
have-nots, not to mention blacks and whites, has been amply docu-
mented. Nor has the South been the only region to exhibit sectional inclinations. The importance of sectional discord in shaping
national political competition has been self-evident. The clashing
interests of the South and New England, the emergence of the
West, the ultimate sectional confrontation that resulted in Civil
War, the antagonisms that flowed from the resort to arms, and
the resilient political regionalism of the twentieth century have
long been obvious. Yet the South remains the nation's most enduring political anomaly; rarely has the region been fully integrated into national politics. This behavioral uniqueness has been
a factor of crucial significance to the course of American politics
and a subject of abiding interest to students of southern history.

The search for a central theme that would best account for the
South's deviant conduct has generated a substantial literature. In
1928 Ulrich B. Phillips depicted the South as "a land with a unity
despite its diversity" and found "the cardinal test of a Southerner
and the central theme of Southern history" to be "a common resolve
indomitably maintained" by white citizens "that it shall be and
remain a white man's country."[5] Phillips failed to evaluate the
impact of this theme on the "common resolve" of black southerners,
and, as Charles Crowe has noted, his candor offended both southern apologists and academic liberals.[6] Nevertheless, the interpretation has gained increasing stature as perhaps the best single explanation of white southernism. Since the publication of Phillips'
essay, few writers have ignored the significance of race in shaping
the identity of southerners, whether white or black, but a number
of scholars have searched for a more encompassing explanation.

---

[4] John Egerton, *The Americanization of Dixie; The Southernization of
America* (New York: Harper and Row, 1974).

[5] Ulrich B. Phillips, "The Central Theme of Southern History," *American
Historical Review,* 34 (October 1928), 31.

[6] Charles Crowe, "Explaining the South," in Crowe, ed., *The Age of Civil
War and Reconstruction, 1830-1900: A Book of Interpretative Essays* (Home-
wood, Ill.: Dorsey, rev. ed., 1975), 2.

David M. Potter suggested the importance of "the folk culture of the South," which survived long after its demise elsewhere in the nation, and Francis Butler Simkins found "the hold of orthodox Protestantism upon Southerners . . . a likely explanation of why the section . . . has kept its identity as the most conservative portion of the United States."[7]   C. Vann Woodward, the most influential of the modern interpreters of the southern past, has emphasized the formative impact of the South's unique and tragic history.   In a land of material abundance, the southern experience "includes a long and quite un-American experience with poverty"; in a nation where history has largely been a "success story," the South has known "frustration, failure, and defeat"; and in an America with a thriving legend of innocence, "the South's preoccupation was with guilt. . . ."[8]   Flowing from these historical experiences has been a regional mythology, which George B. Tindall has speculated may itself be "the central theme of southern history."[9]

Whatever the illusive "central theme," an equally important question relates to the fundamental nature of sectional conflict. Charles A. Beard, of course, found the explanation in economic forces. The greatest of sectional crises, the Civil War, was, according to Beard, "a second American revolution" whereby emergent northern industrial capitalism overturned southern plantation control of federal governmental policy. Within sections, class conflict provided the fundamental stimulus for political competition; between sections, differing economic development was the source of dissension.[10] Frederick Jackson Turner, the great historian of sectionalism, elevated sectional self-consciousness to the status of an independent variable. Each major region evolved "in its own way" and "each had its own type of people, its own geographic and economic basis, its own particular economic and social interests." Internally, geographic subregions, such as small-farm hill country and plantation lowlands, lay at the base of political divisions; externally, "sec-

---

[7] Potter, "The Enigma of the South," 150; Francis Butler Simkins, *The Everlasting South* (Baton Rouge: Louisiana State University Press, 1963), 79.

[8] C. Vann Woodward, *The Burden of Southern History* (Baton Rouge: Louisiana State University Press, rev. ed., 1968), 16-21.

[9] George B. Tindall, "Mythology: A New Frontier in Southern History," in Frank E. Vandiver, ed., *The Idea of the South: Pursuit of a Central Theme* (Chicago: University of Chicago Press, 1964), 1-15.

[10] Charles A. and Mary R. Beard, *The Rise of American Civilization* (New York: Macmillan, 2 vols., 1927), especially II, 52-121.

tional interests" and "sectional antagonisms" were of crucial significance.[11]   The Civil War, then, became a conflict between North and South for control of the West. Although later historians have largely dropped Turner's stress on environmentalism, his basic concepts have been enormously influential.   To the extent that the Civil War was a conflict between two separately evolving and fundamentally incompatible systems, each with an internally generated expansionist drive, struggling for the future of the West, the South's defeat meant northern development of the continent and thus the isolation of the South outside the mainstream of nation evolution.   More recently a new generation of historians schooled in the techniques of quantification have found ethnocultural conflicts of overriding importance in shaping political alignments.   In an ethnically and racially variegated society, tensions between Protestants and Catholics, old-stock settlers and more recently arrived immigrants, blacks and whites, and other divisions have structured political divisions on the mass level.   Locally generated ethnocultural antagonisms, when thrust into national politics, often took the form of sectional strife, as regional groups sought to bring central governmental policy into conformity with their views.   Thus the chain of events that culminated in the Civil War related closely to pietist Protestant endeavors to free the land from sin, including the sin of slavery.[12]

These latter findings seem to offer the best prospect for reconciling the divergent interpretations reviewed above.   Blacks—in this case southern blacks—conform to standard definitions of ethnicity.   The case for treating southern whites within an ethnocultural framework is perhaps less compelling but nevertheless has some merit.[13]   Unlike many other groups who came to the United States possessing a nonwhite skin color or a non-Protestant religion, southern white self-consciousness evolved over time.

Slavery was of course the touchstone of a distinctive white southern identity.   The slave-labor system and the staple-crop economy

[11] Frederick Jackson Turner, The United States, 1830-1850: The Nation and its Sections (New York: Henry Holt, 1935), 11; and Turner, The Significance of Sections in American History (New York: Henry Holt, 1932).

[12] For a review of this literature, see Robert P. Swierenga, "Ethnocultural Political Analysis: A New Approach to American Ethnic Studies," Journal of American Studies, 5 (1971), 59-79.   And see also the article by Louis L. Gerson, "Ethnics in American Politics," in this volume.

[13] Lewis M. Killian, White Southerners (New York: Random House, 1970).

that it supported bound the South together and set the interests of its leadership apart from those of national elites. The system drew a sharp division based on skin color, and, as Wilbur J. Cash observed, the fact that slaveowners, by utilizing the labor of blacks, rarely found it necessary to exploit directly the lesser whites, an arrangement that undermined class conflict and encouraged a sense of white community.[14] Whatever prospects the frontier experience might have had for promoting common-man democracy, the rapid westward push of planters, cotton, and slaves eliminated them. The emergence of the anti-slavery crusade in the North strengthened white unity in the South. By the eve of the Civil War, as Clement Eaton has concluded, conservatism, intolerance, religious orthodoxy, racism, and community ethnocentrism dominated white southern thinking.[15] This regional solidarity was not so much in defense of slavery, since the large majority of whites did not own slaves, and certainly not in support of secession, a step that provoked sharp controversy, but in the general inability of whites to accept the notion that an emancipated biracial society was a feasible possibility.

The Civil War was an epic event in the molding of a white southern ethnocultural identity. It provided the emotionally-fraught unifying symbols—the Confederate flag and "Dixie"—and in time a flourishing Lost Cause mythology. The mythology, more so than the war itself, won converts among those significant numbers of whites who disliked the Confederacy from the beginning. Reconstruction was a forceful attempt to bring social and political reform to the South, an effort not so much to remake the South into the northern image as to reshape it into the image of Republican ideology. The experiment demanded changes too fundamental for a generation of white southerners whose social views had been set by slavery, however, and ultimately Reconstruction strengthened southern defensiveness and permitted conservative elites to unite most of the whites in opposition. The failure of Reconstruction to assure full citizenship to blacks and internal differences within the southern "Redeemer" leadership over the proper course of action left race relations in a state of flux. The issue was finally

---

[14] W. J. Cash, *The Mind of the South* (New York: Vintage Books, 1941), 38-39.

[15] Clement Eaton, *Freedom of Thought in the Old South* (Durham, N. C.: Duke University Press, 1940), especially 300-375.

"settled" by the adoption of de jure segregation and disfranchisement.

Jim Crow segregation, like slavery before it, defined the social
system in terms of skin color. Whether slaves or freedmen, the
presence of large numbers of deprived workers, in addition to the
general poverty of the region, discouraged immigration. While
the rest of the nation during the late nineteenth and early twentieth
century absorbed a vast and heterogeneous immigrant population,
the South remained old stock and Protestant, ethoculturally identi-
fiable as blacks and whites, with that distinction written firmly into
law and vaunted by the "White" and "Colored" signs that adorned
the public facilities across the region. The bulk of the white
population was still the combination of English, Scot, and Scotch-
Irish that it had been at the time of the American Revolution.
Isolated from the mainstream of national developments, southerners
sought solace in a fundamentalist Protestantism, cultivated cotton
and a rural-small town folk culture, and refined the lines of caste
relationships. The massive changes that have swept across the
South since the beginning of World War II, not to mention the
massive out-migration of blacks and whites that has fundamentally
affected the politics of the non-South, have brought the region
closer to national socioeconomic norms than it has been since the
creation of a civilization based on cotton and caste a century and
a half before. But, as Professor Woodward has noted, one thing
that has remained immune from the impact of the "Bulldozer
Revolution" is history, "the collective experience of the Southern
people,"[16] and of course the mythology and group consciousness
that it has produced.

History and southern blacks molded the group identity of southern whites. Somewhat similar forces had their impact elsewhere.
Old-stock New Englanders also possessed a heritage that contained
its distinctive features, and the flood of immigrants that poured
into the region during the nineteenth century heightened the group
cohesiveness of the earlier residents, creating what Duane Lockard
has termed the "two New Englands."[17] The conflicts between the
two—the old-stock Protestants and the more recently arrived, often
Catholic, immigrants—have broadly structured the mass base of

[16] Woodward, The Burden of Southern History, 16.
[17] Duane Lockard, New England State Politics (Princeton: Princton University Press, 1959), 3.

New England politics since the 1850s, the period when the same partisan realignment moved the bulk of southern whites into the Democratic party. A similar political dynamic operated in other areas of the nation, and other ethnocultural groups have demonstrated impressive unity and consistency in partisan politics. The Irish, the first Catholics to arrive in massive numbers, have rather closely paralleled white southerners in their partisan voting behavior since the Civil War period. In fact, the solidly Democratic South appears, generally speaking, to have been less solid than the solidly Democratic Irish. Conversely, the old-stock New Englanders seem to have devoted about as much loyalty to the Republican party during the century after the firing on Fort Sumter as southern whites gave to the Democrats.[18] From an ethnocultural perspective white southern political behavior has not been so unique as it might appear.

The realization of the importance of ethnocultural conflict in the creation of mass partisan coalitions coincided with the formulation of a party systems mode of analysis. The growing number of survey research studies that appeared in print during the post-World War II years consistently demonstrated the importance of party identification and thereby made increasingly obvious the extent of electoral stability in American partisan politics.[19] In normal election years voters overwhelmingly tended to remain loyal to the party with which they identified. The really crucial elections were those that occurred during occasional realigning cycles, when large numbers of voters shifted their loyalty from one party to another. Such partisan upheavals occurred in the 1820s, the 1850s, the 1890s, and the 1930s. Once stabilized, the new party systems thus created tended to be remarkably durable. These realignments, which have occurred about once every generation, have served to readjust political competition to socioeconomic and demographic changes by redistributing power among elites and restructuring mass voter coalitions.

This realignment process has normally coincided with periods

[18] Kevin P. Phillips, *The Emerging Republican Majority* (New Rochelle, N. Y.: Arlington House, 1969), is a convenient summary, if not a notably rigorous study of the political behavior of important groups. See particularly the section on "Northeast Sociopolitical Voting Streams," 82-183.

[19] See the discussion and references in Numan V. Bartley, "Voters and Party Systems: A Review of the Recent Literature," *History Teacher*, 8 (May 1975), 452-469.

of national crisis—the Civil War, the depression of the 1890s, and
the Great Depression of the 1930s—events of sufficient scope and
intensity to affect directly great masses of citizens. With social
tensions quickened by crisis and political elites forced to take stands
or risk being swept aside by events (as the Whigs were in the
1850s), ideological issues have become sharply salient, motivating
basic shifts in the partisan balance of forces. These shifts, far
from being random, have tended to be the result of a group
dynamic primarily though not exclusively ethnocultural in nature.
Religious, ethnic, and even—as was the case with white Protestant
labor union members in the 1930s—organizational values have in
times of economic or cultural stress sufficiently overridden past
party identification to drive previously divided groups solidly into
one party, to break apart previously unified partisan blocs, and
sometimes to shift cohesive groups en masse from one party to
another. The new party system presumably structured on both
elite and mass levels to deal with—though not necessarily to "solve"
—the crisis has, however, lived on long after the occasions that gave
it birth. Consequently, ethnic partisan solidarity has tended to
reflect unity on the one or several issues salient at the time of
realignment, not some monolithic consensus. But once established,
both party identification and the vested interests of political elites
offered powerful supports for continuity.

The first American party system emerged in the 1790s and collapsed prior to the 1820s. The sectionalism inherent in this initial
experiment with partisan politics stemmed primarily from economic and ideological divisions among elites in a new and evolving
nation. Political competition varied substantially from state to
state and turnout in hotly contested elections, particularly in state
and local elections, was far higher than had once been assumed;
nevertheless, the first party system was essentially imposed from
above. Electoral practices, including state legislative selection of
presidential electors in most states (in 1800 two states chose presidential electors through a statewide, at-large vote), insulated national politics from direct popular pressures, while a politics of deference, most notable in the South, allowed wide latitude to political
elites. On the mass level, Federalism tended to be strongest in
static or declining communities while Republicanism thrived best
in growing, dynamic areas. The parties did not divide the electorate along class lines, although some evidence suggests that well-
established elites were more likely to be Federalist and newly

emergent elites Republican.[20] Most fundamental of all was the division between New England, with its Puritan cultural tradition, town settlement pattern, and economic reliance on small-scale agriculture and commercial business enterprise, and the rural, staple-crop, slave-labor South.

The plantation-based southern leadership became increasingly unified against Secretary of the Treasury Alexander Hamilton's plans to remake the United States in England's image. An extraordinarily talented generaton of Virginia aristocrats, led by Thomas Jefferson and James Madison, rallied the anti-Federalist opposition. Hamilton's policies found wide acceptance among merchantilist-oriented New England elites. Following the retirement of George Washington from the presidency, Federalists and Republicans clashed vigorously over fundamental issues concerning federal authority, the development of the West, foreign affairs, and popular democracy. At a time when slavery was still a debatable topic both above and below the Mason-Dixon line, southern elites had far greater opportunity to advance national programs than they were to enjoy later. As the champions of limited government, westward expansion, and popular democracy, the Republicans captured the mood of the times. The politically astute Republican leadership outmaneuvered the inflexible Federalists by cultivating alliances in the Middle Atlantic states. In 1801 the Virginia-New York nexus elevated Thomas Jefferson to the presidency and ushered in the reign of the Virginia dynasty. The generally successful administrations of Jefferson and Madison isolated the Federalists in their shrinking New England and coastal strongholds. Discredited by its association with the ill-fated Hartford Convention, the Federalist party declined rapidly after the War of 1812, permitting President James Monroe to preside over an inappropriately-labelled Era of Good Feeling.

The rapidly expanding trans-Appalachian West, decisively affecting national politics for the first time, generated pressures during the 1820s with which the decaying first party system was unable

---

[20] Richard P. McCormick, "Suffrage, Classes and Party Alignments: A Study in Voting Behavior," *Mississippi Valley Historical Review*, 46 (December 1959), 397-410; McCormick, "New Perspectives on Jacksonian Politics," *American Historical Review*, 65 (January 1960), 288-301; David Hackett Fisher, *The Revolution of American Conservatism: The Federalist Party in the Era of Jeffersonian Democracy* (New York: Harper and Row, 1965), 201-226.

to cope. Monroe's approaching retirement and the inability of the Republican caucus to agree upon a successor in 1824 unleashed the pent-up differences that ultimately splintered the Republican leadership and laid the foundation for the second American party system. At the center of the political conflict was the charismatic Andrew Jackson, who became the rallying point for opposition to the Republican establishment. Jackson was the personification of common-man democracy at a time when liberalized electoral procedures and declining deference to established elites were creating the potential for a more democratic politics. The Jacksonian Democrats displayed impressive inventiveness in the techniques of mass party organization and—following Jackson's successful presidential campaign in 1828—commendable resourcefulness in the use of patronage and political rewards. During the 1830s the southern and western states that had given Jackson solid backing in 1828 and 1832 became increasingly competitive, as opposition forces coalesced into the Whig party. Accepting the implications of common-man politics, the Whigs successfully engineered the classic "Log Cabin and Hard Cider" campaign that elevated the relatively well-born William Henry Harrison to the presidency.

The second party system mobilized the masses of voters and induced an intense partisan involvement that submerged sectional voting patterns. As Richard P. McCormick has observed, "For a very brief period—between 1840 and 1852—the nation, for the only time in its history, had two parties that were both truly national in scope."[21] This was a particularly aberrant period for the South, which had been fully integrated into national politics only during that period. In Georgia Jackson received 96.8 percent of the popular vote in 1828 and 100 percent in 1832 (when he was unopposed in the state), with approximately 20,000 ballots cast in each election; in 1844 and 1848 the Democratic presidential candidates won 51.2 and 48.5 percent respectively of the approximately 90,000 votes cast by Georgians. While somewhat an extreme case, Georgia does accurately illustrate the general pattern that had by the 1840s made mass voter participation and close partisan competition the norm throughout the nation.

Class conflict appears to have been an insignificant factor in

[21] Richard P. McCormick, The Second Party System: Party Formation in the Jacksonian Era (Chapel Hill: University of North Carolina Press, 1966), 14.

structuring mass partisan divisions. In the South plantation owners seem to have been no more inclined toward Whiggery than were yeoman farmers. In North Carolina the Whigs did best in the western hills and mountains, while the Democrats flourished in the lowlands. In Alabama the reverse was true: the Whigs were strongest in the lowlands and weakest in the hill country. But even in Alabama, as Thomas B. Alexander and his students have shown, there was no meaningful relationship between wealth or slave ownership and partisan behavior. Whigs did tend to be more numerous in growing, dynamic Alabama communities, while Democrats fared best in isolated, economically stagnant areas.[22] In any case, local issues and the identification of cultural values with one of the parties seems to have been common nationally. Lee Benson has demonstrated that the sharpest partisan conflict in New York occurred between recently arrived immigrants, with the "New British" flocking to the Whigs and "New non-British" to the Democrats. Old-stock Protestants, including those of New England extraction, showed only a slight Whig bias.[23] In other states the partisan differences between old-stock and newly arrived immigrants may have been greater, but ethnocultural factors seem generally to have been far better predictors of partisan behavior than economic classes.

Given its mass partisan roots and the scope of its organizational network, the second party system collapsed with untimely haste in the 1850s. The injection of sectional issues into partisan politics struck at the Achilles heel of the system. When anti-slavery and anti-southern feeling became interrelated with pressing local social tensions, partisan alignments broke apart. The massive influx of Irish and German Catholics during the late 1840s and early 1850s triggered sharp reactions in northern communities. Such smoldering questions as the place of parochial schools in the educational system, the proper method of observing the Sabbath, and the extent to which established elites possessed proscriptive rights became intensely salient. Pietist Protestants responded with a vigorous reassertion of "American" values, epitomized by the spread of the

---

[22] Thomas B. Alexander, et al., "Who Were the Alabama Whigs?" *Alabama Review*, 16 (January 1963), 5-19, and Alexander, et al., "The Basis of Alabama's Two-Party System," *Alabama Review*, 19 (October 1966), 243-276.

[23] Lee Benson, *The Concept of Jacksonian Democracy: New York as a Test Case* (Princeton: Princeton University Press, 1961).

anti-slavery movement and the campaigns of the Free Soil party, the division of pietist Protestant denominations into northern and southern wings, the enactment of prohibition legislation in thirteen northern states, and the success of the American (Know-Nothing) party.

Unable to withstand the strain, the Whig party fell apart. With southern spokesmen demanding federal protection of slavery in the territories, the emergent Republicans became the defenders of a free-soil West, and the Whigs, forced to choose between their anti-slavery and nativist wings, joined with the American party. By so doing the Whig-American ticket ran a creditable race in the South in 1856, but white southerners, their region and its peculiar institution under attack, gravitated toward the Democratic party, which itself broke into northern and southern branches in 1860. In that election the Republicans championed a program of positive government, including support for Whiggish economic policies, "American" moral values, and a free-soil, homesteaders West, to capitalize on the votes of those who, in Michael F. Holts' words, "hated Catholics and the impudent South, both of which the Democracy represented," and to elect Abraham Lincoln President.[24]

The realignment of the 1850s created and the Civil War solidified the third party system. The crusading zeal of evangelical northern Protestantism found its instrument in the Republican Party, and those who sought protection from the moralistic reformers turned to the Democrats. The Republicans thus relied on the more zealous Protestant denominations—such as the northern Methodists and Congregationalists—and on southern blacks, who identified freedom with Republicanism, for mass partisan support. Catholics, white southerners, and a considerable number of less evangelical northern Protestants, especially those with membership in liturgical denominations, tended to be Democrats. Groups such as the German Lutherans, who approved of Continental Sundays and opposed nativism while at the same time being suspicious of Catholics and southern Confederates, divided sharply and were the source of important "swing" votes.

These conflicts resulted in a restoration of political sectionalism. The Democrats dominated most of the southern and border states; the G.O.P. found reliable support in most of the New England

---

[24] Michael F. Holt, *Forging a Majority: The Formation of the Republican Party in Pittsburgh, 1848-1860* (New Haven: Yale University Press, 1969), 8.

and a number of the western states. Nevertheless, close partisan competition remained the norm in more than a third of the states, including most of those in the Middle Atlantic and Midwestern regions. Nationally, voter turnout continued at high levels. In a more fundamental sense, just as Charles Beard pointed out, the third party system and the Civil War effectively broke southern planter control of national policy, and during the Civil War-Reconstruction period the Republicans enacted a sweeping program of economic nationalism. With the return of the southern states into the Union following Reconstruction, the relatively evenly balanced parties struggled through two decades of stalemate.

In the South the collapse of the Whigs and the Civil War drove most whites into the Democratic party, although this uneasy coalition of former Whigs and Democrats, secessionists and cooperationists, planters and small farmers, business-commercial interests and agrarians was slow to stabilize. During Reconstruction the Republican party, establishing a southern base for the first time, relied upon the newly enfranchised blacks for the bulk of its voting strength, but it also enlisted support from mountain unionists and, for a time, former Whigs. In a sharply fought series of partisan encounters, the Democrats drove the Republicans from the major offices. By the mid-1870s, the South had become heavily Democratic (only North Carolina could be regarded as "competitive" according to a comprehensive study by Paul T. David).[25] Nevertheless, the Republicans continued to mount challenges—sometimes threatening ones—in the upper Southern states, and, elsewhere in the region, periodic if largely futile efforts by Independents and Republicans offered competition to the Democrats. The Independent efforts often resulted from acerbic conflicts among Democratic elites over such issues as payment of state debts, taxing policies, and racial issues. The Civil War and the Thirteenth Amendment did break planter domination of southern politics, with the center of political gravity shifting to the towns and county seats. There, what Jasper B. Shannon has called the "banker-merchant-farmer-lawyer-doctor-governing class" formed the nucleus of the Bourbon Democratic structure.[26] Lacking consistent competition in most

[25] Paul T. David, *Party Strength in the United States, 1872-1970* (Charlottesville: University Press of Virginia, 1972), 46.

[26] Jasper Berry Shannon, *Toward a New Politics in the South* (Knoxville: University of Tennessee Press, 1948), 44.

southern states, the system soon became entrenched. Attending the needs of the haves at the expense of the have-nots, Bourbon policies rarely varied from low taxes and meager services. The decline of staple-crop prices throughout the late nineteenth century depressed the agricultural economy and forced large numbers of southern whites out of the yeoman farmer ranks into tenant status. The festering discontent in the countryside broke into politics in the 1890s in the form of the Peoples party. Bursting forth from the hinterlands, the Populists demanded economic reform, and they flirted with and often fused the Republican blacks. This is not to suggest that Populist elites were racial "liberals"; their views seem not to have differed fundamentally from those of the Bourbon Democrats.[27] The Populists did, however, offer a tangible program of reform, and, most of all, by attempting to mobilize countryside against town and have-nots against haves, they fundamentally challenged the concept of white solidarity and the right of the Bourbons to rule. Responding with a frenzy, the Democrats combined appeals to white supremacy with blatant stuffing of ballot boxes to crush the threat.

But the Populists had raised the spectre of class conflict, and that danger remained after the decline of the Peoples party itself. Displaying remarkable political adroitness, the Bourbons allied with an emergent generation of New South Progressives to sponsor disfranchisement constitutional conventions. The business-oriented Progressive Democrats, anxious to rationalize governmental procedures, expand basic social services, and "purify" the electorate, represented less of a threat to Bourbon rule than did the more radical Populists. Across the South Democrats banded together to eliminate potential opposition.[28] Literacy and understanding tests, poll taxes, and, above all, the "white primary," became

---

[27] On this widely debated point, see Charles Crowe, "Tom Watson, Populists and Blacks Reconsidered," *Journal of Negro History*, 55 (April 1970), 99-116; William F. Holmes, "The Demise of the Colored Farmers' Alliance," *Journal of Southern History*, 41 (May 1975), 185-200; Roger L. Hart, *Redeemers, Bourbons, and Populists: Tennessee, 1870-1896* (Baton Rouge: Louisiana State University Press, 1975), 200-223; and Sheldon Hackney, *Populism to Progressivism in Alabama* (Princeton: Princeton University Press, 1969), 77-88.

[28] J. Morgan Kousser, *The Shaping of Southern Politics: Suffrage Restrictions and the Establishment of the One-Party South, 1880-1910* (New Haven: Yale University Press, 1974), 238-265.

standard suffrage practices. Voter turnout, already in steep decline, fell even more precipitously. By the early twentieth century, the Solid Democratic South was a fully perfected reality. Better than they perhaps realized, the Democrats had created an ideal instrument of one-party rule. The white primary permitted dissident whites to contest primary elections and introduce policy alternatives, but the exclusion of the black masses and most of the lower strata of whites assured that such changes would be appropriately "moderate." The relegation of blacks to their "place" through de jure segregation further restricted the range of white debate. Cleavages between town and country and affluent and nonaffluent did not disappear, as a host of politically successful demagogues testified. But the solid Democratic South was an unquestioned reality.

The declining agricultural economy in the South and West proved a prelude for the general depression of the 1890s. Economic hard times combined with ethnocultural conflicts to create the fourth party system. The depression of 1893, the worst in the nation's history up to that time, came during the early years of the "new immigration." The arrival of a vast wave of non-Protestant Italian and eastern European migrants combined with economic distress and the disruption caused by urbanization and industrialization to restructure partisan voting patterns. The depression followed closely the Democratic sweep in the 1892 elections, and, with voters blaming the party in power, the 1894 off-year elections were a Democratic disaster.

Responding boldly in 1896, the Democrats repudiated incumbent Grover Cleveland and nominated Nebraska's William Jennings Bryan. In an energetic campaign, the Bryan Democrats sought not only to absorb the Populist following by advocating a program of positive government, rural liberalism, and free silver but generally to rally the have-nots, including the northern proletariat. The injection of class conflict into an ethnoculturally-oriented partisan system produced shattering repercussions. Bryan's rural radicalism and Protestant fundamentalism failed to win the support of the ethnically-fragmented northern working class and repelled many of the Catholics and liturgical Protestants who had looked to the Democratic Party for protection from moralistic reformers. William McKinley and the Republicans, promising little more than a return to prosperity, successfully muted their party's image as a vehicle of evangelical zeal and thus smoothed the way to Republicanism for large numbers of former Democrats.

The fourth party system brought political sectionalism to culmination. The realignment of the 1890s decimated the Democratic
party over much of the nation, as such important and previously
competitive industrial states as Illinois, Michigan, Pennsylvania,
and Wisconsin became solidly Republican. The Democrats monopolized the South (or more correctly, the South monopolized the
Democratic party), and partisan competition was largely confined
to some western and border states and to a few significant but
rather isolated northern states.[29]   The Republican party's domination of national partisan politics reflected the concentration of
people and economic power in the northeastern-midwestern states,
and it consolidated the transfer of political power to northern
financial-industrial elites that had begun in the 1850s. The Republican party's accomplishment was the identification of corporate
capitalism with the economic prosperity of the region. The Progressive reforms of the early twentieth century served to stabilize
the "system of 1896" in the non-South as they did in Dixie. The
middle class-oriented Progressives, concerned about immigrant-
based political machines and electoral corruption, sought to make
politics more honest and more responsive to popular rather than
partisan influence. To some extent the Progressives accomplished
their goals but the result also strengthened the anti-party tendencies
of the fourth party system. The adoption of state ballots denied
the parties the important function of printing and distributing the
ballots; primary elections deprived the minority party of its monopoly of the opposition; and the expansion of civil service prevented partisan distribution of the rewards of office on the mass—
though not on the elite—level. Paralleling the decline of partisan
competition and party organization was a significant reduction in
voter turnout.

All of these trends were exaggerated in the one-party South.

---

[29] New York, New Jersey, Indiana, and Ohio were the major competitive
states. David, *Party Strength in the United States, 1872-1970,* 21-54. Except
for its emphasis on ethnocultural factors, this discussion of the "system of
1896" conforms to the interpretation developed by Walter Dean Burnham.
See particularly Burnham, "The Changing Shape of the American Political Universe," *American Political Science Review,* 59 (March 1965), 7-28. See also
the analysis of ethnocultural conflict in Paul Kleppner, *The Cross of Culture:
A Social Analysis of Midwestern Politics, 1850-1900* (New York: Free Press,
1970), and Richard Jensen, *The Winning of the Midwest: Social and Political
Conflict, 1888-1896* (Chicago: University of Chicago Press, 1971).

Whereas by the 1920s voter turnout in presidential elections had
dropped to about 60 percent of the potential nonsouthern electorate,
it had in the South fallen to less than 25 percent, hardly a third of
what it had been during much of the nineteenth century. But the
system did permit southern control of a Democratic party dominated by white southern and Irish Catholic elites. In the early
1880s white southerners became a majority of Senate Democrats,
and, except for occasional Democratic surges, southern whites outnumbered other Democrats in the House after the early 1870s.
This domination became complete during the twentieth century.
By controlling one of the major parties, white southerners effectively possessed the "concurrent majority" that John C. Calhoun
had longed for in antebellum days.[30]

The situation changed dramatically with the coming of the fifth
party system. Dispirited by a decade of electoral failure in
national politics, the Democrats in 1928 nominated Alfred E. Smith,
the Catholic son of New York Irish immigrants. Making no secret
of his disdain for the Ku Klux Klan and prohibition, Smith had a
magnetic appeal to the emerging ethnic and religious minorities in
northern cities. The "new immigration" that in its early stages had
contributed to the destabilization of partisan politics during the
1890s had crowded into the northern industrial centers huge numbers of southern and eastern Europeans. During the 1920s many
of them had drifted toward the Democratic party in state and local
elections, and in 1928 they became a major force in national politics.
Galvanized by the Smith campaign, the ethnics turned out in impressive numbers to swing the larger cities into the Democratic
column. Protestants heavily opposed this new papal offensive,
of course, and Smith lost by a substantial margin nationally. But
the 1928 election proved to be a harbinger of the general realignment of the 1930s. The traumatic impact of the Great Depression
broke Republican domination of national politics and opened the
way for the formation of the New Deal coalition. Joining the non-
Protestant ethnic minorities that had voted for Smith were blacks,
who abandoned the party of Lincoln to support the New Deal,
labor union members, and, of course, white southerners. The Republican party became the home of nonsouthern and nonunion
white Protestants. The fifth party system resurrected partisan com-

[30] This point is developed in David M. Potter, *The South and the Concurrent
Majority* (Baton Rouge: Louisiana State University Press, 1972).

petition in the northern industrial states and fostered a modest upsurge in voter turnout. By bringing spokesmen for the ethnic minorities and labor into leadership positions and by countering corporate dominance with political authority based on bureaucracy rather than political parties, the New Deal broadened the narrow elite base that had marked the previous party system.

These political upheavals had limited immediate impact in the one-party South. Although the Smith campaign had touched off a vigorous anti-Catholic reaction that split the Solid South on the presidential level for the first time since Reconstruction, the region was a land of Democrats and few voters prior to that election and remained so afterward.[31] Yet while Democratic success at the polls nationally elevated veteran southerners to congressional committee leadership positions, the realignment also shifted the mass base of the party from the South to the northern and far western urban centers. Sharp and persistent intraparty conflicts between southern and nonsouthern Democrats soon became a cardinal feature of the fifth party system. Not since the Free Soil and Know-Nothing revolts within the Whig party of the antebellum era had a major party been so racked with open internal dissension. Dixiecrats, Democrats for Eisenhower, States Righters, Independents, American Independents, and Democrats for Nixon flourished in the South following the unifying crises of the depression and World War II. Democratic-sponsored civil rights legislation during the mid-1960s brought intraparty hostilities to the boiling point. The position of the national Democratic party collapsed in the Deep South in 1964, when the large majority of white voters in the southern heartland cast ballots for Republican Barry M. Goldwater. In 1968 the national Democratic presidential ticket failed throughout the region, with lower South whites voting for Wallace and upper South whites favoring Richard M. Nixon. The rout became complete in 1972 when most white southern voters supported Nixon. Black southerners remained Democratic, providing the bulk of the votes for the Democratic presidential ticket in the Deep South in 1964 and throughout the region in 1968 and 1972. The breakdown of the Democratic monopoly in the South provoked acute conflict and pushed voter turnout to levels far above southern twentieth century norms (though still low by nineteenth century standards).

[31] Technically, it should be noted, Warren G. Harding cracked the Solid South in the presidential election of 1920 by carrying Tennessee.

Through five party systems, southern whites have divided, sometimes over basic issues, but only for a brief period prior to the Civil War have these differences been sufficient to sustain stable partisan divisions. Since the 1890s a muted form of class conflict has been relatively common. Democratic primary elections have produced a limited number of liberal Democrats and even in a few instances—notably the case of Huey P. Long of Louisiana—radical Democrats. More recently, the Wallace movement has been overwhelmingly dependent on the votes of lower status and rural whites, as opposed to the Republican proclivities of higher status white suburbanites and the Democratic loyalty of southern blacks.[32] But the history of five party systems strongly suggests the centrality of ethnocultural values, and, as a character in a William Faulkner novel stated, "It's because we [white southerners] alone in the United States . . . are a homogeneous people. I mean the only one of any size."[33] Except for the substantial Latino and Jewish populations in Florida and the Chicanos in Texas, southerners are, on the whole, black and white old-stock Protestants, with the latter massively in the majority. Consequently, whatever the nature of the political system that emerges from the ruins of the New Deal coalition, "the Americanization of Dixie" does not necessarily imply the coming of a viable two-party politics in the South nor a decline of political sectionalism.

[32] Political behavior in the modern South is examined in Numan V. Bartley and Hugh D. Graham, *Southern Politics and the Second Reconstruction* (Baltimore: The Johns Hopkins University Press, 1975), and William C. Havard, ed., *The Changing Politics of the South* (Baton Rouge: Louisiana State University Press, 1972).

[33] Faulkner, *Intruder in the Dust*, 153.

Continuity and Discontinuity:
Dour Reflections
on the
National Security

CHARLES BURTON MARSHALL

A REPORTER who arrived at the very finish of my lecture—billed as "The Prospects for Detente"—in Buffalo a while back asked me to fill him in on what I had said. I declined because, among other reasons, I had to catch a plane. "At least tell me this," the man importuned, "Is dee-TENT-ee a thing or a man?" A short time later I read a quadruple interview on the same subject in one of the country's leading newspapers. Two United States senators and two scholars of repute participating all expressed themselves in favor of detente and then produced a half-dozen diverse and in part contradictory versions of what it was they had endorsed.

The two recollections make a simple point. A foreignism of central significance in discussion about contemporary foreign policy is all too likely to be beyond a listener's cognition and elusive of precision even when used by supposed *cognoscenti* in the field of external affairs. That circumstance is no novelty. The main words in international politics and foreign policy are mostly, and deplorably, fuzzy. I subscribe to a Confucian precept concerning the rectification of names as of paramount importance in governing. As a onetime practitioner and present teacher in the pertinent fields, I have found it necessary to give much time and zeal to trying to be clear about meanings of terms. I always wish, moreover, to know what the cheering—or, for that matter the jeering—is about before I join in. These thoughts suffice to justify my attempt in this essay to present problems of national security in a long perspective. In a definition suitable for our purposes, though not one cast in simple terms, detente denotes a modification—away from anxiety and animosity and toward trust and concord—of attitudes, expectations, and policies between organized societies. The societies concerned in particular are the United States and the Soviet Union. Those who tout detente portray it as an improvement, from the standpoint of national security, over an anterior phase of relationships generally called the Cold War. That idea especially is one I wish to ponder. I shall proceed as succinctly as I can—taking pains to define as I go—to some specific conclusions.

National security signifies the existence of conditions warranting strong expectations of the American people's continuity into a long future as a nation organized through institutions of government sustained by their allegiance and capable of effecting the linked purposes enunciated in the preamble of the Constitution. Those purposes are effectible not in a sense of being brought to conclusion but in a sense of being worked at and maintained as continuous agenda related to the nation as the faculty of liquidity relates to a bank. Five of the matters stated as purposes—perfection of the Union, establishment of justice, promotion of the general welfare, ensuring of domestic tranquility, and securing of liberty to present and oncoming generations—are intrinsic to the nation and presuppose national autonomy. A sixth purpose, fourth in the order given—namely, provision for the common defense—rather than being intrinsic to the nation, looks outward to matters beyond the scope of national jurisdiction, is interdependent with the national autonomy presupposed for the others, and thus is integral to national security as I have defined it. Its implicit components are the fending off of intimidation from without, the preserving of territorial integrity, and the assuring of accessibility of materials essential to national survival and well-being.

Provision for the common defense is an enduring purpose. Fulfilling it entails perception of threats, variant from one epoch to another according to multiple circumstances, and measures to neutralize them—including means for posing counter threats. The root meaning of the infinitive joined to the common defense in the Constitution—*to provide*—is to see ahead. Among the action words in the preamble, it is peculiar in being anticipative. Provi-

dence in the common defense does not consist merely of adjustment
to determined probabilities but inheres rather in adjustment *of*
probabilities perceived as alterable. The function entails discern-
ment of ranges of pertinent possibilities ahead and distinguishing
among them in respect of their benefit or menace, their quotients
of probability, and the responsiveness of such quotients to efforts
to affect them. Next—and this is the heart of the matter—the
common defense requires attempting to raise probability quotients
of possibilities favorable, and to reduce those of possibilities antagonistic, to national security.

Because it basically involves ventures in prediction, providing
for the common defense is constrained by inherent limits of pre-
dictability. Forehandedness is required because foreknowledge is
problematic. The essence is not preemption of decisions in foreseeable exigencies but timely allocation of resources so as not to
foreclose choice—power to cope—for those later on to bear responsibility for the common defense in face of exigencies as yet
unforeseeable. The aim is to forestall surprise in the sense both
of the manifestation of the unforeseen and, more importantly, of
being foreclosed from choice and overwhelmed.

In an open society with accountable governing institutions, the
entity functioning at any stage in providing for the common defense is an indeterminate human aggregate varying, according to
the particular at hand, from a small number with official status
to the populace as a whole. What at any stage is critical, in a
sense of being decisive, is not individual capacity for percipiency
but what the group in a determining portion perceives together.
Whatever the group—whether consisting of the President and a
small number of counselors, inclusive of some necessary portion
of Congress, or engrossing the nation as a whole—the scope and
accuracy of its perceptions must depend on pertinent judgments
and standards, major premises and norms, accepted in general.
Such a pattern of common, or shared, sense about what really
counts constitutes what I shall term as such a group's operational
code—an expression borrowed from Nathan Leites' writings and, in
my judgment, preferable in this context to ideology, which denotes
a particular kind of operational code.

An operational code should reflect experience, direct or received.
In that sense memory is a constituent of capacity to perceive—and
herein I pay my respects to Thomas Aquinas for having included
a good memory among attributes required in governing. Good

memory is discriminating memory, meaning memory capable of distinguishing between the applicable and the inapplicable past. That kind of memory, maintained in common, is essential to forehandedness in providing for the common defense. Coherence in related policies—an indisputably necessary quality—requires shared perceptions, and those in turn require a shared operational code, among the aggregates involved in decisions. Otherwise authority is fragmented, and measures become bogged in contradiction. Another obvious essential is effectuality, which requires, besides coherence, correctness of perceptions.

Because of the character of problems pertinent to providing for the common defense, coded norms pertinent to concord and peace, conflict and war, and the nexus among them are of particular pertinence. Points of reference for making analytic distinctions among such coded norms are whether or not concord and peace are assumed to be inherent general conditions and what values are assigned to them or, in contrast, to conflict and war. The functions and contents of operational codes in the American experience as distinguished from those of other aggregates of mankind are relevant here. In my judgment, no element in the American psyche presents a record more remarkable for consistency and continuity.

Pertinent norms in the traditional American outlook were derived from a sense of apartness and new beginnings associated with the colonial experience. Those norms were reflections also of intellectual doctrines of the Enlightenment strongly influential in American thought in connection with the establishment of national independence. Circumstances in the nation's early epochs seemed to vindicate those norms. With the end of Napoleonic times, important military potential in Europe, which had been the locus of active strategic rivalries, had become diffused among diverse states of similar magnitudes. Such forces as some of them had maintained in the American hemisphere had been substantially withdrawn and from positions an ocean's width away no longer posed an appreciable threat here. Europe itself had entered a phase of relative tranquility. What wars occurred in Europe or elsewhere were generally local in scope, brief in duration, and conducted for modest stakes.

The United States experienced its share of conflict, including a huge internal war in the 1860s. It was plausible, nevertheless, to regard concord and peace as the inherent conditions. By a corollary, conflict and war were seen as aberrant and deviant—as results of breakdowns of normal order. The causes of war were discerned as relatively superficial and readily rectifiable maladjustments. The channeling of human thought and energy into higher and better—and normal—endeavors was assumed to be a sensible means for abating conflict and ending war. Harmony of interest, taken to be inherent, would be given its chance to prosper through encouragement of good will, reason, knowledge, communication, understanding and the like. The attitude was abolitionary of war in a mild, reformish way. Considerations of strategy were disjointed from conditions of peace. Strategy consisted of a set of concepts relevant to the common defense only in rare contingencies of belligerency and out of mind during normal reigns of peace.

Such ideas were consistent elements underlying a diversity of attitudes and initiatives in United States foreign policy. The long attachment to isolationism articulated in President Washington's Farewell Address and maintained for a century prior to and two decades subsequent to World War I was consistent with such norms. President Theodore Roosevelt's overtures in 1907 looking to the second of the peace conferences at The Hague, President Taft's program of arbitration treaties, Secretary of State Bryan's network of conciliation treaties in Wilson's first term, and the Kellogg-Briand Pact in 1929 for renunciation of war stemmed from similar premises. So did the successive neutrality acts of 1935-37. More to the point, United States policies in both of the World Wars reflected the same assumptions in a different way.

In its fashion, each of those wars was portrayed in United States policy as a war to abolish war. The character of the nation's enemies lent plausibility to the notion. By a code of norms antithetic to the one already summarized, war, seen as the inherent phenomenon, alone gives scope to human potentialities, whereas peace is regarded as a deformation that enchains and impoverishes the human spirit. A succession of German scriveners had written variations on that romantic-militaristic theme during the nineteenth century. Discourses from the imperial throne in William II's time echoed their dour sentimentalities. A generation later, Hitler drew upon an exaggerated version of kindred ideas in doing his dramatic, dogmatic and aggressive utmost. These observations are not intended as explanations of the historic causes of the two World Wars —matters much too complex for explication here. What is in point, the Kaiser as personification of the Central Powers and, even more so, the Fuehrer as personification of the Axis, made it easy to believe that victory would mark an overthrow of bellicosity itself and open a way for limitless peace.

In both instances, strategic considerations were applied for subduing enemies but not beyond. National leadership articulated conditions of peace in terms avowedly transcending strategic considerations. The central element to which national leadership hoped to entrust national security was an international organization—first the League of Nations and then the United Nations—designed to universalize a code of norms such as those nurtured among Americans in the country's period of privileged detachment. President Franklin D. Roosevelt and his Secretary of State, Cordell Hull, in their time—just as President Wilson in his—portrayed international organization as an arrangement to abolish war and thus to outmode strategy. As in Wilson's earlier version, the organization was supposed to institutionalize so overwhelming a consensus for such a code of norms that strategic competition would be consigned to an obsolete past, and thenceforth international politics would be conducted, and international differences reconciled, under conditions free of any intimidating shadow of hostilities.

Roosevelt counted on indefinite continuity for the coalition drawn together to overthrow the Axis—an unequivocally committed United States associated with a robust and purposeful Britain, a rehabilitated France, an amicably disposed China at last autonomous and capable of participating in general affairs as a great power, and finally a Soviet Union in a durable collaborative mood. Back from the Yalta conference—marking the high point in the dream of collaboration between the United States and its Soviet ally—Roosevelt in early 1945 depicted to Congress a post-war world freed from needs "for spheres of influence, for alliances, for balances of power, or any other special arrangements." All such strategic devices, he promised, would be consigned to "the unhappy past."

It would be pointless to dwell upon the fatuities—as they seem now—in Roosevelt's depiction of that aspiration and his confidence of his ability to give effect to it. As they illustrate, in foreign policy as in so much of life, believing is seeing. Roosevelt's faith in his postulates was strong because the need seemed great. His foundations for peace to follow upon defeat of the Axis were completely consonant with the American operational code. Critics have often leveled charges of dissimulation against him as a policy leader, but not, I think, with respect to his project for an organized, pacified postwar world. Regarding that aim, he was forthcoming, and he was supported by a wide consensus among his countrymen in official life and in general.

"It is not the fact that we believe"—to quote a truism from Morris Raphael Cohen's *Preface to Logic*—"or how intensely we believe, that determines probability, but the content of what is asserted." However strong the convictions sustaining them, Roosevelt's expectations proved unprophetic respecting British strength, China's political character after victory, and—of special importance here—the Soviet Union's postwar intentions. A divergence of purposes, positioning the United States and the Soviet Union as adversaries, soon materialized as an impediment to the hoped-for collaboration. The divergence was rooted in an antithesis between respective codes of norms, and so a consideration of the Soviet outlook is pertinent.

At a high level of abstraction—and one should always be wary of truths which hold only at such a level—the respective codes of norms are alike in postulating concord and peace as inherent and conflict and war as aberrant. The Soviet outlook, however, holds such aberrations as give rise to conflict and war to be characteristics knotted into the very fabric of human societies. Accordingly, a drastic reordering of relationships, a redoing of human awareness and culture, is necessary—in the senses both of being instrumental and of being inevitable—to the end of eliminating war-making aberrations and giving rein to inherent human peaceableness. At a theoretic final reckoning, on completion of the processes of redoing, war will be permanently abolished and absolute peace installed. Meanwhile the quest of purported peace must be forwarded by pressing antagonisms overtly or covertly against human aggregates of distinguishable outlook, regarded as having vested interests in aberrant conditions underlying conflict. The performers of that mission profess to regard themselves as agents of historic necessity rather than as mere executors of their own interests. Constituting the Communist Party hierarchy whose base is the Soviet Union and whose instrument is the Soviet state apparatus, those executors must strive above all to hold onto that position. That aim requires monopoly of the country's public life, control of intellectual, artistic, spiritual, and economic aspects of existence, and the forestalling of any internal challenge to "the little self-perpetuating clique of men at the top"—an apt description from

George Kennan's famous 1947 article in *Foreign Affairs* on "The Sources of Soviet Conduct." Beyond that paramount aim of self-perpetuation, the ruling group strives to maintain Communist rule wherever established elsewhere and awaits and encourages, as it can, opportunities tending toward an eventual universal triumph professed as inevitable.

The phase of relationships known as the Cold War began concomitantly with a shift among United States policy makers to that perception of the Soviet Union. A government—I refer specifically to our own—is not a disciplined and coordinated outfit responsive to authoritative direction with the unison of a football team executing a signal sent in from the bench. An attempt to time precisely the pertinent shift in perception would be misleading. Recognition of divergence over conditions of peace between the United States and its former main ally against the Axis—involving disappointment of the Roosevelt dream of collaboration in world order—developed in stages beginning within a year after Roosevelt's death and continuing for several years.

No span of peace in the nation's past matched the new circumstances. The accustomed practice of postulating concord and peace as inherent, and conflict and war as aberrant interruptions of normal courses, did not fit the situation. For the first time in national experience it had become necessary to consider peace and war not as disjoined aspects of experience but as contrasting and sometimes concurrent products of differing combinations of the same factors.

An external probability adverse to national security is a threat. An alterable probability countervailing a threat is a strategic opportunity. A concern to make use of such an opportunity is a strategic interest. An obligation to uphold such an interest is a commitment. Considerations despite which commitments are entered into and effectuated—that is to say, considerations which test will—are costs, which may be computable or noncomputable. Computable costs are expressible as resources. Commitment—expressing an inner resolve on contingent action, the manifestation of such a resolve as a pledge to influence others' wills and actions, and finally the actual venturing of resources—is the key term, for it represents linkage between matters intrinsic and matters external to the United States.

The conduct of policy in strategic terms is a business of maintaining coherence among perceived threats, recognized opportunities, defined interests, and acknowledged and accepted costs, including resources provided. All of these matters in combination have a bearing on questions constantly in mind among those who make policy for governments in strategic rivalry and for those in the status of watchful bystanders. What would happen in the event hypothetical war should become actual? Who would be drawn in? Who would stay out? What havoc would be wrought? Who would prevail in the final issue? From their answers to such questions—and from their estimates of adversaries' answers and of adversaries' perceptions regarding their own answers—potential enemies derive their assumptions concerning thresholds of hostilities, their sense of how far it is safe to push an issue, and their grasp of when it is prudent to temporize or, in extremity, to back down.

Strategic stability derives from a proximate match between the respective sides' perceptions of those questions. When both sides perceive the outcome of hypothetical war as a toss-up and are reciprocally aware of each other's perceptions, the degree of constraint on them is about equal. When ultimate advantage is perceived as accruing to one and the same side, that side is less under constraint in any confrontation. Strategic instability and high danger of war obtain when each side assumes the ultimate advantage and the other side's concurrence in that assumption.

It is pertinent to recall here the country's situation at the time of first undertaking the conduct of strategic competition as a settled part of policy in nonbelligerency and of creating an array of institutions—DOD, JCS, NSC, CIA, AER, and the others—whose acronyms symbolize various aspects of the novel mission. As of now, one can comprehend the circumstances only against a background of experiences in World War II.

As convincingly related in Geoffrey Perrett's *Days of Sadness, Years of Triumph,* that war produced a series of prodigious successes for national policy. Revitalization of the national economy— an aim zealously but ineffectually striven for in nine years of the New Deal—had become realized in a surpassing degree. Despite huge diversions of manpower into military service, manufacturing and agricultural production had exceeded all experience and expectation. Rates of upward mobility, both economic and social, had been unprecedented. Yet inflation had been minimal. After some initial reverses, military operations of unimagined scope and complexity had been carried through to definitive results precisely on schedule. As never before, the nation had become united in recognition of common enemies, all of whom were brought to unequivocal defeat.

At the conclusion, the country's capital plant, far from having suffered net damage, was expanded, diversified, and modernized far beyond the prewar situation. Agriculture had achieved new levels of efficiency. The country's food reserves were sufficient to meet any conceivable domestic or foreign demand. The value of a dollar steady at 35 to an ounce of gold provided the standard measure for the trading world's currencies. The nation's commercial shipping resources were unrivaled. The nation had a short-run monopoly and a longer-run headstart in nuclear technology. Its naval power and air power far surpassed any possible combination. The nation itself and its army and other services were attuned to victory. The country's public life had escaped damage by defeat, invasion, and occupation. Civil morale was high.

I have neither sympathy nor patience with current tendencies, characteristically misinformed, to find evidences and promptings for a feeling of national guilt because of the extent of national power or in the way it was put to use in that epoch. The scope and quality of this government's endeavors to help in rehabilitation of public life and in restoration and enhancement of economic vitality among scores of long-established nations in the wake of the war and to assist various newcomers to statehood in trying to get off to a good start were, everything considered, creditable. I must forgo details on diverse aspects, however, for the focus here is on strategic considerations.

For the time being, the elements of strength in the American situation afforded the United States ultimate strategic advantage vis-a-vis the Soviet Union. The United States brought within the scope of assurance provided by that advantage certain other countries which, lacking United States support, would find themselves under intimidation from the Soviet Union.

The scope of the vast and varied strategic commitments abroad into which the United States contracted itself was further enlarged after the Communist accession to power in continental China. As a Senate Foreign Relations Committee report of a few years ago described the magnitudes:

> With an eagerness and a "can-do" philosophy, the United States expanded its military presence abroad, to the point where it assumed, almost inad-

vertently and without notice, a role that has been described as the policeman of the free world.

As a result . . . the United States was firmly committed to more than 43 nations by treaty and agreement and had some 375 major foreign military bases and 3,000 minor military facilities spread all over the world, virtually surrounding the Soviet Union and Communist China. . . .

The effort included the tendering of military equipment and training and the deployment of United States forces abroad where considered necessary to make guarantees sufficiently dissuasive to adversaries, persuasive to allies. In the Korean and Southeast Asian cases, United States forces were pitted against Communist forces in a dozen cumulative years of peripheral combat. Here, however, our concern is less with magnitudes and events than with underlying concepts.

A perception of peace and war as complementary variables across a continuum of existence rather than as disjoined and antithetic slabs of time can be a basis for a quite plausible code of norms. In such a view, a concept of war as a breakdown of peace shares validity with a concept of peace as a breakdown of war. The attitude does not glorify war and certainly may prefer peace. Such an outlook defines the condition of peace in strategic terms— as a situation achieved and preserved by taking account of factors which in a distinguishable perspective would be integers of war plans. Karl von Clausewitz's *On War* is a classic epitome of such an approach. Geoffrey Blainey's *The Causes of War* ably portrays it in our own time. Without presuming to put myself in a class with either, I own to having long shared the outlook. What seemed exceptional to me was that fragile past during which peace and security had been bestowed on the United States. Wilsonianism and the Rooseveltian adaptation of it struck me as ill-founded. The re-embodiment of world organization seemed to me delusory and diversionary. I took the advent of strategic competition called the Cold War to be only what should have been expected in the circumstances, and not deplorable.

Not my personal outlook but the premises underlying national policies then undertaken are what matter here. In a sense such premises were consonant with the strategic view of peace as described, but such a view was adopted in addition, rather than in succession, to the traditional coded norms. The point brings up a problem in the logic of policy. How can an operational code involving a postulate of concord and peace as inherent, along with a corollary of conflict and war as aberrant, come to terms with an antithetic set of purposes linked to an irreconcilable code? The problem did not arise in relation to challenges posed by rampant adversaries encountered in the two world wars, for they could be coped with as aberrant interruptions. The challenge posed by a Soviet rulership "under no ideological compulsion to accomplish its purposes in a hurry"—a regime, in Kennan's description, in a position to "afford to be patient" and to "look forward to a duel of infinite duration"—was of a different sort. How cope with such a challenge without altering the operational code into the obverse of the adversary's? Projectors of United States policy handled the matter by postulating the adversary's malleability. The aim was not overthrow but reform of the other side. Persevere long enough in denying the Kremlin opportunity while taking care to avoid general war, and eventually—so went the rationale—the adversary must desist from frowardness and become more tractable.

Variations on the theme were multiple. President Truman's enunciation of the Truman Doctrine in 1947 envisioned eventual Soviet cooperation in efforts for "peaceful development of nations, free from coercion." Kennan's famous article of the same year declared it to be within the United States' "power to increase enormously the strains under which Soviet policy must operate, to force upon the Kremlin a far greater degree of moderation and circumspection than it has had to observe in recent years, and in this way to promote tendencies which must eventually find their outlet in either the break-up or the gradual mellowing of Soviet power." Secretary of State Dean Acheson's testimony before the Senate Foreign Relations Committee explained the North Atlantic Treaty, far from being a regional alliance in any sense known to the past, as a device for moving toward vindication of the United Nations Charter's promise of a world gentled by a universally shared preference for peace. President Eisenhower professed to anticipate that happy eventuality within "the foreseeable future." President Kennedy's speech at American University in 1963 all but announced its advent. President Lyndon Johnson's speech of April 7, 1965, ostensibly committing the United States to realizing unmolested independence for South Viet Nam, dwelt upon a goal of achieving Communist collaboration in realization of "a very old dream . . . of a world where disputes are settled by law and reason."

In their own fashion the Soviet Union's policy-makers have also looked beyond the Cold War. Stalin's successors soon abandoned his professed anticipation of an inevitable epoch of unequivocal war antecedent to final victory for the Soviet Union's purposes. In their preferred version, opposition would gradually be degraded to ineffectuality.

Both the United States' and the Soviet Union's conceptions of a subsequence to the Cold War represent in their respective ways a reversion to Yalta. In the American version, the Soviet Union will have become at least tacitly desistant from revolutionary opportunism, inclined instead to define its aims in terms of national interests traditionally perceived, and won over to seeing the advantages of collaborating in good faith toward realization of mutual benefits in a stabilized world—much the way Roosevelt perceived "Uncle's Joe's" Russia. In the Soviet version, the United States—preoccupied with thoughts of peace, pliable about conditions, careless of strategic considerations, treasuring super-power collaboration as good per se, and trusting and acquiescent about the nature and scope of Soviet ambition—will have become tacitly disposed to acquiesce in legitimization of Soviet purposes, or at least abashed to press issues about them. Such was about the way Marshal Stalin must have sized up Roosevelt's America in early 1945.

"As a state of mind"—Adam Ulam writes in his excellent biography, *Stalin*—"the Cold War had its origin in the Americans' fear of things and people they do not understand and in Soviet Russia's fear of being understood." One must apply care in analyzing those words, for in them the meaning of the verb *understand* shifts subtly from "empathize" to "comprehend." American policy-makers long to empathize. Soviet policy-makers dislike being comprehended. The thought reveals much. For American policy-makers the Yalta mood epitomized a reassuring sense of empathizing with the Soviet Union. Reciprocally, awareness of that felt empathy must have brought Soviet policy-makers an encouraging sense of being misunderstood—along with a consciousness of diminishing risks and an expectation of expanding opportunities.

Such was the psychological interaction interrupted by the Cold War, which both sides have striven to end in ways suitable to their respective outlooks. Hoped-for turns toward amity have been heralded at nine junctures beginning with the lifting of the first Berlin blockade in 1949. The pertinent word in American usage then was "thaw." Later on "relaxation of tensions" enjoyed vogue.

In the early 1960s that awkard phrase gave way to the briefer French equivalent. "Detente" has become accepted also in Soviet usage as an occasional synonym for a more customary phrase, "peaceful coexistence."

It has remained for the Nixon administration and its legatee to portray detente as a great realization in policy, for which credit is claimed and applause acknowledged—a fragile achievement, however, for the very ones vaunting it as a benign reality warn us that detente, like the heaven-sent knight Lohengrin, is likely to leave in a huff if questioned. Like Lohengrin's bride, I have in mind some queries to put even under pain of disenthrallment.

How does one account for the preoccupation with personality in the conduct of foreign policy currently being mainfested among communicators and within the magistracy? As for the networks and the press, the answer is not difficult. Characteristically a superficial lot in a hasty vocation, journalists are romantically predisposed. So long as it works or seems to work, shuttle diplomacy fits in with the theatricalizing which is a specialty of TV news. The printed hyperbolizing—as when a weekly news magazine hails the Secretary of State as "Super-Secretary," another alludes to his negotiatory "miracles," or a third credits him with having "a magic touch"—is on a par, for insight and erudition, with a beauty queen's description of him as "the greatest man produced in the modern age." How the Aladdin-and-lamp motif has caught on at high levels of authority is more significant. I, for one, was astounded on learning of President's Ford's public pledge to the United Nations General Assembly against correcting an overconcentration of roles in that one official. Had the world's governments actually been on tenterhooks lest the President should correct what was obviously an organizational anomaly? Why should details so intrinsic to our own executive branch be made international business? If they are properly so, then I see no basis for a rebuke later on to the Organization for African Unity for trying to nose into a third-echelon appointment within the Department of State.

The overappraising of personality attests, I suspect, a fancy that the United States may luck through its troubles on virtuosity in lieu of resolve and forehandedness. Secretary Kissinger's knowledge, energy, and deftness as negotiator are not in question. One may acknowledge those attributes without being moved to touch

the hem of the man's garments. Yet most of the Secretary's celebrated achievements—and this is the rub—seem fated to prove out
as ephemeral wonders. As their transiency becomes revealed by
events, one can wish at least that certain lessons not be lost on
general awareness. For one, even when deftly maneuvered, rear-
guard actions are not triumphs. For a second, miracles and a magic
touch are irrelevant to the conduct of foreign policy. Competence
for practitioners is indeed vastly preferable to incompetence, but
will and tangible resourcefulness, not prodigies, are the ingredients
of salvation.

The grasp of foreign policy underlying detente does unduly
accentuate personality as a component in international relations.
Rapport among statesmen is taken to signify compatibility of interests between the states which they are supposed to represent.
Yet rapport is preserved by confining attention to matters susceptible of being agreed on and passing over such matters as divide.
The aura engendered by thus dwelling on points of agreement, to
the exclusion of controvertible matters, tends to suggest more
concord than warranted by the situation as a whole. Detente is
an exercise in atmospherics carried on with a view to reducing
basic divergencies and, pari passu, transforming animosities.

That observation does not necessarily impugn the process. All
civility—I must concede this point—rests upon deemphasis of
antagonisms. On the other hand—and this point I must stress—
not all repression of antagonism promotes civility. The point has
a connection with the Confucian principle concerning the importance of using right names. That principle leads me to discuss
the phenomenon of euphemism and its potential for mischief.

Euphemism was exemplified in former Senator Fulbright's call
for Israel to acknowledge the Palestine Liberation Front as a
"bargaining partner"—prompting me to consult my dictionary in
vain for an authentic definition to justify the key term, partner, in
such a context. Senator Humphrey euphemized in alluding to a
prospective "transfer of power" in Cambodia—as if an impending
sanguinary conquest were to be a constitutional devolution of
authority. Euphemism denotes a practice of using auspicious
terms, terms of good omen, to make reality seem better than warranted—a practice, to paraphrase a contemporary barbarism, of
telling it like it isn't. What is harmful in it is, obviously, a tendency
to obscure what needs to be done.

Detente, as I see it, is an extended exercise in euphemism. One needs only to revert to former President Nixon's broaching of detente by announcing an end to an era of confrontation and the beginning of an epoch of negotiation with the Soviet Union. The implied disjunction between diplomatic processes and contests of will was at variance with experience. In fact, also, negotiations with the Soviet Union focusing on the conditions of peace had been going on for a quarter century, with lapses only in Stalin's final phase and in the last seven months of the Eisenhower presidency—producing a record of diplomatic interchange unsurpassed for volume and scope in the history of relationships between great powers. No one was, or is, in position to rule out further face-to-face tests of will between the United States and the Soviet Union.

In phrases from Robert Conquest writing in *Foreign Affairs*, such an approach assumes "the Soviet polity . . . whose characteristics are almost extravagantly different from our own"—"an almost unbelievably aberrant and deviant political culture"—to be "just another foreign state, a powerful rival no doubt, but little more: a country whose rulers certainly conduct their internal affairs in a way we can only deplore, but . . . in the international field are to be regarded as more or less like anyone else." A change of the Soviet Union's character to conform to that assumption would confirm success for the United States' version of a proper sequel to the Cold War and, again in Conquest's words, "would indicate the total transformation of the world scene; would be the one single event which would bring true and lasting peace to our planet."

Detente begs a question. In an application of Ulam's formulation, are those who govern in the United States properly content at last in truly understanding the Soviet Union, while those ruling in the Soviet Union have reformed so as to have become happy at last about being truly understood, or are our magistrates deluding themselves with euphemisms while those who rule in the Soviet Union, still our steady adversaries, feel reassured in a renewed awareness of being misunderstood? That disenthralling question—which gets to basic differences between incompatible versions of how to end the Cold War—has to be asked, and those guiding United States foreign policy should be pressed to answer it candidly.

My own answer is, at least to me, not reassuring. Virtually all of the elements of strength supporting undertakings in United States policy at the outset of the Cold War either have lapsed or appear to have come into serious question—a conclusion which I state without elaborating in dismal detail. The country's general attitude reminds me of a description in George Santayana's *Dominations and Powers* concerning another nation in regression:

. . . . she could no longer be warlike with a good conscience; the virtuous thing was to bow one's way out and say: My mistake.   Her kings were half-ashamed to be kings, her liberals were half-ashamed to govern. . . . All became a medley of sweet reasonableness, stupidity, and confusion.   Being a great power was now a great burden.   It was urgent to reduce responsibility, to reduce armaments, to refer everything to conferences, . . . to let everyone have his own way abroad, and to let everyone have his own way at home. Had not England always been a champion of liberty?   But wasn't it time now for the champion to retire?   And wouldn't liberty be much freer without a champion?

With minor revisions, those reflections would apply now to the United States.   So far as general awareness is concerned, the epoch of strategic concern seems to have become a parenthesis in national experience.   The nonstrategic operational code of our longer past seems to have endured without having been more than temporarily affected.   Certainly the postulates of a strategic outlook took hold, if at all, only tentatively and ambiguously among large portions of Americans.

As well as to Americans in general, the last observation is applicable in part also to policy-makers.   My reproach here is not to their folly of getting involved in Vietnam, whence we wanted out, against an enemy determined to get in—a certain formula for eventual defeat and a defiance of precepts of sound strategy.   My reproach, rather, is to the improvidence of having desisted a decade ago from maintaining ascendancy in strategic nuclear power in a belief that the Soviet adversary would reciprocate our wish to settle for a strategic stalemate and thus—with strategic factors neutralized —help vindicate in a roundabout way our dream of a world pacified by the disjoining of peace from the contingencies of war.

A problem before us now is that of rallying will and assigning resources to maintain a strategic balance and to prevent a determinative advantage from slipping away to an adversary who, besides being willing to bide time, has no intent to settle for indeterminate results.   That problem is all the more difficult because of a lack of general awareness of the dangers.   That lack in turn is due in large part to preoccupation with detente, misperception of its effects, and misrepresentation of its accomplishments at the apex of political authority.

Surveying trends and estimating prospects from the Kremlin's standpoint, I think I would on balance feel quite assured. Casting up those matters from an American outlook, I see adverse trends everywhere and perceive ahead great dangers of slippage into strategic subordination, with all the dire corollaries of that relationship. We must do the things necessary to avoid that plight, but that is not to say we shall do them. Unless and until we break free of the fashion of agreeing on the goodness of detente, it seems unlikely that we shall. In my view, detente is a conceptual snare because of its ambiguity, as illustrated in the following sentence quoted from the lead of a dispatch datelined from Moscow and published in the *New York Times*, April 7, 1975: "Despite a tide in foreign affairs apparently running in Moscow's favor in Indochina, the Middle East and Portugal, the overriding theme in Soviet foreign policy remains that of detente." With "because of" substituted for "despite" the sentence makes sense.

Democracy and Tyranny in America: The Radical Paradox of the Bicentennial and Blacks in the American Political System

SAMUEL DuBois COOK

AMBIGUITY, AMBIVALENCE, TENSION, paradox, irony, tragedy, contradiction, and schizophrenia have always governed the status of the black man in the American political system and process—as indeed they have presided, somewhat like Platonic essences and pure forms, over his position and lot in the total institutional firmament and public and private life of the country. Politics is, after all, a function of culture—the values, presuppositions, world-view, ethos, style, materiality, and vision of the whole web and heart's desire of a people and culture. Racism and its ideology have informed, inspired, and guided the broad sweep of American culture. In a tortuous and anguished way, racism has been, on the ultimate level, both the affirmation and the negation of the American Dream.

Inevitably, therefore, political life has reflected the subjugation and oppression of blacks in the total framework of American culture. At home but a stranger, free but bound, citizen but alien, agent but spectator, involved but tyrannized, participant but victim, embraced but exiled, a "Thou" but an "It," a person but a thing, in the company of the blessed but cursed, a part of the elect but condemned—that has been the substance, if not always the form and intention, of the black man's experience and journey in the celebrated New World experiment in freedom, equality, justice, dignity, and self-government.

Like the black experience and journey in general, black politics represents and symbolizes the most radical paradox, ambiguity, and contradiction in American life, thought, character, and ideals. Involved are the marriage and harmonization of democracy and tyranny, freedom and slavery, liberty and despotism, idealism and racism, humanism and the negation of black humanity, pluralism and oppression, stability and seething alienation, optimism and pessimism, universalism and particularism, perfectionism and "original sin," liberalism and authoritarianism, experimentation and doctrinaire dehumanization, and progressivism and reaction. Sensitive and perceptive minds from Tocqueville and Bryce to David Spitz have commented on the "tyranny of the majority," the "tyranny of public opinion," or the "fatalism of the multitude." But the tyranny of racism has been the worst form of tyranny of the American social order, political system, and mind.

The tyranny of the collective pride, self-worship, and supreme tragedy of racism, however, has been equated with the presence and reality of democracy as well as the blessed and natural inheritance of freedom, dignity, and equality. Generally speaking, this set of presuppositions and framework of meaning, value, understanding, and interpretation have fostered an easy, complacent, and satisfied conscience. The brutal realities have been more than obscured. They have been identified with the order of authentic idealism and universal humanism and thus accepted and celebrated as normative. Creative tension between the "is" and the "ought" has been minimized. In a strange and persistent way, the oppressed position of black human beings has been rationalized, moralized, justified, and even sanctified and glorified.

Myrdal perceived the contradiction and moral ambiguity as a deep moral dilemma, a clash between vigorous commitment to the democratic form of government and way of life, on the one hand, and the harsh reality of the oppression of black people, on the other. The problem almost transcends the realm of rational intelligibility. According to Myrdal,

The American Negro problem is a problem in the heart of the American. It is there that the interracial tension has its focus. It is there that the decisive

struggle goes on. . . . Though our study includes economic, social, and politi-
cal race relations, at bottom our problem is the moral valuations on various
levels of consciousness and generality. The 'American Dilemma,' is the ever-
raging conflict between, on the one hand, the valuations preserved on the
general plane which we shall call the 'American Creed,' where the American
thinks, talks, and acts under the influence of high national and Christian pre-
cepts, and, on the other, the valuations on specific planes of individual and
group living, where personal and local interests; economic, social, and sexual
jealousies; considerations of community prestige and conformity; group preju-
dice against particular persons or types of people; and all sorts of miscellaneous
wants, impulses, and habits dominate his outlook.[1]

Myrdal is profoundly and enduringly correct in viewing the "race problem" as a moral problem. It is indeed, from beginning to end, whatever the institutional manifestation, behavioral configuration, or ideological consideration, at heart a moral problem. It has always been and will continue to be, in substance, a moral issue. The moral dimensions, presuppositions, and content of the political process are both timely and timeless. As in other aspects of culture, the ethical basis of politics is inescapable. The fundamental questions are those of humanity and citizenship. Who is to be called a human being and treated as one? Who is to be called an American citizen and treated as one? In other words, who is a citizen of the American commonwealth and of what Kant called the "commonwealth of humanity"? The moral basis of the American political system and process is critical to any rational approach to, and understanding of, the black political experience.

Yet Myrdal's analysis and model are, while suggestive and necessary, insufficient. His framework does not touch the radical depths; indeed, it helps to obscure them. Conceptually and perceptually, the radical contradiction between the black man's status and experience, on the one hand, and the American Dream, on the other, has been denied. The oppression of blacks has been made, operationally and otherwise, to square with the presuppositions, character, content, and meaning of the American Dream. The best has been perverted into the worst. In terms of the radical depths of experience and interpretation, blacks have been excluded from the very promise of American life. The intrinsically incompatible was not only made compatible but such compatibility received glorification and sanctification. Thus, in the thought of many, slavery was a necessary condition of freedom; hence the enslavement of

---

[1] *An American Dilemma* (New York: Harper & Brothers, 1944), xlvii.

black humanity was a presupposition of the freedom of white humanity. Perhaps Reinhold Niebuhr would call this an example of "ideological taint" and "egoistic corruption." The harmonization of black oppression with American freedom and the consequent acceptance of the "dominant-submissive" or "superordinate-subordinate" model by students of American politics have had far-reaching results.

From another angle of vision, one confronts the tyranny of the liberal democratic illusion which has exercised profound influence on the American mind and experience. Democracy and freedom, according to this perspective, are an integral part of the "givenness" of the American experience and way, an inheritance of the land and its people, self-evident truths.

In a famous passage of *Democracy in America*, Tocqueville, the brilliant French observer of the American scene in the early 1830's, asserted: "The great advantage of the Americans is that they have arrived at a state of democracy without having to endure a democratic revolution, and that they are born equal instead of becoming so."[2] This is the typical view of the American condition: Americans are born free and equal; democracy is a "given" of social and political existence, a reflection of the nature of things. There is, hence, no need for a democratic revolution. It is utterly irrational to seek and to struggle for a self-evident inheritance of principles, premises, institutions, and other conditions of freedom and equality. What is essential is the glorification, celebration, and preservation of the richness and wonders of democratic and equalitarian grace.

And that is precisely what has happened. With the falsification of experience and the awesome union of reality and illusion, fact and myth, empiricism and sentimental idealism, political scientists have generally celebrated the achievements and ignored the defects —at least with reference to the black political experience—of American democracy. They have sanctified stability, consensus, pluralism, continuity, harmony, shifting alliances, competing centers of power, and the *status quo* mentality rather than the need for institutional change, social reform, and creative tension between promise and fulfillment. Thoughtful and sustained self-criticism has been out of the question.

Morris observes that

---

[2] Alexis de Tocqueville, *Democracy in America*, Henry Reeve text (New York: Vintage Books, 1959), II, 108.

. . . American political scientists have been deeply committed to certain flattering conceptions of the American political system and have been inclined to ignore, or treat as incidental aberrations, evidence that seems to disrupt or contradict these conceptions. The popular image of a democratic polity committed to the principles of justice and equality for all could not tolerate the reality of inequality and systematic oppression that has been the experience of blacks.[3]

Generally speaking, the liberal democratic illusion has generated and sustained a complacent, easy, and satisfied conscience. Such a conscience militates against change. It has been, perhaps, the greatest barrier to change in the American political system with reference to blacks. But if all is well, if Americans are born free and equal, why change in the political system? Change for what? If our society is truly democratic, the obligation is not to change it but to preserve and strengthen it. The illusion of a democratic culture is a mighty and effective hurdle to the achievement of a truly democratic society.

Another significant perspective in seeking to understand the role of the black man in the American political system is the recognition, over the long haul of the history of the New World, of another awesome paradox, irony, and contradiction. Blacks, since colonial times and the early days of the fledgling Republic, have had a profound and enduring impact on the American political system and process. They have done so unwittingly and not of their own will. Black people have not deeply influenced the American political system and public process as political agents, participants, citizens, movers, shakers, or actors in the great drama of political life but as political subjects, victims, issues, centers and sources of conflict, tension, and compromise, and objects of manipulation, control, fear, and exploitation. The phenomenon has been peculiar. The very presence of black people has had far-reaching consequences for the political and governing process. Black presence has been constantly "troublesome," thorny, gnawing, and a source of uneasiness.

Consider, for example, the politics of the slave controversy, from the early colonial period to the Declaration of Independence, Revolutionary War, Constitutional Convention, bitter struggle over the ratification of the Constitution, Westward expansion, the admission of new states to the Union, various compromises, the Abolition Movement, and routine character of group and electoral politics.

[3] Milton D. Morris, *The Politics of Black America* (New York: Harper & Row, Publishers, 1975), 4.

Slavery was a haunting specter on the American political system. The tragedy of the slave controversy kept the political system under constant threat, strain and tension and led, in the end, to its collapse and the Civil War. Consider, too, the Confederacy, the Civil War itself, the Democratic split in 1860, the birth of the Republican Party (and several minor short-lived parties as well), the Compromise of 1877, Reconstruction, the Bourbon Redemption, the establishment of various restrictive voting laws, the Black Codes, the rise and perpetuation of the one-party system in the South,[4] the birth and death of Populism,[5] the emergence and continuity of the Solid South, the Dixiecrat Movement of 1948, the numerous quadrennial independent electors scenarios, the Wallace movement, the resurgence of modern Southern Republicanism, and so forth. Consider the impact of racism and race on the American party systems, national conventions, presidential campaigns, electoral laws and processes, various political movements, legislative and administrative procedures and decisions, the Presidency, the courts, and state and local government and politics.

Racism has exerted a tyranny over the mind of the white South. In his classic study, *Southern Politics*, V. O. Key observed:

In its grand outlines the politics of the South revolves around the position of the Negro. It is at times interpreted as a politics of cotton, as a politics of free trade, as a politics of agrarian poverty, or as a politics of planter and plutocrat. Although such interpretations have a superficial validity, in the last analysis the major peculiarities of southern politics go back to the Negro. Whatever phase of the southern political process one seeks to understand, sooner or later the trail of inquiry leads to the Negro.[6]

And Heard asserted that "Southern concern over the Negro is the most deeply rooted source of political contention in American politics."[7]

[4] Alexander Heard, *A Two-Party South?* (Chapel Hill: University of North Carolina Press, 1952), 9, 145-146; J. B. Shannon, *Toward a New Politics in the South* (Knoxville: University of Tennessee Press, 1949), 8-9, and Harry S. Ashmore, *Epitaph for Dixie* (New York: W. W. North & Company, Inc., 1957), 15.

[5] See, for example, C. Van Woodward, *Tom Watson: Agrarian Rebel*, Galaxy ed. (New York: Oxford University Press, 1963), chs. 13 and 20, and Anna Rochester, *The Populist Movement in the United States* (New York: International Publishers, 1943), 59-60. See, in particular, Tom Watson's tragic and bitter comment in T. Harry Williams', *Romance and Realism in Southern Politics* (Athens: University of Georgia Press, 1960), 55.

[6] *Southern Politics*, Vintage ed. (New York: Alfred A. Knopf, Inc., 1949), 5.

[7] Heard, *op. cit.*, 27.

In large part because of the historic power and influence of the South in national politics and in part because of racism in the North, the sheer black presence has been a continuous and almost universal force in American politics. Thus, while essentially outside and powerless, black people have profoundly and indelibly influenced the American political system and process as a source of issues, contention, meaning, direction, dynamism, motivation, manipulation, power, tension, unity, division, strategy, symbols, and inspiration. The sad controversy over "busing," "racial balance," and the "ethnic purity" of neighborhoods during the presidential election campaign of this Bicentennial year is a dramatic, grim, and menacing reminder of the aching continuity of the very presence of black people as an endless issue and object of exploitation and manipulation in the brutal struggle for power and its fruits—real and imagined.

In the quest for a meaningful perspective on the black man and the American political system, a final observation is necessary. The American political system is a function and reflection of American culture and history. As Louis Hartz noted, America has neither a genuine revolutionary tradition nor a "tradition of reaction: lacking Robespierre it lacks Maistre, lacking Sydney it lacks Charles II. Its liberalism is what Santayana called, referring to American democracy, a 'natural' phenomenon."[8]

The American political system, in general, has not been reactionary but progressive, forward-looking, optimistic, in search of higher possibilities and greater promises, deeper and broader expectations—at least in terms of social and humanitarian reforms, movements for greater popular participation, expanded situations and opportunities of personal responsibility and choice, and enlarged equality, benefits, and rewards. Never revolutionary or radical but gradualist, centrist, experimental, practical rather than dogmatic and doctrinaire. Almost always, the thrust and movement of events, public policies, orientation, and outlook have been inexorably forward, not backward, upward, not downward. The rhythm of the American political system has been progressive, not reactionary. The two major exceptions—in social and human terms —involve black people—the 1830's and the post-Reconstruction era. Reactionary, regressive, and repressive movements prevailed in both situations.

[8] *The Liberal Tradition in America* (New York: Harcourt, Brace & World, Inc., 1955), 5.

Ironically, during the great popular stirrings and democratic reforms of the Jacksonian period—involving universal white manhood suffrage, abolition of property qualifications for voting and public office-holding, popular and frequent elections, apportionment of representation as well as constitutional revision and amendment—there was a reversal of the political status of free Negroes. The very state conventions which extended the suffrage of whites constitutionally withdrew the vote from free men of color.

Virginia and North Carolina joined Maryland and Kentucky in taking from the free Negro the ballot he had heretofore possessed. In like manner all new states of the period, North as well as South, denied suffrage to free Negroes. The action of the old southern states was paralleled by that of the northern states. Delaware, Connecticut, New Jersey, and Pennsylvania took the ballot from the Negro. And New York in 1821 limited Negro suffrage by requiring that he possess a freehold valued at two hundred and fifty dollars over and above all indebtedness.[9]

With the end of the Civil War and the adoption of the Reconstruction Amendments, blacks, in large numbers, participated in the Southern political process. Following, however, the Compromise of 1877, a massive reaction set in and blacks were systematically excluded from participation in the political process.

There is some evidence that a third movement of social and humanistic reversal is under way. The momentum toward racial equality has been lost. Not only is great progress increasingly difficult, but the consolidation and even retention of gains are in grave jeopardy. There is some talk of the tragic end of the Second Reconstruction.

A GLANCE AT THE PAST

Pre-Civil War

Whatever the polarity of interpretation, the fragmentary character of the data, and the ambiguity of experience, the conclusion seems inescapable that black politics in colonial America was of a very limited nature and consequence—reflecting the status of blacks in the social order. Gosnell asserts that the "direct political import-

---

[9] Fletcher M. Green, "Democracy in the Old South," in George B. Tindall, ed., *The Pursuit of Southern History* (Baton Rouge: Louisiana State University Press, 1964), 186.

ance of the Negro prior to the Civil War was slight."[10]   Moon
argues that "the vote of the Free Negro was everywhere small and
in most places insignificant."[11]   "As a political power," says Myrdal,
"the free Negroes were, of course, inconsequential, both in the
South and in the North."[12]

Voting is the most elementary property of citizenship.   Before
the Civil War, even free blacks were, on the whole, systematically
excluded from suffrage.   That fact, especially in view of the small
number of free blacks, reveals much about the character and persistence of the American political tradition as regards black human
beings.   Again, there were the uncharacteristically American epi-
sodes of humanistic and social reaction, reversal, and retreat in the
context of progressivism and the thirst for social improvement.

Significantly, at the time of the adoption of the Constitution, only
South Carolina and Georgia of the original states withheld suffrage
from free blacks.[13]   But haunting reaction set in.   "Prior to the
Civil War, Negroes had the right to vote in only four northern
states—Massachusetts, New Hampshire, New York, and Vermont.
One southern state, North Carolina, for a period allowed free slaves
to vote."[14]   The voting laws of New York discriminated against free
blacks.[15]   When the Fifteenth Amendment was ratified in 1870,
blacks could vote in only seven northern states.[16]   "During the
period between the Philadelphia conventions of 1787 and 1865,
only Maine, New Hampshire, Vermont, Rhode Island and Massachusetts permitted Negroes to vote on equal terms with whites.   All
other states, at some time, have barred Negro Americans from the
suffrage."[17]

[10] Harold F. Gosnell, *Negro Politicians* (Chicago: University of Chicago
Press, 1967), 3.

[11] Henry Lee Moon, *Balance of Power: The Negro Vote* (New York:
Doubleday and Company, 1948), 55.

[12] Myrdal, *op. cit.*, 429.

[13] *Ibid.*

[14] Howard Penniman, *The American Political Process* (New York: D. Van
Nostrand Company, Inc. 1962), 14. Myrdal and Green, however, say that
blacks could vote in five Northern states.   Myrdal, *op. cit.*, 430, and Green,
op. cit., 187.

[15] Myrdal, *op. cit.*, 430.

[16] Penniman, *op. cit.*, 14.

[17] G. James Fleming, "The Negro in American Politics: The Past," in
John P. Davis, ed., *The American Negro Reference Book* (Englewood Cliffs:
Prentice-Hall, Inc., 1966), 418.

Yet, to the extent that free blacks were allowed to participate in the political process of colonial America, there is a dramatic reminder both of the hunger in the hearts of blacks for involvement in public life and of the continuity and depth of the American Dream as a driving force, inspiration, and passion in the "souls of black folk." Oddly, there was no affirmation of the futility of participation in the political process as a means of improving their lot and the lot of their brothers in bondage. Perhaps when human beings have virtually nothing, the hope and expectation of small gains mean a lot. It is also suggestive of the inexhaustible capacity of the human spirit, in the face of overwhelming odds, to hope, believe, protest, and affirm human life and aspirations. This is one of the central and persistent themes of the black experience in politics and culture.

"Black politics flourished in colonial America,"[18] according to Hanes Walton, Jr. Blacks were engaged in, he goes on to say, pressure or nonelectoral as well as electoral politics. "Both these categories revolve around the shifting status of blacks in the American colonies."[19]

The pressure or nonelectoral political activities of blacks evolved from attempts to attain freedom, to maintain the status of a 'free man of color,' to remove discriminatory practices from different communities, and to have suffrage rights given, extended, or returned. On the other hand, black electoral politics in colonial America tended to support those who championed the idea of 'suffrage for all regardless of color,' those political parties (major or minor) that espoused equalitarian legislation favorable to free blacks.[20]

In this restricted and hostile social environment and massively oppressive civic and political culture, what were the tactics of social change for the purpose of freedom, equality, and dignity? Tactics were multi-dimensional.

Significant black political activity began with the establishment of the slave status. Black petitions, memorials, resolutions, and proclamations were presented to local public officials, state governments, and courts. Finally, in 1800, blacks not only petitioned Congress for a redress of their grievances, but also called upon Congress to act against the slave trade, the Fugitive Slave Act of 1793, and the institution of slavery itself.

[18] Hanes Walton, Jr., *Black Politics: A Theoretical and Structural Analysis* (New York: J. B. Lippincott Company, 1972), 17.
[19] *Ibid.*
[20] *Ibid.*, 17-18.

286

These petitions, which began around 1661, were presented to public officials not only by free blacks but by slaves as well. Not all of the earliest protest activity took the form of petitions. Some was violent, destructive, lacking in coordination. The slave revolts and insurrections definitely attest to this. Moreover, not all of the petitions and pressure activity were focused on freedom. Numerous black protestors cried out for equal educational facilities, and some protested against being taxed without having the right to vote. In 1791, when South Carolina levied a heavy poll tax upon free blacks, two petitions were sent to the state legislature signed by 23 blacks from Camden, South Carolina, and 34 blacks from Charleston protesting these laws and the disadvantages they placed upon the free black populace. Neither petition accomplished its purpose, but the poll tax law in the state was amended in 1809 to exclude blacks who were physically incapable of earning a livelihood. Petitions like this often met with limited success; some even obtained complete success.[21]

The significance of black politics in colonial America cannot be grasped from the quantitative perspective. The really important reality is that, from the very beginning of their experience in the New World, black people developed a romance with the American Dream of freedom, equality, and human dignity; they developed a political consciousness, will, and determination to use whatever frail methods and tactics at their disposal, and they became practitioners of the politics of protest against injustice and oppression. But protest is ultimately affirmation. In protesting against injustice and oppression, blacks were affirming the vitality, power, dignity, beauty, and creativity of freedom, justice, and equality.

The issue of colonization is a dramatic example of the depth and persistence of the love affair blacks have always had with America and their determination to achieve freedom and justice on the American shores.

The first major issue on which blacks protested after the Revolutionary War was colonization—removal of free blacks outside of U.S. territorial units. Along with agitating against colonization, blacks condemned discrimination throughout the northern states.[22]

Finally, blacks played a vital role in the politics of the antislavery crusade. "The numerous tactics that black abolitionists employed in seeking to destroy slavery ran from moral suasion to the support of John Brown's raid at Harper's Ferry."[23]

[21] *Ibid.*, 18-19.
[22] *Ibid.*, 27.
[23] *Ibid.*

The Day and Night of Reconstruction

With legal emancipation and the ratification of the Civil War Amendments, the hope and expectation prevailed that, at long last, the four million former slaves would become, in reality as well as in theory, citizens, free men, and therefore full and equal participants in the Southern political and governmental process. Hopes, among the freedmen and their friends and allies, soared. Expectations and aspirations took wing. The human spirit sparkled with a sense of renewal, freedom, vitality, spontaneity, and wonder at the loss of chains and the vision of entering the Promised Land. Reconstruction got under way with a bang and with characteristically American optimism, triumph, innocence, and tragic illusion.

Despite the tragically scarred legacy of slavery, Southern resentment and hostility, political chaos, and partisan wrangling for the advantages of power and privilege, blacks plunged deeply into the muddy waters of Southern politics. They registered and voted in large numbers. They filled significant elective and appointive offices. They were familiar figures at state constitutional conventions, in state legislatures, and in local positions of responsibility. Between 1869 and 1880, sixteen black men served in Congress from the South—two of whom, Hiram R. Revels and Blanche K. Bruce, represented Mississippi in the Senate. When George H. White of North Carolina left the House of Representatives in 1901, after serving two terms, he was the last black person to be a member of that chamber until the election of Oscar S. DePriest of Chicago in 1929. White was the 20th black Congressman from 1870 to 1901.[24]

Many myths have been created and perpetuated about "Negro domination" during Reconstruction—powerful myths that have been used to justify the political oppression and degradation of black men. The facts, however, are quite different. As John Hope Franklin observed,

No group has attracted more attention or has had its role more misrepresented by contemporaries and by posterity than Southern Negroes during the Radical Reconstruction. The period has been described as one of Negro rule, as one of gross perfidy with the Negro as the central figure, since the reins of misgovernment were supposedly held by black militiamen. Negroes were in the South. They held public office and, at times, played important parts in the

[24] Chuck Stone, *Black Political Power in America* (Indianapolis: The Bobbs-Merrill Company, 1968), 30-35.

public life of their respective states. But it would be stretching a point to say that their roles were dominant, and it would be hopelessly distorting the picture to suggest that they ruled the South. It was in South Carolina that they had the greatest numerical strength. In the first legislature there were eighty-seven Negroes and forty whites. From the outset, however, whites controlled the state senate and in 1874 the lower house as well. At all times the governor was white. There were two Negro lieutenant governors. . . .[25]

Negro public officials, during Reconstruction, were neither better nor worse than their white counterparts. Both virtues and defects, both successes and failures were shared. Black men made real contributions.[26] A major contribution was to the establishment of public education for both races. "It is fair to say," asserted DuBois, "that the Negro carpetbag governments established the public schools of the South."[27]

The Nadir

The robust hopes of Reconstruction were dashed for a variety of complex reasons. The shattered dream was a tragic nightmare in the collective experience, consciousness, and memory of black people. In a profound sense, the loss of existential hope and concrete expectations, the anguish of spirit, and the inevitable feeling of despair and betrayal were worse than slavery itself. Slavery at least had the sad virtue of generating and sustaining a culture of hopelessness.

The failure of the national government and the American people to make a genuine, sustained, and massive commitment to make freedom and equality empirically real and functioning for the freedmen was responsible for the derailment of Reconstruction. It was more than a failure of the political system. It was an American failure of will, skill, nerve, and authenticity of commitment to incorporate black people within the content of the American Dream. This land continues to reap the tragic harvest of that failure.

More specifically, the national government failed to enforce the Civil War Amendments—especially the Fourteenth and Fifteenth—and failed to develop and implement a comprehensive and creative plan of genuine social, economic, and human reconstruction de-

[25] *Reconstruction* (Chicago: University of Chicago Press, 1961), 133.
[26] Fleming, *op. cit.*
[27] W. E. B. DuBois, *Black Reconstruction in America, 1860-1880,* Meridian ed. (New York: The World Publishing Company, 1964), 664.

signed to give flesh and blood and concrete content and substance to legal emancipation. Freedom means power to do or not to do, to act or not to act. The demand for freedom is, among other things, the demand for power.

Besides, partisan calculations, exploitation, and manipulation, Southern determination to make the political process once again the exclusive prerogative of whites, the low economic, social, and educational status of the ex-slaves and their inadequate political experience, civic education, and sophistication, and a multiplicity of other forces conspired to end the Reconstruction experiment in shared power, responsibility, freedom, and democracy.

With the Compromise of 1877, and the consequent withdrawal of federal troops from the South, black people were abandoned to their worst enemies. "White Power" was restored with vengeance and collective self-righteousness and a salvationist syndrome.

Force, violence, threats, economic pressure and reprisals, psychological and emotional torture and coercion, and various and endless "legal" devices, constitutional mechanisms, and other "respectable" techniques were employed to reduce black people, once more, to the status of object and victim. Virtual slavery was returned. As Hanes Walton, Jr. has well stated,

> In 1890, Mississippi called a state convention for the purpose of eliminating the black electorate; its plan for disfranchising the black voter became the model for the other southern states. In fact, the Mississippi precedent of not submitting the new constitution to the electorate for ratification, but simply proclaiming it the law of the land was followed by all the southern conventions except that of Alabama.
>
> With the arrival of the era of disfranchisement, the black electorate was reduced to insignificance in the South. Once again a struggle to regain and retain the vote ensued. The struggle has continued unabated to the present day.
>
> Before the struggle to regain the vote commenced, however, blacks attempted to have the federal government protect their right to vote.[28]

A NOTE ON THE PRESENT AND FUTURE

Owing to Supreme Court decisions, executive action, various Civil Rights Acts, constant pressure from blacks and their white allies, the Civil Rights Movement, attitudinal changes in the land, demographic factors, the world situation, the revolution in mass

---

[28] Walton, op. cit., 35.

media of communication and transportation, and a host of other considerations and influences, the American political system has become increasingly sensitive and responsive to black insistence on sharing the American Dream. The Civil Rights Act of 1964, in effect, reinstituted the 14th Amendment, and the Voting Rights Act of 1965, in substance, re-enacted the 15th Amendment. The decade between the mid-fifties and the mid-sixties was one of remarkable and unprecedented gains for blacks. For blacks, it was the most creative, constructive, and humane period in their long experience with the American political system. In the late sixties, however, the cold winds of conservatism, reaction, and "benign neglect" began blowing again. They continue.

Of special significance during that decade of enormous progress was the Voting Rights Act of 1965. Largely because of that legislation, black people today hold more major and minor, elective and appointive offices, than at any time since Reconstruction. In the 11 states of the Old Confederacy, nothing less than a democratic revolution has taken place. Since the establishment of the Voter Education Project in 1962, 3½ million blacks have been added to the registration books. More than 1½ million blacks have registered since the enactment of the Voting Rights Act.

The most dramatic part of the democratic revolution in the South, however, lies in the increase in the number of black elected officials. In 1962, there were fewer than 50 black office-holders in Dixie.[29] In 1965, the watershed year, only 72 blacks held public office.[30] But according to a recent VEP press release, there are today 1,944 black elected officials in the South.

The public offices now held by southern blacks include: U.S. House of Representatives, 3; state senators, 3; state representatives, 88; county officials, 294; mayors, 68; municipal officials, 827; law enforcement officials, 204; and education officials, 445.[31]

Even so, the 1,944 black elected officials represent only 2.5 of the total number of public offices in the South, and blacks constitute more than 20 percent of the population of the region. One must also remember that (1) no blacks hold statewide office in the South; (2) few of the black officials hold major offices; and (3)

[29] Voter Education Project, *1974 Report of the Executive Director,* Atlanta, 1.
[30] Voter Education Project Press Release, Atlanta, May 11, 1976, 1.
[31] *Ibid.* Also see John Lewis and Archie E. Allen, "Black Voter Registration Efforts in the South," *Notre Dame Lawyer,* 48 (October 1972), 114.

virtually all of the black officials basically represent black constituencies. Whites generally "bloc vote" against black candidates or fail to vote at all. There is not a single black member of the federal bench in the South—district or appellate.

Of the approximately 15 million blacks of voting age in the nation, it is estimated that only about 8½ million are registered voters.

On the national scene, blacks have increasingly won election to public office; percentagewise, however, the number is not impressive. There are 17 black members of the House of Representatives —a total of 4 percent. There is only one black member of the U.S. Senate—a total of 1 percent. There is no black governor in the 50 states. There are only two lieutenant governors—in California and Colorado. A few other blacks occupy state-wide positions of varying significance.

According to the 1975 edition of the Joint Center for Political Studies' *National Roster of Black Elected Officials,* 3,503 black persons held elective offices as of May 1, 1975. It is sobering to remember, however, that the 3,503 blacks represent less than 1 percent of the total number of elective offices in the United States. There are more than 500,000 elective offices in the country. "For whites, that adds up to approximately 287 elected officials for every 100,000 people. The 3,503 BEO's add up to about 16 for every 100,000 people."[32]

Another observer comments that "despite the high number of blacks holding elective office, they represent only 0.05 percent of the total of elective offices in the country."[33]

'We're electing blacks at a rate of 464 per year,' reported Eddie N. Williams, president of the Joint Center for Political Studies, a Washington-based organization that conducts research into minority politics.

At that rate, by the year 2000 there will be 15,000 blacks in public office, but that figure will be 3 percent of the total. So even when we're running fast we don't seem to be moving much.[34]

There are numerous black appointed public officials—ranging all the way from a Supreme Court Justice and a member of the President's Cabinet to several members of the lower federal courts to

[32] "Black Elected Officials: Is There a Measurable Difference?", *Black World,* October, 1975, 49.

[33] Paul Delaney, "Blacks Gaining Politically But Still Feel Frustrated," *New York Times,* June 1, 1976.

[34] Quoted in *ibid.*

local members of boards and commissions. But blacks in the political system must be evaluated from a much broader perspective—
especially how the masses of black people fare. Haunting the black
community are serious problems of unemployment, underemploy-
ment, comparative income with whites, education, welfare, housing,
health, and discrimination. The response of the American political
system to these woes has been and continues to be insufficient and,
indeed, largely insensitive. Part of the problem is rooted in the
illusions of black progress and part in a feeling of "fatigue" about
the "black problem." Unlike during the great decade of progress,
the black agenda is being ignored. The country does not want to
be reminded of the urgently unfinished business of racial and social
justice.

Can the American political system be made to work for black
people on a consistent and sustained basis? Must there be a "new
politics"? Can the political process be made to "payoff" in terms
of the basic needs and aspirations of the black community? These
questions are being hotly debated today. Conventional politics is,
in the view of Mervyn Dymally, a part of the problem.

It is part of the problem because the political system is the major bulwark
of racism in America.

It is a part of the problem in the sense that the political system is structured
to repel fundamental social and economic change.

We hear a great deal about the deficiencies, real or imagined, of certain
black leaders, but not enough attention, it seems to me, is paid to the framework within which they operate. That framework prevents radical growth and
innovation—as it was designed to prevent radical growth and innovation.[35]

Thus, in this typical view, the defect is systemic, in the very political system itself. Some talk of the "violent overthrow" of the system or of "revolution." But, in terms of the cold realities of power,
apart from all else, such is a prescription for collective suicide of
black people. In the American context, violence simply will be
counter-productive as an instrument of social change, as Martin
Luther King, Jr. asserted time and again. Violence is a disaster
for all.

From the long perspective of history, a new factor in the equation
of blacks in the American political system is that today blacks can

[35] "The Black Man's Role in American Politics," in Lenneal J. Henderson,
Jr., ed., *Black Political Life in the United States* (San Francisco: Chandler
Publishing Company, 1972), 23.

take the initiative to formulate and press issues and help define the terms of the public dialogue and agenda. The ability to take the initiative is a striking development of immense significance. It means that blacks can be creative participants and subjects rather than mere objects and victims of the political process. In *Negro Politics: The Search for Leadership*, James Q. Wilson asserted,

Negroes are, in a very real sense, the objects rather than the subjects of civic action. Things are done for, or about, or to, or because of Negroes, but they are less frequently done *by* Negroes.[36]

Again,

Few civic issues are initiated by Negroes, but many are responded to by them; Negro civic leadership is more often defensive than assertive. Negroes, to use Riesman's phrase, are often—though not always—a 'veto group.' When they are not a veto group, the reasons can most frequently be found in the constraints that affect civic leaders themselves. . . .[37]

But today, blacks are, more and more, insisting on acting rather than merely reacting, and are desperately seeking to identify, define, and dramatize the issues for public discourse, priority, and decision. The implications are far-reaching.

In the initiation, definition, and elaboration of the issues and the development of a "black agenda," several organizations, in addition to the traditional civil rights groups, are involved: the Congressional Black Caucus, the National Black Political Convention, the National Black Political Assembly, and the Southern Conference of Black Mayors, to name only a few. During this Bicentennial year, the Caucus of Black Democrats met for the first time to formulate black issues and insist on their consideration in the Presidential campaign.

There is a profound feeling in the black community and among black leadership that the issues of greatest concern to black people are being ignored. There is a deep conviction of insensitivity and indifference to the black agenda. Many blacks feel that not only is there a failure to consolidate the great gains of the Civil Rights Movement, but that the gains are being eroded by a variety of forces.

How to translate political gains into economic gains and political

---

[36] James Q. Wilson, *Negro Politics: The Search for Leadership* (Chicago: The University of Chicago Press, 1960), 133.
[37] *Ibid.*, 135.

power into economic power is one of the basic issues confronting the black community. Can the political system be an effective instrument of economic justice? If so, how?

In black politics today, there is a profound and somewhat painful and melancholic groping for power and meaningful participation in the heart of the American political system. There is a strange mixture of alienation, hope, despair, confidence, frustration, apathy, feeling of the futility of effort, and feverish activism about political things.

There is a groping for direction, issues, priorities, funds, organization, leadership, inspiration, affirmation, protest, and movement. Above all, there is a groping for strategies of social, political, and economic change. Black politics, in this Bicentennial year, is characterized, also, by a deep sense of frustration, anguish, drift, wandering, and a tinge of cynicism and hopelessness. There are problems of the mobilization of power, factionalism, the payoff, the forcing of black issues on the national agenda, of coalitions versus separatism and nationalism.

The role of blacks in the American political system is heightened and dramatized by Bicentennial collective memory and reflection. What does American mean and stand for? What is Americanism? What are the ideals and promises of the land? Are the American political system and American history and culture redemptive as well as creative? Will history "repeat" itself in terms of the Second Reconstruction? Will the tyranny of racism defile the next century as it has the past two? What are the grounds and sources of hope for the American ideals of freedom, democracy, justice, and equality being applied meaningfully to all?

As in the past, black politics will, in large measure, continue to be shaped by white politics. After all, the basic power and resources —including those for social change and social justice—are in white hands. Is it not time, on the occasion of the celebration of the Bicentennial, for American freedom and justice to be extended and applied equally to all

Women's Place
in
American Politics:
The Historical Perspective

Louise M. Young

T HE POLITICAL ROLE of American women is the outcome of a process of social and political change involving millions of women over three centuries of time. The political saliency of sex conflict surfaced in the 17th century when cultural entrepreneurs felt impelled to play roles beyond sanctioned limits, and the resulting conflict was politicized.[1] Again, in the 19th century, as the net of interaction between the sexes was cast over a wider area, a succession of women found means to affect the course of events by politicizing their subject status. In varied and often fortuitous ways they interacted with political, social and religious institutions to forward social change and advance their own sex from political non-existence to a degree of individual autonomy and collective awareness justifying claims to be regarded as values in themselves, independent of their biological function.[2]

A consideration of women and politics in an historical context finds it useful to define political participation as "those voluntary activities by which members of a society share in the selection of rulers, and, di-

---

[1] Political saliency "refers to any heightening of awareness of a particular group membership at the time when the individual is oriented to the political world." Angus Campbell, et al, *American Voter* (New York: John Wiley & Sons, 1960), 311.

[2] It was not, in fact, until the present generation of feminists that this claim was pressed to the exclusion of other claims.

rectly or indirectly, in the formation of public policy;"[3] and of political behavior as including "acts, orientations to action, identifications, demands, expectations, evaluations."[4]   While these definitions are commonly applied to the analysis of groups, the assumption is that groups are composed of individuals acting in a context in which political action occurs; i.e., where relationships between rulers and ruled, affected by social, political and personal factors, require choices at points where social and political goals clash.

With latitude so generous, it can be said that American women began participating in politics and fashioning patterns of political behavior soon after Anne Hutchinson stepped ashore at Boston in 1634. Across the gulf of three centuries she stands: a symbol of an age prepared to test the ultimate consequence of the Protestant Reformation. A child of the Puritan Revolution, she carried the virus of revolt to the New World and politicized a strong dissent to the religious, political, social, and psychological restraints imposed on women when she challenged the assumption of the theocracy that no woman could have a voice in the "Divine Polity."[5]

The Puritan belief that divine law was superior to all other laws and binding on all, ruler and ruled alike, interlacing religious and political thinking, subtly re-shaped the institution of the family as the political unit of the state: the "little Commonwealth" in which the wife was a "great officer," taking precedence over her children, but without legal identity: "Husband and wife are one, and he is that one." Both common law and the biblical account of Creation, in the Puritan view, decreed that the husband, created in God's image, "has ever been lord and lawful king."   "The Common Law here shaketh hand with Divinitie."[6]

---

[3] Herbert McClosky, "Political Participation," *International Encyclopedia of the Social Sciences*, 12, 203.

[4] Heinz Eulau, "Political Behavior," *Ibid.*, 252.

[5] For biographic and bibliographic material on all of the women mentioned in this article, see *Notable American Women* (NAW), ed. Edward and Janet James, 3 vols. (Cambridge: Belknap Press of Harvard University Press, 1971).

[6] The first treatise on the complicated status of English women in the 15th and 16th centuries was compiled in the Tudor period but not published until 1632: *The Lawes Resolutions of Women's Rights.*   Because of "Adam's sin," the compiler explained, "Women have no voyse in Parliament.   They make no Lawes, they consent to none, they abrogate none.   All of them are understood either married or to be married and their desires are subject to their husband. . . .   The Common Lawe here shaketh hand with Divinitie. . . ."   Women had virtually no rights under "public law."   Under "private law" ("rights" developed through time and feudal custom though not affirmed in statutes),

This concept of the "divinely ordained" family as the political unit of the state was transferred intact to the New England settlements and charted the course of their social and political development. The spirit of individualism released by the Reformation, reinforced in England by the secular break with Rome and the rise of Puritanism, encouraged those who could read the Bible to make their own interpretation of man's (and woman's) relation to God. Forwardness among women was on the rise, subtly encouraged by the example of Queen Elizabeth who represented the old but faced toward the new paths women were being stirred to follow. Within the family—the "little Commonwealth"—women could exert all the influence which qualities of mind and character enabled them to exert, but where the family touched the community, they were not permitted to forget that subjection was forever the portion of Eve's daughters.

An outpouring of hortatory and admonitory tracts on the blessings of matrimony and the duties of the "good wife" to be subservient and obedient to her "monarch-husband" indicated the social ferment arising from public discussion of scriptural injunctions against women speaking in public, or teaching, or "usurping power over men"—partly provoked by an unusual spate of queens in the 16th century.[7] The ground was well prepared for the revolution in the status of women, which became "the most far-reaching change of modern times," though "the process was as slow as it was inexorable."[8]

Four thousand families migrated to the English settlements in the New World during the "Puritan Hejira" (1631-1643): mature and venturesome men and women with children coming along to carry forward the beliefs and customs brought with them from the mother country, as well as the searching debate regarding the religious and political ordering of the sexes.[9] One of these families was that of William and Anne Hutchinson and their twelve children. Anne Hutchinson was not prepared to be patient when she discovered she had merely exchanged the tyranny of Archbishop Laud for that of the "godly fathers"

---

spinsters and widows had practically the same rights as men of similar social and economic station. See Pearl Hogrefe, *Tudor Women* (Ames: University of Iowa Press, 1975) ch. 2; Doris Stenton, *The English Woman in History* (New York: Macmillan, 1957) ch. 1; Carl Bridenbaugh, *Vexed and Troubled Englishmen, 1590-1642* (New York: Oxford University Press, 1968), 27-38.

[7] Hogrefe summarizes this material, 4-9.

[8] Bridenbaugh, 27-28.

[9] *Ibid.*, 463.

of the Boston congregation. The motives that had impelled her to
follow her pastor, John Cotton, to Boston, urged her to seek a further
phrasing of her spiritual needs. A woman of commanding intellect, a
"peculiarly magnetic temperament" and a persuasive tongue, fortified
by a knowledge of the Bible as well as of Puritan doctrine, she gathered
her neighbors around her and explicated the weekly sermons, maintaining that a "covenant of grace" was a logical culmination of the doctri-
nally orthodox "covenant of works."[10]

Her ingratiating doctrine of the "indwelling Spirit" and "universal
grace" tapped a current of discontent among those not of the Elect,
which soon became a politically disruptive following that threatened
the very basis of the oligarchy's authority to be the sole promulga-
tors of the law. Anne Hutchinson was ordered to cease her meetings
and be silent. When she refused, the resultant strife became the issue
of the stormy election of 1637 in which the Hutchinsonian party was
defeated.

With Winthrop restored as Governor, the Ecclesiastical Synod has-
tened to examine the Hutchinson doctrines and found them heretical.
When she refused to abandon them, Winthrop declared she "walked
by such a rule as cannot stand with the peace of any state."[11] Hetero-
doxy was treason; the issue was both civil and theological. In November 1638 she was charged with heresy and "traducing the ministry,"
i.e., insubordination. "We have a few things against you," charged
the General Court, ". . . of dangerous consequence . . . the dishonor you
have brought unto God by these unsound tenets." To which Mistress
Hutchinson replied, "It was never in my heart to slight any man but
only that man should be kept in his own place and not be set in the room
of God." The verdict was inevitable. She was excommunicated and
sentenced "as a leper" to withdraw from the Colony.

Anne Hutchinson stands alongside Roger Williams in asserting the
right to liberty of conscience and planting the "seeds of incipient democracy,"[12] but more important for the future emergence of her sex,
she had organized a following to promote her views. Her persecutors

[10] Charles M. Andrews, *The Colonial Period of American History* (New Haven: Yale
University Press, 1964) I, 477-486; Thomas J. Wertenbaker, *The Puritan Oligarchy*
(Princeton University Press, 1947), 219-224; Charles F. Adams, *Antinomianism in Massa-
chusetts Bay, 1636-1638*, Prince Society Publications, v. 21, 1894.

[11] See Charles F Adams, *op. cit.* for a detailed account of the trial.

[12] George P. Gooch, *The History of Democratic Ideas in the 17th Century* (Cambridge:
Cambridge University Press, 1898), 84-90.

had stopped her meetings when they perceived that free assembly lent itself to collective action; but the Puritan clergy had forgotten the lesson two generations later when they sanctioned the formation of little circles of devout women for spiritual improvement and good works as a "most indearing exercise of social piety."[13] They had approved a mode of social action that took women out of their homes into the community, broadened their minds and their interests, helped them develop rudimentary organizing skills, and accustomed society to the spectacle of women engaging in social action.

Institutionalizing the principle of association in the earliest church-related societies laid the basis for women's political socialization through the independent exercise of organizing talents outside the church; and served as the primary means of transforming them from social pawns to autonomous individuals. More than a century later, Alexis de Tocqueville perceived that there was a "necessary connection between the principle of association and that of equality in a democracy."[14] Individuals "can do hardly anything by themselves," he wrote, ". . . if they do not learn voluntarily to help one another." Indeed, "the art of pursuing in common the object of their common desire" is "the only means they have of acting." The "art of associating together" became a practiced skill among women in the 18th and 19th centuries.

A few years after Anne Hutchinson perished in an Indian massacre, heresy in a highly dangerous form once more raised its head in Boston in the guise of George Fox's earliest missionaries to the New World: Anne Austin and Mary Fisher.[15] The zeal of the Quakers penetrated the Puritan armor at no point more painfully than in their insistence on the equality of the sexes. Both men and women were "children of Light," subject to direct call from God to become "publishers of truth," since "man can not limit the power of God by conceiving it as existing in his sex only." The egalitarian principle worked its way into outward practices. The marriage ceremony was stripped of its patriarchal and

---

[13] Mary Sumner Benson, *Women in Eighteenth Century America: A Study of Opinion and Usage* (New York: Columbia University Press, 1935), 178-179.

[14] Alexis de Tocqueville, *Democracy in America*, ed. Phillips Bradley, Vintage Book (New York: Random House, 1945) II, 115.

[15] Mabel R. Brailsford, *Quaker Women, 1650-1690* (London: Duckworth & Co., 1915), 94-113. See also Ishbel Ross, *Margaret Fell: Mother of Quakerism* (New York: Longmans, Green, 1949), ch. 19. The most distinguished of Fox's converts, Margaret Fell is mainly responsible for the egalitarian practices.

sacerdotal elements; the paid ministry was abolished, taking with it the last remnant of priestly authority; and church business was divided between men's and women's committees, equal in importance but specialized in function. Women enjoyed genuine representation in the governing of the community.

The dynamic influence of the egalitarian principle ran deeper than outward practices to shape the very processes of thought. The privilege of serving as ministers presupposed women's right to speak in public and justified equal access to education. Training in the conduct of church business taught organizational skills and familiarity with deliberative policy-making. The encouragement of "approved example" furnished warmth for ambition. The early exercise of public responsibilities developed a tradition of leadership among Quaker women scattered in small settlements over most of the colonies during the 17th and 18th centuries. Imbued with equalitarian values which were latently revolutionary in the social climate of the time, these women prepared the way for four of the outstanding pioneer feminists: Lucretia Mott, Sarah and Angelina Grimké, and Susan B. Anthony.[16] Anne Hutchinson furnished an ineluctable example and a mode of social action. A galaxy of Quaker women set in motion the ideological revolution that eventually restructured women's relation to the family, the state, religion, and education.

The *Mayflower* wives were more typical of the women in the Great Migration than Anne Hutchinson and the zealous Quakers, and furnished historians with the archetypal model of the pioneer wife as brave and resourceful as she was anonymous. Thirty four women embarked on the *Mayflower*; at year's end eleven had survived. None had been asked to sign the Mayflower Compact. Their husbands' daring in drawing up a civic covenant was offset by prudent adherence to custom in domestic relations. A year earlier (1619), the Virginia House of Burgesses in its initial meeting under the "charter of grants and liberties" declared that since "it is not knowen whether man or woman be the most necessary" in establishing plantations, it granted a hundred acres to wives as well as husbands.[17]

As it turned out, the first generation of English women who peopled the wilderness found they had an unaccustomed degree of freedom in

---

[16] A sampling of these early women includes Mary Dyer, Mary Coffin Starbuck, Hannah Penn, Elizabeth Haddon, Elizabeth Harris.

[17] Andrews, I, 183-184.

the New World, including freedom to endure incredible hardships and contrive a thousand shifts to survive. Husbands and wives were mutually dependent partners in an exacting enterprise. Old World attitudes were loosened in fact if not in law. Sharing the common perils entitled women to a voice in the decision making and many of them exercised it by intruding in public affairs. The valiant wives in Bacon's Rebellion not only assisted but helped instigate the insurgency of the frontiersmen against the tidewater aristocrats; while Lady Frances Berkeley played a major role on the side of the aristocrats, journeying to London to lay the "facts" before the King.[18]

From the earliest settlements, wives were both homemakers and partners of their husbands in their breadwinning activities, whether as farmer, merchant, trader, printer, pewterer, or a dozen other crafts. It was a functional society with few underutilized resources. Equipped with a power of attorney, women frequently served as agents for their husbands in business transactions. The courts customarily appointed women as executrices of their husbands' estates. As widows they were free to carry on their husbands' enterprises and frequently retained control after marrying again. As heads of families they had options of a semi-public sort; and in a surprising number of cases inherited their husbands' posts as public printers, tax-treasurers, prothonotaries.[19] Women's participation in litigation as attorneys-in-fact is scattered over court minutes in all of the colonies, until the growth of the paid legal profession in the mid-18th century shut them out of contact with the legal profession and the judicial process: a political fact of great importance to women as the profession tightened its hold on the political process.[20]

The pressure of reality tended to contravene the Puritan principle of women's subject status and to democratize the institution of the family

---

[18] Julia C. Spruill, *Women's Life and Work in the Southern Colonies* (Norton Library, New York: W. W. Norton & Company, 1972), 233-235. The durable and politically gifted Lady Frances was wife to three royal governors in succession, and a leader of the "Green Springs faction" in Virginia politics for a generation. See also NAW, I, 135.

[19] Eugenie Leonard, *The Dear-Bought Heritage* (Philadelphia: University of Pennsylvania Press, 1965), 232 ff.

[20] Sophie H. Drinker, "Women Attorneys of Colonial Times," *Maryland Historical Magazine*, Vol. 56, No. 4, December 1961, 351. The legal profession was the last of the learned professions to admit women (1869), while the judicial process has been the most resistant of governmental institutions to women's participation. Not until the Civil Rights Act of 1967 were women made eligible for jury duty in all of the states.

in communities which were being constructed de novo. Much of what women did was "unscriptural," but law deferred to expediency as women's productive value created an enlarged mentality regarding their social and economic function.[21] As towns grew to cities in the 18th century, however, the distinction between the roles of homemaker and breadwinner grew sharper and tradition tended to reassert itself, with a denigration of women's status.

The situation was similar in the matter of voting. Women were mainly left out of account in provisions for voting in the 17th century but were not explicitly denied the right in New England and the Middle Atlantic Colonies. Careful sifting of local records has produced evidence that women proprietors of large landholdings could and occasionally did vote in New Jersey, New York, Connecticut, and several towns in Massachusetts.[22]

In the four colonies with landed institutions, voting was customarily restricted to possessors of large landholdings. While land-owning women voted for members of the Virginia House of Burgesses until 1699, the growing unwillingness to share this form of power is evidenced in the experience of Margaret Brent, whose claim to a vote in the Maryland Assembly was indisputable. Calvert's Proprietorship was free of the royal prerogative; his power was absolute. His brother, Leonard Calvert, was vice-regent.

In 1638, Margaret Brent and her sister Mary, non-juring Catholics from Gloucestershire, arrived at the Maryland Palatinate armed with a large grant of land from Lord Baltimore.[23] They established a manor and exercised seignorial power. With an extensive knowledge of English law, Margaret Brent engaged in court action as attorney-in-fact in 124 cases between 1640 and 1650, and managed her affairs with such acumen that she became the most conspicuous figure in the troubled early years of the Palatinate. As a proprietor she was entitled to "voice, seat and place" in the Assembly, but the legislative body had little or no power and met only when it was convoked. She did not press her claim to membership until after she became executrix and residuary legatee of Leonard Calvert's estate (1647).

In January, 1648, Brent appeared before the Assembly and demanded

---

[21] Leonard, ch. 5.

[22] Sophie H. Drinker, "Votes for Women in 18th Century New Jersey," *Proceedings, New Jersey Historical Society*, LXXX, January, 1962. 15-33.

[23] Andrews, II, 283-322; Spruill, 234 ff.

"voice and two votes" in order to carry out her responsibilities. Governor Greene acknowledged the Assembly's debt to her, but found the courage to deny her the vote as being outside her "ordained sphere," although granting her voice and seat. No doubt her sex furnished a convenient pretext for removing her from her polar position between the prerogative and the Assembly's uncertain authority, but the action was significant as anticipating the leveling of the feudal status of the landowning feme sole to the status of feme covert. The traditional division between women with husbands and those without—feme covert and feme sole—was yielding to a new division between men and women —the political polarization of the sexes—which constituted the essence of women's formal relation to public life in the late 18th, 19th and early 20th century.

As the principle of representation advanced to include greater numbers of males, it declined correspondingly for females, ending somewhat ingloriously for the latter in the State of New Jersey early in the 19th century. New Jersey was sensitive to unusual pressures from within and without, with politically liberal Quakers dominant in the West and a mix of Dutch, German and English colonizers in the North and East. From the beginning its electoral processes were "experimental." The hastily written constitution on the eve of declaring independence (June, 1776) enfranchised all inhabitants worth fifty pounds or more. Legislative enactment in 1790 confirmed the inclusion of women in "all inhabitants." Recent scholarship affirms that the provision was probably a survival of an old practice, in a colony with many land-owning women, reinforced by the presence of Quakers in West Jersey.[24] Women rarely exercised the privilege, however, until an Essex County election in 1796 when a "regiment of women" descended on the polls in a vain attempt to save a Federalist candidate. Again in 1803 and 1807, "widows and maids" came forward to save the Federalist ticket. So fraudulent was the 1807 election that the legislature set it aside as void, and the state made haste to rewrite the Constitution, disfranchising women. History records no complaint from the women.

New Jersey's action in 1807 marks the end of a century-long process. Property holding men gradually ceased being willing to share the ruling with property holding women. After the Revolution, as the electoral process became democratized, and the right to vote inhered in the per-

[24] Drinker, op. cit.; see also, Richard P. McCormick, *History of Voting in New Jersey*, 1664-1911 (New Brunswick: Rutgers University Press, 1953).

son rather than in property, male voters gradually ceased being willing to consider that any woman as an individual had a stake in society. Along with a leveling of class was a redistribution of power. All males became rulers; all females the ruled. No special significance is attached to the date, 1807, but it marks the point at which the principle that "all free and rightful government rests on the consent of the governed" was ready for clarification.

II

The half century of political disequilibrium accompanying the rebellion against the Crown might have been expected to produce some individuals sufficiently discontented to press for an enlarged role for women. Many notable women—Abigail Adams and Mercy Otis Warren are only the most renowned—played vigorous roles in sustaining the rebellion but primarily as partners of their husbands in the common effort. Mercy Warren, with an inborn talent for politics and restless ambition, saw deeply into the incongruities in the position of women and held bold views that women's deficiencies and consequent political deprivations were altogether the result of a lack of education. As self-appointed "historical apologist" for the Rebellion, she wrote her history of the "mighty commotion" because she had been denied an active role, and desired to be "the first of her sex . . . who taught the reading world in matters of state policy and history."[25]

Abigail Adams' importance in the evolution of women's role rests, not on her views of women's liberation, but on the model she furnished for a participant's role in a husband-wife political partnership. The part she played both complemented and supplemented that of her husband. She was forthright, shrewd, an independent political entity. Her intellectual vigor was as great as her husband's; her social perceptions much keener. From no other political couple have we so deftly woven a tapestry of shared views regarding the vital issues of the day; and from no other woman except Eleanor Roosevelt do we have so complete a record of a political partner's experiences as they impinge on public life.

Although Abigail Adams held advanced views on women's education, she probably shared John Adams' view that suffrage should be confined

[25] Moses Coit Tyler, *Literary History of the American Revolution* (New York: G. P. Putnam's Sons, 1898), II, 420-421.

to the property-owning class; though she probably also agreed when he asked, "Why exclude women? Women have as good judgment, as independent minds, as those men who are wholly destitute of property." The witty exchange between husband and wife which some have taken as sounding the tocsin of revolt seems rather a demand for relief from common law disabilities, spiced with a characteristic barb at Adams' slaveholding colleagues who do not share her "passion for liberty" being "accustomed to deprive their fellow creatures of theirs."[26] She was an outspoken foe of slavery.

The potential political significance of the role of the President's wife as a political partner became evident soon after the establishment of the republic. The intimate records of the early presidents reveal the part played by their wives in patterning the role of the President as a symbol of the power of the sovereign people. This involved a complex process of personification phrased in the social aspects of the role. The President's official home became the seat of his power; his public life was superimposed on his private life; his wife's role was that of his official partner; his accessibility, his manner of entertaining, his ceremonial observances were joint decisions of the President and his official partner.

The first three women to occupy this role represented three important cultural strands in American life. Martha Washington, a plantation aristocrat, behaved as naturally as "queen of the republican court" as she had as mistress of Mount Vernon. The Washingtons invested the Presidential role with dignity hedged round with deference. The Adams, more republican in their tastes and habits, strove to maintain a presidential posture "sufficiently elevated and independent" to establish the proper social distance from the aristocratic Senate and the democratic House. As the first occupants of the White House, they made the President's House the first home in the nation: the President's place of business as the people's sovereign.

Abigail Adams' successor was Dolley Payne Madison, a Philadelphia Quaker temperamentally fitted to encompass wider social and political relationships. Unlike Abigail Adams, she had little interest in partisan differences or political distinctions. Her effortless urbanity during a reign of sixteen years, eight as wife of the Secretary of State and official hostess for widower Jefferson, and eight as First Lady during Madison's

[26] *Familiar Letters of John Adams and His Wife Abigail Adams*, ed. Charles Francis Adams (New York: 1871), 118.

terms "pleased everyone and offended no one." Jefferson, concerned to introduce the "manners of democracy," did away with levees, birthday celebrations, weekly receptions and other trappings of courtly ceremony. The political revolution was not complete until the new republic had made trial of the social implications of its principles. Theoretically he was accessible to the people at all times, but practically he led a bachelor's life.

It was left to the wife of the Secretary of State to hold weekly receptions at her home and hospitably receive all who cared to come. During her tenure as First Lady she made the role of the First Lady a vocation, pre–eminent in status, the apotheosis of Everywoman, and filled this position in a manner designed to contribute to the political success as well as the personal popularity of the President.

As First Lady, Dolley Madison exercised a masterful social authority in creating a "society" in the rude unfinished capital, formulating an unwritten code of social behavior for a political society that was under the constant critical surveillance of representatives of older nations. Her republican salons were intimate meeting grounds where both partisan and social barriers might be transcended and diplomats rub shoulders with frontiersmen. To her rather than to Jefferson may be accorded the credit for translating the spirit of the Jeffersonian era into social forms. The value of her hospitality was heightened by the fact that members of the early Congresses were a "transient, heterogeneous, compulsively democratic" aggregation of men, separated from their families, living in boarding houses, and congregating mainly with the likeminded.[27] For such men the White House served as a social center which they were privileged to enjoy if they chose. During the Madison and Monroe Administrations, increasing numbers of Congressmen brought their wives and daughters to Washington for the Congressional sessions and social life became more varied and animated. Under the long social sway of Dolley Madison, numerous salons were established by wives of Cabinet members and more or less permanent residents such as Mrs. Albert Gallatin, Mrs. William Thornton, and Margaret Bayard Smith.

III

The democratic principle remained an abstraction until the expansion of electoral participation dissolved the deferential society of the

[27] James S. Young, "Community and Society," in *American Political Behavior: Historical Essays and Readings*, ed. Lee Benson et al. (New York: Harper & Row, 1974), 87-109.

18th century, but expansive notions of equality and liberty were plainly signalled by the riotous mobs in Philadelphia and New York in 1792 and 1793. "Both men and women seemed for a time to have put away their wits and gone mad with republicanism."[28] Mob action is an extreme statement of the fact that the "consent of the governed" includes a wide range of political behavior and almost unlimited opportunities for political action. The ballot, in fact, is only a symbol of the real business of participation, which is a "continuous, unrecorded plebiscite on the personalities and policies and administration of government."[29] It has been in plebiscitary activities that women have unmistakably registered their presence in the political environment, beginning soon after the nation's founding.

From 1807 until 1838, women had no electoral privilege in any state. These same years saw their entry into almost every avenue of political activity except that ending at the polling place.

In the absence of law forbidding it, women collectively and individually pre-empted numerous quasi-political rights: (a) socializing the political environment not only by their presence at partisan rallies but at such formal Federalist gatherings as the Washington Benevolent Societies' annual parades and banquets; and laying the foundations for a satellite relationship to the political parties; (b) organizing pressure groups for bringing pressure on legislatures and shaping public opinion on political issues; (c) discussing political issues on public platforms, despite scriptural injunctions and public disapproval; (d) transforming a political faction into a political party with a slate of candidates; (e) canvassing for political candidates; (f) editing partisan newspapers; (g) addressing state legislative committees with prescriptive advice; (h) petitioning and personally addressing state legislatures demanding statutory reforms in the common law regarding married women's disabilities; (i) engaging in civil disobedience by refusing to pay taxes; (j) and loosing a hail storm of petitions in the House of Representatives for the abolition of slavery, under the aegis of their knightly champion, John Quincy Adams, which finally provoked the House to seek relief by passing the Pinckney Gag Rule, raising the constitutional issues of free speech and right of petition.[30]

---

[28] John Bach McMaster, *History of the American People* (New York: D. D. Appleton, 1909), II, 50-51, 93-95.

[29] Charles E. Merriam, *Systematic Politics* (Chicago: University of Chicago Press, 1933), 230.

[30] (a) Beginning with the Adams-Jackson campaign in 1828, women were visibly present

Women were visibly part of the political environment from the inno-
vative beginnings of modern political campaigns. The extra-constitu-
tional devices for consulting and informing the electorate and "dispos-
ing minds to the right candidate," out of which party organizations
grew, were grass roots socio-political activities in which whole families
were involved. In the Cumberland region and the Ohio Valley, political campaigning borrowed the attributes of the early 19th century religious revivals. It was only a step from camp meetings to political mass

---

in presidential election campaigns: helped shape grass roots campaign methods and tactics; and established the pattern of partisan volunteerism, ironically, in the period when
the spoils system of rewards for services was developing. Incidentally, the spoils system
had a significant and enduring effect on the role of the political wife.

(b) The Female Anti-Slavery Societies, 1833. Church-related societies were also active as pressure groups on such issues as Cherokee removal and anti-Masonry.

(c) Frances Wright: July 4th address, New Harmony, Indiana, 1828. A. J. G. Perkins
and Theresa Wolfson, *Francis Wright: Free Enquirer* (Harper & Brothers: New York,
1939), 208 ff.

(d) With her dynamic speeches and editorials in the *Free Enquirer*, Wright developed an effective political organization of working men. *Ibid.*, Ch. V. See also Samuel
Eliot Morison, *Oxford History of the United States* (London: Oxford University Press) I,
432 ff.

(e) Wright campaigned in several cities for Van Buren in 1836. Ostrogorski names
Wright and Van Buren as the first "professional politicians". See M. Ostrogorski, *Poli-
tics and People: The Ordeal of Self-Government in the United States* (New York: Arno
Press, 1974), ch. 2. Wright saw labor as the potential political force.

(f) Wright, *Free Enquirer*, New York; Anne Royall, *The Huntress*, Washington.

(g) In 1838, Angelina Grimké addressed a legislative committee of the Massachusetts
Legislature; presented 20,000 petitions from Massachusetts women demanding abolition
of slavery and asserted, "I hold that American women have to do with this subject, not
only because it is moral and religious, but because it is political, inasmuch as we are citizens of this republic. . . ." The status of women as citizens was at issue in the right of
petition.

(h) Ernestine Rose, New York State Legislature, 1835. NAW, II, 196.

(i) Seven women in a Universalist community in Geauga County, Ohio, refused to pay
their taxes in 1828, since they were denied representation. Sufficient property was
seized to satisfy the levy. This became a popular form of protest among feminists, including Lucy Stone, Abby Kelly Foster, Harriet Hunt and Dr. Mary Walker. It always
led to property seizure and therefore publicity.

(j) The petition campaign began among Quaker women in 1830 or earlier; increased
steadily and reached floodtide in 1837-1840 with the "Fathers and Rulers" petition, ex-
acerbating opinion in both North and South, and helping "to place the whole dread-
fully perplexing problem beyond the point where peaceful and considered plans of restriction . . . could be examined." Andrew C. McLaughlin, *Constitutional History of the
United States* (New York: D. Appleton-Century Co., 1935), 476-482.

meetings, and women took the step along with the men. The presence of women and children helped shape the communal character of the grass roots campaigns. Rival candidates, like revivalists of competing sects, traveled in groups from one wilderness rally to another, electioneering at rallies lasting a day or more. Between speeches, the candidates moved among the crowds, not to pray and exhort, "but to shake hands, kiss babies, as if they had known us all our lives . . . they all promised a great deal of good things if we would elect them."[31]

The Adams-Jackson campaign in 1828 had all the lineaments of modern electoral campaigns. Women were present at the mass meetings, the torchlight parades, the all-day rallies and barbecues, listening to political harangues in which political information was blended with a rich mix of demagoguery that excited partisan involvement. Jackson typified the aggressive individualism and egalitarianism of the frontier. The conviction that "one man was as good as another"—the mystique of the "plain people"—was common property, reflecting a "spirit and sense of popular power and of popular competence" developed to the point of self-consciousness.[32] As Tocqueville observed, politics was a "universal preoccupation" with the people. Their greatest delight was "to take a hand in the regulation of society and to discuss it . . . even the women frequently attend public meetings and listen to public harangues as a recreation."[33] "Every fresh truth . . . every new idea became a germ of power placed within reach of the people."

In the Adams-Jackson campaign, probably the most scurrilous in our history, the easy morality and egalitarianism of the frontier was pitted against the narrow morals of the older states. Adams partisans extracted every advantage from Jackson's chequered career and irregular marriage, while the Jackson partisans were no kinder to the life style of the Adams, assailing Louisa Adams' "monarchical tendencies" and assumption of an "exalted station."[34] The resentment of men and

[31] Report of election of 1810 in Kentucky Gazette, Sesquicentennial History of Kentucky, ed. Frederick A. Wallis (Hopkinsville, Ky.: Historical Records Association, 1945) I, 290.

[32] McLaughlin, 401.

[33] Tocqueville, I, 250.

[34] Louisa Adams was driven to defend herself in a presumably autobiographic memoir published in the Saturday Evening Post, February 24, 1827, 1. On the 1828 election, see Florence Weston, The Presidential Election of 1828 (Washington, D. C.: Ruddick Press, 1935), 142 ff; Samuel Flagg Bemis, John Quincy Adams and the Union (New York: Alfred A. Knopf, 1956), 126-128.

women living in wilderness cabins was easily triggered by tirades against "presidential palaces" and fashionable clothes paid for with their taxes. "Politics ran high at this time," said Elizabeth Oakes Smith in Portland, Maine, "and every man . . . and every woman was partisan." The partisan enthusiasm of the women found bizarre ways to express itself, such as calico dresses and aprons "imprinted with medallions of the very unhandsome head of their hero," symbolic of one aspect of the role, both obtrusive and irresponsible, that women were assuming in the world of partisan politics, on the fringe of the parties. Their capacity for partisan involvement developed long before it occurred to those who were participants in campaigns that a predisposition toward a favored candidate should find expression at the ballot box.

If the wives of the frontiersmen helped elect Jackson in 1828, it was a different kind of wife who assured Van Buren's election eight years later.[35] Rachael Jackson's death soon after the 1828 election was blamed by the embittered President on the scurrilous attacks of the opposition, and furnished the emotional setting for the social war between Jackson and the indignant wives of his Cabinet over the recognition of "the hussy," Peggy Timberlake Eaton, a tavern keeper's sprightly daughter who married Senator John Eaton after Jackson had named Eaton to his Cabinet as Secretary of War. Precipitated by Mrs. John C. Calhoun, a tempest blew up over the social recognition of Mrs. Eaton in which Jackson's entire Cabinet was forced to resign and two ambassadors were sent home. Calhoun, despite his close ties with Jackson and strong aspirations for the presidency, countenanced if he did not approve his wife's action, thus making his own narrow moral judgment on a disgraceful incident.

In the boisterous election of 1840, editors from Maine to Florida noted that women "had become the very life and soul of these movements of the people"; attracted, it was inferred, "by the parades and the singing and the rest of the mummery."[36] The unprecedented outburst of political enthusiasm that carried more voters to the polls than ever before was attributable to the character of the candidates as well as the nature of the audiences, both artfully exploited by the Whigs to unify a coalition of diverse interests by papering over dangerous and

---

[35] The best account of the "Eaton imbroglio" is in Margaret L. Coit, *John C. Calhoun: American Portrait* (Boston: Houghton Mifflin Co., 1950), ch. 13; see also Bemis, 196.

[36] Robert Gray Gunderson, *The Log Cabin Campaign* (Frankfort: Kentucky University Press, 1957), 135 ff.

threatening issues. The techniques tried in 1828 were elaborated and new ones invented. Slogans, symbols, and monster rallies contributed to the "glorious excitement and uproar." Women held campaign teas, made speeches, participated in monster parades, reportedly attended the two and three-day rallies by the thousands. Whig managers organized glee clubs of men and women that traveled from town to town, combining the power of song with the fun of a hayride. The campaign of 1840 institutionalized campaign techniques that survived until the invention of radio and television.[37]

This aspect of the development of the political behavior of woman was patterned by the same influences that shaped her position in the family along the line of settlement when the political center of gravity had shifted to the frontier states west of the Alleghenies. Her freedom in the family, which was the only structured institution in the initial stages of settlement on the westward-moving frontier, had taken on cultural attributes. Around her had gathered legends of courage, resourcefulness, and endurance—a legacy from the 17th century—individualizing the frontier woman on a heroic scale as a symbol of a "new woman" in an egalitarian society. She came to be regarded as the carrier of civilization and, increasingly, as the custodian of morals. In her wake came settlements, churches, schools.

The further west the culture symbol traveled, the more powerful it became, offering one explanation for the fact that the first surrender of the male monopoly of the ballot came in the frontier state of Kentucky in 1838, when white widows with children in school (probably not a numerous class) were granted school suffrage; and the first grant of full suffrage to women any place in the western world came in the newly organized Territory of Wyoming in 1869. Kentucky's concessive yielding of school suffrage, the political value of which is minimal, marked the beginning of the incremental progress toward full suffrage. Persuasively as women learned to argue the case for suffrage as an "inalienable right," the point was never conceded. The tedious advance was a matter of inching forward, step by step, through concession of partial suffrage at points strategic to the interest of the dominant group in maintaining social control. School suffrage advanced gradually, especially west of the Mississippi. Suffrage on tax and bond issues was slower; municipal suffrage slower still.

---

[37] See Mrs. John A. Logan, *Reminiscences of a Soldier's Wife* (New York: Charles Scribners' Sons, 1913) for a running account of electoral campaigns from 1856 to the end of the century.

IV

Foreign visitors came to see and appraise. The first of them, the
Scottish heiress, Frances Wright (1818), who followed the "rising star of
liberty" to the New World to see for herself what it portended, concluded on her first visit that it was "impossible for women to stand in
higher estimate than they do here." Returning in the entourage of General Lafayette in 1824, she saw reason to amend her early views and
stayed on to become the champion of the slave, the working man, en-
gulfed in the rising tide of industrialism, and woman, oppressed by marriage and religious institutions.

A second visitor was the radical British journalist, Harriet Martineau,
for whom her sex had been no barrier to fame. She came, she said, "to
judge American society in its spirit and method," by its own test—"the
Declaration of Independence and the constitutions based on its principles."[38]   Her opinion of American women was decidedly astringent.
They had the shadow of freedom but not the substance; were free to get
their heads turned by religion, to keep them away from "morals, philosophy and politics."[39]   They exalted education but, while some became "gorgeous pedants," others filled their minds with inferior French
novels.   Instead of justice they were given indulgence.   Possessing far
more of "the machinery of freedom" than her British sisters, they were
hoodwinked into not using it.

A third visitor, Alexis de Tocqueville (1831), was more perceptive.
He observed that the "general equality of condition" had not only
shaped political institutions but had modified all aspects of social life,
including the relations between the sexes, "making woman more and
more the equal of man."[40]   But the sensitive-minded Frenchman also
noted that "constant care" had been taken "to trace two distinct lines of
action for the two sexes to make them keep pace one with the other . . .
in two paths that are always different." His "binocular vision" enabled
him to envisage phenomena from different and opposing angles and
comprehend a subtle process going on before his eyes: the "general
equality of condition" had fostered adaptive adjustments to the inescapable fact of bi-sexuality, an insight that furnishes an analytical perspective useful in tracing women's path across American political history.

[38] Harriet Martineau, *Autobiography* (London: Saunders & Otley, 1837) I, 405.
[39] Harriet Martineau, *Society in America* (London: Saunders & Otley, 1837) I, 238,
III, 108-110.
[40] Tocqueville, II, 222.

Tocqueville's gaze rested longest on the astonishing spectacle of the young woman, educated far beyond European practice, surrendered at an early age to her own guidance, enjoying sufficient contact with reality to exercise her own judgment and accept responsibility for her own actions, intellectually and morally "enlightened." She was a product of the institution of the American family shaped by a century of frontier experience: the Puritan family democratized by the "general equality of condition," egalitarian, nuclear, affectional and cooperative, in which both parents were "mild authority figures." Her marital choice was freely made, but once made, it was sternly adhered to.[41] In short, the American woman was at once the freest and the most circumscribed: a paradox that engaged his deepest interest.

Martineau gathered her observations in the easy freedom of Washington drawing rooms, fashionable New York boarding houses, Southern plantation mansions, and the homes of the New England intellectual aristocracy. Tocqueville traveled more widely and observed women not only in urban settings but in frontier settlements and wilderness clearings where the conditions of their existence and the role they played were revelatory. There was truth in the observations of all three visitors. The context of the lives of American women had no parallel elsewhere. It was in fact, as Martineau said, "a very singular society."

V

Paralleling the seemingly spontaneous partisan activities of women in the 1830s and 1840s that laid the foundations for a satellite relationship to the political parties were purposeful initiatives of individual women intent on women's liberation from their subject status. It was a period of intellectual ferment and confusion when a people "not yet welded into a society nor refined into a civilization" yielded popular authority to a succession of men and women who voiced their hopes and aspirations.[42] Among those who discovered the exhilaration of possessing the public ear were the feminist pioneers, Frances Wright, Lucretia Mott, Sarah and Angelina Grimké and Margaret Fuller. A feminist orientation had been anticipated by Mercy Warren and Judith Murray, but the new generation added action to analysis and put their sex in the

[41] *Ibid*, II, 212-214.
[42] Constance Rourke, *Trumpets of Jubilee* (New York: Harcourt Brace & Co., 1927), vii-ix.

thick of the struggle for power in a critical period, despite the denunci-
ations of the clergy, the conservative press and outraged members of
Congress.

First in order of time among these women was Frances Wright, intellectual offspring of Mary Wollstonecraft, who advanced a range of
explosive ideas from public platforms beginning in 1828 that would engage the public mind for the next fifty years, including abolition of slavery, reforms in marriage and divorce laws, birth control, universal public education, abolition of imprisonment for debt; and became the first
woman in American political life to gain and use political power.[43] A
revolutionary by temperament, her major theme was universal state-
supported education, "the reform without which all other reforms are
but idle or temporary . . . the only pledge of equal and invaluable
rights."[44] Her natural element was politics, her philosophy a mix of
Godwinian rationalism, Benthamite utilitarianism and Owenite socialism, which could not fail to be ingratiating with the discontented "mechanics and artisans" who were her main target. A woman of privilege,
she adopted the cause of the underdog, of whatever color or sex, and
soon had an immense following as well as an instant set of enemies. Her
example was inspiring to the avant-garde feminists, and at the same
time counterproductive because of the hostility aroused by the sensa-
tional radicalism of many of her ideas. As an unspoken tribute, a steel-
engraved portrait of Frances Wright serves as a frontispiece to the five-
volume *History of Woman Suffrage*, compiled by Susan B. Anthony,
Elizabeth Cady Stanton and others (1883-1902).

Margaret Fuller stands alongside Frances Wright as a source of the
leavening ideas from the Enlightment that helped shape the feminist
faith in the potentiality of women. The Transcendental author and
critic forms a triumvirate with Mary Wollstonecraft and George Sand
in phrasing the aspirations of the feminist revolution. The most thoroughgoing individualist in the Concord circle, she perceived the special
significance, for her sex, of the Emersonian glorification of the individual. The time was ripe for a woman who would embody the rebellions
as well as the visions of the age and add to them the bitterly personal
grievances of women, which she did in *Woman in the Nineteenth Century* (1845). For Fuller as for Wright, education, grandly conceived,

---

[43] See Morison, supra, n30. Perkins and Wolfson, ch. V.

[44] Wright's rounded platform emphasized free education, free religious inquiry, free
marital unions, but most important of all was free education.

was the key to releasing women from their habitual willingness to be taught and led by men: to her views on education she added the liberating concept that only women could help women. Her justly famous "Conversations" (1838-1840) were consciousness-raising seminars on an exalted level that radicalized a score of eminent women in Boston's intellectual circles, including several who became feminist leaders.

Even stronger than the leavening ideas from the Enlightenment was the moralistic impulse that found expression in the wave of religious enthusiasm that swept over New England, New York, Pennsylvania and Ohio in the 1820s and 1830s, and sought outlet in politically oriented humanitarianism: temperance, anti-slavery, anti-Masonry, and eventually feminism; and established the permanent character of women's independent social action. The "shackles of sin" had to be struck off the slaveholder, the intemperate or licentious man, the exploiter of women and children, the supporter of the double standard of morality, the "machine politician," before women could be liberated. The philosophic basis of the "fettered sex's" aspirations was profoundly moral, and had its roots in the Puritan acknowledgment of man's hopeless depravity.

In 1833, when several small anti-slavery societies with many women members in New England and the Middle Atlantic states met in Philadelphia to form the American Anti-Slavery Society (AASS), the male members unintentionally provided the brilliantly persuasive Lucretia Mott, "imbued with the rights of women from her earliest childhood at Nantucket,"[45] with an opportunity to organize the latent feminist impulse identified by Frances Wright, and make of it a political instrument. Although the constitution of the AASS declared that all dues-paying members were entitled to vote at the meetings, there was acrimonious debate regarding the status of women members in the new organization, led by the wealthy Tappan brothers (reincarnations of 17th century Puritans) and Congregational clergymen, who pressed successfully for denial of status to women and restriction of their activities to work among women. Several women were present during the debate regarding their proper role, including the principled nonconformist, Lucretia Mott.

A week later she assembled a score or more of Quaker women abolitionists in Philadelphia, "to consider the propriety" of an independent Female Anti-Slavery Society to promote abolition by means of their own devising. Their long preoccupation with the cause of the slave

[45] Otelia Cromwell, *Lucretia Mott* (Cambridge: Harvard University Press, 1958), 125.

gave them a purpose profoundly shared; the cavalier rejection of their status as voting members in the AASS furnished a motive. Mott subtly elicited a sense of group identity among these women already accustomed to speaking in public, to organizing boycotts and collecting petitions in their own way, and a sense of solidarity that prepared them for an expanded range of social and political interaction. By 1836 a network of Female Anti-Slavery Societies had become the political nerve center of the feminist enterprise. They developed an esprit de corps through correspondence; and prepared for a national convention in May, 1837 (when the AASS was in session), that set up the special petition campaign for circulation among women in every town and county in the North, addressed humbly to their "Fathers and Rulers," "pleading" in behalf of a long oppressed and deeply injured class of native Americans—under your exclusive control. . . . We should be less than women if the nameless and unnumbered wrongs of which the slaves of our sex are made the defenceless victims, did not fill us with horror, and constrain us—in agony of spirit—to pray for their deliverance."[46] This petition (drafted by Theodore Weld), with its intimations of the brutalities visited upon slave women, was the greatest single propaganda effort of the abolition campaign, starting backfires in small towns and country districts where the leading citizens were either "timorous" or "apathetic," but their wives were easily aroused to respond with their signatures and the formation of new Female Anti-Slavery Societies. The petitions poured into Washington in the tens of thousands. Special clerks had to be hired to stuff them in boxes for storage at the Capitol.

In the meantime, Lucretia Mott had launched the careers of Sarah and Angelina Grimké, members of a wealthy and distinguished South Carolina family whose personal knowledge of slavery and impassioned protest against it was not matched until Harriet Beecher Stowe's *Uncle Tom's Cabin* cast a wider net to catch the conscience of the North.[47] The Grimkés traveled on to Massachusetts where they found the atmosphere "elastic" under the spell of William Lloyd Garrison and his ardent lieutenants, the abolitionist women surrounding Maria Weston Chapman. The Grimkés' success before audiences of women soon led to

---

[46] Gilbert H. Barnes, *The Anti-Slavery Impulse* (New York: D. Appleton Century, 1933), 130-146.

[47] See the excellent biography of the Grimké sisters by Gerda Lerner, *The Grimké Sisters from South Carolina; Rebels Against Slavery* (Boston: Houghton Mifflin Company, 1967), 7, 166-167, 189, 274.

audiences composed of both men and women, which led inevitably to severe censure by the clergy in the Pastoral Letter of the Council of Congregational Ministers, read in all Congregational churches in July, 1837, warning against these women "who so far forget themselves as to itinerate in the character of public lecturers and teachers" threatening "permanent injury to the female character."

The framers of the Pastoral Letter had unwittingly broken the barrier between the slave's cause and the woman's cause. They prompted Sarah Grimké's biting "Letters on the Equality of the Sexes," the first disputatious feminist polemic; and impelled Angelina in her speeches to link the cause of the slave with that of women, since both were chattels. Criticism from moderate elements among the male abolitionists, including Theodore Weld (whom Angelina married in 1838), urged the sisters to consider the woman's cause as "derivative" to the great "central cause of human freedom," but criticism only hardened the sisters' intransigence, and ended in sharpening the division within the AASS that split it asunder in 1840 over the "woman question."[48]

It was in this atmosphere that delegates were chosen to attend the World Anti-Slavery Convention held at London in 1840. Eight women were selected by the militant elements, including Lucretia Mott. The controversy within the AASS was carried to the floor of the Convention by the American opponents of women's credentials, led by James Birney, and consumed an entire day of the Convention's time, but ended in denial of their credentials. The spectacle of the abolitionist women sitting in a curtained alcove, and joined there by prominent British women naturally elicited wide interest that furthered the feminist cause in both countries. An additional fortuitous event was the meeting of Lucretia Mott with Elizabeth Cady Stanton, bride of Henry B. Stanton, not herself a delegate. Elizabeth Cady Stanton was exactly the right fuse for the older woman's practiced hand, ready with the spark. Their conversations were discussions of principles. The right of women, said Lucretia Mott, to take part in the "deliberations of government" was the basic principle of freedom.[49] "I move that the phrase 'be allowed to' be stricken from our vocabulary." Women's freedom has too long been "by sufferance and at will of a superior." The relationship cemented in London found expression at Seneca Falls.

---

[48] Aileen Kraditor, *Means and Ends in American Abolitionism*, (New York: Pantheon Books, 1969), ch. 3.

[49] Cromwell, 123-126.

VI

Eight years elapsed before the paths of Mott and Stanton crossed again, fortuitously, in July, 1848.[50] Both the setting and the date of the Seneca Falls Convention furnished an appropriate context for launching a revolution. The small town in western New York lay in a region congenial to political dissidence and reformist activities, with a liberal sprinkling of Quakers. It was a year of revolutions in Europe and a presidential election in the United States. The organized abolition movement had virtually ended after the split in 1840, with the moderate abolitionists turning to political organization while the Garrisonians, including most of the women activists, with their no-government principles, standing outside the political process. The sectional controversy had been diverted to political channels by the war with Mexico and the annexation of Texas.

The abolition movement had produced thousands of women who had emerged in political life as a group because of the interest they asserted. The time was ripe for a manifesto that voiced their sense of their own worth and competence. Elizabeth Cady Stanton, Lucretia Mott, her sister Martha Wright and Mary Ann McClintock issued a Call to a Woman's Rights Convention (July 19, 1848) "to discuss the social, civil and religious condition of women." The Call conveyed the dual nature of "rights," both legal and moral. Three days later 300 men and women assembled to discuss a Declaration of Sentiments regarding women's grievances and Resolutions for redress.

The Declaration of Sentiments was the outcome of the "intolerable" encroachments on women's "inalienable rights" as human beings: the rejection of their petitions by Congress, the denial of their right to share in policy making in the abolition movement, the severe censure of the clergy, and the rejection of their credentials in London. Like the Coercive Acts of the British Parliament in the 1770s that inflamed the colonists' will to resist and led to the Declaration of Independence, these oppressive reminders of their subject status had created a demand to assert their independence. After two days of discussion, more than a hundred men and women signed the Declaration of Sentiments and the Resolutions, including the resolution naming it "the duty of the women of this country to secure to themselves the sacred right to the elective franchise."

[50] A good account of the Seneca Falls meeting, with supporting documents, is in Alice Rossi, *Feminist Papers* (New York: Columbia University Press, 1973), 413 ff.

The framers of the Declaration of Sentiments borrowed both the words and the lofty moral tone of the Declaration of Independence. To Jefferson's long preamble they added only the word "women":

We hold these truths to be self evident, that all men and women are created equal; that they are endowed by their Creator with certain inalienable rights; that among these are life, liberty and the pursuit of happiness; that to secure these rights governments are instituted, deriving their just powers from the consent of the governed. Whenever any form of government becomes destructive of these ends, it is the right of those who suffer from it to refuse allegiance to it, and to insist upon the institution of a new government . . . such has been the patient sufferance of the women under this government, and such is now the necessity that constrains them to demand the equal station to which they are entitled. . . .

The history of mankind is a history of repeated injuries and usurpations on the part of man toward woman, having in direct object the establishment of an absolute tyranny over her. To prove this, let facts be submitted to a candid world.

Eighteen grievances were listed as "proof." Twelve of the eighteen detailed women's statutory disabilities under common law. As a result of their legal subjection, women have been denied opportunity for education, for economic opportunity; they have been denied entry to professions and excluded from the ministry. Finally, man has usurped the prerogative of Jehovah Himself, "claiming it as his right to assign for her a sphere of action, when that belongs to her conscience and to her God."

The Declaration of Sentiments was a serious document that tore away the semantic veil from the meaning of equality. Jefferson had no intention of including either women or slaves among those "created equal." The women at Seneca Falls sought the equality tacitly phrased in the Declaration of Independence and embodied in the principles of the Constitution. Those who signed the document understood they had made a commitment to the principle that men and women were created equal; that men had no intrinsic right to exercise authority over women except with their consent; and that the presumption of male superiority would hereafter be challenged.

The Declaration of Sentiments was criticized, ridiculed and denounced in the press. A few who had signed withdrew their names. But the die had been cast. The gathering at Seneca Falls established a pattern for consciousness-raising conventions to interpret and promote the revolution it called for. The concern of the growing woman's rights societies, running alongside the Female Anti-Slavery Societies, was to serve the cause of human freedom by transforming woman's status while delivering the slave from bondage. When war came, the Northern women, already organized in church-related and reform-related soci-

eties, threw themselves into service on the civilian front. For the first
time in American experience, the female population was effectively mobilized as a valuable part of the war machine on the Union side.

On the political front during the war, women's services in the now
dominant Republican Party were unstinted, and for the most part unre-
warded. Susan Anthony was the principle organizer of the Women's
National Loyal League that collected thousands of petitions demanding
emancipation of the slaves. Anna Dickinson, the Quaker lass whose
power to arouse partisan emotion was one of the most valuable assets
of the Republicans in the doubtful states of New York and Connecticut in the elections of 1863 and 1864, was credited with having carried
them.[51] As recognition and reward, she was asked to address Congress
on war policies in 1863, before an audience that included Lincoln and
his Cabinet. The bizarre career of this remarkable woman—the use and
abuse of her talents—is a footnote on the developing relationship between partisan women and party organizations.

Political campaigning by women had developed informally while the
Republican Party was still in the issue-oriented organizational phase in
the 1850s. Henry Blackwell, an astute politician was quick to perceive
the value of articulate women as a source of interest and emotional appeal on the hustings. His wife, Lucy Stone, campaigned for the Liberty
ticket in 1852 (in bloomers), the Free Soil and Republican tickets in
1856 and 1860. She was joined on the campaign trail by Mary Liver-
more, Anne Dickinson, Susan Anthony, Elizabeth Cady Stanton, and
several others. The opportunity to campaign for issue-oriented third
parties recurred in the 1880s and 1890s in the Populist coalition, and
again in the Progressive Party in 1912, when Jane Addams was one of
Theodore Roosevelt's most persuasive campaigners.

The satellite relation of women to the major parties, on the other
hand, is the most complex of their political relationships. Partly it derives from the fact that, from the beginning of women's participation
in the 19th century, specialization and division of labor in political activity developed along heterosexual albeit culturally determined lines in
the subtly shaded activities by means of which political control is inter-
woven with social and economic control. The legacy of three quarters
of a century of party work and party allegiance as auxiliaries established

---

[51] Giraut Chester, *Embattled Maiden* (G. P. Putnam's Sons: New York, 1951), chs. 4,
5, 8.

habits of political volunteerism which are still reflected in women's tolerance of various forms of institutionalized discrimination which bar full status in party organizations.

VII

The woman's rights movement prior to the Civil War served mainly as a corollary to the issue of slavery. Once the war had ended, the nation's need to re-weave the constitutional bonds and assimilate the freed slave crowded the issue of woman's status into the background as a subject of negligible interest compared with racial equality. Nevertheless, the feminists ardently supported the 13th Amendment, which declared the slave free and overruled the Dred Scott decision, but did not define his or her citizenship.

The purpose of the 14th Amendment, so people thought, was to abolish the conditions of slavery and make the black race a component part of American society: to nationalize "the fundamental rights of citizenship."[52] But the insertion of the adjective "male" three times in the 'representation' clause (section 2) of the amendment was clearly exclusionary. It left the black female and her white sisters in a constitutional limbo, and marked the culmination of a half century of drift toward defining the principle of equality as applicable to the male half of the population.

Susan Anthony took instant alarm at the inclusion of "male" in the draft of the amendment, and moved heaven and earth to persuade their old abolitionist allies, including Senator Charles Sumner and Representative Thaddeus Stevens to remove it. The effort failed, and the women's cause became hopelessly entangled in the complex politics of the 14th and 15th Amendments, doomed never to escape their consequences.

During the controversy over ratification of the 14th Amendment, a fateful election in Kansas offered a significant test of public opinion (1867).[53] The ballot included referenda on Negro suffrage and woman suffrage. The Republicans lobbied hard for Negro suffrage and against woman suffrage. The Democrats opposed both. Both lost by a wide margin, though woman suffrage did better than Negro suffrage. The

[52] McLaughlin, 678-680. See also James M. McPherson, *The Struggle for Equality* (Princeton: Princeton University Press, 1964), chs. 15, 18.

[53] Rossi, 431-470.

failure to win suffrage in an ideologically liberal state by vote of the male population offered a preview of the magnitude of the job facing women, though none would have guessed that a "pauseless campaign" of 52 years lay ahead.

The unhappy outcome in Kansas aggravated differences already existing between the Boston-based group clustered about Henry Blackwell, Lucy Stone, Julia Ward Howe, Henry Ward Beecher and Wendell Phillips, and the New York-based Stanton-Anthony group. The former agreed to withdraw opposition to the 14th Amendment, aligning themselves with the Radical Republican Party. Stanton and Anthony rejected such a proposal as a politically degrading betrayal, which split the Equal Rights Association in two (1869). The Stanton-Anthony followers were organized as the National Woman Suffrage Association (NWSA), with membership limited to women and a program of aggressive tactics. The New England group, organized as the American Woman Suffrage Association (AWSA), staked their future on working within the then dominant element in the Republican Party. Lucretia Mott kept a foot in both camps.

The wording of the 14th Amendment created a gathering fog of legal ambiguities calling for challenge.[54] Lawyers and a few Congressmen encouraged a belief that a declaratory act of Congress could affirm an interpretation extending the suffrage to women. Acting on legal advice, 150 women in ten states and the District of Columbia attempted to vote in the 1871 and 1872 elections. In a few cases they succeeded, or at least escaped arrest. In most cases their right to register was ceremoniously denied. Two cases were appealed to the U. S. Supreme Court, both represented by able counsel as important test cases. The first dealt with the 70 women in the District of Columbia who attempted to vote. Counsel argued that the 15th Amendment did not confer a right; it voiced a solemn mandate not to deny a right that was an already existing fact, and expressly recognized that citizens of the United States have the right to vote. The Court unanimously rejected this interpretation.

A second appeal carried this argument a step further. Virginia Minor, St. Louis, Missouri, appealed against the rejection of her right to vote by the Missouri Supreme Court.[55] Her husband, a St. Louis lawyer, served as counsel. The Minor brief asked where, between the 13th

---

[54] Carrie Chapman Catt, *Woman Suffrage and Politics* (New York: Charles Scribner's Sons, 1926), 92-95.

[55] *Ibid.*

and 15th Amendments, did "the colored man come into the possession of the right of suffrage which he was now exercising?" Chief Justice Cartter delivered the unanimous opinion of the Court (Minor v. Hapersett, 1875) that the 14th Amendment "advanced women to full citizenship and clothed them with the capacity to become voters"; but this "constitutional capacity lies dormant, as is the case of an infant, until made effective by state action." In short, the states retained the power to define the composition of the electorate, as long as race discrimination was not present.

A related case tested the "privileges and immunities" clause of the 14th Amendment and further exposed the glacial inertia of the judicial mind. Myra Bradwell, founder and editor of the *Chicago Legal News* and partner of her lawyer husband, applied for admission to the Illinois bar, citing as precedent the admission of Mrs. Arabella Mansfield to the Iowa bar (1869). Her application was rejected. On appeal, the Illinois Supreme Court ruled that Illinois law did not permit a married woman to enter into contracts or have business dealings. "It would not promote justice to permit women to engage in trials at the bar." Bradwell carried the case to the U. S. Supreme Court, on the grounds that she had been denied the "privileges and immunities" protected by the 14th Amendment. Justice Miller, speaking for the majority, concurred with the decision of the Illinois Court, and turned aside from the issue to discourse on the "defect of sex" and the "historic sphere of women."[56]

Litigation was probably less effective in promoting change than the well-planned attempt of Susan B. Anthony, accompanied by 13 Rochester (N. Y.) women, to register and vote in November 1872.[57] It was a deliberate and widely publicized text of constitutional provisions for the rights and privileges of citizens. The women were arrested, along with the registrars, and indicted. Anthony alone was brought to trial in an extraordinary judicial proceeding in the U. S. District Court, and found guilty by Judge E. L. Hunt without a poll of the jury. She refused to pay the levied fine, but was thwarted in her hope of appeal for a writ

[56] A few years later the Illinois Legislature enacted legislation providing that no profession could be closed to individuals who met the criteria for admission, and admitted Myra Bradwell by special statute. See NAW I, 223 for biography of Myra Bradwell; II, 492 for Arabella Mansfield.

[57] Eleanor Flexner, *Century of Struggle* (Cambridge: Belknap Press of Harvard University Press, 1959), 165-168. A contemporary newspaper account of the Proceedings and Anthony's rebuke is in *Radical Feminism*, Anne Koedt, Ellen Levine, Anita Rapone, eds. (New York: Quadrangle, New York Times Publishing Co., 1973), 17-20.

of habeas corpus when the State made no attempt to collect the fine. The Anthony trial, and her impassioned rebuke to the presiding judge focused public attention sharply on the fundamental constitutional issue created when the adjective "male" was written into the Constitution.

The Dred Scott decision had to be over-ruled by the Reconstruction amendments;[58] the latter in turn by the 19th and 23rd amendments. The Anthony amendment was introduced in both Houses of Congress in 1878; and re-introduced in every Session thereafter until its passage in 1919 and ratification in August 1920. The politics of constitutional change regarding the composition of the polity offers a gritty view of history. Most amendments tend to deal with extreme situations when other methods have failed a frustrated cause; their path is often a treacherous one because the parties to the action represent aspects of wider social conflicts.[59] At issue in the struggle for the 19th amendment was the definition of a constituency; not the qualifications of the aspirants for admission to the electorate but the desirability of their presence there—the issue raised by Anne Hutchinson three centuries earlier.

Deeply divided among themselves, and pinched in the chill winds of reaction after the antebellum wave of reform, the two suffrage associations remained small, deviant groups during the 1870s and 1880s. Both associations were the targets of the bitter resentment engendered in the South by the Reconstruction policies: a resentment that hardened into an emotional block against enfranchising women that was never dissolved. Political circumstances grew still more intractable after the compromise of 1877, which ended the reign of the carpetbaggers and established a sectional truce between southern interests eager to restore white ascendancy and northern economic interests desiring favorable legislation. Both opposed women suffrage.

The political initiative during these years came primarily from the Stanton-Anthony partnership, remarkable for its union of complimentary talents, personalities and circumstances. Susan Anthony was fashioned on an heroic scale. Forceful, outgoing, with no husband to exercise restraints, she was free to devote her inexhaustible energies to the cause. She possessed both moral enterprise and political acumen, sustained by an indomitable will that drove her radical cause forward in an unfriendly world. Her Quaker background and supportive family made her invulnerable to ridicule and ostracism.

[58] McLaughlin, 655.

[59] Clement E. Vose, *The Politics of Constitutional Change* (Lexington, Mass.: D. C. Heath, 1972), 341.

Elizabeth Cady Stanton, tied down with a husband and seven children, nevertheless found time to voice her brilliant iconoclasms from the shelter of her own home. Susan Anthony's rebellion was not only approved by but a living-out of the lofty values of her family. Stanton rebelled first of all against her family, and fed her inner rebellions by an activist life. She was a bold and original thinker, with a gift for the rhetoric of argument and a sense of irony that embellished her literary gifts. Her sharp and mordant wit offset Anthony's lack of a sense of humor. Stanton's career offers an interesting instance of the revolutionary possibilities when a politically oriented personality structure clashes with sex-related political deprivations, as in the later instance of Carrie Chapman Catt.

Working together, Stanton and Anthony prepared and presented the arguments designed to enlighten public opinion on the conditions of women's subjection, to explore the premises on which their subjection rested, the scope of their grievances, the fundamental contradictions between democratic principles and the political bondage of women. Stanton was a master of irony, and few stumblings of the "sons of Adam" went unrecorded. In conventions, legislative hearings, or on the lyceum circuit they conducted their unflagging campaign through the 1870s and 1880s, developing the concept of oppression as a corollary of group identity, a concept revived by today's neo-feminists. Although American women were, and still are, probably the freest in the world, as Tocqueville observed, they feel considerable role strain which motivates a search for the oppressor, or for a solution to the fundamental contradiction between democratic principles and their application: "the fallacy lurking between the premise and the conclusion."

During these stormy years the ballot took on mythic aspects. In forcibly enfranchising the freedmen, the architects of Reconstruction policies had deliberately set aside the principle of representation and made the ballot a symbol of a value system that included all males and and excluded all females. The "Republican betrayal," memory of which Stanton and Anthony kept alive, channeled the feminist grievances into the single demand for the ballot. The compulsion to sustain their passionate conviction, against the surrounding pressures, that their exclusion was illegitimate and unjust wove a mythic web about the denial of the ballot as a symbol of all grievances demanding redress and the possession of it as a symbol of all things hoped for. The longer the struggle lasted, the more millenial became the feminists' faith in the inexpressible value of the right to vote. Not until Carrie Chapman Catt came on the national scene in 1890 did the delegates to the annual conventions find release from the tensions and frustrations generated by the prolonged recital of their wrongs and turn their attention from agitation to organization.

VIII

In 1873 a group of women highly placed in literary and social circles, including Julia Ward Howe and Charlotte Wilbur, organized the Association for the Advancement of Women, ostensibly to promote women's liberation but actually to rescue the feminist cause from the opprobrium arising from the Beecher-Tilton scandal and trial, and such "rash and gaudy" acts as Susan Anthony's attempt to vote and subsequent trial. Among those invited to join was a young woman named Frances Willard, on the strength of her current but short-lived status as Dean of the Ladies College of Northwestern University. At the same time bands of praying churchwomen were closing three thousand saloons across Ohio and Indiana in a spontaneous outburst of moralistic piety. In 1874 the anarchic zeal of the women was harnessed in the Women's Christian Temperance Union, in which Frances Willard found her vocation.[60]

Temperance organizations dominated by men already had a long history in the East. The spread of temperance to the West was partly a response to immigration from Germany and Italy, but even more, to the rise of feminism because it offered a natural channel for feminine concerns. The drunkard became a scapegoat for the more generalized consequences of man's "natural depravity," and provided the most unanswerable arguments for reforms in marriage and divorce laws, child custody laws and property disabilities. Frances Willard politicized the moral issue arising from intemperance as Lucretia Mott and the Grimké sisters had the slavery issue, and transformed a cause to a political movement that became the first centrally controlled, nationwide and politically effective organization of women in American political history. From 1879 until her death in 1898 she was president of an organization with a peak membership of 200,000 in 15,000 tightly controlled unions scattered nationwide but predominantly in the Middle West and the

---

[60] Flexner, ch. 13. The cross currents in 19th century feminism are admirably dealt with in Flexner's comprehensive, pathbreaking study.

South, exercising national power and influence in promoting a wide range of reforms.[61]

During the 1870s and 1880s, when the suffrage movement was weak, divided and regarded as radical, Frances Willard applied a combination of psychological insight, eclectic imagination and personal magnetism to draw women out of their homes to engage in political activities under the benign aegis of "protecting their homes." Pressing for an awareness that society finds its ends obstructed by women who do not understand that they are members of a larger social order than the family, or even the community, she found means to help women escape from the "swathing femininity" imposed by the "cult of domesticity" in provincial towns and cities that had long outgrown the influence of the pioneering phase of settlement.[62] She organized the Unions under thirty-nine departments, ranging from temperance, woman suffrage, and economic reforms to child care and nutrition, with an appeal sufficiently varied that women from every level of education, social outlook and political awareness could find a congenial niche.

Her method was first to captivate and then disarm women of their "fear of public work," which, she reasoned, was a rationalization of their husbands' insistence on their need of protection, by persuading them to roll up huge petitions demanding the vote on liquor questions.[63] "It's much easier to see a drunkard than a principle" was her axiom. For those who saw the relation between means and ends, it was only a step to perceive that full suffrage was necessary, since most reforms had their temperance aspect. Admired by her followers, approved by the clergy and the press, and actively supported by influential middle class women who became the mainstay of the General Federation of Women's Clubs, Frances Willard became a legend in her own time. When her grip was loosened, the legend disintegrated into a cult perpetuated by the most

[61] Mary Earhart, *Frances Willard: From Prayers to Politics* (Chicago: University of Chicago Press, 1944). A detailed biography that places Willard in historical perspective as a major force in cultivating, among women who shrank from radicalism, a political orientaton that was congruent with women's self-image as housewives and mothers. She prepared the way for Jane Addams, while Anthony prepared the way for Carrie Chapman Catt. On Willard's methods, see also Flexner, 181-185.

[62] Mary Austin, *Earth Horizon* (Boston: Houghton Mifflin, 1932), 132 ff. The undertow of anti-feminization, described as the "cult of domesticity" as men's and women's roles became sharply differentiated after the frontier phase had ended, was countered by Willard's psychological approach. Austin's autobiographic account is perceptive.

[63] Flexner, 183-184.

conservative of her temperance followers. Most of the aggressive women whom she trained in her Franchise Department, including Anna Howard Shaw, Zerelda Wallace and Belle Kearney, transferred their energies after 1895 to the suffrage movement.

The year 1890 was a crucial year, politically speaking, in the struggle for equality. Social change and time's healing had narrowed the differences between the rival suffrage associations in perceived goals and methods, as the first generation of leaders was nearing the end of the course. In 1890 the associations merged as the National American Woman Suffrage Association (NAWSA).

In the same year, Jane Croly, founder of Sorosis (1868), invited representatives of 94 women's literary and civic clubs to form the General Federation of Women's Clubs, the largest and most diverse organization of women in the United States, with several million members and the nucleus of a worldwide association.[64] Excellent leadership between 1890 and 1920 broadened the social and literary character of the clubs to embrace political and social concerns. Local clubs were encouraged to have politically oriented civic programs. Because of its size and diversification, the General Federation played an effective role in the socialization of American women, synchronizing with the Chautauqua movement, the adult education and university extension movements.

Organization and education were the twin paths to liberation. The church-related societies had mediated between women and the community in the 17th and 18th centuries in a rudimentary way. The first reported organizations of women, in the 18th century, to shape opinion on slavery, influenced by Quaker practices, mediated between women and the state. Again in the Revolutionary period, women organized effectively to promote the cause of independence. Before the end of the 18th century, the first independent philanthropic organizations of women appeared in eastern cities,with a particular concern for ameliorating the lot of the socially and economically injured members of their own sex. In the 19th century and thereafter women's organizations proliferated on an immense scale, and served to integrate them into the political culture by providing functional representation for women's concerns, and contributing to political pluralism.

[64] Jane Cunningham Croly, *History of the Woman's Club Movement in America* (New York: H. G. Allen & Co., 1898); Mary I. Wood, *History of the General Federation of Women's Clubs* (New York: General Federation of Women's Clubs, 1912). See also Flexner, 179-181.

Out of organizational activities came the most characteristic aspect of women's political role: pressure on the holders of power by lobbying. Long denied the right to express their convictions at the ballot box, women found lobbying a natural channel for exercising influence. It took many forms, from personal pressure to petitioning legislatures. The petition was not only an opinion-shaping strategy but an invaluable means of political socialization involving the interaction between those whose opinion the petitioners sought and the recipients of the petition. Practical involvement in political action developed local leadership, and represented a mode of organizing for social action, with an evangelical quality which found political expression later in the century in the movement for direct legislation, the initiative, referendum and recall. The leaders of the abolition movement and the WCTU polished this strategy to a high luster.

Lobbying for policy change tended to supplant petition campaigns as women's familiarity with political action increased, especially in local affairs. But along this path there lay snares. The less radical organizations such as the General Federation and the WCTU, fearful of limiting their growth by nationally endorsing so divisive an issue as woman suffrage, developed the concept that pressure by indirection was woman's traditional way of getting things done. Their absence from the polling place they came to regard as a positive advantage, since their male rulers were more susceptible to pressure if their self-image was not disturbed.[65] This confusion of ends and means, sometimes referred to as "electoral schizophrenia"—delayed the formation of a massive coalition of women's organizations until 1914, after the battle had been fairly won by the fortunate interposition of the Progressive Party's campaign in 1912, which broke the hold of the eastern wing of the Republican Party on Congress; but lived on in vestigial attitudes still visible among older women.

IX

The impulse to reform, snuffed out in the East by the economic and political aftermath of the Civil War, sprang up anew on the pioneer-

[65] Despite Frances Willard's strong commitment to woman suffrage and to political activism, a strong conservative element within the WCTU prevented national endorsement of woman suffrage until 1914, although several state branches endorsed it. A similar situation existed in the General Federation and the Association of Collegiate Alumnae (later the American Association of University Women). A vote on the divisive issue was simply avoided in national conventions.

ing fringe of western settlement signalling the agrarian revolt that carried feminism aloft in a new surge of development. The frontier context of the Plains states resembled that of the Ohio Valley in the 1830s, with the exception that the terms of survival were far more severe and selective. Once again the family was initially the only structured institution in frontier areas, and women were indispensable not only in organizing resources to meet primal needs but in creating new communities and new political groupings.[66] The Patrons of Husbandry, the Farmers' Alliance, the Greenbackers and Populists welcomed women as voting members of their dissident third parties and drew heavily on their moral energies. Many of the activist women in the agrarian parties were educated eastern women who had gone West to teach after the war—and found husbands. Historians never fail to mention the tall Irish woman with the magnificent voice—Mary Ellen Lease —whose anguish over her own blighted dreams roused prairie audiences to a feverish pitch of rebellion against the railroads and the mortgage holders.

Paralleling these developments was the granting of full suffrage to the women in the newly organized Territory of Wyoming by the Territorial Legislature (1869).[67] Men outnumbered women six to one on this last and rawest of the frontiers, and transients outnumbered settlers ten to one. The need was for rapid conquest to establish a stable society and forestall anarchy. The territory had no unifying ethnic base nor common code of behavior. Many of the permanent settlers had come from the East, with educated wives who were well prepared to make trial of the experiment. Feminist Esther Morris, an Anthony convert, played a part in securing the legislation and was promptly named justice of the peace, presiding over a court with women jurors.

Both the exercise of the franchise and of the judicial function were innovations; but it is a matter of interest that no woman was elected

---

[66] Most of the suffrage leaders of the generation that won the vote were raised on the plains frontier: Catt, Willard, Shaw, Addams, Lathrop, the Abbott sisters.

[67] Allan G. Grimes, *The Puritan Ethic and Woman Suffrage* (New York: Oxford University Press, 1967). Grimes professes to see a "fundamental change in social values concerning the role of women," rather than, as it appears to this writer, a gradual shift arising from frontier experience as the frontier moved westward, with innovations in women's political participation at each line of settlement. Tocqueville's perception that some cultural baggage was gained, some lost on each successive frontier, seems accurate. In the baggage gradually jettisoned was the Puritan conception of the family.

to the state legislature until 1912, and no woman from Wyoming has ever been elected to Congress. One Governor's wife, Nellie Tayloe Ross, was appointed to replace her husband at his death, and served acceptably—an early instance of the "widow's succession," but the pioneering state has set no records for women's participation, although geographic factors must be taken into account. Nevertheless it is axiomatic that concessionary grants of the right to vote involve few lessons in political socialization, and participation thrives where the soil of political socialization is deep.[68]

In 1870 the women of Utah were enfranchised, partly as the result of a misguided effort on the part of Congress to get rid of plural marriage by giving women the vote. But Mormon society was not threatened by anarchy. It was both socially and ethnically unified with an even ratio between the sexes. The Mormons' confidence in their wives led them to enfranchise women themselves by action of the Territorial Legislature. When Utah entered the Union in 1894, it followed Wyoming's example by insisting on a suffrage provision in its first Constitution.

Suffrage victory in the adjacent states of Colorado (1893) and Idaho (1896) was won partly by the Mormon example and partly by the women themselves with the aid of the Populist Party. Not for fourteen years did the next incremental advance come when women in the State of Washington won suffrage, this time with the help of the insurgent Republicans. Thereafter came California, Oregon, Kansas, Arizona, Montana and Nevada. The election of 1916 was decisively affected by the fact that 13 states had either full suffrage or presidential suffrage.[69]

Opposition to the enfranchisement of women was far more widespread and strategically located than is remembered, although opponents were slow to phrase an ideology of resistance. Southern bitterness toward the abolitionists and their descendants was never allayed. The opposition of the Democratic Party in the South to the Anthony Amendment was monolithic, and remained so to the end.[70] The states of the former Confederacy were also impervious to incremental ad-

---

[68] Since 1920, the level of women's participation in politics has been highest in those industrial states where resistance before 1920 was most stubborn.

[69] Catt's state-by-state account of winning the vote is in *Woman Suffrage and Politics*. See supra.

[70] David Morgan, *Suffragists and Democrats* (Lansing: Michigan State University Press, 1972). A detailed account of the opposition of the Democratic Party, especially in the Wilson Administration.

vance through partial suffrage. None ratified the amendment when it was finally submitted for ratification in 1920.

In the North and middle states the opposition represented factions within parties; the "wet" element in the industrial states; the trade associations representing textile and agricultural interests that were employers of women and children; the coalition of brewers and distillers associations; and the conservative eastern wing of the Republican Party.[71] In 1910, the political forces arrayed against woman suffrage were so formidable and strategically located in Congress and in the hostile trade associations, in the Catholic hierarchy and certain ethnic groups, that victory could have been long postponed.

Opposition of a more "respectable sort," intellectually speaking, became vocal in the East in the 1870s. Lawyers, scholars, editors, presidents and many faculty members on Ivy League campuses strenuously opposed woman suffrage. The *North American Review*, the *Nation*, the *Outlook* and the *New York Times* were vehicles for the anti-suffrage views of Francis Parkman, Richard H. Dana, Lyman Abbott, Elihu Root, E. L. Godkin. Their arguments dwelt on their noble motives in wishing to protect women from the "dirty business" of politics; on God's ordinance regarding woman's sphere as being the home; "the empire of the heart"; on woman's physical weakness and emotional instability; on the threat to the family arising from the influence of the "socialist and pacifist" women such as Florence Kelley and Jane Addams. A multitude of well-financed anti-suffrage associations sprang up in all parts of the country but especially in New York and Massachusetts. The Man-Suffrage Association and the American Constitutional League (later the Sentinels of the Republic) furnished witnesses at hearings, spread propaganda leaflets and newspaper advertisements, and conducted a more insidious lobby through their ties with economic interests and political leaders.

Socially prominent women organized Committees of Remonstrants against womens' "liberation" in Boston and New York in the 1870s. Later the National Association Opposed to Woman Suffrage headed first by Mrs. Arthur Dodge and later by Mrs. James W. Wadsworth repeated the arguments advanced by their conservative husbands, arguments seemingly even more imbedded in prejudice and a cynical distrust of government than when voiced by the male opponents. Woman's right to political equality was never debated on its merit. The fact that

[71] Flexner, ch. 22; Vose, ch. 3; Catt, chs. 10, 14, 15 and 18.

substantial economic interests might be endangered, or acknowledgment that the possessors of power never desire to share it, were never mentioned.

It came down to woman's place is in the home, by male decree! Because of the tensions created, the preoccupations on both sides of the controversy over the "oligarchy of sex" became a focus of bitter and unyielding hostility.

X

The decade of the 1890s was one of quickening political concerns among the first generation of women college graduates, groping to put human welfare at the center of politics. Higher education was a potent factor in shaping patterns of expectation and political socialization. The struggle for political rights and for entry to the professions went hand in hand, fostering the growing solidarity among educated women.

Since exclusion from professional schools in the eastern universities remained entrenched, some of the most able and ambitious women rounded out their education in more sophisticated centers abroad. The resultant intellectual awakening had ironic consequences for the eastern educational establishment bent on retaining male supremacy. Among those driven abroad, either to acquire a professional degree or find a pattern for their life work were several whose European experience enabled them to broaden the intellectual and ideological dimensions of the suffrage movement. The subsequent careers of Jane Addams, Florence Kelley, Julia Lathrop, and Carey Thomas introduced advanced European social thinking into the feminist ideology.

These young women established their identity in the social enterprise with a formula for a broadened interpretation of equality and democracy in terms of "social justice." They rejected the material values of the prevailing laissez faire individualism of the economic establishment as well as the settled domesticity of the urban middle class family pattern. Industrialization had widened the gap between husbands and wives as well as between rich and poor. The struggle in the market place was cruelly unfair to working women and children, but even more deplorable was the parasitism it induced in the middle class housewife. The highly charged reformist zeal of these women produced a proliferation of social and political innovations, including the settlement house movement, which represented a significant adaptation of the principle of association to the functional activities of the individual home.

Jane Addams went to live at Hull House in 1889; and thrust out its walls to enclose the community. Urbanization had destroyed the home as an independent fortress, and had robbed the homemaker of most of her functions. Both by precept and example, Addams made a persuasive case for politicizing the role of the homemaker by urging her to follow her traditional functions into the political world as the "municipal housekeeper": in short, to take control of local government.[72] The motivation of Addams and those in her orbit was the "subjective necessity" to express and institutionalize women's deepest concerns for human welfare. Their activities touched the political process at innumerable points. They penetrated the neighborhood by policy-oriented investigations of social and economic conditions; organized community pressure to secure improved public services, and on state legislatures to secure ameliorative legislation; finally on the federal government to undertake inquiries into living and working conditions of women and children. Hull House and its sister settlements in other cities institutionalized the concept of "social responsibility."

In the same decade, Carrie Chapman Catt rose to leadership in the national suffrage association and turned its face in a new direction.[73] She transformed the annual conventions from recitals of grievances to programmed discussions of the current debasement of politics by electoral corruption, and the usurpation of power by political machines. The featured speakers were the municipal and governmental reformers who called for civil service reform, direct legislation, direct primary, municipal home rule, proportional representation, the Australian ballot. Each speaker had a prescription for returning power to the people, and in so doing, to provide access to those numbering half the population denied a share in the ruling. The organization was swung into the orbit of the progressive movement.

Catt and Addams towered over all other women in this period. Each represented a major aspect of the progressive movement where it intersected the feminist movement. The question had ceased to be justifying women's right to the vote, so long proved futile, but demonstrating society's urgent need for women's social energies. They agreed that women had a two-pronged responsibility in public life. Catt

[72] Jane Addams, *Forty Years at Hull House* (New York: Macmillan Co., 1935). See also Proceedings, NAWSA Convention, 1906, for Addams' speech on "Municipal Housekeeping."

[73] Mary Gray Peck, *Carrie Chapman Catt* (New York: 1944).

believed women had a specific responsibility to share with other social forces in forming a countervailing power capable of opposing the dominance of economic interests with their oligarchic tendencies. Addams held that women had a "peculiar responsibility" for the social welfare aspect of government. Politically speaking, these twin concerns would enable women, as a new group, to carve out a place for themselves in the political-social order—a task which they left to the next generation.

Ethnics
in
American Politics

Louis L. Gerson

America, a nation of nationalities, is currently experiencing a surge of ethnic pride and identity. Ethnicity is in great vogue. The mass media pay homage to it. Federal and state governments fund ethnic heritage studies. Private prestigious foundations, like the Rockefeller and Ford, subsidize a variety of ethnic projects, stimulating and, indeed, enticing scholars and organizers in American universities and hyphenated communities into what seems a promising and expanding new frontier of research. Books, monographs, articles are being published in increasing numbers—some scholarly and cautious, many more polemical and hasty—hailing the revival of ethnocentricity and the rise of the unmeltable ethnics.

What are the causes for the dramatic awakening of ethnic feelings? Is it present in all of America's ethnic groups? Is it, as some have hinted, a reaction to black pride, black power, and, perhaps, a cover for racism? Is it genuine, or another typical American mood, soon to fade away? And what about the effects: will it help eliminate discrimination, end divisiveness, or will it bring more alienation and more tension within the American society?

These questions and more cannot be answered with certainty. We do not have solid empirical studies. The literature on ethnic groups, large as it is, is spotty. Studies on specific immigrant groups vary in quality, quantity, and subject matter. And one can only hope that the present heightened interest in ethnicity will help and encourage, especially, the newer immigrant groups in the

United States—Poles, Slovaks, Czechs, Lithuanians, Italians, and others—to examine in greater depth, intensity, and objectivity their past and present history in America.

There is much talk and writing about the reawakening of ethnic feelings. Of marked interest are those Catholic intellectual writers, particularly of Polish, Slovak, and Italian origin, who are rediscovering with greater pride and new importance their immigrant roots and who speak glowingly about the revival of dormant ethnic cultures and ethnic political power. As yet, however, there is no proof that they reflect the feelings of ordinary members within any or all ethnic groups.

It is doubtful that the current revival of ethnicity will be sustained at today's level of intensity, or that it will fulfill the expectations of those who have hailed it. Americanization—the acculturation and assimilation of immigrant groups within the developing American society—has been a great and progressive achievement, and it is unlikely to be reversed. The evolution of that process has, of course, varied from one immigrant group to another, depending on the country of origin, time of arrival, education and skills, kind of leadership, resistance to change, and place of settlement in the United States. Despite great difficulties, frustrations, and contradictory pressures encountered in the process of Americanization, there is no evidence of deprivation when non-English-speaking immigrant groups had to learn a new language and sublimate, partially or fully, their old cultures for an emerging new one in America. Without exception all immigrant groups wanted to be integrated into the American society and gain full access to its values. This stands out in sharp contrast to the experiences of ethnic minorities in other societies who, fearing extinction, continue to seek protection from a dominant culture.

The record of immigrant acculturation and assimilation supports the idea that the United States is a melting-pot nation, and further needed research should confirm it. To be sure, there have been times when the melting pot cooled and crystallized, but the process was never in danger of ending. Some immigrant groups have been fully absorbed, leaving only symbolic residues; others, particularly the newer ones, have not. Upheavals like the First and Second World Wars, and the Cold War, and domestic turbulence like the decade of the 1960s have catalytic effects. In times of heightened stress even many nationality groups that have shown tendencies to blend into American life during times of domestic and interna-

tional tranquility respond to reawakened memories and pressures
from their leaders and from American politicians of both parties
and react on the basis of origin, race, and, at times, creed. And
this is to be expected, given the nature of the American pluralistic
society that recognizes and accepts, and, indeed, encourages the
concept of group differentiation and group political action.

From that historic day of the Declaration of Independence,
America has been the hope and the asylum of the oppressed, the
persecuted, the hungry, the poor, the adventurous. It has attracted peoples of all nations, all races, all creeds. No other country has had such appeal. The United States, the "distant magnet,"
in Lord Acton's evocative phrase, has been and continues to be a
nation of immigrants.

By 1976, the Bicentennial Year, nearly fifty million representatives of almost all nations of the world have settled in the United
States. From early in the nineteenth century to 1930 approximately 60 percent of total world migration flowed to America.
In 1970 one-sixth of the population was either foreign born or born
of foreign parentage, and more than 30 million Americans claimed
a foreign language as their mother tongue. These figures only
suggest the ethnic composition of America. In sheer numbers this
movement of peoples toward America has been an important factor
of modern world history, and of American history in particular.

The largest and most concentrated wave of immigration came
at the turn of the nineteenth century, mostly from Southeastern
Europe. During the four decades from 1870 to 1910 the total
foreign white stock (including foreign-born white and native white
of foreign or mixed parentage) increased by more than 21 million.
In the decade 1861-1870 the percentage of immigrants from Southeastern Europe was 1.5; that from Northwestern Europe, 87.8. In
the decade preceding the First World War the percentages were
almost reversed: 70.8 and 21.7. Following the passage of the Immigration Law of 1965, which changed the 1924 law with its
"national origin" quota designed to favor white, Anglo-Saxon, northern European immigrants, a new wave of immigrants began. In
the decade 1965-1975 more than four million legal new immigrants
settled in America. (In addition millions of illegal immigrants are
pouring in.) This time most of them are Asians, Latin Americans,
and West Indies. Averaging more than 400,000 a year, they are
altering the racial and ethnic composition of the nation, and are

being absorbed with scarcely any publicity and with little public assistance.

This latest influx of newcomers, the largest in more than a half a century, will not have the same impact on the American population as did that in the 1900s. At that time the population was about 75 million; today it is over 215 million. The mighty confluence of new arrivals in the 1900s occurred on the eve of America's emergence as a great world power and her eventual participation in the World Wars of the twentieth century. It also coincided with the change from the nature of the liberal revolutionary movements of the 1840s to the radical, communist, anarchist, and socialist movements of the first quarter of the century. This was also the period when racial theories derived from Social Darwinism, the championing of the superiority of the Anglo-Saxon peoples, had become increasingly popular. The sudden presence of great numbers of alien peoples from Europe beyond the Elbe, an area with myriad cultures and languages, revived the anti-foreignism of the Know-Nothing movement of the 1850s and raised concern for future American homogeneity and culture. Few of the newcomers were Protestant, most were unskilled and even illiterate in their own language. They were not the immigrants that men like Henry Adams and Woodrow Wilson considered best for the country. Their fear mirrored the anxieties, as well as the ignorance, of their contemporaries.

The experiences of these immigrants in this pivotal period inevitably affected the course of acculturation and assimilation of immigrant peoples within the American society. The most immediate and traumatic event was, of course, the outbreak of the First World War, which heightened the nationalistic fervor and aspirations of subjugated minorities in Austria-Hungary, Russia, and Germany, and found concern and support among their former nationals living across the seas—the majority of whom had left their homelands within the previous three decades. The war in Europe produced a "hyphenated uproar" in the United States, and many were quick to claim that the melting pot, the symbol of the transforming of the immigrant into an American, had failed—a charge, by the way, that would be repeated at the outbreak of the Second World War and the Cold War that followed.

By 1914 ethnic Americans had become strongly interested in their native countries, invariably influencing American politics. Many of the immigrants who had had no patriotic feeling toward their native lands discovered it in America. The roots of immigrant nationalism were found not only in the affection for the native countries, often absent at the time of emigration, but perhaps even more in the compressed ghettos where group consciousness was fostered by loneliness, poverty, and the animosities of nativists and other ethnic groups. In the two or so decades before the First World War the immigrants from Eastern and Southern Europe came mainly from strata of society in which the national consciousness was not fully developed. Only a small proportion came from the educated and middle classes. Most of them were peasants, uneducated and unskilled but nevertheless men and women of courage and energy enough to brave the unknown in the alien New World. Throughout that part of Europe, as well as in the Ireland of the 1840s, patriots saw in the breaking away of thousands of countrymen a threat of depopulation and the weakening of revolutionary activities, whereas the entrenched ruling elite saw it as a safety-valve.

Once in the United States many an immigrant who in his native land had been restricted in the study of his history, the use of his language, and participation in politics, found the first opportunity for self-expression, rediscovery of his heritage, and freedom to practice his way of life. It was this freedom in the adopted land that paradoxically enough led to ethnic-group identification and solidification. In the countries of their origin, the Italians, Slovaks, Slovenes, Poles, Croatians, Ruthenians, and many others had considered themselves more as citizens of distinct localities and adherents of certain churches than as members of national states. For a great many of them ethnic nationalism and affection toward the old country emerged only after arrival in the United States.

The first concern of the immigrant was the transplanting of his Church. More than any other factor, the Church united and transcended old-country attachments and identification with local villages, towns, or regions. It was the strongest link with the past and the first bridge to the future. It was natural that the non-English-speaking immigrant would want priests or ministers of his own stock and would insist that his own language be used in his Church and parish. The Church played a central role: it was a source of guidance and talent; it was also the foremost instrument for promoting educational growth and social adjustment. To the immigrant parent, the Church meant continuity between his old life and the new in America, and he was understandably most anxious that his children enroll in parochial schools and remain true to the faith.

The demand for foreign-language subdivisions within the established churches in the United States confronted their leaders with difficult problems. Many American churches of the same denomination as that to which immigrants belonged refused to accede to the demand, and this led many immigrant groups to set up their own churches, with their own ministers and priests. The Catholic Church, however, was the one most affected. Here in America it has been almost entirely made up of successive waves of immigrant groups, each of which insisted on services in its native tongue and priests of its own nationality. The conflict began with Irish-American resentment of the "anti-foreignism" of the then strongly entrenched French clergy and continued when the Irish, once they controlled the hierarchy, balked at the request of the newer arrivals. This reaction of the Irish-dominated Catholic Church, as well as the uncompromising desire of the ethnic groups to retain their language, their own priests, their own parishes, and their own parochial schools, may well account for the birth and development of intense ethnic nationalism among American Roman Catholics. If so, then the Catholic Church in America, itself a universal church, by its failure to resolve pressures from its multilingual and multicultural members became, unwittingly, an important factor in the rise of ethnicity.

Resentment toward Irish clericalism was further accentuated by the political power of Irish-Americans. Immigrant groups moving into the cities found the Irish in control of jobs, police, church. Relations worsened when injudicious Irish priests criticized some nationalities for anticlericalism (Italians, Czechs) and castigated others for clannishness (Poles, French, Canadians, Ukrainians). In time, the Irish clergy and politicians learned to accommodate themselves to the wishes of the newer immigrant groups; continued refusal risked wholesale defection and the weakening of the Church and political alliances.

Religious freedom in America encouraged the emergence of ethnic solidarity. The first differentiation was on religious lines. The parishes and churches of distinct nationalities organized, regulated, and preserved ethnic ways of life, and thus fostered group consciousness and group pride that at times strayed into ethnic nationalism. When acculturation and assimilation began to make inroads among second and third-generation ethnic-Americans, "ethnic" Catholicism continued to keep them together. Affiliation with the "ethnic" Church and religious beliefs have continued to serve long after the ethnic language and culture were forgotten or lost.

The Church was not the only preoccupation of the newcomers. The others were economic, social, and political. A great many of the immigrants were unskilled and uneducated, and this made it difficult to obtain decent jobs and adequate wages. Native workers feared them as a potential threat to their livelihood. Reaction to these attitudes was inevitable. Low social status and the sense of being exploited and resented led to development of an inferiority complex and intensified ethnic feeling. In the immigrants' search for social and economic security, they insulated themselves in urban ghettos—Little Polands, Little Italys, Little Hungarys. Their isolation was further compounded by the transplanting of Old World distrusts. Historic grievances and wrongs were bitterly aired when they found themselves living in the same city blocks with Ukrainians, Czechs, Slovaks, Lithuanians, Jews. These enforced contacts revived bygone rivalries and fostered pride in the homelands. Here the attachment to the native village or province was transformed into a stronger identification with native countries, and thus was forged a stronger ethnic identity than the immigrants had ever had before. The revival of virulent anti-Semitism in Russia and in many parts of Eastern Europe at the end of the nineteenth century and its importation by many of the immigrants from these areas extended Zionism among many American Jewish groups that had formerly rejected the appeals of Jewish nationalistic movements. Zionism originated in the desire of the Jewish people to put an end to national and social inferiority and economic persecution. It was to find, particularly during times of suffering abroad, the birth of Israel and subsequent threats to its security, many adherents in the United States.

The American party system has been the most important contributing factor to the hyphenization of Americans. The major parties have consistently and actively sought the support of ethnic groups. This persistent attention to the immigrant vote, markedly accelerated with the arrival of large numbers of Irish in the 1840s, was expanded at the turn of the century when multitudes of immigrants from Southeastern Europe began to settle in strategic urban areas. At first the "capture" of the ethnic vote was relatively easy. Finding employment and adjusting to the new environment overshadowed the immigrants' political interests or concerns. The newcomers wanted jobs, friends to ease assimilation, help in obtaining citizenship—the local ward leaders provided all these, and more, in return for a lifetime of fealty to the party.

Local political activity to organize ethnic Americans was soon elevated to the national level and then expanded. The Democratic and Republican National Committees began organizing nationalities divisions in the 1880s, a practice that is still going on. Though the names of these divisions have changed, their purposes have remained the same. (The current title of the Democratic party's division catering to the ethnic vote is "All American Council"; that of the Republican, "Heritage Groups.") Through these units both parties continuously reinforce, or hope to reinforce, the ethnocentricity of Americans of foreign origin—an ethnocentricity originally cultivated by ethnic churches and ethnic social or fraternal organizations. Passage of time, decreased flow of immigration since 1924, and the assimilation of immigrant groups have not diminished the activities of the nationalities divisions. On the contrary, any indication of breakdowns of traditional ethnic patterns or failure to respond to ethnic-oriented issues or candidates has led to more refinement of the organizational machinery and operational methods to stir and then to solidify group consciousness.

At the end of the Second World War ethnic-Americans began to defect from the Democrtic party, or so it was thought by party leaders. Hitherto loyal and submissive foreign-language groups were, as one county chairman put it, "definitely off the reservation." The loosening of ethnic ties to the Democratic party encouraged the Republicans to expand their efforts to liberate ethnic groups from Democratic containment. Competition between the parties for the elusive ethnic vote increased. Stimulated by party strategists and nourished by the Cold War and the coincidental emergence of the newer ethnic groups whose native lands were occupied or threatened by Communist Russia, the intensity of political appeals for ethnic involvement in American politics was unprecedented for peacetime. Beginning with the national campaign of 1948 the domestic, and especially, the foreign policy planks of both parties reflected what directors of their nationalities divisions believed were the emotions, desires, hopes, historic memories, and half-buried loyalties of ethnic-Americans. In their efforts to win the ethnic vote, each party found it more and more difficult to outdo the other in promises or stands on issues.

By the time of the presidential campaign of 1956, both parties' planks touching upon issues of ethnic interest were remarkably similar. The Hungarian Revolution and the Suez Canal crisis— two nearly simultaneous events occurring on the eve of the election —shattered the developing consensus. The Soviet victory in Hungary and America's alignment with the Soviets against Israel, Great Britain, and France produced consternation among Americans of East European origin and Jewish-Americans. The promise of "liberation" of Eastern Europe ended with the Russian "reconquest" of Budapest, and so too the belief of automatic United States support of Israel. Although few perceived it at that time, the intensity of ethnic influence on American foreign policies was markedly weakened. The high cost of American military intervention with the ever more likely possibility of a major war with the Soviet Union has had a most sobering effect.

After 1956 the Democratic party began to concentrate on economic and social issues, while the Republicans continued their appeals to ethnics with hackneyed anti-communist approaches that lost their credibility and vigor. Following President Richard Nixon's rapprochement with Communist China and avowed desire to improve relations with the Soviet Union, the strategy of the Republican party to attract ethnic votes may well begin to resemble that of the Democrats.

Do Americans vote on the basis of their national origin? There are as many answers to this question as there are experts—be they sociologists, historians, political scientists, political strategists, ethnic leaders, journalists. Some believe that Americans of foreign descent vote *en bloc,* that they can be swung to either of the parties by proper baits. There are some who qualify such opinions by distinguishing the voting behavior of the urban ethnics from the rural ethnics, the "new" immigrants of Southeast European origin from the "old" Northwest Europeans, and the foreign-born from the first, second, or third generation offspring of immigrants. And then there are those who concede that this may have been true in the past, but it is no longer true today.

Indeed, the very phrase "ethnic politics" may no longer be, if it ever was, a meaningful or appropriate term for the political behavior of today's hyphenated Americans. To some political analysts the word "ethnic" is a euphemism for "working class," a coalition of white Americans of similar socioeconomic condition, age, education, homeownership, and religion who also happen to be of ethnic background but who no longer have much or anything to do with "ethnic" nationalistic considerations. The chief issues that concern these Americans are housing, secure employment, new job opportunities, neighborhood schools, and resentment that their fear of losing jobs to blacks and their worry about crime and the future of their neighborhoods is equated with racism and bigotry.

American political leaders are most reluctant to change their opinions and attitudes about Americans of foreign descent. Many of them who fervently avow their belief in the melting pot during patriotic celebrations ignore it at election times. Politicians who think in terms of the farm vote, the labor vote, the business vote, the veteran vote are convinced of the ethnic vote. No study or presentation, however dispassionate and objective, seems to shake or weaken their persistent credence in the unassimilability of ethnic Americans. Data that negate the ethnic vote are dismissed as evidence of wrong appeals and the need to find new issues to bewitch the hyphenates.

And what about ethnic influence on American foreign policies? Here too the student of ethnic political behavior is confronted with a wide range of diverse conclusions. Ethnic groups have, of course, complete liberty to urge the government to support their ancestral homelands. This is an acknowledged and recognized prerogative of elements within the American political system, and, moreover, clearly encouraged by the parties, its most important political instruments.

Pressures of hyphenated Americans on American foreign policies have been directed toward the fruition of national hopes, retaining or seeking the return of national territories, winning and preserving national independence, and cessation of persecution and oppression of minority ethnic and religious groups in other nations. The question of Ireland, the threat of Nazism and Fascism, the birth and security of Israel, the expansion and fear of Communism, the problem of "captive peoples," foreign aid, the application of the historic principles of isolationism, self-determination, anti-imperialism, anti-colonialism, and more have been areas where ethnic influences have been felt.

Throughout its history the United States has been tolerant of political activities of its immigrant peoples. Premature, abortive, or successful loyalist, liberal, Communist, or Fascist revolutions have brought exiles and refugees to its shores. From the very first

day of the American Revolution, Latin American exiles have plotted
to overthrow their home governments and at times invaded their
native lands from American bases. Here the nationalist aspirations
of the Irish, Jews, Poles, Czechs, Lithuanians, Latvians, Ukrainians,
Greeks, Chinese, and many others have received political and
material support from their American compatriots. Here future
prime ministers, presidents, and dictators of resurrected or newly
established nations the world over have appealed to ethnic or racial
pride and occasionally intervened in the electoral process.

It is not surprising that foreign or indigenous ethnic leaders in
this hospitable and congenial "nation of nations" should seek to
influence American foreign policies in the interest of their father-
lands. What is noteworthy is that despite all these activities often
encouraged by American political leaders, including presidents and
members of Congress, there is no hard documentary evidence that
the course of American diplomacy has been directed or altered by
the influence of a specific ethnic group.

Ethnic pressures on foreign policies with accompanying claims
of success or failure have led to false beliefs at home and abroad
that the policies were based on domestic ethnic considerations.
Seldom, if ever, have American major foreign policy decisions been
affected by purely ethnic considerations. More often than not,
ethnic interests have been advanced within the guidelines of historic principles and stated objectives. In this era of detente with
a powerful Soviet Union and the determined desire of the American people to limit involvement in world affairs, yesterday's slogans
that were designed to win the ethnic vote—"liberation," "containment," "Ukrainian independence," "Free Lithuania"—are out of
tune with the times.

To be sure, additional research is needed before one can answer
with any degree of conviction and certainty the question of the
role of ethnicity in American politics and diplomacy. As we await
more substantive studies, it seems evident that the ethnic nationalism of hyphenated Americans is less related to the winning of
political power, the championing of the old country, the exalta-
tion of culture and religion than it is to the achievement of dignity,
equality, respectability, and unhampered access to American values
and benefits.

Contributors to This Issue

Numan V. Bartley is professor of history at the University of Georgia.

Walter Dean Burnham is professor of political science at the Massachusetts Institute of Technology.

George W. Carey is professor of government at Georgetown University and editor of the *Political Science Reviewer.*

Samuel DuBois Cook is President of Dillard University.

Manning J. Dauer is Distinguished Service Professor of political science at the University of Florida and managing editor of *The Journal of Politics.*

Louis L. Gerson is professor and head of the department of political science at the University of Connecticut.

Alan P. Grimes is professor of political science at Michigan State University.

Robert J. Harris is the James Hart Professor of Government at the University of Virginia and was the first editor of *The Journal of Politics.*

Ralph K. Huitt is Executive Director of the National Association of State Universities and Land Grant Colleges.

Charles Burton Marshall is the Paul H. Nitze Professor of International Politics at the School of Advanced International Studies, Johns Hopkins University.

James McClellan is a member of the Washington staff of Senator Jesse Helms of North Carolina.

ROBERT J. MORGAN is professor of political science at the University of Virginia.

VINCENT OSTROM is professor of political science at Indiana University.

GEORGE E. REEDY is dean of the College of Journalism at Marquette University and former press secretary to President Lyndon B. Johnson.

JASPER B. SHANNON is professor emeritus of political science at the University of Nebraska.

LEWIS P. SIMPSON is the William A. Read Professor of English Literature at Louisiana State University and co-editor of the *Southern Review*.

RENÉ DE VISME WILLIAMSON is professor of political science at Louisiana State University and a former editor of *The Journal of Politics*.

LOUISE M. YOUNG is professor emeritus of American University with a primary interest in social history.